EARLY SUFI WOMEN

EARLY SUFI WOMEN

Dhikr an-Niswa al-Mutaʿabbidāt aṣ-Ṣūfiyyāt

BY

ABŪ ʿABD AR-RAḤMĀN AS-SULAMĪ

◆

EDITED AND TRANSLATED FROM THE
RIYADH MANUSCRIPT WITH
INTRODUCTION AND NOTES BY

RKIA ELAROUI CORNELL

FONS VITAE

Fons Vitae Edition published 1999

Printed in the United States of America

Library of Congress Catalog Card Number: 99-67569

ISBN-1-887752-06-4

Fons Vitae
49 Mockingbird Valley Drive
Louisville, KY 40207-1366
email: grayh101@aol.com
website: www.fonsvitae.com

To my father, who instilled the love of the *awliyāʾ Allāh* in me—
And to my husband, who nurtured it through his teaching.

To my mother, who embodied their qualities—
And to my daughter, who is trying to carry on their legacy.

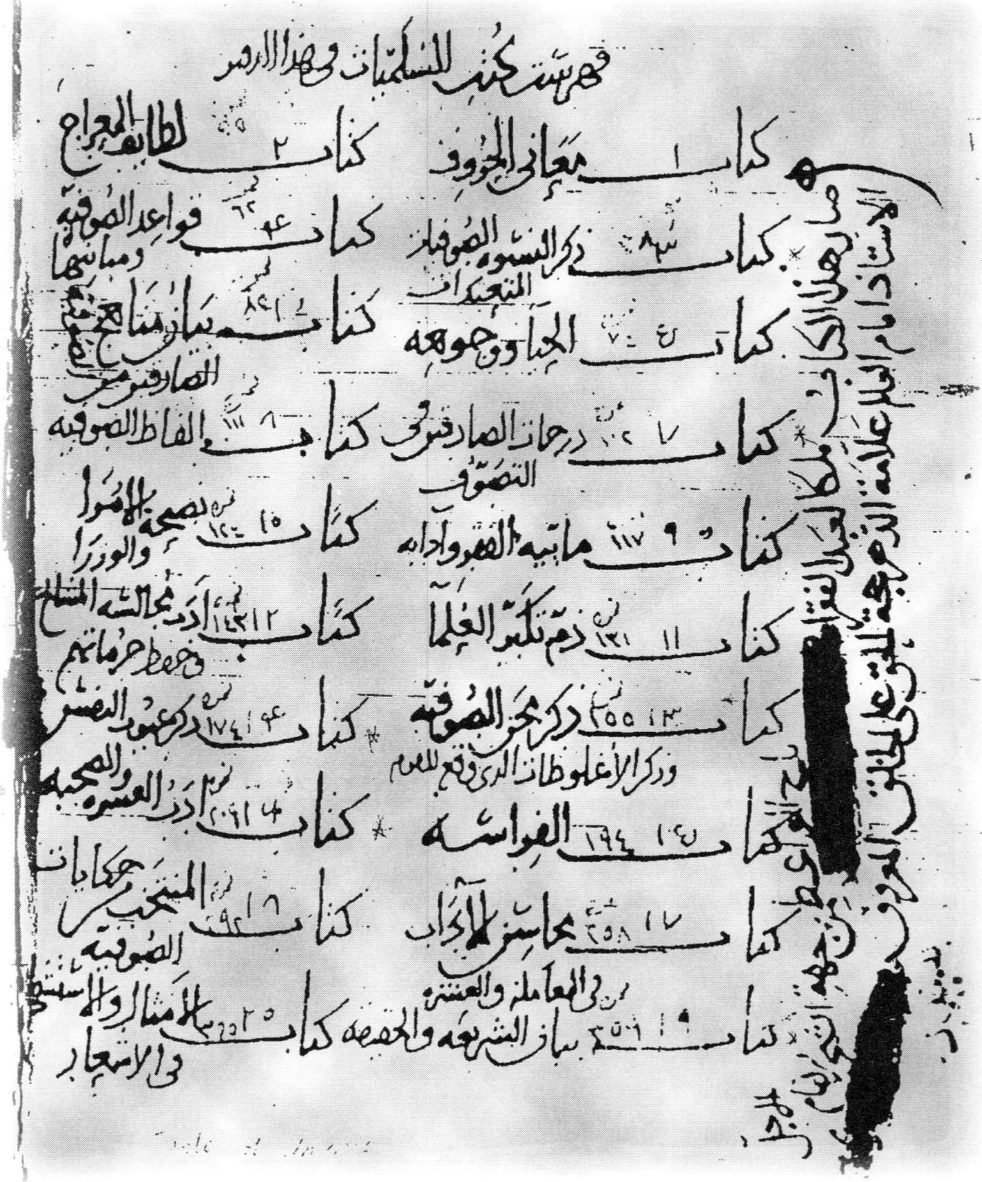

فهرست كتب السلميات في هذا الدفتر

كتاب معاني الحروف — كتاب لطائف المعراج

كتاب ذكر النسوة الصوفيات المتعبدات — كتاب قواعد الصوفية ومبانيها

كتاب الحياء ووجوهه — كتاب بيان مناهج الصادقين

كتاب درجات الصادقين في التصوف — كتاب ألفاظ الصوفية

كتاب ما بينه الفتوة وآدابه — كتاب نصيحة الأمراء والوزراء

كتاب ذم تكبر العلماء — كتاب أدب مجالسة المشايخ وحفظ حرماتهم

كتاب ذكر محن الصوفية وذكر الأغلوطات الذي وقع للقوم — كتاب ذكر عيوب النفس

كتاب الفراسة — كتاب أدب العشرة والصحبة

كتاب محاسن الآداب في المعاملة والعشرة — كتاب المنتخب من حكايات الصوفية

كتاب بيان الشريعة والحقيقة — كتاب الأمثال والاستشهاد في الأشعار

Title page of Riyadh *Sulamiyyat* Manuscript.

CONTENTS

Map: The World of as-Sulamī's Women 8

Acknowledgments 9

Foreword by Carl Ernst 11

Introduction: As-Sulamī and His Sufi Women 15
- A Veiled Tradition 15
- As-Sulamī's World 20
  - Competing Caliphates 20
  - Khurasan and Nishapur in the Tenth Century C.E. 23
  - Turkish Influence 26
  - Sectarian Conflicts 27
- As-Sulamī's Life and Works 31
  - Primary Influences 31
  - Later Influences 33
  - Major Works 37
- As-Sulamī's Book of Sufi Women 43
  - Recovering the Text 43
  - Organization of the Text 47
  - A Hermeneutic of Remembrance 48
- As-Sulamī's View of Women's Sufism 54
  - A Theology of Servitude 54
  - Institutions of Women's Sufism 60

A Memorial of Female Sufi Devotees 72

Appendix: Entries on As-Sulamī's Early Sufi Women Found in *Ṣifat aṣ-Ṣafwa* 263

Index 328

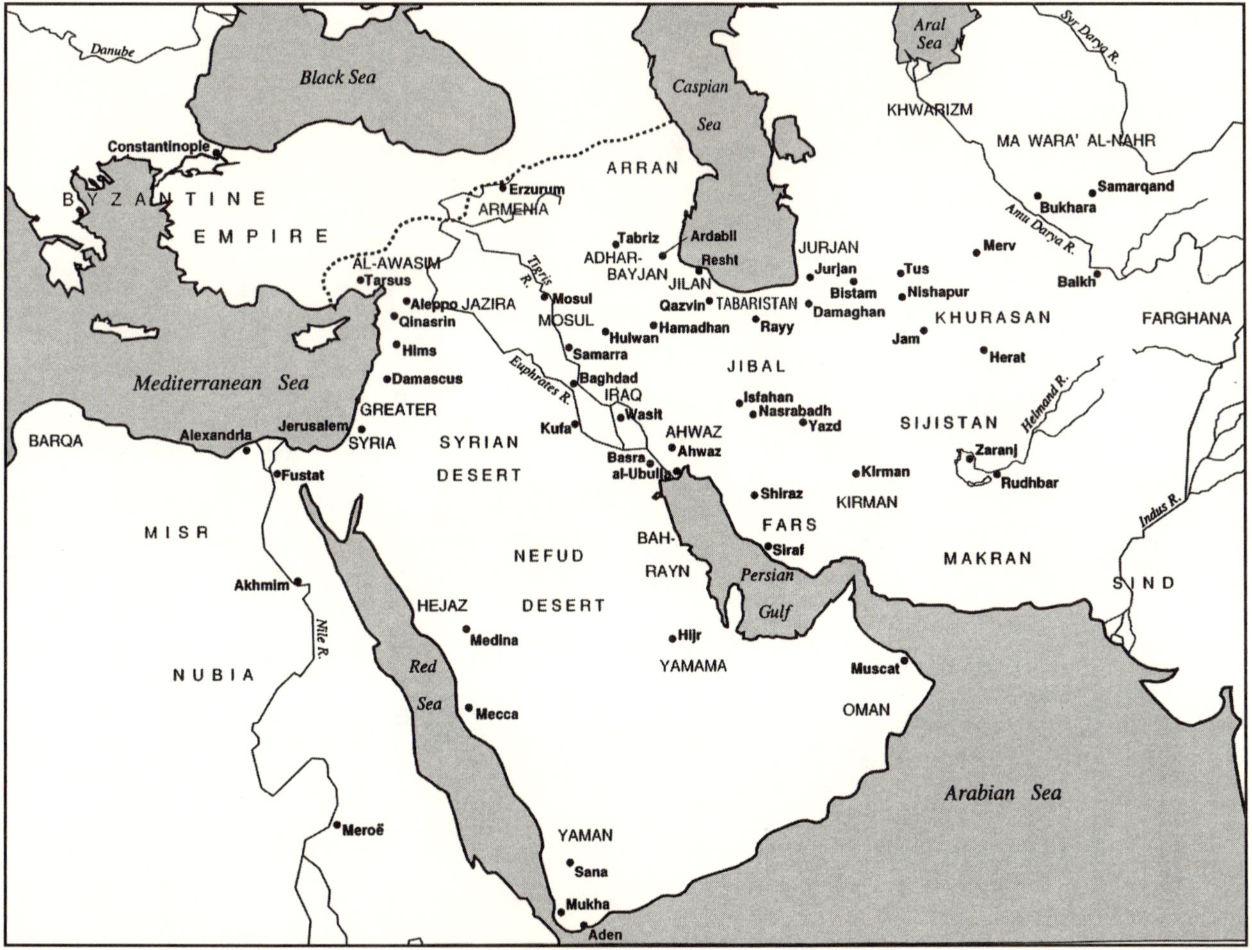

The World of as-Sulami's Women

ACKNOWLEDGMENTS

This book could not have been written without the assistance of three people. The first is Muṣṭafā an-Nājī, the proprietor of Librairie Dar al-Turath in Rabat, Morocco. When my husband and I were conducting the Duke in Morocco summer program in 1994, Muṣṭafā pulled the 1993 Arabic edition of as-Sulamī's *Dhikr an-niswa al-muta*ᶜ*abbidāt aṣ-ṣūfiyyāt* from the shelves of his bookstore and said to me: "Do something with this." Had Muṣṭafā not said this, I would not have thought of pursuing my interest in the women of Islam in a way that could be both intellectually and spiritually rewarding.

The second person who was responsible for this book is Gray Henry, the Editor and Publisher of Fons Vitae. Were as-Sulamī alive today, he would certainly include Gray in a book about modern women devoted to the spiritual. Without her assistance, I could not have obtained a photocopy of the Riyadh "Sulamiyyāt" manuscript that enabled me to produce a critical edition and translation of as-Sulamī's book of Sufi women. Without her friends in Saudi Arabia and the kindness of the Faisal Foundation Library, this earliest Sulamī manuscript and vital contribution to the history of Sufism might have remained hidden for many more years. Gray is also responsible for designing the cover of this book and for discovering the unique artwork used there that evokes so well the spiritual women of the Islamic past.

The third person who helped bring this work to fruition is my husband, Vincent J. Cornell. As my partner, teacher, critic, and copy editor, he was indispensable to its completion. For more than two years, "my ladies" seduced him away from his own projects, enticing us to spend countless hours discussing ideas, following leads, arguing points, and immersing ourselves in as-Sulamī's world. I especially value the memory of the long car trips that we took to Northwestern University, taking our daughter Sakina to and from college. These days were filled with discussions of as-Sulamī and his Sufī women, and I am sure that their *baraka* (grace or blessing) helped get us safely to our destination. Sometimes, even Sakina got caught up in my obsession and helped me revise portions of the translation and Introduction.

Other people have been involved in this work as well. I am especially grateful to Carl Ernst of the University of North Carolina, Chapel Hill, who read and commented on an early draft of the translation and gave me invaluable advice on what to include in the Introduction. Special thanks should also go to my friend and colleague Miriam Cooke of Duke University, who read a draft of the Introduction and suggested a number of useful revisions. Thanks are also due to Daniel ᶜAbd al-Ḥayy Moore, the Muslim-American poet, who helped revise my translation of poems in al-Sulamī's book of Sufi women and in the *Ṣifat aṣ-Ṣafwa* Appendix. I must also acknowledge my student and teaching assistant, Omid Safi, who is now an assistant professor of religion at Colgate University. His help was crucial in elucidating the occasional Persian term in as-Sulamī's text and in translating selections from al-Jāmī's *Nafaḥāt al-uns*. Finally, I should mention Rebecca Dobbs of the the Geography Department of the University of North Carolina, Chapel Hill, who produced the map, "The World of as-Sulamī's Women," and Rob Baker, Chris Bandy, and Molly Rannells for their collective effort in designing, producing, and proof-reading of the text.

R.E.C.
Duke University
Department of Asian and African
Languages and Literature
June, 1999

FOREWORD

"Muslim women are oppressed." How often does one encounter this stereotype? This statement is so commonly asserted, and so rarely questioned, that it passes for general knowledge and is accepted as undisputed fact. Yet the people who accept this dictum by and large have never met with or spoken to a Muslim woman. They might consider themselves liberal, and would never dream of making racial slurs about blacks or Jews. Yet somehow it is comforting for Europeans and Americans to consider themselves superior to Muslim men, who seemingly are never content until they oppress women. It is not often that Westerners pause to consider that the ideals of our society are frequently betrayed in practice, and that it may not be fair to compare our ideals to the practice of others.

When considering examples closer to hand, it is easy to acknowledge that facts such as class, ethnicity, the state, or urban or rural location may play decisive roles in determining the status of women. But for some reason it has become axiomatic to assert that Muslims are exempt from all such historical, social, and political factors. They alone among all the peoples of the world are believed to be ruled exclusively by religion—and that religion is of course identified only with the fundamentalism that is so eagerly sought after by media news outlets. Even though Muslim countries like Pakistan and Bangladesh have had female prime ministers, while the United States is still very far from having a woman president, this somehow does not alter their impressions about oppressed Muslim women.

Most people would agree that a strongly negative opinion about a large group of people, which is supported neither by evidence nor by reason, should be considered as a prejudice and nothing more. But most Americans and Europeans have been exposed throughout modern history to an endless stream of negative images and sweeping assertions about Muslim women. These images were part of the massive complex of colonial discourse that justified European domination over the rest of the world on the grounds of civilizational superiority. This colonial discourse was nourished by the harem fantasies of travel writers and Orientalist painters (almost all male), and it was sustained by the image of the veil as a depersonalizing and frightening restriction. In the absence of any access to the voices of real live Muslim women, it is perhaps understandable that such abstractions and stereotypes have dominated their perception in the West.

It is therefore truly exciting that the text of as-Sulamī's long lost book on Sufi women has unexpectedly come to light in Saudi Arabia. At a time when feminist scholars have been unearthing tremendous riches of female spirituality in the Christian and Jewish traditions, it should not be surprising that the Islamic religion conceals similar treasures. As Rkia Cornell aptly points out, traces of this important early Sufi work lingered in Islamic literature for a thousand years. Major scholars such as Jāmī and Ibn al-Jawzī drew upon it for their own biographical writings on Sufism, yet it suffered the fate of falling into oblivion until now.

What does this rediscovered text tell us about women's spiritual lives in the early Islamic period? Rkia Cornell sensitively describes this as a "veiled tradition," in which the privacy claimed by modest and saintly women has in effect conspired to cloak them in mystery. At the same time, she reveals the existence of several schools of ascetic and mystical practice among early Sufi women. There is, of course, one Sufi woman whose name is widely recognized by students of mysticism: Rābiᶜa of Basra, whose life and sayings are well known due to the labors of Margaret Smith. Yet Rābiᶜa was one among many women mystics, and her hagiographic treatment has oddly served to obscure the contributions of others. Often the mere mention of Rābiᶜa sufficed as a minimal reference to women, and authors frequently felt no obligation to say any more after this obligatory gesture. The larger biographical dictionaries of Sufism generally offer only a handful of biographies of women next to hundreds or even thousands for men. As Cornell demonstrates, one can indeed find misogynistic tendencies among some Muslim authors (although the reality is far from the universal stereotype commonly subscribed to).

But what is important about this text is that it displays distinctive feminine traditions of spiritual practice summarized under the central Islamic category of service to God. This did not mean subservience to men, however, as we can see from the women who taught men and criticized the shortcomings of well known male Sufis. There was also a distinctive tradition of female chivalry (*niswān*), corresponding to the widely spread institution of ethical teachings known among men as *futuwwa*. All this was carried out in the atmosphere of intense asceticism that characterized the early Sufi movement in general.

This text also provides another example of the way in which early Sufism was formulated in terms of the central concerns and scriptural resources of Islam. In the past two centuries, the rise of modern fundamentalist movements has led to an unprecedented questioning and even rejection of Sufi spirituality as un-Islamic. Yet the example of as-Sulamī, a scholar of profound attainments in scholarship on the Qurʾān and hadith, shows Sufism as a spiritual enterprise that constituted the capstone of Islamic learning and piety.

Rkia Cornell has meticulously translated and annotated this rich document, and her introduction clarifies the importance of the text in relation to the extensive writings of its author as-Sulamī. She explains how to read its laconic style, and she teases considerable information from it with the aid of historical context and comparative observations. This translation is a model of how early Arabic texts can be interpreted, and students of Arabic will also be grateful for her clear edition of the original text. But the real payoff of this detailed scholarship has been to reveal this gem of feminine spirituality to a new audience. I hope that this lifting of the veil will provide readers with an opportunity to gauge the profound religious choices made by Muslim women a thousand years ago, and that this important document will help lead western readers to a new appreciation of the religious lives of Muslim women today.

Carl Ernst
University of North Carolina at Chapel Hill

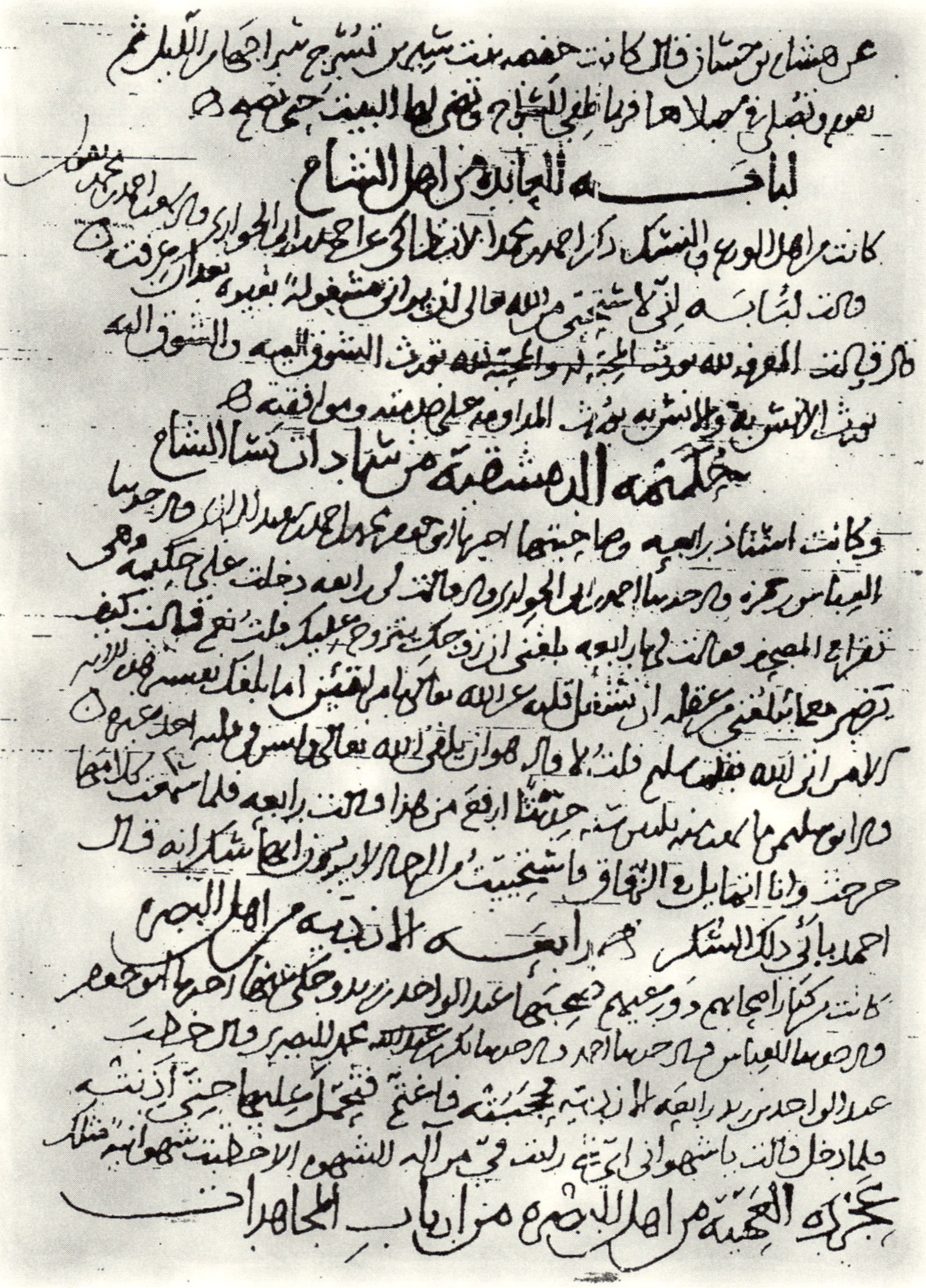
عن هشام بن حسان قال كانت حفصة بنت سيرين تسرج سراجها بالليل ثم
تقوم وتصلي في مصلاها فربما طفي السراج فيضيء لها البيت حتى تصبح
لبابة العابدة من اهل الشام
حكيمة الدمشقية من عابدات نساء الشام
رابعة الازدية من اهل البصرة
عجردة العمية من اهل البصرة من ارباب المجاهدات

Dhikr an-Niswa al-Muta 'abbidat as-Sufiyyat: Notices on Lubaba al-'Abida, Hukayma ad-Dimashqiyya and Rabi'a al-Azdiyya.

INTRODUCTION
AS-SULAMĪ AND HIS SUFI WOMEN

A VEILED TRADITION

Few terms in Islam have been more widely debated than "Sufi." To this day, scholars still disagree over the origins of the Sufis, the nature of their practices, and the meaning of their doctrines. One of the earliest and most influential treatments of these subjects is found in *Kitāb at-taᶜarruf li-madhhab ahl at-taṣawwuf* (Introduction to the Methodology of the Sufis) by Abū Bakr al-Kalābādhī of Bukhara (d. ca. 380/990). An extensive discussion of the word "Sufi" can be found in the opening chapter of this work. After giving a long list of possible etymologies for the term and quoting a number of famous mystics on the attributes of the Sufis, al-Kalābādhī closes the chapter with a description of an encounter between the famous Egyptian Sufi Dhū an-Nūn al-Miṣrī (d. 246/861) and an unnamed Sufi woman on the cost of Syria:

> Dhū an-Nūn said: I saw a woman on the coast of Syria and asked her: "Where are you coming from (may God have mercy on you)?" She replied: "From a people who 'are moved to rise from their beds at night [calling on their Lord in fear and hope].'"[1] Then I asked: "And where are you going?" She said: "To 'men whom neither worldly commerce nor striving after gain can divert from the remembrance of God.'"[2] "Describe them for me," I said. And she recited:
>
> "A people who have staked their aspirations on God,
> And whose ambitions aspire to nothing else.
>
> The goal of this folk is their Lord and Master,
> Oh what a noble goal is theirs, for the One beyond compare!
>
> They do not compete for the world and its honors,
> Whether it be for food, luxury, or children,
>
> Nor for fine and costly clothes,
> Nor for the ease and comfort that is found in towns.

1. Qurᵓān 32 (*as-Sajda*), 16. the portion of this quotation in brackets is not in the text of *at-Taᶜarruf.*

2. Qurᵓān 24 (*an-Nūr*), 37.

> Instead, they hasten toward the promise of an exalted station,
> Knowing that each step brings them closer to the farthest horizon.
>
> They are the hostages of washes and gullies,
> And you will find them gathered on mountain-tops."[3]

By concluding one of the most important chapters of his book with this poem, al-Kalābādhī reveals his high regard for its anonymous author's understanding of Sufism. Dhū an-Nūn, who created the Sufi doctrine of spiritual states (*aḥwāl*) and stations (*maqāmāt*), is reminded by this woman that the essence of Sufism is not to be found in paranormal states but in spiritual practice, an idea that mirrors al-Kalābādhī's own view of Sufism as a "way of proceeding" or methodology (*madhhab*). True Sufis are Muslims whose hearts vibrate with the spirituality of the Qurʾān. They "rise from their beds at night," devoted to the remembrance of God. They "stake their ambitions on God" and aspire to nothing else. Their goal is God alone. Only by ignoring the world and its honors can they "hasten to the promise of an exalted station." Seeking solitude in their devotion to God, they are to be found in washes and gullies, or gathered on mountain-tops. In short, the Sufi is the best of Muslims: if a woman, she is a person who differs from her fellow believers mainly to the extent that her devotion to God is an all-consuming vocation.

In al-Kalābādhī's day, nothing proved the quality of a person's background better than a well-turned phrase or an elegantly composed poem. Scholars, courtiers, and other intellectuals would demonstrate their proficiency in the *belles-lettres (adab)* by displaying their knowledge of rhetoric, metaphor, and similar literary devices. Poetry was especially valued as a medium of expression because of its ability to present ideas in an evocative and economical manner. As spiritual intellectuals, Sufis provided some of the most noteworthy examples of this art. Whether in works of sacred biography, collections of Sufi poetry, or doctrinal treatises, Sufis such as al-Kalābādhī's anonymous woman would be depicted as extemporaneously composing verses in a variety of poetical forms.

3. Abū Bakr Muḥammad ibn Isḥāq al-Bukhārī al-Kalābādhī, *Kitāb at-taʿarruf li-madhhab ahl at-taṣawwuf*, ed. A. J. Arberry (Cairo, 1415/1994 reprint of 1352/1933 first editon), 10. See also *The Doctrine of the Ṣūfīs* (*Kitāb al-Taʿarruf li-madhhab ahl al-taṣawwuf*), trans. A. J. Arberry (Cambridge, 1991 reprint of 1935 first edition), 11. What is quoted here is my translation. Although Arberry accuses the Arabs of being prolix in their literary expression (xiii), his own awkward translation of this poem suffers form the same defect. For an overview of al-Kalābādhī's life and works, see Paul Nwyia, "al-Kalābādhī," *Encyclopaedia of Islam* second edition, hereafter (*EI*^{2}), 467.

In the context of such a literary tradition, a poem that was good enough to be included in a major treatise on Sufism could be composed only by a person who was recognized as having attained the highest level of Sufi knowledge. Yet despite the fact that she had attained such knowledge, al-Kalābādhī never informs his reader of the identity of the woman who so impressed Dhū an-Nūn al-Miṣrī. By remaining anonymous, she poses no challenge to the unique status of her more famous interlocutor. In citing only Dhū an-Nūn al-Miṣrī by name, al-Kalābādhī causes the Egyptian master to appropriate the Sufi woman's wisdom as his own.

This veiling of women's voices is typical of al-Kalābādhī's approach to Sufi history. In *Kitāb at-ta^{c}arruf*, the only Sufi woman cited by name is Rābi^{c}a al-^{c}Adawiyya (d. 185/801), the famous saint of Basra, who is mentioned three times.[4] But these short citations do little or nothing to provide Rābi^{c}a with a voice. For al-Kalābādhī, Rābi^{c}a al-^{c}Adawiyya is more of a trope, a rhetorical device, than a real person. In his opinion, most women are deficient in their knowledge and practice of Islam. As such, they cannot speak authoritatively for either Islam or Sufism. Although he claims that this deficiency is not part of a woman's essential nature (*fī a^{c}yānihinna*), it is still apparent in women's religious practices. Women are deficient in religion, says al-Kalābādhī, because during their monthly periods they are prohibited from praying or fasting. Furthermore, he adds, anyone who is deficient in religion is also deficient in faith: "The practice of religion is faith itself. The two are the same, even in the view of those who do not see faith as based entirely on works."[5]

Al-Kalābādhī's low opinion of women was not unique among sufis in the Islamic Middle Period. He was not the worst, but merely one of the earliest in a long line of male authorities on Sufism who hid the teachings and even the existence of Sufi women behind a veil of obscurity.[6] Instead of serving as exemplars for other women to follow, Rābi^{c}a al-^{c}Adawiyya and Dhū an-Nūn's anonymous Sufi woman appear in *Kitāb at-ta^{c}arruf* as exceptions to the norm of female inadequacy. Because such women were so rare, their wisdom and high standing among men served as a rebuke to

4. On Rābi^{c}a al-^{c}Adawiyya, see as-Sulamī, *Dhikr an-niswa al-muta^{c}abbidāt aṣ-ṣūfiyyāt,* section I below.

5. al-Kalābādhī, *at-Ta^{c}arruf,* 53; Arberry, *Doctrine,* 68–69.

6. Another Sufi writer who sought to minimize the contributions of women was the poet Abū al-Majd "Ḥakīm" Sanā^{c}ī (d. 525/1131) of Ghazna in modern-day Afghanistan. The most he could say about women was: "A pious woman is better than a thousand bad men." Since even one ordinary man is better than a thousand bad men, this statement does little to enhance the status of women. See Annemarie Schimmel, "The Feminine Element in Sufism," Appendix to idem, *Mystical Dimensions of Islam* (Chapel Hill, North Carolina, 1975), 426.

the majority of Muslim women, who were considered unable to attain the same level of spirituality.

However, not all Sufis had such a negative opinion of women. Sufi writers who included Sufi women in their works clearly had a higher regard for women than those who excluded them. For example, in *Nafaḥāt al-uns* (Breaths of Intimacy), ᶜAbd ar-Raḥmān al-Jāmī of Herat (d. 899/1492) opens his appendix on Sufi women with a verse by the poet al-Mutanabbī (d. 354/965), which appears to assert that women and men are equal:

> If all women were as those whom we have mentioned,
> Then women would have been preferred over men.
>
> The femininity of the word "sun" (*shams*) is not a rebuke,
> And masculinity is not an honor for the crescent moon (*hilāl*).[7]

Yet, even this poem is not as positive as it seems. The assertion of gender equality in the second verse is contradicted by an implication of gender inequality in the preceding verse. The use of the conditional (Ar. *law kāna*) in the first verse of the poem does not really imply that women are equal to or superior to men. Rather, it states a grammatical impossibility: most women will never be "as those whom we have mentioned." Although a few exceptional women might surpass men in their qualities, women in general are not preferred over men because they do not measure up to their male counterparts. While masculinity should not in itself be a source of pride, and femininity should not in itself be a mark of shame, gender inequality remains a fact of life. Instead of elevating the status of women, al-Mutanabbī's poem provides but another example of Carolyn G. Heilbrun's observation that "exceptional women are the chief imprisoners of nonexceptional women, simultaneously proving that any woman could do [remarkable things] and assuring, in their uniqueness among men, that no other woman will."[8]

Today, the situation is little different. Outside of the United States or Western Europe, it is rare to find a Sufi order that accepts women as a

7. ᶜAbd ar-Raḥmān ibn Aḥmad Jāmī, *Nafaḥāt al-uns min ḥaḍarāt al-quds*, ed. Mehdī Tawḥīdīpūr (Tehran, 1337/1917),615. With a slight change of wording ("If all women were as those whom we have lost"), this verse can be found in *Dīwān al-Mutanabbī* (Berlin,1861), 388. It is cited in the new edition of Jāmī's *Nafaḥāt al-uns* (Tehran, 1992), 612 and np. 926. The verse was part of an elegy that al-Mutanabbī composed on the death of the mother of his patron, Sayf ad-Dawla al-Hāmādānī in 337/948. I am grateful to Professor Carl Ernst of the University of North Carolina Chapel Hill, for providing this information.

8. Carolyn G. Heilbrun, *Writing a Woman's Life* (New York, 1988), 81. quoted in Denise A. Spellberg, *Politics, Gender, and the Islamic Past: The legacy of ᶜA'isha bint Abi Bakr* (New York, 1994), 59.

matter of policy.[9] While many women are the disciples of Sufi masters, many others do not have the same access to Sufi teaching as do men. In many Muslim countries, women's participation in Sufism is marginal: often, women are confined to seeking blessing at the shrines of saints or participating in public festivals. Women may also be the keepers of saints' shrines and, in South Asia, may even become itinerant *qalandars* or *malangs* who exist on the margins of both Sufism and Islam.[10] However, within the context of institutionalized Sufism, the segregation of the sexes remains the norm. In Morocco, for example, women can be found among the "lovers" (*muḥibbīn*) or hangers-on who attend the public rituals of popular Sufi orders such as the ᶜĪsāwa or the Ḥamadsha.[11] But few women, if any, are to be found among the adepts (*fuqarāʾ*) of these orders. In Egypt, the Supreme Council of Sufi Orders officially bans female membership. In Egyptian cities such as Cairo and Alexandria, women who follow the teachings of Sufi masters must often practice their Sufism semi-covertly, meeting in houses or other locations that are separated from the places where men's devotions are performed. Occasionally, as a compromise, sessions of invocation might be organized under the auspices of womens's sections in Sufi voluntary associations, such as Egypt's ᶜAshīra Muḥammadiyya.[12] Although Sufi masters may give lectures for female audiences, one seldom finds women and men participating together in the circles of teaching and invocation that characterize the doctrinal aspect of Sufism.

The continued mistrust of women and their spirituality among many Sufis is a major reason why as-Sulamī's book of Sufi women is so important to the study of both Sufism and Islam today. It is the earliest extant work to give a sense of identity to the numerous Sufi women who served their male brethren, studied with them, supported them financially, and even, at times, surpassed them in their knowledge. As-Sulamī's book of Sufi women challenges the legitimacy of modern restrictions on women's

9. Partial exceptions to this rule could be found in Turkish Sufism, where a Sufi woman was called "sister" (Turk. *baci*), and in the Jazūliyya Sufi order of Morocco (fifteenth to seventeenth centuries C.E.), whose shaykhs initiated educated women. See Annemarie Schimmel, *My Soul is a Woman: The Feminine in Islam*, Susan H. Ray, trans. (New York, 1997), 44–45; and Vincent J. Cornell, *Realm of the Saint: Power and Authority in Moroccan Sufism* (Austin, Texas, 1998), 248–49.

10. For a description of a female *malang*, see "The Qalandar Confronts the Proper Muslim," in Katherine Pratt Ewing, *Arguing Sainthood: Modernity, Psychoanalysis and Islam* (Durham, North Carolina and London, 1997), 201–29.

11. See, for example, Vincent Crapanzano, *The Ḥamadsha: A Study in Moroccan Ethnopsychiatry* (Berkeley and London, 1973).

12. For an overview of women's Sufism in contemporary Egypt, see Valerie J. Hoffman, *Sufism, Mystics and Saints in Modern Egypt* (Columbia, South Carolina, 1995), 226–54.

participation in Sufism by demonstrating that in Sufism's formative period, women were not so often excluded from the public aspects of spiritual life. As-Sulamī portrays Sufi women as full equals of their male counterparts in religion and intellect, as well as in their knowledge of Sufi doctrines and practices.[13] Unlike al-Kalābādhī, who preferred to keep the contributions of Sufi women hidden, as-Sulamī insists on revealing both their identities and the content of their teachings.

One of the Sufi women whom as-Sulamī unveils for us is the woman al-Kalābādhī quotes to illustrate the meaning of the term "Sufi." This was Fāṭima of Nishapur, a Sufi woman who spent many years in Mecca, far from her home in eastern Iran, and traveled widely in Palestine and Syria.[14] According to as-Sulamī, it was in Mecca or Jerusalem, and not on the Syrian coast, where she met Dhū an-Nūn al-Miṣrī and taught him such subjects as the doctrine of truthfulness (*ṣidq*) and the exegesis (*taʾwīl*) of the Qurʾān. Significantly, as-Sulamī depicts Fāṭima of Nishapur as correcting Dhū an-Nūn often. Because of her wisdom, Dhū an-Nūn accorded her the highest praise that a Sufi master could give to a colleague: "She is a saint (*walīya*) from among the saints (*awliyāʾ*) of God." As-Sulamī also mentions that another giant of early Sufism, Bāyazīd al-Bisṭāmī (d. 261/875 or 264/877–78), who once said that "it is the same to me whether I walk past a woman or a wall,"[15] had an equally high opinion of Fāṭima of Nishapur. "In all of my life," said Bāyazīd, "I have seen only one true man and one true woman. The woman was Fāṭima of Nishapur."[16]

AS-SULAMI'S WORLD

Competing Caliphates

Like Fāṭima the teacher of Dhū an-Nūn, as-Sulamī was born in the eastern Iranian city of Nishapur. The fourth century A.H. (tenth century C.E.),

13. See, for example, *Dhikr an-niswa,* section LI below, where as-Sulamī notes that ʿAbda and Āmina, the sisters of the Sufi Abū Sulaymān ad-Dārānī, attained "an exalted level of intellect (*ʿaql*) and religious observance (*dīn*)."

14. For as-Sulamī's notice on Fāṭima of Nishapur, see *Dhikr an-niswa,* section XXX below.

15. Tor Andrae, *In the Garden of Myrtles: Studies in Early Islamic Mysticism,* trans. Birgitta Sharpe (Albany, New York, 1987), 47.

16. For another account of the relationship between Fāṭima of Nishapur and Dhū an-Nūn al-Miṣrī and Bāyazīd al-Bisṭamī, see Annemarie Schimmel, *Mystical Dimensions,* 427. Unfortunately, because of mistakes in her original sources (al-Hujwīrī, al-ʿAṭṭār, and Jāmī), Schimmel conflates accounts of Fāṭima of Nishapur with those of Umm ʿAlī Fāṭima of Balkh, the wife of Aḥmad ibn Khaḍrawayh (See *Dhikr an-niswa,* section XLI below).

during which as-Sulamī passed most of his life, was a period of political, religious, and intellectual ferment that for a time propelled Nishapur to the center of the Islamic world. Sometimes known as the "Shi^{c}ite century," this era witnessed no less than three competing caliphs, political successors to the Prophet Muḥammad, who claimed the right to rule over Islam.[17] In the west, Muslim Spain had been controlled since the middle of the eighth century C.E. by Umayyad emirs, descendants of the Umayyad caliphs who ruled Islam from Damascus in the first and second centuries A.H. In 317/929, less than a decade before as-Sulamī's birth, the Umayyad emir ^{c}Abd ar-Raḥmān III (r. 301–50/912–61) proclaimed himself caliph in his capital of Córdoba.

The Umayyads of Spain were Sunni Muslims who followed the Mālikī school of Islamic law. ^{c}Abd ar-Raḥmān III created his caliphate as a defence against the religious and political influence of Shi^{c}ism, which had spread into Islamic Spain as a result of the missionary activities of the Fatimids.[18] The Fatimid revolt arose in North Africa at the beginning of the tenth century C.E. The first Fatimid caliph, ^{c}Ubayd Allāh (r. 297–322/ 909–34), was a follower of the Ismā^{c}īlī sect of Shi^{c}ism and a descendant of the Prophet Muḥammad through the Prophet's daughter Fāṭima. Upon taking power, he proclaimed himself the *Mahdī* (The Guided One), a divinely-inspired leader who would inaugurate a new era of justice and salvation. Over the next sixty years, ^{c}Ubayd Allāh's successors established a powerful state in North Africa, which they governed from their capital of al-Mahdiyya in present-day Tunisia. In 358/969, the Fatimid caliph al-Mu^{c}izz sent an army under the Sicilian commander Jawhar to conquer Egypt. To commemorate this victory, Jawhar founded a new capital city called al-Qāhira (The All-Conquering), today's Cairo.

After al-Mu^{c}izz moved his court from al-Mahdiyya to Cairo, the new Egyptian capital of the Fatimids quickly grew into a major metropolis. Basing their prosperity on the control of the eastern Mediterranean and dominance over the trade with India, the Fatimids commanded vast resources and spent lavishly on the construction of palaces, public works, and centers

17. On the concept of the "Shī^{c}ī century," see Marshall G. S. Hodgson, *The Venture of Islam: Conscience and History in a World Civilization,* Vol. 2, *The Expansion of Islam in the Middle Periods* (Chicago, 1974), 36–39.

18. For detailed information on the development of the Fatimid state and Fatimid Ismā^{c}īlism. see Farhad Daftary, *The Ismā^{c}īlīs: Their History and Doctrines* (Cambridge, 1990), 144–255.

of religious instruction.[19] One of the most important of these projects was the mosque-university of al-Azhar, which was created as the intellectual center of Ismāᶜīlī Shiᶜism. As-Sulamī's life coincided with the reigns of some of the most important Fatimid caliphs, starting with al-Qāᵓim (r. 322–34/934–46), and ending with al-Ḥākim (r. 386–411/ 996–1021), whose mysterious disappearance into the Egyptian desert occurred just before as-Sulamī's death.[20]

The third caliphate to claim authority over the Muslim world was that of the ᶜAbbasids, who defeated the Umayyad caliphs in 132/750. The ᶜAbbasids were descendants of the Prophet's uncle al-ᶜAbbās, and started out as supporters of the Shiᶜa. Once they gained power, however, they excluded the Shiᶜa from their circle and adopted the role of Sunni caliphs. As a means of gaining legitimacy, they patronized religious scholars and promoted the rule of Islamic law *(ash-Sharīᶜa).* By allowing non-Arab Muslims to attain high positions in their administration, they also fostered the development of a multi-ethnic Islamic civilization. At the height of their power in the ninth century C.E., the ᶜAbbasids presided over the greatest empire in the world. This empire was ruled from their new capital of Baghdad, which was founded in 145/762. In less than a century, Baghdad would become an enormous trade emporium with hundreds of thousands of inhabitants.

In as-Sulamī's day, however, the ᶜAbbasid caliphate was but a shadow of its former self and Baghdad was no longer the most important city in the Muslim world. Many regions, such as Egypt, Syria, Iran, and Central Asia had become independent of ᶜAbbasid control. Even more importantly, the ᶜAbbasid caliphs themselves were no longer in charge of their own affairs. Real power was in the hands of Buyid emirs, who governed most of present-day Iraq and Iran as military dictators. The Buyids were a family from Daylam, in the Alborz mountains of Iran, who were converted to Islam by Shiᶜites of the Zaydī sect. After taking power in 334/945, shortly after as-Sulamī's birth, they divided the ᶜAbbasid provinces in Iraq and southern and central Iran among themselves. The administrators of the Buyid regime came from Fars, the heartland of ancient Persia. The significance of Fars to the Buyids is reflected in the fact that they maintained courts in the Persian cities of Shiraz and Isfahan that were nearly as important as the court in Baghdad.[21]

19. For a good summary of Fatimid trade and administrative organization, see M. A. Shaban, *Islamic History: A New Interpretation,* Vol. 2, A.D. 750–1055 A.H. 132–448 (Cambridge, 1976), 199–206.

20. Ibid., 206–10.

21. On the Buyids, see Ibid., 159–87 and Hodgson, *Venture of Islam,* vol. 2, 35–36.

Under the Buyids, the ᶜAbbasid caliph was practically stripped of his sovereign rights and privileges. All major administrators, from the governors of provinces to the Vizier *(wazīr),* who actually ran the ᶜAbbasid state, were appointed by the caliph only after first being approved by the Buyids. Even the caliph's daily allowance was set by the Buyids. If a Buyid emir asked for money from the caliph's account, he could not be refused. Under the emir ᶜAḍuḍ ad-Dawla (r. in Baghdad, 367–72/978–82), the caliph was even forced to add the Buyid's name to his own at the end of the Friday sermon.[22]

The Imāmī or "Twelver" sect of the Shiᶜa (the dominant Shiᶜite sect today) was favored by the Buyids. In Baghdad and the Iranian city of Qom, scholars such as Jaᶜfar ibn Qawlawayh (d. 369/979) and Shaykh Ṣaduq (Muḥammad ibn Bābawayh, d. 381/991) produced theological works that were to become foundational for contemporary Shiᶜism.[23] Yet despite their patronage of Shiᶜism, the Buyids did not overthrow the ᶜAbbasid caliph. When the emir Muᶜizz ad-Dawla (r. 334–56/945–67) sought to replace the caliph with a Shiᶜite descendant of ᶜAlī, his advisers counseled him against it, saying: "If trouble were to arise between yourself and the ᶜAbbasid caliph, your followers, who do not believe him to be the rightful claimant, will not hesitate even if you order them to kill him. But in case of an ᶜAlid caliph, they will not hesitate to carry out his commands even if it be to kill you."[24]

Khurasan and Nishapur in the Tenth Century C.E.

As-Sulamī's home city of Nishapur was in Khurasan, a region of eastern Iran that also included parts of present-day Turkmenistan, Uzbekistan, and Afghanistan. The vanguard of the army that conquered Khurasan for Islam was made up of warriors from as-Sulamī's tribe of Banū Sulaym. Although the Banū Sulaym were supported by other Arab tribes such as

22. Amir H. Siddiqi, *Caliphate and Kingship in Medieval Persia* (Philadelphia, 1977), 34–36. This is a reprint of a series of articles that first appeared in *Islamic Culture,* vols. 9–11 (Hyderabad, 1935–37).

23. On the importance of the Buyid period to the development of Imāmī Shīᶜīsm, see Moojan Momen, *An Introduction to Shiᶜi Islam: The History and Doctrines of Twelver Shiᶜism* (New Haven and London, 1985), 75–84.

24. Siddiqi, *Caliphate and Kingship, 35.* This account was transmitted by the historian Ibn al-Athīr (d. 631/1234) in *al-Kāmil fī at-taʾrīkh.*

Tamīm, Azd, and Khuzāᶜa, they were still prominent in Khurasan during as-Sulamī's lifetime.[25]

Today, Nishapur is only a minor city. However, from the time of the Muslim conquest until the twelfth century C.E. it was one of the most important cities in the Islamic world. Other important cities of Khurasan included Merv (in modern Turkmenistan) to the northeast, Herat (now in Afghanistan) to the southeast, and Balkh (now a ruin in Afghanistan) to the far east. The key to Khurasan was the Iranian city of Rayy (near modern Tehran) to the west, which controlled the major east-west trade routes into the region. Nishapur was a large city by the standards of the time. In as-Sulamī's day its population numbered about 100,000. Lying at the crossroads of major trade routes, it functioned as a commercial center and gained additional wealth from the surplus, rents, and taxes of more than one thousand villages.[26] The mercantile elites of Nishapur, which included as-Sulamī's family, owned country estates from which they derived much of their wealth. These elite families financed religious endowments, which paid for public buildings and supported students of the Islamic sciences. Many of these elites were Arabs, the descendants of 50,000 Arab families from Iraq that settled in Khurasan during the Umayyad period.[27] Others were Persian in origin, the descendants of rural landowners who controlled Khurasan at the time of the Muslim conquest.

In the tenth century C.E., Khurasan was ruled by the Samanids, a family of Sunni Muslims descended from Persian notables whose capital was at Bukhara in present-day Uzbekistan.[28] In pre-Islamic times the region of Bukhara had been the homeland of the Sogdians, a people who acted as middlemen in the profitable trade between Europe and China. Like the Sogdians, the Samanids also prospered from trade with Europe. The Samanid trade route passed from Khurasan through Tabaristan (present-day Mazandaran) and Daylam on the southern shore of the Caspian Sea, to Azerbaijan and Armenia, and finally to the lands of Byzantium. Another Samanid trade route went north up the Caspian Sea and the Volga River to the lands of the Bulgars and the Viking Rus, who supplied sables and other valuable furs. Within this Samanid trade network, Bukhara was a center for agricultural produce, Merv supplied manufactured goods, and

25. On the Muslim conquest of Khurasan, see M. A. Shaban, *The ᶜAbbasid Revolution* (Cambridge, 1970), 16–34.

26. For a description of medieval Nishapur see Richard W. Bulliet, *The Patricians of Nishapur: A Study in Medieval Islamic Social History* (Cambridge Mass., 1972), 3–19.

27. Shaban, *The ᶜAbbasid Revolution,* 31–32.

28. On the Samanids, see Hodgson, *Venture of Islam* vol. 2, 32–34.

Nishapur served as a military base and commercial center whose merchants maintained close ties with their counterparts in Tabaristan to the west.[29]

Because their prosperity was based on commerce, the Samanids maintained good relations with their neighbors and avoided involvement in sectarian disputes. The tolerance of the Samanids was an important reason why so many Sufis, philosophers, and other intellectuals were able to flourish under their rule. Their main concern was not the purity of Islam, but control of the city of Rayy, which allowed access to the Byzantine trade routes. The Buyid conquest of Rayy in the middle of the tenth century C.E. started a long, fifty-year decline that eventually led to the collapse of the Samanid state. To the extent that there was an ideological aspect of the Samanid dispute with the Buyids, it was over Shi^{c}ism. As Sunnis, the Samanids had a high regard for the ^{c}Abbasid caliphate and ruled their domains as nominal ^{c}Abbasid governors. Although succession to the Samanid throne was hereditary and the ^{c}Abbasids had no hand in the appointment of new rulers, the Samanids maintained their oath of allegiance *(bay^{c}a)* to the caliph and governed their territories according to the Ḥanafī school of law. Islamic scholars enjoyed such a high reputation among the Samanids that one of their first emirs, Ismā^{c}īl ibn Ahmad (r. 279–95/892–907), is reported to have moved seven steps backward whenever he was in the presence of a learned and pious man.[30]

Yet despite their reputation for good government, the Samanids could not gain support for their cause when they were threatened by the Turkish Qarakhanids and Ghaznavids at the end of the tenth century. Samanid preachers in Bukhara mounted the pulpits of their mosques and called on the people to rally to their defence, saying: "You are aware of how well we have conducted ourselves and how cordial have been the relations between us. This enemy now menaces us, and it is your manifest duty to help us and fight on our behalf. So ask God's grace in succouring our cause." However, when the people of Bukhara consulted their local religious leaders on this matter, they received the following reply: "If the Khān's followers were at variance with you on religion, it would be a duty to fight them. But where the object of dispute is temporal, no Muslim has a right to risk his life and

29. On the Samanid trade system, see Shaban, *Islamic History,* vol. 2, 175–79 On the Samanid embassy to the Volga Rus, see Ibid., 149–51. According to the geographer al-Muqaddasī (ca. 378/988), the Samanid army was headquartered in Nishapur. See Abū ^{c}Abdallāh Muḥammad al-Muqaddasī, *The Best Divisions for Knowledge of the Regions: A Translation* of Ahsan al-Taqasim fi Ma^{c}rifat al-Aqalim, trans. Basil Anthony Collins (Reading, United Kingdom, 1994), 297.

30. Siddiqi, *Caliphate and Kingship,* 59.

expose himself to bloodshed. These [Turks] are well-conducted and orthodox; it is better to keep away from the fray."[31]

Turkish Influence

The lack of support for the Samanids illustrates the wide gulf that separated the ruling dyansties of this period from their subjects. Besides being a Shiᶜite century, the tenth century C.E. also inaugurated the so-called Turkish period of Islamic history, in which power increasingly came into the hands of Turkish horsemen from Central Asia, who were either recruited as soldiers by regional dynasties or trained as military slaves (sing. *mamlūk)* for the personal service of caliphs and emirs.

Because of the widespread use of military slaves, and also because elite families used slaves as trusted managers and assistants, terms associated with the culture of servitude were used in many areas of discourse, including Sufism. Words such as *mamlūk, ᶜabd* (slave), *ama* (slave-girl), or *ghulām* ("boy" or personal servant) were often used to describe any person who served another, whether it be a human being or God. Sufis and other religious devotees commonly used such terms to refer to themselves. In his book of Sufi women, as-Sulamī emphasizes the concept of *taᶜabbud,* the disciplined practice of servitude. The official title of the Buyid emir of Baghdad, a person of free birth, was "Slave of the Commander of the Faithful" *(ᶜAbd Amīr al-Muᵓminīn),* even though the caliph was more his servant than the other way around. Similarly, historical accounts portray Sebüktigin (r. 366–87/977–97), the founder of the Ghaznavid dynasty, as having been a slave, although he was more likely a clan leader from the region of Ghaznīn in Afghanistan who only called himself a slave as a way of showing his loyalty to Alptigin, his original patron.[32]

The economic basis of Turkish power was the *iqṭāᶜ*, a land grant that was given to military commanders instead of a salary. The *iqṭāᶜ* was originally created to generate revenues from agricultural surpluses when currency was in short supply. At first, the emirs allowed their commanders

31. Ibid., 59–60.

32. Shaban, *Islamic History,* vol. 2, 180–81. On Sebüktigin, see the translation of the passage on the Ghaznavids from *Ra's māl an-nadīm* by Ibn Bābā al-Qāshāni (d. after 500/1106–7) in Clifford Edmund Bosworth, *The Later Ghaznavids: Splendour and Decay, The Dynasty in Afghanistan and Northern India, 1040–1186* (New York, 1977), 134. In this work, Sebüktigin is portrayed as a "slave" of the chamberlain (*ḥājib*) Alptigin. Sebüktegin's son, Sultan Maḥmūd of Ghazna (d. 421/1030), was so enamored with Ayāz, his military slave, that he called himself "the slave of his slave." See Schimmel, *My Soul Is a Woman,* 18–19.

to make private use of agricultural surpluses in their regions in order to support their troops and retinues. Later, they hired tax farmers who paid the state an agreed-upon cash sum in return for the profits they could gain from the collection and sale of agricultural produce. Eventually, entire villages and their productive lands (sometimes confiscated from local elites) would be given over for the use of military commanders.

In Iraq, the economic decline of Baghdad in the second half of the tenth century created a severe shortage of hard currency, as gold and silver flowed increasingly toward Fatimid Egypt. In order to compensate themselves for this lack of currency, the Buyids exploited the institution of the *iqṭāᶜ* to an unprecedented degree. During as-Sulamī's lifetime, the *iqṭāᶜ* system spread throughout the eastern half of the Islamic world, as Buyid and Turkish emirs took over more and more lands and villages to oufit and maintain their military forces. These forces were primarily loyal to the local commander who maintained them, and acted as a double-edged sword that both promoted and threatened the interests of regional rulers. In the end, it was the Turkish beneficiaries of the *iqṭāᶜ* system, the Qarakhanids, the Ghaznavids, and eventually the Seljuqs, that brought down the Samanid and Buyid regimes.[33]

Sectarian Conflicts

The open market for goods that characterized Samanid commercial life was matched by a similarly open market of ideas, as Imāmī and Ismāᶜīlī Shiᶜites, Sufis, philosophers, partisans of Sunni doctrines, and adherents of different schools of law all competed for the hearts and minds of local rulers and their subjects. This climate of sectarian competition led many Sufis in Khurasan to reform Sufi doctrines and practices in order to bring them more into line with a universal standard of Sunni Islam. Both al-Kalābādhī and as-Sulamī were major contributors to this process. Richard Bulliet has traced the outlines of sectarian conflict in Nishapur, where religious disputes were so serious that they led to the downfall of the city in the twelfth century C.E.[34] The Palestinian geographer al-Muqaddasī, who visited Khurasan in the year 369/980, remarked that sectarian violence was the main drawback of this region, which otherwise surpassed the rest of the Islamic world in its high level of culture and learning:

33. For an introduction to the *iqṭāᶜ* system, see Hodgson, *Venture of Islam,* vol. 2, 101–2, and Shaban, *Islamic History,* vol. 2, 95–96 and 163–64. The *iqṭāᶜ* did not constitute a true feudal system, since lands reverted to the state upon the death of the person who utilized them.

34. See Bulliet, *Patricians of Nishapur,* 28–46.

> There is partisanship between the western half of Nishapur—it is the higher half and pertains to Manīshak—and the other half, pertaining to al-Ḥīra: there is frightful bigotry against any other sect. And now it has arisen between the Shiʿa and the Karrāmiyya. There is fanaticism in Sijistan between al-Samakiyya, they being the followers of [the jurist] Abū Ḥanīfa—may God have mercy on him—and al-Ṣādiqiyya, they being the followers of [the jurist] al-Shāfiʿī—may God be pleased with him. Blood is shed in these discords, so that the ruler intervenes. In Sarakhs the discord is between al-ʿArūsiyya, who are follwers of Abū Ḥanīfa, and al-Ahliyya, who are followers of al-Shāfiʿī; in Herat, between al-ʿAmaliyya and al-Karrāmiyya; in Merv, between the city people and those of al-Sūq al-ʿAtīq (the old market); in Nasā between the people of al-Khāneh and those of the extremity of the market; in Abīward, between the Kurds and the extremity of the town. I heard a man say, "An owl has not drunk from the water without becoming a fanatic." In Balkh there is bigotry against any other sect, similarly Samarqand. Of all the towns there are few that are free of fanaticism.[35]

Al-Muqaddasī's first-hand information partly confirms Bulliet's contention that conflict in Nishapur took two major forms—between partisans of Muʿtazilī and Ashʿarī theology on the one hand, and between followers of the Ḥanafī and Shāfiʿī schools of law on the other. While there seems to have been a tendency for Muʿtazilite theologians to be trained in Ḥanafī law and for Ashʿarites to be Shāfiʿīs, loyalty to a school of theology did not always follow loyalty to a school of law. While scarcely any Shāfiʿīs in Nishapur were Muʿtazilites, at least some Ḥanafīs were Ashʿarites. At times, even Shiʿites might belong to a Sunni school of law. This was the case, for example, with the Zaydīs, the sect to which the Buyids belonged, who often followed Ḥanafī law. More important is the fact that as-Sulamī and most other reformist Sufis in Khurasan were both Shāfiʿī in their legal orientation and Ashʿarī in theology, and that the Shāfiʿī school of law showed particular growth and vigor during as-Sulamī's lifetime.[36]

Although Bulliet traces the roots of sectarian conflict in Nishapur to ethnic and class differences, there were also doctrinal reasons why Shāfiʿīs would not approve of Muʿtazilī theology. The founder of the Shāfiʿī school of law, Muḥammad ibn Idrīs ash-Shāfiʿī (d. 204/820), is credited with developing the concept of the "roots of jurisprudence"

35. al-Muqaddasi, *Best Divisions,* 296–97.

36. See Bulliet, *Patricians of Nishapur,* 42–43, especially n. 23, where he finds twenty-three Sufis of Nishapur associated with the Shāfiʿī school of law, as opposed to only one who was Ḥanafī, two who were Mālikīs, and two who were Ẓāhirīs.

(uṣūl al-fiqh). In its most basic form, *uṣūl al-fiqh* is a method of legal reasoning that privileges certain types of knowledge *(ᶜilm)* over others.[37] The truest form of knowledge is that which comes from God. Thus, in solving a legal problem, the Shāfiᶜī jurist first had to look to the Qur᾿ān, which contains the revealed word of God. If the answer to a specific problem could not be found in the Qur᾿ān, the next best form of knowledge was that which was divinely inspired. This type of knowledge can be found in the *Sunna,* the Tradition of Islam as defined by the Prophet Muḥammad. By as-Sulamī's day, the content of the Sunna had been codified in collections of Prophetic traditions known as *ḥadīth.* Only when the desired answer could not be found in either the Qur᾿ān or the hadith was the jurist allowed to resort to his own reasoning *(ijtihād).* But even then, his decision had to be based on strict analogy *(qiyās)* with a text of either the Qur᾿ān or the hadith. To help him in his reasoning, the Shāfiᶜī jurist might also turn to supplementary traditions *(āthār)* of the Prophet's Companions or their successors. For as-Sulamī, who was trained in Shāfiᶜī law and closely followed the *uṣūl* method, the authoritativeness of tradition was so important that he felt obliged to document the accounts in his book of Sufi women with hadith-style chains of transmission.

The *uṣūl* approach to knowledge was opposed to that of the Muᶜtazilites, who relied less on tradition and more on reason and formal logic as bases of interpretation.[38] Calling themselves the "people of [divine] justice and unity" *(ahl al-ᶜadl wa at-tawḥīd),* they resisted any attempt to place intermediaries between God and His creatures. For the Muᶜtazilites, Allāh was a God of justice, who could do no evil, and created the universe and set it in motion according to laws of His own making. The world was a moral testing-ground for the human being, where each person was judged on the basis of freely made choices of good or evil. Also belonging to this world was the Qur᾿ān, which was seen by the Muᶜtazilites as a revelation created by God and sent down to the Prophet Muḥammad at a specific time and place. For Shāfiᶜīs and other adherents of the *uṣūl* method, the danger of this belief was that it undermined the authority of the Sharīᶜa by allowing the possibility that certain rulings of the Qur᾿ān could be altered if conditions changed enough to justify such a move.

37. For a good introduction to the *uṣūl al-fiqh* method, see Mohammed Hashim Kamali, *Principles of Islamic Jurisprudence* (Cambridge, 1991).

38. On the history and doctrines of Muᶜtazilism, see Richard C. Martin, Mark R. Woodward, and Dwi S. Atmaja, *Defenders of Reason in Islam: Muᶜtazilism from Medieval School to Modern Symbol* (Oxford, 1997), esp. 25–115.

Despite strong anti-Muᶜtazilite sentiment among Sunni scholars, Muᶜtazilism was favored by the Buyid emirs of Baghdad and Fars and remained influential throughout the region of Khurasan. Zaydī and Imāmī Shiᶜites were particularly attracted by the Muᶜtazilī doctrines of justice and free will, because they justified the right of an Imam from the family of the Prophet to rise against oppression and injustice. Given the widespread interest in Muᶜtazilism in this period, opposition to Muᶜtazilī theology by the Sufi reformers of Khurasan and their non-Sufi *uṣūlī* allies should be seen as directed at two sets of opponents—the Muᶜtazilites themselves, who could be found among the Ḥanafī scholars of the Samanid state, and the Zaydī and Imāmī Shiᶜites, who represented a threat to Sunni Islam because of Buyid patronage.[39]

Ashᶜarī theology was favored by many uṣūlīs and Sufis as an alternative to Muᶜtazilism. The founder of Ashᶜarism, Abū al-Ḥasan al-Ashᶜarī (d. 323/935), was himself a former Muᶜtazilite. Criticizing the Muᶜtazilites for limiting their conception of the Absolute to the conventions of human reason, he created a theology that simultaneously maintained God's transcendence and God's immanence. For al-Ashᶜarī, God was more than a Creator and Law-Giver who allowed humans to chart their own course. Instead, God was an active participant in all human and worldly affairs, an eternally recreating Creator, who refashioned the world at every moment in time. For the Sufis, this theology provided a justification for the continuity of divine inspiration (*ilhām*) and the miracles of saints (sing. *karāma*). To most Muᶜtazilites, anything other than a prophetic revelation or a prophetic miracle was inconceivable because each miracle or act of revelation required an extraordinary interference in the natural order of things. For Ashᶜarī Sufis, however, such miraculous "rendings of the fabric of custom" (sing. *kharq al-ᶜāda*) were much less extraordinary because each moment in time was a miracle in itself. Since God continuously recreated the world at each moment, the creation of a miracle or the opening of a channel of divine inspiration involved no more than adding a minor wrinkle to the fabric of creation. For as-Sulamī, the most important miracles were revelatory in nature. In his book of Sufi women, the only miracles mentioned are *ilhāmāt*, instances of divine inspiration.[40]

39. For an excellent overview of the Muᶜtazila-Sufi dispute, see Florian Sobieroj, "The Muᶜtazila and Sufism," *Islamic Mysticism Contested: Thirteen Centuries of Controversies and Polemics,* ed. Frederick de Jong and Bernd Radtke (Leiden, 1999), 68–92.

40. A similar emphasis on knowledge-based or "epistemological" miracles can be found in early Moroccan Sufism, which was influenced by the Khurasanian Sufi tradition. See Cornell, *Realm of the Saint*, esp. 115–16.

AS-SULAMĪ'S LIFE AND WORKS

Primary Influences

Abū ᶜAbd ar-Raḥmān Muḥammad ibn al-Ḥusayn as-Sulamī was born on 10 Jumāda II, 325 (4 April, 937), according to his disciple and biographer Muḥammad al-Khashshāb (d. 456/1054).[41] His father, al-Ḥusayn ibn Muḥammad al-Azdī, was an ascetic who followed *ṭarīq al-malāma*, the Sufi "path of blame." He was trained in this method by ᶜAbdallāh ibn Munāzil (d. 329/941), the leader of the *malāmatiyya* in Nishapur.[42] The *malāmatiyya* are well known in the history of Sufism for seeking public disapproval by appearing to break the rules of the Law, the Sharīᶜa. Ibn Munāzil, however, did not follow such an antinomian approach to Sufism. His approach to the *malāmatiyya* was based on the Qur'ān and the Sunna and involved a strongly ethical interpretation of Islam.[43] As-Sulamī's father was also a specialist in ethical conduct.[44] When his son Abū ᶜAbd ar-Raḥmān was born, al-Ḥusayn ibn Muḥammad took all of his possessions, sold them, and gave the money to the poor, saying to himself: "A son has been given to you and you have nothing to give him. If he becomes righteous, he will be a patron for the righteous. But if he becomes an evildoer, he has been given no means to do evil."[45] Actions such as this were typical of the *malāmatiyya*. By giving away his possessions, as-Sulamī's father did not mean to deprive his son of his livelihood. Rather, he desired to sanctify him according to the words of the Qur'ān: "Of their possessions take alms, that you may purify and sanctify them."[46]

41. Gerhard Böwering, "al-Sulamī," *EI²*, 811–12; and Abū ᶜAbd ar-Raḥmān as-Sulamī, *Ṭabaqāt aṣ-Ṣūfiyya*, ed. Nūr ad-Dīn Shurayba, 18 (the Common Era date is incorrect in this latter source.) Much of al-Khashshāb's information on as-Sulamī can be found in Shams ad-Dīn Muḥammad adh-Dhahabī (d. 748/1374), *Siyar aᶜlām an-nubalā'*, ed. Shuᶜayb al-Arna'ūt et. al. (Beirut, 1996), vol.17, 247–55. Adh-Dhahabī also cites another source which claims that as-Sulamī was born in 330/942.

42. Jāmī, *Nafaḥāt al-uns,* 312. On Ibn Munāzil, see as-Sulamī, *Ṭabaqāt aṣ-ṣūfiyya*, 326–29; and ᶜAbd al-Karīm ibn Hāwāzin al-Qushayrī, *ar-Risāla al-Qushayriyya fī ᶜilm at-taṣawwuf*, ed. Maᶜrūf Zurayq and ᶜAlī ᶜAbd al-Ḥamīd Bilṭarjī, (Beirut, 1410/1990), 435. For information on Umm Kulthūm, a female disciple of Ibn Munāzil, see *Dhikr an-niswa,* section LXXIII below.

43. For as-Sulamī's *uṣūl*-based view of the *malāmatiyya,* see idem, "Risāla al-Malāmatiyya," in Abū al-ᶜAlā al-ᶜAfifi, *al-Malāmatiyya wa aṣ-ṣūfiyya wa ahl al-futuwwa*, 86–160.

44. Jāmī, *Nafaḥāt al-uns*, 312. The Persian text reads: *dar ᶜulūm muᶜāmaleh kāmil bud.*

45. Ibid.

46. Qur'ān 9 (*at-Tawba*), 103.

Al-Ḥusayn ibn Muḥammad al-Azdī died in the year 345/956–57, leaving little to support his wife and son.[47] This did not prove to be a problem, however, because as-Sulamī's mother was from one of the most important families of Nishapur. The Sulamīs, his mother's family, controlled villages and large amounts of land in the region of Ustuvā, north of the city.[48] This may have been a reason why her son took the name of as-Sulamī, rather than al-Azdī, the name of his father. By doing so, he continued a tradition started by his great-great grandfather, Aḥmad ibn Yūsuf as-Sulamī (d. 264/878), who was the premier hadith scholar of his time in Khurasan. Like Abū ᶜAbd ar-Raḥmān as-Sulamī, Aḥmad ibn Yūsuf took the name of as-Sulamī from his mother, although his father was an Azdī. He is said to have stated: "I am not a Sulamī but an Azdī. But my house is Sulamī."[49] This practice of tracing a man's primary line of descent through his mother, which Ruth Roded has termed "semimatrilineal ascription," was common in the early centuries of Islam, especially in cases like that of as-Sulamī, where the mother's social status was higher than that of the father.[50]

Upon his father's death, the responsibility for as-Sulamī's education passed to his mother's father, Ismāᶜīl ibn Nujayd (d. 365/976–77), who had no living son of his own. Like Aḥmad ibn Yūsuf as-Sulamī, Ibn Nujayd was a specialist in hadith, and counted among his teachers the son of Aḥmad ibn Ḥanbal.[51] He was initiated into Sufism as a youth by Abū ᶜUthmān al-Ḥīrī (d. 298/910) and met the great Sufi shaykh Abū al-Qāsim al-Junayd (d. 298/910) in Baghdad. Like as-Sulamī's father, Ibn Nujayd was a *malāmatī* Sufi, although he was not a disciple of Ibn Munāzil. However, his "path of blame" was similarly ethical and was based on the principles of *futuwwa*, which he learned from al-Ḥīrī.[52] Al-Ḥīrī, who was

47. Jāmī, *Nafaḥāt al-uns*, 312. Böwering's contention that as-Sulamī's father left Nishapur to settle in Mecca ["al-Sulamī," *EI*², 811] is apparently mistaken. Although Nūr ad-Dīn Shurayba, the editor of *Ṭabaqāt aṣ-ṣūfiyya*, says that as-Sulamī's father "went off to be God's neighbor" (*intaqala . . . ilā jiwār Allāh*), this is a euphemism for death. See as-Sulamī, *Ṭabaqāt aṣ-Ṣūfiyya*, 17.

48. On the land-holdings of the Sulamīs and the related clan of the Qushayrīs in Ustuvā see Bulliet, *Patricians of Nishapur*, 151.

49. adh-Dhahabī, *Siyar aᶜlām an-nubalāᵓ*, vol.12, 385.

50. See Ruth Roded, *Women in Islamic Biographical Collections: From Ibn Saᶜd to* Who's Who (Boulder, Colorado and London, 1994), 12, 56–57, 140–41. The most famous example of semimatrilineal ascription is that of the Shiᶜite Imams, who trace their descent from the Prophet Muḥammad through the Prophet's daughter Fāṭima

51. adh-Dhahabī, *Siyar aᶜlām an-nubalāᵓ*, vol.16, 146. On Ibn Nujayd see also, as-Sulamī, *Ṭabaqāt aṣ-ṣūfiyya*, 454–57 and al-Qushayrī, *ar-Risāla*, 435–36.

52. In *Dhikr an-niswa*, as-Sulamī mentions five female disciples of al-Ḥīrī: a wife of Ibn Nujayd known as Fakhrawayh bint ᶜAlī (section XLI V), Fāṭima al-Ḥajāfiyya (section XLV), ᶜĀᵓisha the daughter of al-Ḥīrī (section XLVII), ᶜĀᵓisha of Merv (section LII), and Fāṭima bint Aḥmad al-Hānīᵓ (section LIII). All were practitioners of *futuwwa*.

originally from Rayy, had been a disciple of the great Persian master of *futuwwa*, Shāh ibn Shujāᶜ al-Kirmānī (d. before 300/912–13). *Futuwwa* is a type of Sufi chivalry that stresses altruism and brotherhood. According to as-Sulamī, one of his grandfather's favorite sayings about *futuwwa* was: "Putting virtue to work (*tarbīyat al-iḥsān*) is better than virtue itself."[53]

Ismāᶜīl ibn Nujayd did more than just teach his grandson *futuwwa*, he also practiced it in all aspects of his life. For example, he would never take credit for acts of charity.[54] When Ibn Nujayd's father died and left him a large inheritance, he anonymously gave it all away for the maintenance of scholars and ascetics. Once, when al-Ḥīrī asked for money to be donated for the defence of Islam, Ibn Nujayd gave him two thousand silver dirhams. But when al-Ḥīrī told his Sufi disciples about the gift, Ibn Nujayd asked for it to be returned, saying, "I have given you money that belonged to my mother, so give it back." Later that night, he gave the money once again to al-Ḥīrī, but asked the shaykh to keep the gift concealed. Afterwards, al-Ḥīrī stated, "I stand ashamed before the spiritual motivation (*himma*) of Abū ᶜAmr[ibn Nujayd]."[55]

Later Influences

As-Sulamī learned respect for scholarly authority from his teacher of Shāfiᶜī jurisprudence, Abū Sahl as-Saᶜlūkī (d 369/980). As-Saᶜlūkī was the most important teacher of Shāfiᶜī law in Nishapur and was also an Ashᶜarī theologian.[56] It was said that his knowledge was vast and that his standards were uncompromising. In one session that as-Sulamī attended, when the students were reciting the Qurᵓān, as-Saᶜlūkī suddenly changed the style of recitation to rhythmic chanting. Feeling irritated at

53. As-Sulamī, *Ṭabaqāt aṣ-ṣūfiyya*, 455. This saying is a paraphrase of the verse of the Qurᵓān: "Is there any reward for good other than good (*hal jazāᵓu al-iḥsān illā al-iḥsān*)?" Qurᵓān, 55 (*ar-Raḥmān*), 60.

54. Anonymous acts of charity are recommended in the Qurᵓān: "If you disclose acts of charity, it is well; but if you conceal them and make sure that they reach the poor (*al-fuqarāᵓ*), it is better for you, for it will absolve you of your evil deeds; and God is fully aware of what you do." Qurᵓān, 2 (*al-Baqara*), 271. Because the term, *al-fuqarāᵓ* (the poor), is commonly used by Sufis to refer to themselves, this injunction may be understood as recommending that charity be given to the Sufis.

55. adh-Dhahabi, *Siyar aᶜlām an-nubalāᵓ*, vol.16, 147.

56. On Abū Sahl as-Saᶜlūkī (also known as "as-Suᶜlūkī"), see Bulliet, *Patricians of Nishapur*, 115–17. Böwering's contention that as-Saᶜlūkī followed the Ḥanafī school of jurisprudence ["al-Sulamī," *EI²*, 811] is incorrect. He was known as "al-Ḥanafī" only because he was descended from the Arab tribe of Banū Ḥanīfa.

this, as-Sulamī asked himself, "Why?" Later, his teacher said to him: "Do you not know that whoever says to his master 'Why?' will never meet with success?"[57] As-Saᶜlūkī also said: "Disobedience toward parents can be erased by forgiveness; disobedience toward teachers can be erased in no way."[58]

After his father and grandfather, the most influential teacher of Sufism for as-Sulamī was his spiritual master, Abū al-Qāsim Ibrāhīm an-Naṣrābādhī (d. 367/977–78), who resided in Nishapur between the years 340/951 and 365/976.[59] It was probably from an-Naṣrābādhī that as-Sulamī developed his interest in sacred biography, for he tells us that the former was educated in many disciplines, including the biographies (*siyar*) and history (*taʾrīkh*) of the Sufis.[60] ᶜAlī ibn ᶜUthmān al-Hujwīrī (d. ca. 469/1076–77), the author of *Kashf al-maḥjūb* (Unveiling the Veiled), calls an-Naṣrābādhī the most learned and devout man of his age and "the master of the later shaykhs of Khurasan."[61]

There is no doubt that as-Sulamī and an-Naṣrābādhī were close; as-Sulamī quotes an-Naṣrābādhī extensively on the subject of Sufism and accompanied him when he left Nishapur for Mecca in 366/977. Thus, it is somewhat surprising that in his book of Sufi women he subjects his shaykh to criticism from Umm al-Ḥusayn al-Qurashiyya, a female disciple of an-Naṣrābādhī who came from one of the most powerful families of Nishapur. Acting as her teacher's conscience, Umm al-Ḥusayn reproaches an-Naṣrābādhī for his personal failings, such as when she says to him during one of his lectures: "How fine are your words and how ugly are your morals!"[62] In an account related by the biographer Muḥammad adh-Dhahabī (d. 748/1374), as-Sulamī mentions that despite an-Naṣrābādhī's high reputation as a Sufi master, he was beaten, humiliated, and even jailed for his views, such as when he was accused of telling his followers to circumambulate the tombs of saints in the same way that one would circumambulate the Kaᶜba in Mecca.[63]

57. Bulliet, *Patricians of Nishapur*, 116. For the exact text of this report, see adh-Dhahabi, *Siyar aᶜlām an-nubalāʾ*, vol.17, 251.

58. Bulliet, *Patricians of Nishapur*, 117.

59. Ibid., 150. In *Dhikr an-niswa*, as-Sulamī mentions three female disciples of an-Naṣrābādhī: Umm Kulthūm, who was previously mentioned as a disciple of Ibn Munāzil (section LXXIII); Umm ᶜAlī, the daughter of the Sufi ᶜAbdallāh ibn Ḥamshādh (section LXXV); and Jumᶜa bint Muḥammad, also known as Umm al-Ḥusayn al-Qurashiyya (sections LXVI and LXXVIII).

60. as-Sulamī, *Ṭabaqāt aṣ-ṣūfiyya*, 484.

61. ᶜAlī b. ᶜUthmān al-Jullābī al-Hujwīrī, *The Kashf al-Mahjūb: The Oldest Persian Treatise on Sufism*, trans. Reynold A. Nicholson, (London, 1976 reprint of 1911 first edition), 159.

62. *Dhikr an-niswa,* section LXVI below.

63. adh-Dhahabī, *Siyar aᶜlām an-nubalāʾ*, vol.16, 264–65.

Another important Sufi who influenced as-Sulamī was Muḥammad ibn Khafīf of Shiraz (d. 371/982). Although Ibn Khafīf lived in the region of Fars in southwestern Iran, his wife was a native of Nishapur and came from a family that was known to the Sufis of Khurasan.[64] As-Sulamī clearly held Ibn Khafīf in the highest regard. He describes him as "knowledgeable in the outward and inward sciences" and praises him as the "foremost Sufi shaykh of his time in his spiritual states, his knowledge, and his morals."[65] As-Sulamī also informs us that he visited Ibn Khafīf and obtained from him a written authorization (*ijāza*) to transmit both Sufi and Prophetic traditions. This most likely occurred during as-Sulamī's return from his pilgrimage to Mecca.

It may also have been through Ibn Khafīf that as-Sulamī met the famous Ash^c^arī theologian Abū Bakr al-Bāqillānī (d. 403/1012–13). When al-Bāqillānī visited Shiraz during the reign of the Buyid emir ^c^Aḍuḍ ad-Dawla (r. in Fars 338–72/949–83), he dropped in on Ibn Khafīf while the latter was teaching *Kitāb al-luma^c^* (The Inspired Treatise), a work on theology written by al-Ash^c^arī. When al-Bāqillānī told Ibn Khafīf to continue his lesson, the Sufi refused, saying: "I am like one who is forced to make his ablution without water. If one finds water, there is no need to make the ablution without it." "You are not a person who makes his ablution without water," al-Bāqillānī replied. "On the contrary, you possess great knowledge and are on the right path, so may Allah give you success!"[66] At least one account claims that as-Sulamī studied Ash^c^arī theology under al-Bāqillānī in Shiraz during this same period.[67]

As-Sulamī left for Mecca with an-Naṣrābādhī in the year following his grandfather's death. Since Ibn Nujayd had no eligible male heirs, his entire inheritance, which consisted of estates, trade goods, and three shares in a village, passed to as-Sulamī's mother.[68] Although he was nearly forty years old at the time, as-Sulamī could not go to Mecca without his mother's permission. Being her trustee and heir, he could not undertake such a long and potentially dangerous journey without ensuring that she would be taken care of in case he did not return. Instead of preventing

64. as-Sulamī, *Ṭabaqāt aṣ-ṣūfiyya*, 462. A female disciple of Ibn Khafīf was al-Wahatiyya Umm al-Faḍl. See *Dhikr an-niswa,* section LXVII below.

65. as-Sulamī, *Ṭabaqāt aṣ-ṣūfiyya*, 462.

66. Introduction to Abū Bakr Muḥammad ibn aṭ-Ṭayyib al-Bāqillānī, *I^c^jāz al-Qur^ɔ^ān*, ed. Aḥmad Ṣaqr (Beirut reprint of 1954 Cairo edition), 21. This account was related by al-Bāqillānī himself.

67. Ibid., 32.

68. adh-Dhahabī, *Siyar a^c^lām an-nubalā^ɔ^*, vol.17, 249. Böwering's contention that as-Sulamī left for Mecca before his grandfather's death ("al-Sulamī," *EI*^{2}, 811) is contradicted by this source.

her son from making the journey, as-Sulamī's mother willingly gave her permission and told her son to take an advance on his inheritance to finance his pilgrimage. This consisted of one share in a village, which as-Sulamī sold for one thousand gold dinars. Before he left, his mother said to him: "You have set yourself toward the House of God. So make sure that your guardian angels do not write down anything that you will be ashamed of tomorrow."[69]

The name of as-Sulamī's mother does not appear in any extant source on his life, nor does it appear in his book of Sufi women. Similarly veiled from public view is the name of his maternal grandmother or any information about his own wife and children. Since Fakhrawayh bint ᶜAlī, a wife of as-Sulamī's grandfather who was not related to as-Sulamī, is mentioned in his book of Sufi women, this lack of information must be taken as intentional.[70] In Islamic culture, the mother is respected to the point of reverence.[71] She is the most important female companion to her son other than his wife, and is an intimate presence whose counsel is so highly valued that in biographical accounts it is often used for the voice of one's conscience. Because of this intimacy, the mother, like one's wife and children, is included within the sacred domain of the *maḥram*, the inner domain of the family, which must be protected from the prying gaze of the outside world. If as-Sulamī wanted to use his mother as an example, respect demanded that he preserve her *ḥurma,* her honored status, by concealing her identity. Since she did not choose to reveal herself to others, he had no right to publicize her identity.

Nūr ad-Dīn Shurayba, the editor of as-Sulamī's *Ṭabaqāt aṣ-ṣūfiyya*, mentions a total of twenty-eight teachers of as-Sulamī, whose specialties ranged from the Arabic language to Qurᵓānic studies, hadith, jurisprudence, and Sufism.[72] In order to complete his studies, as-Sulamī traveled throughout Khurasan, Iran, and Iraq, spending long periods of time in

69. Ibid. This account is similar to another related about the mother of Sufyān ath-Thawrī (d. 161/777–78), a famous legist whom as-Sulamī mentions in his notice on Rābiᶜa al-ᶜAdawiyya (*Dhikr an-niswa,* section I below). Sufyān's mother used the profits from her spinning to pay for her son's education. "Oh my son," she counseled him, "Whenever you put ten letters down on a page, think back on your progress and see whether you have grown in spirit, maturity, or dignity. If you have not progressed in this way, then know that your learning will neither harm nor benefit you." Jamāl ad-Dīn Abū al-Faraj ibn al-Jawzī (d. 597/1201), *Ṣifat aṣ-Ṣafwa*, ed. Maḥmūd Fākhūrī and Muḥammad Rawwās Qalᶜanjī (Beirut, 1406/1986), vol. 3, 189. See also, Nelly Amri and Laroussi Amri, *Les femmes soufies ou la passion de Dieu* (St. Jean de Braye, France, 1992), 89.

70. See *Dhikr an-niswa,* section XLIV below.

71. On the importance of the mother in Islamic culture, see Schimmel, *My Soul Is a Woman*, 89–97.

72. See Shurayba, introduction to as-Sulamī, *Ṭabaqāt aṣ-ṣūfiyya*, 19–24

Merv and Baghdad. He reached the western limit of his travels during his pilgrimage to Mecca with an-Naṣrābādhī, most likely returning to Nishapur by way of the cities of Isfahan and Shiraz in the region of Fars. Apart from the individuals already mentioned, the most important of as-Sulamī's teachers and associates were the Shāfiᶜī jurist and theologian Abū Bakr ash-Shāshī (d. 366/976–77) and the Sufi biographer Abū Nuᶜaym al-Iṣfahānī (d. 430/1038–39), a younger contemporary of as-Sulamī who saw himself more as the latter's student than as his colleague. As-Sulamī also may have known Abū Naṣr as-Sarrāj at-Tūsī (d. 378/988), the author of *Kitāb al-lumaᶜ fi at-taṣawwuf* (The Inspired Treatise on Sufism), for this work contains accounts about Abū ᶜUthmān al-Ḥīrī that were transmitted by as-Sulamī's grandfather.[73]

Major Works

Although as-Sulamī has long been seen as an important systematizer of Sufi doctrine, he has not been regarded as significantly more important than his immediate predecessors, such as as-Sarrāj or al-Kalābādhī, or his immediate successors, such as al-Iṣfahānī or his student Abū al-Qāsim al-Qushayrī (d. 465/1072–73). However, Gerhard Böwering's recent publication of as-Sulamī's shorter Qurᵓān commentary and the discovery of previously unknown treatises by as-Sulamī should lead to a reassessment of his legacy.[74] As an indication of his importance to Sufi doctrine, one need only refer to al-Qushayrī's *ar-Risāla fi ᶜilm at-taṣawwuf* (Treatise on the Science of Sufism). A close examination of this work reveals the teachings of both as-Sulamī and his Sufi master an-Naṣrābādhī, who was also the teacher of al-Qushayrī's primary shaykh, Abū ᶜAlī ad-Daqqāq (d. 405/1015).[75]

As-Sulamī's attempt to systematize Sufi doctrines can be characterized as an "uṣūlization" project, because it involved bringing Sufism into

73. Abū Naṣr al-Sarrāj, *Kitāb al-Lumaᶜ fi'l-Taṣawwuf*, ed. R. A. Nicholson, (London, 1963 reprint of 1914 first edition), xviii. Nūr ad-Dīn Shurayba (Introduction to as-Sulamī, *Ṭabaqāt aṣ-ṣūfiyya*, 48) sees as-Sarrāj as a major link between al-Junayd and as-Sulamī. While such a connection may have existed, as-Sulamī was already linked to al-Junayd via both an-Naṣrābādhī and his grandfather, Ismāᶜīl ibn Nujayd.

74. Gerhard Böwering, *The Minor Qurᵓān Commentary of Abū ᶜAbd ar-Raḥmān Muḥammad b. al-Ḥusayn as-Sulamī* (d. 412/1021) (Beirut, 1995). As-Sulamī's newly discovered treatises will be discussed below.

75. Bulliet, *Patricians of Nishapur*, 150–53. Al-Qushayrī was so much a part of as-Sulamī's circle that he chose to go on the pilgrimage to Mecca with two friends who were also students of as-Sulamī. These were Abū Muḥammad al-Juwaynī (d. 431/1039–40) and Abū Bakr al-Bayhaqī (d. 458/1066). Ibid., 152, and Shurayba, introduction to as-Sulamī, *Ṭabaqāt aṣ-ṣūfiyya*, 25–26.

agreement with the Sunna of the Prophet Muḥammad, as defined by the methodology of uṣūl.[76] As-Sulamī's role in this project is described in the following passage by al-Iṣfahānī, who provides a clear account of as-Sulamī's aims and objectives:

> Abū ᶜAbd ar-Raḥmān as-Sulamī was one of those whom we met. He was a person who took utmost care in systematizing and correcting the methodology of the Sufis (*tawṭiʾat madhhab al-mutaṣawwifa wa tahdhībihi*) according to the doctrines of the earliest generations of Muslims. This was to be accomplished by emulating their characteristics, making their spiritual practices obligatory, and following the traditions of their teachings, distinguishing them from the teachings of those who are defective in their practices and confused about the Way among the ignorant followers of this school. [As-Sulamī] disapproved of these [latter Sufis] because, for him, the reality of this method lay in emulating the Messenger of God (may God bless and preserve him) in his statements, his laws, his directives, and his proclamations, and in following the example of the most knowledgeable scholars of Sufism, the transmitters of tradition, and the wisest of the legal specialists.[77]

According to al-Khashshāb, as-Sulamī had written nearly seven hundred works on Sufism by the time of his death in 412/1021.[78] Since books in this period were often composed of separate sections that were counted individually, it is best to think of this number as referring to "chapters" rather than to actual books. There is no doubt, however, that as-Sulamī was a prolific writer. This was due in part to the fact that he inherited a library of considerable size from his grandfather, Ismāᶜīl ibn Nujayd. In *Taʾrīkh Baghdād* (The History of Baghdad), the biographer al-Khaṭīb al-Baghdādī (d. 463/1071), who knew as-Sulamī's student al-Qushayrī, provides a view of as-Sulamī seated in his library surrounded by books, which included an alchemical work by the Sufi martyr al-Ḥallāj (d. 309/921–22).[79] As-Sulamī's works were apparently the Sufi "best-sellers" of their day. Al-Khashshāb says that they were in high demand in as-Sulamī's lifetime, and that even a copy of one of as-Sulamī's treatises in al-Khashshāb's poor handwriting could sell for up to twenty gold dinars.

76. I am indebted to my husband, Vincent J. Cornell, for the concept of "uṣūlization."

77. Abū Nuᶜaym Aḥmad ibn ᶜAbdallāh al-Iṣfahānī, *Ḥilyat al-awliyāʾ wa ṭabaqāt al-aṣfiyāʾ*, ed. Abū Hājir Saᶜīd ibn Basyūnī Zaghlūl (Beirut reprint, n.d.), vol. 2, 25.

78. adh-Dhahabi, *Siyar aᶜlām an-nubalāʾ*, vol. 17, 247.

79. Abū Bakr Aḥmad ibn ᶜAlī al-Khaṭīb al-Baghdādī, *Taʾrīkh Baghdād aw Madīnat as-Salām*, ed. Muṣṭafā ᶜAbd al-Qādir ᶜAṭā (Beirut, 1997), vol. 2, 245. The work by al-Ḥallāj was entitled *aṣ-Ṣayhūr fī naqḍ ad-duhūr* (The Smelting Process in the Contravention of Time).

He further reports that a copy of as-Sulamī's Qur'ān commentary was sold in Egypt for one thousand dinars and that a child was crushed to death by a crowd that rushed to attend a public reading of one of as-Sulamī's biographical works in the city of Hamadan.[80]

As-Sulamī's works can be divided into three types: (1) sacred biographies[81] or works on the lives and teachings of famous Sufis, (2) treatises on Sufi institutions and practices, and (3) commentaries on the Qur'ān. His book of Sufi women belongs to the category of sacred biography. As-Sulamī wrote this work as a supplement to his famous *Ṭabaqāt aṣ-ṣūfiyya* (Generations of the Sufis), which originally contained one hundred notices about Sufi men.[82] Most scholars believe that *Ṭabaqāt aṣ-ṣūfiyya* was itself an abridgment of a much larger work entitled *Ta'rīkh aṣ-ṣūfiyya* (History of the Sufis). This earlier compendium, which is now lost, contained one thousand biographical notices.[83] Another lost work in this genre was *Sunan aṣ-ṣūfiyya* (Traditions of the Sufis). Its contents were partly integrated into the writings of as-Sulamī's student, the traditionist Abū Bakr al-Bayhaqī (d. 458/1066).[84] Al-Khaṭīb al-Baghdādī mentions a fifth biographical work by as-Sulamī, *al-Ikhwa wa al-akhawāt min aṣ-ṣūfiyya* (Brothers and Sisters among the Sufis), about which little is known at the present time.[85] All of as-Sulamī's biographical works, including his book of Sufi women, contributed to the program of uṣūlization by tracing the origins of Sufi practices to the example set by the Prophet Muḥammad, his Companions, and other major figures from the first generations of Islam.

As-Sulamī's most widely disseminated works were his treatises on Sufi practices and institutions. These can be found throughout the Muslim world and are still regarded as authoritative. As-Sulamī appears to have been more concerned in these writings with Sufi practice (*ᶜamal*) than with the intellectual aspects of Sufi doctrine (*ᶜilm*). Although all of the Sufi reformers of this period discussed both doctrine and practice, each

80. adh-Dhahabī, *Siyar aᶜlām an-nubalā'*, vol.17, 248.

81. "Sacred biography," comes from Thomas Heffernan, who defines the term as: "a narrative text of the vita of the saint written by a member of a community of belief." Idem, *Sacred Biography: Saints and Their Biographers in the Middle Ages* (Oxford, 1988), 15–16.

82. This work has been published in two edited editions: that of Nūr ad-Dīn Shurayba and an earlier edition by Johannes Pedersen (Leiden, 1960). The edited editions of *Ṭabaqāt aṣ-ṣūfiyya* now contain 105 biographical notices.

83. On this work see Böwering, "al-Sulamī," EI^2, 811. It is unclear whether *Ta'rīkh aṣ-ṣūfiyya* contained any notices on Sufi women.

84. Ibid., 811–12.

85. al-Baghdādī, *Ta'rīkh Baghdād,* vol.7, 115.

gave a distinct emphasis to one or the other in his works. In *Kitāb al-luma*^c^,for example, Abū Naṣr as-Sarrāj is primarily concerned with situating Sufism within the theological and juridical sciences of Islam.[86] For him, Sufism was a distinct school of thought (*madhhab*), whose roots could be found in the Qur^ɔ^ān and the Sunna. Thus, he portrays the Sufis as religious specialists (*^c^ulamā^ɔ^*) who share a common cause with the jurists and theologians of normative Islam. As-Sarrāj's argument in favor of orthodox mysticism is heavily indebted to the scholastic-theological (*kalām*) tradition of Islamic thought. By contrast, al-Kalābādhī, the author of *Kitāb at-ta^c^arruf*, takes Sufism's status as a school of Islamic thought for granted, and is more concerned with tracing Sufism's intellectual origins and providing definitions of mystical stations and states. The doctrinal emphasis of this work is reflected in A. J. Arberry's translation of its title: *The Doctrine of the Ṣūfis*. Abū Nu^c^aym al-Iṣfahānī returns to as-Sarrāj's more apologetic agenda in *Ḥilyat al-awliyā^ɔ^ wa ṭabaqāt al-aṣfiyā^ɔ^* (Adornment of the Saints and Generations of the Pure). Unlike as-Sarrāj and al-Kalābādhī, but more like as-Sulamī, he makes his case for Sufism's place in normative Islam through the medium of sacred biography, creating a massive compendium of the heroes of Islamic spirituality which culminates in the Sufis as the true followers of the Prophet Muḥammad and his Companions. Like other authors of sacred biography, his tendency also was to foreground practice instead of doctrine.

Thus, if as-Sarrāj can be seen as the theologian of the Sufi uṣūlization project, al-Kalābādhī was its doctrinal specialist and al-Iṣfahānī was its biographer. As-Sulamī played a crucial role in this project by defining the boundaries of Sufi practice. First, he sought to purge the Sufi method of its deviant practices and distinguished Sufism from other forms of Islamic devotion and asceticism.[87] Second, he developed normative models for new approaches to Sufism, such as *futuwwa*, the popular institution of Sufi chivalry. These interests are illustrated in the titles of his most famous treatises, such as: *Kitāb al-malāmatiyya wa ghalaṭāt aṣ-ṣūfiyya* (The Path of Blame and the Errors of the Sufis), *Kitāb al-futuwwa* (Book of Sufi Chivalry), *Kitāb ^c^uyūb an-nafs wa mudāwātuhā* (The Faults of the Soul and

86. For an overview of this work, see R. A. Nicholson's introduction to *Kitàb al-Luma*^c^, i-lxiv.

87. A predecessor of as-Sulamī in this role may have been Ja^c^far al-Khuldī (d. 348/959), who excluded a number of famous mystics of Khurasan, such as al-Ḥakīm at-Tirmidhī (d. ca. 295/908) from the ranks of the Sufis. As-Sulamī relied on al-Khuldī as a source for his information on Sufi women. See below and Sara Sviri, "Ḥakīm Tirmidhī and the *Malāmatī* Movement in Early Sufism," *Classical Persian Sufism: from its Origins to Rumi*, ed. Leonard Lewisohn (London and New York, 1993), 592–94.

Their Cures), *Manāhij al-ᶜārifīn* (Approaches of the Gnostics), and *Darajāt al-muᶜamalāt* (Degrees of Ethical Conduct).[88] The Riyadh manuscript of as-Sulamī texts, in which as-Sulamī's book of Sufi women is to be found, contains a number of previously unknown treatises of the same type, such as *Kitāb alfāẓ aṣ-ṣūfiyya* (Book of Sufi Terms), *Kitāb al-firāsa* (Book of Clairvoyance), and two works of an ethical and political nature, *Naṣīḥat al-umarāʾ wa al-wuzarāʾ* (Advice for Princes and Viziers) and *Dhamm takabbur al-ᶜulamāʾ* (Condemnation of the Arrogance of Scholars).

Apart from the biographical *Taʾrīkh aṣ-ṣūfiyya*, the most extensive work that as-Sulamī produced was his exegesis of the Qurʾān, *Ḥaqāʾiq at-tafsīr* (Realities of Exegesis).[89] This book, which still exists in numerous manuscript copies, has not yet been edited, although a shorter version entitled *Ziyādat ḥaqāʾiq at-tafsīr* (Addendum to "Realities of Exegesis") was published by Böwering in 1995.[90] Ironically, the popularity of this commentary among the elites of Iran and Khurasan caused as-Sulamī considerable inconvenience. Once, when he was on the road to Hamadan, a Buyid emir demanded that he stop his journey and make a copy of *Ḥaqāʾiq at-tafsīr* for him. In return for his trouble, which caused as-Sulamī to miss a pilgrimage to Mecca, the emir gave him a fine horse, one hundred gold dinars, and several robes of honor. The Ghaznavid prince Naṣr ibn Sebüktigin, the brother of Sultan Maḥmūd of Ghazna (r. 388–421/998–1030), was so impressed with *Ḥaqāʾiq at-tafsīr* that he had it copied in ten volumes, with the Quranic passages written in gold. However, his persistence in demanding that as-Sulamī teach the work to him personally was so irritating to the shaykh that he fled from the prince's messenger whenever the latter called on him. In order to regain his peace of mind, as-Sulamī finally agreed to authorize Naṣr ibn Sebüktegin to teach *Ḥaqāʾiq at-tafsīr* on his own behalf.[91]

Despite this acclaim from the rulers and elites of his day, as-Sulamī and his works also had their detractors. Al-Khaṭīb al-Baghdādī mentions a scholar from Nishapur named Muḥammad ibn Yūsuf al-Qaṭṭān, who

88. For a list of as-Sulamī's edited treatises, see Böwering, "al-Sulamī," EI^2, 812. As-Sulamī's *Kitāb al-futuwwa* has been rendered into English as Ibn al-Husayn al-Sulami, *The Book of Sufi Chivalry: Lessons to a Son of the Moment, Futuwwah,* trans. Tosun Bayrak al-Jerrahi al-Halvati (New York, 1983).

89. For a description of this work see Gerhard Böwering. "The Qurʾān Commentary of as-Sulamī," *Islamic Studies Presented to Charles J. Adams*, ed. Wael B. Hallaq and Donald P. Little (Leiden, 1991), 41–56.

90. See note 74 above.

91. adh-Dhahabī, *Siyar aᶜlām an-nubalāʾ*, vol.17, 248–49.

claimed that as-Sulamī lied about the length of time he spent with certain teachers of hadith.[92] Since al-Qaṭṭān appears to have come from a Ḥanafī-Muᶜtazilī family of scholars, it is probable that his accusation had more to do with anti-Sufi or anti-Shāfiᶜī sectarianism than with any of as-Sulamī's actual shortcomings.[93] Another criticism of as-Sulamī is voiced by the biographer adh-Dhahabī, who claims that *Ḥaqāʾiq at-tafsīr* contains traditions from "one of the Imams of the *bāṭinī* heresy" (*baᶜḍ al-aʾimma min zandaqat al-bāṭiniyya*), an obvious reference to the Fatimid Ismāᶜīlis.[94] This view was shared by adh-Dhahabī's teacher, the Ḥanbalī jurist Ibn Taymiyya (d. 728/1328), who reports that a scholar of the Qurʾān named Abū al-Ḥasan al-Wāḥidī went so far as to claim that anyone who approved of *Ḥaqāʾiq at-tafsīr* was an unbeliever.[95]

These criticisms by Ibn Taymiyya and other scholars of the Ḥanbalī school were due to the fact that in his Qurʾān commentary as-Sulamī frequently cites Jaᶜfar aṣ-Ṣādiq (d. 148/765), the sixth Shiᶜite Imam and the source of tradition to whom the Ismāᶜīlī Shīᶜa most often refer.[96] Despite the fact that as-Sulamī sought to identify Sufism with Sunni Islam, he does not appear to have been against all aspects of Shiᶜism. Like other Sufi reformers of his time, including al-Kalābādhī and al-Iṣfahānī, as-Sulamī considered the first six Shiᶜite Imams from ᶜAlī through Jaᶜfar to be forerunners of the Sufis, and thus included them among *as-Salaf aṣ-Ṣāliḥ*.[97] Although this position was fully consistent with tenth-century uṣūlī doctrine, it did not satisfy later Sunni sectarians, who were not prepared to accept any Shiᶜite—even an honored Imam such as Jaᶜfar—as a valid source of Islamic tradition.

92. al-Khaṭīb al-Baghdādī, *Taʾrīkh Baghdād*, vol.2, 245.

93. Bulliet, *Patricians of Nishapur*, 135. Abū al-Ḥasan ᶜAlī al-Qaṭṭān (d. 405/1015), a probable relative of Muḥammad ibn Yūsuf al-Qaṭṭān, held the post of imam of the congregational mosque of Nishapur.

94. adh-Dhahabī, *Siyar aᶜlām an-nubalāʾ*, vol.17, 252.

95. Ibid., 255.

96. See Gerhard Böwering, "The Major Sources of Sulamī's Minor Qurʾān Commentary," *Oriens* (35), 1996, 38–39 and 52–56.

97. See, for example, al-Iṣfahānī, *Ḥilyat al-awliyāʾ*, vol.3, 192–206. See also, al-Kalābādhī, *at-Taᶜarruf*, 11, and Arberry, *Doctrine*, 12. According to as-Sulamī's disciple, the famous malāmatī Sufi Abū Saᶜīd Abū al-Khayr (d. 440/1049), as-Sulamī traced his chain of doctrinal transmission (*silsila*) from the Prophet Muḥammad through ᶜAlī, al-Ḥusayn, and the first Shiᶜite Imams to the sixth Imam, Jaᶜfar aṣ-Ṣādiq, who then passed it on to Maᶜrūf al-Karkhī of Baghdad. Although there is a problem with this account, since Maᶜrūf al-Karkhī is known to have been an associate of the eighth Shiᶜite Imam, ᶜAlī ar-Riḍāʾ (d. 203/818), it confirms the importance of Jaᶜfar aṣ-Ṣādiq's teachings to as-Sulamī. See Muḥammad ibn al-Munawwar, *Les Étapes mystiques du shaykh Abu Sa'id: Mystères de la connaisance de l'Unique* (Asrar al Tawhid fi Maqâmât e al shaykh Abu Sa'id), trans. Mohammed Achena, (Paris, 1974), 49.

AS-SULAMĪ'S BOOK OF SUFI WOMEN

Recovering the Text

Like the scent of perfume in an abandoned palace, as-Sulamī's book of Sufi women has left its traces in Islamic sacred biography since it was first written around the turn of the eleventh century C.E. Rare even in its own time, passages from this work would occasionally appear in later biographies from different parts of the Muslim world. Such works include *Ṣifat aṣ-Ṣafwa* (The Nature of the Elect) by Abū al-Faraj ibn al-Jawzī of Baghdad (d. 597/1201), *Nafaḥāt al-uns* by the Afghani Sufi al-Jāmī, who relied on a Persian translation of as-Sulamī's *Ṭabaqāt aṣ-ṣūfiyya* by ᶜAbdallāh al-Anṣārī of Herat (d. 482/1089),[98] and *al-Kawākib ad-durriyya* (The Glittering Spheres) by the Egyptian Sufi ᶜAbd ar-Raᵓūf al-Munāwī (d. 1031/1622).[99] Curiously, none of these authors seems to have known the original title of as-Sulamī's book of Sufi women. Although it is now clear that Ibn al-Jawzī copied several of as-Sulamī's notices on Sufi women exactly, he merely cites as-Sulamī as one of his sources. Al-Jāmī comes closer to providing a title, but because he learned about as-Sulamī's writings through the translations of al-Anṣārī, he could do no more than give an approximation, stating that as-Sulamī wrote a book "mentioning the states of worshipful women and female gnostics" (Pers. *zikr aḥvāl nisveh-yi ᶜābidāt va nisāᵓ ᶜārifāt*).[100]

In the age before the printing press, when books had to be copied by hand, it was not unusual for a rare work to become the subject of hearsay. The full title might be forgotten, parts of the manuscript might be lost, the name of the author might be confused with another person, and parts of two or more different works might be combined. Yet seldom does the title of a known work disappear completely. Since the titles of several of as-Sulamī's lost works, such as *Taᵓrīkh aṣ-ṣūfiyya* and *Sunan aṣ-ṣūfiyya*, have been passed down accurately for nearly a thousand years, why did this not happen with his book of Sufi women? Might this amnesia of Islamic scholarship have been due to the fact that unlike his other works, as-Sulamī's book of Sufi women did not include men, but was written exclusively about women?

98. Schimmel, *Mystical Dimensions of Islam*, 90.

99. Margaret Smith, *Rabiᵓa: The Life and Work of Rabi'a and Other Women Mystics in Islam* (Oxford, 1994), 11.

100. Jāmī, *Nafaḥāt al-uns*, 615. Jāmī was also mistaken about the title of as-Sulamī's *Ṭabaqāt aṣ-ṣūfiyya*, calling it instead, "*Ṭabaqāt al-mashāᵓīkh*" (Generations of the Shaykhs). Ibid.

References to as-Sulamī's book of Sufi women can also be found in modern studies of Sufism, where it is portrayed as an appendix to *Ṭabaqāt aṣ-ṣūfiyya.* This tradition can be traced to al-Jāmī, who, perhaps again following al-Anṣārī, placed his section on Sufi women at the end of *Nafaḥāt al-uns*. The first modern scholar to refer to as-Sulamī's book as an appendix was Margaret Smith, who, in a 1928 study of Rābiᶜa al-ᶜAdawiyya, states: "Another missing authority which would undoubtedly be of great value is the section on women devotees and gnostics at the end of the 'Ṭabaqát al-Ṣúfiyya' of Abú 'Abd al-Raḥmán al-Sulamí, to which Jámí refers and to which there is also a reference in al-Munawwar's [sic., al-Munāwī's?] book, especially referring to Rábiᶜa."[101] The same assumption is made in a 1992 French work on Sufi women by Nelly and Laroussi Amri, who write: "Nous ne pouvons que déplorer la perte de l'ouvrage . . . d'Al-Sulamī consacré aux femmes; il s'agirait plutôt de la section féminine de ses *Ṭabaqāt al ṣūfiya* . . . qui, malheureusement, ne nous a été conservée que par les emprunts faits par Jāmī."[102] Finally, Ruth Roded, in a 1994 study of women in Islamic biographical collections, remarks: "The earliest extant dictionary of Sufis, compiled by al-Sulami . . . contained a number of women to whom later writers refer, but the section on women in his work has apparently been lost."[103]

It was thus a discovery of great importance when, in 1991, Maḥmūd Muḥammad aṭ-Ṭanāḥī came across this long-lost work in a collection of treatises by as-Sulamī in the library of Muḥammad ibn Saud Islamic University in Riyadh, Saudi Arabia.[104] Aṭ-Ṭanāḥī seems to have been interested in this collection primarily for antiquarian reasons. First, he notes that among its twenty-six titles are a number of previously unknown works by as-Sulamī. Second, it may be the oldest Sulamī manuscript in existence. The section on Sufi women contains a copyist's notation stating that it was completed ten nights before the middle of Safar in the year 474. This corresponds to a Common Era date of July 17, 1081, only sixty years (or sixty-two Islamic lunar years) after the death of as-Sulamī himself. Finally, the manuscript is a rare eleventh-century example of Arabic

101. Smith, *Rabi'a*, 12.

102. Amri and Amri, *Femmes soufis*, 35.

103. Roded, *Women in Islamic Biographical Collections*, 92. One may also mention the notices, originally from as-Sulamī's book of Sufi women, that were copied and translated from Jāmī and al-Munāwī in Javad Nurbakhsh, *Sufi Women*, trans., Leonard Lewisohn (New York, 1983). However, since this latter work was not written for a scholarly audience, there is no critical analysis of either its contents or its sources.

104. The catalogue number of this manuscript is 2118.

calligraphy, which contains stylistic elements that are usually associated with later forms of calligraphy.[105]

As a student of Ḥanbalī scholarship, aṭ-Ṭanāḥī recognized that the third work in this collection, *Dhikr an-niswa al-muta*ᶜ*abbidāt aṣ-ṣūfiyyāt* (Memorial of Female Sufi Devotees), was a source for Ibn al-Jawzī's notices on women in *Ṣifat aṣ-Ṣafwa*.[106] Since the Riyadh collection of Sulamī texts does not include a copy of *Ṭabaqāt aṣ-ṣūfiyya*, it is now apparent that as-Sulamī's book of Sufi women was not written as an appendix, but was composed as a separate work. Being aware of the interest that a work on Sufi women would arouse among the general public, in 1993 aṭ-Ṭanāḥī published an edited version of *Dhikr an-niswa al-muta*ᶜ*abbidāt aṣ-ṣūfiyyāt* through the Cairo publishing house of al-Khānjī.

Students of Sufism and Islamic Studies should be grateful to Dr. aṭ-Ṭanāḥī for discovering as-Sulamī's book of Sufi women and revealing its contents for the first time. However, his Arabic edition of this work cannot be considered definitive. First, a comparison of this edition with the original manuscript reveals several transcription errors, including missing portions of text, which require correction. Second, neither aṭ-Ṭanāḥī's introduction nor his footnotes contextualize as-Sulamī's book of Sufi women as part of either Sufism or Sufi literature. Third, aṭ-Ṭanāḥī's unfamiliarity with the Sufi tradition of sacred biography causes him to misunderstand or overlook important points. For example, when Dhū an-Nūn al-Miṣrī calls Fāṭima of Nishapur "my [male] teacher (*ustādhī*)," he dismisses this as a "linguistic anomaly" (*ṭurfa lughawiyya*).[107] More than just an anomaly, this use of gendered terminology is an example of what was to become a recurring trope in Sufi literature: that of elevating exceptional women to the ranks of honorary men.[108] Even more importantly, aṭ-Ṭanāḥī passes over in silence the unique technical vocabulary of women's Sufism that as-Sulamī employs in this work. Gendered technical terms such as *niswa* and *niswān*, which clearly have specific meanings for as-

105. See the introductory discussion in Abū ᶜAbd ar-Raḥmān as-Sulamī, *Dhikr an-niswa al-muta*ᶜ*abbidāt aṣ-ṣūfiyyāt*, ed., Maḥmūd Muḥammad aṭ-Ṭanāḥī (Cairo, 1993), 7 and 18. Böwering's assertion that the editor of this work is named "ᶜIrāqī" ("al-Sulamī," *EI*², 812) is mistaken.

106. In his introduction to *Dhikr an-niswa*, aṭ-Ṭanāḥī incorrectly states that this work is the second in the "as-Sulamiyyāt" collection. Ibid., 7.

107. Ibid., 19.

108. The practice of elevating exceptional women to the status of honorary men is reflected in the following comment by Farīd ad-Dīn al-ᶜAṭṭār (d. ca. 627/1230), who was also from Nishapur: "When a woman is a man on the path of the Lord Most High, she cannot be called a woman." See Michael Sells, *Early Islamic Mysticism: Sufi, Qur'an, Mi'raj, Poetic and Theological Writings* (Mahwah, New York, 1996), 155.

Sulamī, are significant and need to be examined in detail. Finally, aṭ-Ṭanāḥī does not see as-Sulamī's Sufi women as noteworthy in themselves, but only because they are associated with famous Sufi men.[109] While as-Sulamī does indeed identify many Sufi women as the wives, daughters, sisters, or associates of famous men, he clearly intended to say more than that "Behind every great Sufi man is a Sufi woman." On the contrary, rather than being validated by Sufi men, as-Sulamī's Sufi women just as often validate their male colleagues by educating them in Sufi doctrines and practices.

It was to address such issues, as well as to make this work available to a wider audience outside of the Arab world, that I decided to translate as-Sulamī's *Dhikr an-niswa al-muta*ᶜ*abbidāt aṣ-ṣūfiyyāt* into English and to re-edit the Arabic text from the original manuscript. As an appendix, I have also added the sections on as-Sulamī's Sufi women from a published edition of Ibn al-Jawzī's *Ṣifat aṣ-Ṣafwa*. This latter work, which was written about two hundred years after as-Sulamī's, contains information from sources that were not used by as-Sulamī. Also, comparing as-Sulamī's and Ibn al-Jawzī's depictions of Sufi women will help the reader appreciate as-Sulamī's unique concern with disproving Muslim stereotypes about woman's supposed lack of religion and intellect.

Although Ibn al-Jawzī's Sufi women are depicted as being more emotional and "woman-like" than those of as-Sulamī, this should not diminish Ibn al-Jawzī's importance in documenting the participation of women in Islam. This Ḥanbalī scholar, who is best known as an opponent of Sufism, was raised from a young age by his mother and paternal aunt and developed a strong interest in women's spirituality.[110] This interest was fostered by a female teacher of Ibn al-Jawzī named Shuhda bint al-ᶜIbarī (d. 574/1178), who was one of the foremost hadith scholars of her age.[111] No less than 240 notices, or 23 percent of the entries in *Ṣifat aṣ-Ṣafwa*, are dedicated to women, including many of the Sufi women discussed by as-Sulamī.[112] In the Introduction to this work, Ibn al-Jawzī even criticizes as-Sulamī's colleague Abū Nuᶜaym al-Iṣfahani for ignoring women in *Ḥilyat al-awliyā*ᵓ. In a remarkable passage for its time, Ibn al-Jawzī claims that al-Iṣfahānī's failure to appreciate women's spirituality perpetuates the negative stereotyping of women among Muslim men: "Except

109. See, for example, aṭ-Ṭanāḥī's introduction to as-Sulamī, *Dhikr an-niswa*, 9.

110. Ibn al-Jawzī, *Ṣifat aṣ-Ṣafwa*, vol.1, 8.

111. Joseph N. Bell, *Love Theory in Later Ḥanbalite Islam* (Albany, New York, 1979), 12.

112. On the notices that Ibn al-Jawzī devotes to women in *Ṣifat aṣ-Ṣafwa*, see Roded, *Women in Islamic Biographical Collections*, 3 and 92.

for only a few cases, [al-Iṣfahānī] did not mention pious women at all, even though it is well known that given women's apparent shortcomings, failing to mention female devotees causes men to ignore women in general. Yet [the jurist] Sufyān ath-Thawrī learned from Rābiᶜa [al-ᶜAdawiyya] and followed her teachings."[113]

Organization of the Text

As-Sulamī's *Dhikr an-niswa al-mutaᶜabbidāt aṣ-ṣūfiyyāt* contains eighty-two notices on Sufi women. Although they are part of the genre of sacred biography, these notices are not biographies in the modern sense of the word. Rather, they are more like literary collages, which are made up of a few to a dozen or so individual accounts or vignettes. When taken together, these vignettes provide a composite portrait of the spirituality of each Sufi woman mentioned in the work. Two portraits, those of Zubda and Muḍgha, the sisters of Bishr al-Ḥāfī of Baghdad (section L), and ᶜAbda and Āmina, the sisters of Abū Sulaymān ad-Dārānī of Syria (section LI), are of pairs of sisters. Four portraits, those of Lubāba al-Mutaᶜabbida of Jerusalem (sections II and XXII), Unaysa bint ᶜAmr al-ᶜAdawiyya of Basra (sections XII and XXXIX), Umm al-Aswad bint Zayd al-ᶜAdawiyya of Basra (sections XIII and XL), and Jumᶜa bint Aḥmad or Umm al-Ḥusayn al-Qurashiyya of Nasā (sections LXVI and LXXVIII), appear in two different places. In all, eighty separate women are treated in this text.

Unlike Ibn al-Jawzī, as-Sulamī does not arrange his portraits of Sufi women in a strictly chronological manner. Instead, they are arranged in regional clusters that roughly correspond to three chronological periods. For example, the first twenty-nine portraits of Sufi women alternate between Basra and Syria, with the single exception of Yemen. These women represent the earliest Sufi women discussed by as-Sulamī. For the most part, they are figures of the late Umayyad and early ᶜAbbasid periods who flourished between the years 100/718–19 and 230/844–45—a chronological period that transcends both centuries and dynastic periods. At times, one or two portraits appear out of order. It is difficult to determine whether this was intentional or whether it was due to the copyist of the Riyadh manuscript mistakenly collating the wrong material. However, since we know that as-Sulamī originally arranged the notices in *Ṭabaqāt*

113. Ibn al-Jawzī, *Ṣifat aṣ-Ṣafwa*, vol. 1, 31.

aṣ-ṣūfiyya into five "generations" of twenty notices each, it is likely that he would have organized his book of Sufi women in a similarly systematic manner.[114]

Geographically, the largest cluster of Sufi women (twenty-three individuals) includes both the city of Basra and regions close to Basra, such as the port city of al-Ubulla at the head of the Persian Gulf. The next largest cluster (twenty-one individuals) is from as-Sulamī's home city of Nishapur and its surrounding regions. The next two clusters include Syria (a region) and Baghdad (a city), each represented by eleven individuals. Finally, a few other regions also receive significant mention, such as Damaghan (five individuals), Egypt (two individuals), and Khurasan beyond Nishapur (four individuals). On the provincial level, Iraq is the most often cited region, with thirty-four Sufi women represented, followed by Khurasan, with twenty-five women represented. Chronologically, the order of the clusters is as follows: (1) Basra and Syria, (2) Baghdad, Damaghan, and Egypt, (3) Nishapur and Khurasan.

A Hermeneutic of Remembrance

For as-Sulamī, the Sufi women who are memorialized in *Dhikr an-niswa al-muta^{c}abbidāt aṣ-ṣūfiyyāt* are fully the equals of the Sufi men in *Ṭabaqāt aṣ-ṣūfiyya*. As spiritual exemplars, they too are "masters of the realities of divine oneness, recipients of divine discourses, possessors of true visions and exemplary conduct, and followers of the ways of the prophets."[115] However, unlike their male counterparts, they run a greater risk of being overlooked. As women, they are more likely to be misunderstood and their teachings are more likely to be ignored. Because they are less socially visible than Sufi men, Sufi women need their own "hermeneutic of remembrance."[116] In the introduction to *Ṭabaqāt aṣ-ṣūfiyya*, as-Sulamī hints at his intention to create such a hermeneutic by citing the following Quranic verse: "And what about the *believing men and believing women* whom you did not know and that you might have fallen upon [in enmity], and upon whose account a crime would have

114. See as-Sulamī's introduction to *Ṭabaqāt aṣ-ṣūfiyya*, 3 (following the editor's introduction).

115. Ibid., 2.

116. This term was originally used to characterize feminist-historical works that sought to recover the "secret history" of women's authority in early Christianity. See Lynda L. Coon, *Sacred Fictions: Holy Women and Hagiography in Late Antiquity* (Philadelphia, 1997), xix–xx.

accrued to you without your knowledge? [God caused them to exist] so that He might admit to His mercy whom He will.'"[117] Later on in the same discussion, as-Sulamī quotes a hadith that further supports the case for a hermeneutic of remembrance of Sufi women by implicitly contradicting the belief that later generations of Muslims are worse than those who preceded them: "[The Prophet Muḥammad] (may God bless and preserve him) said: 'The similitude of my community is like the rain; no one knows whether the benefit is in the first of it or in the last of it.'"[118]

As-Sulamī's book of Sufi women, like *Ṭabaqāt aṣ-ṣūfiyya,* is an example of *ṭabaqāt* ("levels" or "classes") literature, one of the oldest styles of Muslim historical writing.[119] The *ṭabaqāt* genre originated as part of the field of hadith criticism and arose out of the need to assess the backgrounds of hadith transmitters and the bearers of tradition. The authors of *ṭabaqāt* works grouped the earliest bearers of tradition (*rijāl al-ᶜilm*) into three chronological classes known as the "Righteous Predecessors" (*as-Salaf aṣ-Ṣāliḥ*): the Companions of the Prophet Muḥammad (*aṣ-Ṣaḥāba*), the Followers of the Companions (*at-Tābiᶜūn*), and the Followers of the Followers (*Tābiᶜ at-Tābiᶜīn*). As the genre developed, *ṭabaqāt* works began to be organized by region as well as by chronology, and the list of authorities was expanded to include the scholars and piety-minded of contemporary times. This expanded form of *ṭabaqāt* literature became the model for Sufi sacred biography. In the Sufi tradition, such works can be identified by the presence of one or more of the following terms in their titles: *ṭabaqāt* (categories or generations), *taʾrīkh* (history or chronology), *dhikr* or *tadhkīra* (recollection or memorial), *rijāl* ("men," the bearers of tradition), or *tarjama* (translation, in the sense of "translating" or "carrying over" exemplary virtues or teachings from one generation to another).[120]

Because of its origin in the field of hadith criticism, *ṭabaqāt* literature often followed a hadith-style format and employed hadith-type chains of

117. Qurʾān, 48 (*al-Fatḥ*), 25. Italics added.

118. as-Sulamī, introduction to *Ṭabaqāt aṣ-ṣūfiyya*, 2.

119. For a historical overview of the *ṭabaqāt* genre, see Franz Rosenthal, *A History of Muslim Historiography* (Leiden, 1968), 93–95; and Claude Gilliot, "Ṭabaḳāt," *EI*², 7–10. This latter article, which closely follows Ibrahim Hafsi, "Recherches sur le genre 'Ṭabaqāt' dans la littérature arabe," *Arabica* xxiii (1976), 228–65; xxiv (1977), 1–41 and 150–86, takes little notice of the importance of *ṭabaqāt* literature in Sufism. The same is true for R. Stephen Humphreys, *Islamic History: A Framework for Inquiry* (Princeton, 1991), 187–208, which otherwise provides a good overview of *ṭabaqāt* literature as part of the discipline of "ulamology."

120. Tarif Khalidi, *Arabic Historical Thought in the Classical Period* (Cambridge, 1994), 204–10.

authority, even when its subject matter had little or nothing to do with hadith. The likely prototype for the first Sufi *ṭabaqāt* works was *aṭ-Ṭabaqāt al-kubrā* (The Greatest Generations) by Muḥammad ibn Saᶜd (d. 230/845). Before composing this work, Ibn Saᶜd had been the assistant of Muḥammad al-Wāqidī (d. 207/823), a famous biographer of the Prophet Muḥammad. In *aṭ-Ṭabaqāt al-kubrā*, Ibn Saᶜd included portraits of all bearers of tradition from the time of the Prophet until his own day, including many women.[121]

As-Sulamī's portraits of Sufi women are similar in form to those of Ibn Saᶜd and are prefaced by similar hadith-style chains of authority (sing. *isnād*). For each account, one or two to several individuals are cited as passing down information from an original source (preferably an eyewitness) to the author. Thus, for as-Sulamī as well as for Ibn Saᶜd, the chain of authority acted in a way that was analogous to the modern footnote, for it mediated between the historical past, in which the interpretive presence of the author was not supposed to appear, and the actual present of the work being composed, in which the author's presence is inevitably involved.[122]

In a work of sacred biography, each chain of authority constitutes a chain of evidence, whose "reality effect"[123] depends on the reliability of each authority cited.[124] This is particularly important when an account describes paranormal phenomena or when the author makes an assertion that goes beyond expectations. Although as-Sulamī's book of Sufi women is not, strictly speaking, a hagiography and as-Sulamī seldom portrays his subjects as miracle-workers, he does attempt to demonstrate that Sufi women possess levels of intellect (*ᶜaql*) and wisdom (*ḥikma*) that are equivalent to those of Sufi men. Since this assertion contradicts cultural expectations, the "footnoting" that he employs by citing chains of authority is crucial to his argument. Just as in a modern academic work, the strength of as-Sulamī's argument depends both on his own rhetorical skills and on the prior knowledge of his audience. This prior knowledge is

121. Ibid., 44–48. Among Ibn Saᶜd's notices are the earliest accounts of some of the women mentioned by as-Sulamī. Cross-references to Ibn Saᶜd can be found in the footnotes to al-Sulamī's *Dhikr an-niswa*. below.

122. I am grateful for this insight to my student Catherine Chin, who brought up the *isnād*-footnote analogy in a class paper entitled, "Between Two Worlds: Past and Present in the Source-Citations of Eusebius and Tabari" (Duke University, Fall, 1998).

123. See Roland Barthes, "The Reality Effect," trans., R. Carter, in *French Literary Theory Today*, ed., T. Todorov (Cambridge, 1982), 11–17.

124. On the evidentiary nature of accounts in Muslim sacred biography, see Cornell, *Realm of the Saint*, 63–66.

crucial in the case of the *isnād*, for the truth-value of an *isnād* can be assessed only by a reader who is aware of each authority's background and reputation as a transmitter of tradition. This unspoken, subtextual dimension of the hermeneutics of remembrance, in which an authority's name stands for an entire body of background information, is an important aspect of the rhetoric of sacred biography, both in Islam and in Christianity. [125]

In order to help the modern reader approximate the experience of an informed reader in as-Sulamī's time, I have included in the footnotes to *Dhikr an-niswa al-muta*ᶜ*abbidāt aṣ-ṣūfiyyāt* background information on most of the transmitters cited in the text. Whenever possible, I relied on information supplied by as-Sulamī himself in *Ṭabaqāt aṣ-ṣūfiyya* or on the works of his students or contemporaries, such as al-Iṣfahānī and al-Qushayrī. This background information, which tends to be ignored by most modern editors and translators of Islamic sacred biography, adds an important sub-narrative to the main text of as-Sulamī's work. It allows the reader to gain a deeper understanding of the work as a whole by providing historical, intellectual, and doctrinal contexts in which to situate the author's arguments.

As-Sulamī was not the first Sufi author to make use of the *ṭabaqāt* genre. In fact, this type of literature had become so common by as-Sulamī's time that in many cases he could dispense with oral tradition entirely and rely on written sources alone. The fact that he felt able to do so is a strong indication of the extent to which literacy and the culture of the written word had penetrated Nishapur by the beginning of the eleventh century C.E. Elsewhere in the Muslim world, oral tradition was still preferable to the written word, and written works were not considered properly transmitted unless a text had been verbally recited to an interlocutor by its author or by someone whom the author had designated. Although as-Sulamī was a product of the same intellectual tradition, and felt obliged to support most of his accounts with oral chains of transmission, he in fact used written materials on a regular basis. Occasionally, he is explicit in his use of the written word, such as when he states: "I found [this account] in the handwriting of my father," or "I found this in the handwriting of [the Sufi shaykh] Abū Jaᶜfar Aḥmad ibn Ḥamdān."[126] In most cases, however, he omits the titles of written works and cites their

125. See, for example, Coon, *Sacred Fictions*, 6–13.

126. See the notices on Muʾmina the Daughter of Bahlūl (section IV), Muᶜādha bint ᶜAbdallāh al-ᶜAdawiyya (section V), and ᶜĀʾisha the Wife of Abū Ḥafṣ of Nishapur (section XXXVI) in as-Sulamī, *Dhikr an-niswa,* below.

authors only as names within an apparently "oral" chain of authority, leaving it to the reader to decide whether the information was transmitted orally or by means of a book.

Four of the authorities cited by as-Sulamī were Sufis who produced their own *ṭabaqāt* works. The earliest of these was Muḥammad ibn al-Ḥusayn al-Burjulānī of Baghdad (d. 238/852), who documented the lives and exploits of Muslim ascetics in a book called *Kitāb ar-ruhbān* (Book of Monks).[127] According to al-Iṣfahānī, al-Burjulānī saw Muslim and Christian ascetics as following similar spiritual methods, and considered the Christian practice of self-denial through hunger to be particularly attractive to Muslim sensibilities.[128] Al-Burjulānī appears as a source for as-Sulamī in ten portraits of Sufi women, whose subjects all come from the regions of Basra or Baghdad. In one account (section XXXIX), as-Sulamī cites al-Burjulānī directly, indicating that he probably copied his information from the latter's book. That this book came from the library of as-Sulamī's grandfather is suggested in section XII, where Ismāᶜīl ibn Nujayd is mentioned as the final transmitter of al-Burjulānī's information.

Another Sufi author of *ṭabaqāt* literature cited by as-Sulamī was Ibrāhīm ibn al-Junayd (d. before 270/883–84), who also resided in Baghdad.[129] Ibn al-Junayd was a student of al-Burjulānī who composed his own *Kitāb ar-ruhbān*. According to the bibliographer Muḥammad an-Nadīm (ca. 380/990), Ibn al-Junayd was noted in Iraq as a major authority on the history of Sufism.[130] He appears three times in as-Sulamī's book of Sufi women, twice as a source for al-Burjulānī, and once (section X) as a unique source, indicating that as-Sulamī may have possessed at least part of his book as well. In all three cases, the Sufi women he mentions were from either Basra or Baghdad.

A Sufi biographer from as-Sulamī's grandfather's generation was Jaᶜfar al-Khuldī of Baghdad (d. 348/959–60).[131] Al-Khuldī was a disciple of the two masters of the Baghdad school of Sufism, Abū al-Qāsim

127. On al-Burjulānī, see Andrae, *In the Garden of Myrtles*, 8–12 and 32, and Louis Massignon, *Essay on the Origins of the Technical Language of Islamic Mysticism*, Benjamin Clark, trans. (Notre Dame, Indiana, 1997 translation of 1968 Paris edition), 160. See also, al-Baghdādī, *Taʾrīkh Baghdād*, vol.2, 219, where Aḥmad ibn Ḥanbal cites al-Burjulānī as a reliable source for information on Muslim ascetics.

128. al-Iṣfahānī, *Ḥilyat al-awliyāʾ*, vol.10, 150–51.

129. al-Baghdādī, *Taʾrīkh Baghdād*, vol.6, 119.

130. Abū al-Faraj Muḥammad ibn Abī Yaᶜqūb Isḥāq al-Warrāq an-Nadīm, *Kitāb al-fihrist*, ed., Ibn ᶜAlī ibn Zayn al-ᶜĀbidīn al-Ḥāʾirī al-Mazandarānī (Beirut, 1988), 237.

131. On Jaᶜfar al-Khuldī see as-Sulamī, *Ṭabaqāt aṣ-ṣūfiyya*, 434–39; al-Iṣfahānī, *Ḥilyat al-awliyāʾ*, vol.10, 381–82; and Ibn al-Jawzī, *Ṣifat aṣ-Ṣafwa*, vol.2, 468–69.

al-Junayd and Abū al-Ḥusayn an-Nūrī (d. 295/908). Besides being a Sufi poet who composed more than 150 mystical poems, al-Khuldī was also known for a *ṭabaqāt* work entitled *Ḥikāyāt al-awliyāʾ* (Tales of the Saints), which al-Khaṭīb al-Baghdādī called "one of the three wonders of Baghdad."[132] A small portion of this work is reproduced in the section on Sufis in an-Nadīm's *Kitāb al-fihrist* (Bibliographical Index).[133] Unfortunately, this section of an-Nadīm's bibliography is itself incomplete and appears to consist only of the latter's notes and not of al-Khuldī's actual text. As-Sulamī cites al-Khuldī three times in his book of Sufi women, twice as a source for al-Burjulānī, and once (section LXII) as a transmitter of information from al-Junayd's associate Ibrāhīm al-Khawwāṣ (d. 291/904). It is impossible to determine whether as-Sulamī possessed his own copy of *Ḥikāyāt al-awliyāʾ*, because every reference to al-Khuldī is mediated by another authority. However, the Riyadh manuscript contains a text attributed to as-Sulamī entitled *Kitāb al-muntakhab min ḥikāyāt aṣ-ṣūfiyya* (Selections from "Tales of the Sufis"), which may be an abridgment of al-Khuldī's book.[134]

The only *ṭabaqāt* work that as-Sulamī cites by name is *Ṭabaqāt an-nussāk* (Categories of the Ascetics) by Abū Saᶜīd ibn al-Aᶜrābī (d. 341/952–53).[135] Ibn al-Aᶜrābī was originally from Basra but died in Mecca, where he served as Imam of the Sacred Mosque. Although he is mentioned only once (section VI), he is one of the most important authorities to be cited in as-Sulamī's book of Sufi women. In his unique position as both a respected Sufi master and the holder of one of the most honored teaching posts available to a scholar of his time, Ibn al-Aᶜrābī influenced an entire generation of Sufis from Khurasan to Muslim Spain.[136] His work of sacred biography, which is now lost, is the earliest recorded use of the term *ṭabaqāt* in a Sufi work. It would thus be of great value to the history of Sufism if this work were to be found, like as-Sulamī's *Dhikr an-niswa al-mutaᶜabbidāt aṣ-ṣūfiyyāt*, in some overlooked corner of a major library.

132. al-Baghdādī, *Taʾrīkh Baghdād*, vol. 7, 235.

133. an-Nadīm, *al-Fihrist*, 235–38. For a translation of this section, see *The Fihrist of al-Nadīm: A Tenth-Century Survey of Muslim Culture*, ed. and trans. Bayard Dodge (New York, 1970), vol.1, 455–61.

134. I am indebted to Professor Carl Ernst of the University of North Carolina at Chapel Hill for this insight.

135. On Abū Saᶜīd ibn al-Aᶜrābī, see as-Sulamī, *Ṭabaqāt aṣ-ṣūfiyya*, 427–30, and al-Iṣfahānī, *Ḥilyat al-awliyāʾ*, vol.2, 25. See also Ali Hassan Abdel-Kader, *The Life, Personality and Writings of Al-Junayd: A Study of a Third/Ninth-Century Mystic* (London, 1976), x–xii.

136. Portions of Ibn al-Aᶜrābī's *Kitāb al-wajd* (Book of Ecstasy) can be found in Nicholson, ed., *The Kitáb al-Lumaᶜ*, 300–314. On Ibn al-Aᶜrābī's influence on Sufism in Islamic Spain, see Manuela Marin, "Abū Saᶜīd ibn al-Aᶜrābī et le Développement du Soufisme en al-Andalus," *Revue du Monde musulman et de la Mediterranée*, 63–64 (1992), 28–38.

AS-SULAMĪ'S VIEW OF WOMEN'S SUFISM

A Theology of Servitude

In as-Sulamī's book of Sufi women no theme is more prominent than that of servitude. In fact, servitude is so central to as-Sulamī's understanding of women's spirituality that he enshrines the concept in the title of his work: *Dhikr an-niswa al-muta^cabbidāt aṣ-ṣūfiyyāt*. This title tells the reader that as-Sulamī's subjects are a distinct group of women (designated by the collective term *niswa*) who are to be included among the Sufis because they practice *ta^cabbud*—literally, "making oneself a slave" (*^cabd*)—the disciplined practice of servitude. For as-Sulamī, *ta^cabbud* is the essence of women's Sufism. For Sufi women, it is their means to divine inspiration and the spiritual method that distinguishes them from their male Sufi colleagues.

Although as-Sulamī makes *ta^cabbud* the distinguishing characteristic of women's Sufism, the concept for which it stands has long been part of Sufi piety, regardless of gender. The Arabic term for worship (*^cibāda*), which applies to all Muslims, Sufi or otherwise, means "servitude." This concept is also expressed in hadith. For example, in the *Musnad* (Collection of Authenticated Traditions) of Aḥmad ibn Ḥanbal (d. 241/855), the Prophet Muḥammad states that the names most favored by God are ^cAbd Allāh (Slave of God) and ^cAbd ar-Raḥmān (Slave of the Bestower of Grace).[137] In the Qur^oān, *islām*—the submission of oneself to the will of God—is frequently expressed in terms of servitude. This "selling of oneself to God" is the quintessential attribute of the true believer and is one of the spiritual traits that Islam shares with both Judaism and Christianity:

> Verily God has purchased from the believers their persons and possessions in return for Paradise. They fight in the cause of God and slay and are slain. It is a binding promise on God, stated in truth in the Torah, the Gospel, and the Qur^oān. And who is more faithful to His promise than [God]? So rejoice in the sale of yourself which you have concluded; for it is the supreme achievement.[138]

In *Ḥaqā^oiq at-tafsīr*, his exegesis of the Qur^oān, as-Sulamī discusses the concept of servitude through the words of Aḥmad ibn ^cAṭā^o (d. 309/921),

137. Ibn Ḥanbal, *Musnad*, 14/245.

138. Qur^oān 9 (*at-Tawba*), 111.

a famous Sufi of Baghdad who was an associate of al-Junayd. In these passages, another term for servitude is used: *ᶜubūdiyya*, which literally means "slavery." In his commentary on the Qur᾿ān's Chapter on Women (*Sūrat an-nisā᾿*), as-Sulamī quotes Ibn ᶜAṭā᾿ as saying: "ᶜUbūdiyya is a combination of four traits: to be true to one's covenants, to preserve moral rectitude, to be satisfied with whatever one finds, and to patiently bear what has been lost."[139] Elsewhere, Ibn ᶜAṭā᾿ states that the "sale of oneself" to God, to which the Qur᾿ān refers, means the suppression of the lower soul or human ego (*nafs*): "[The prophet] Joseph was sold by his enemies, who were his adversaries. Likewise, you sell yourself to your adversaries: these are your lusts and your passions. The worst of your enemies is the *nafs* that is between your two sides."[140] Salvation from the *nafs,* says Ibn ᶜAṭā᾿, can only be purchased with servitude: "The *nafs* is driven toward impropriety. But the slave is commanded to behave properly. The *nafs* by its nature hastens toward disobedience. But through effort the slave restrains its evil desires. He who abandons effort has given free rein to the *nafs* and ignores discipline. However much you aid it, you become a partner in its desires. For this reason al-Junayd has said: 'He who helps his *nafs* attain its desires is a partner in the actions of his *nafs*.' This is because servitude is in the observance of propriety while the essence of sin is in impropriety."[141]

A similar understanding of servitude can be found in *Slavery as Salvation* (1990), Dale B. Martin's study of the rhetoric of slavery and status inversion in early Christianity. Realizing that the metaphor of slavery in the Gospels and the epistles of the Apostle Paul stood for more than just humility, Martin examined slavery in late antiquity in its full socio-historical context and found that it was a more complex institution than most readers of the New Testament assumed. For example, in the later Roman Empire, where social, economic, and political ties were often based on patronage, slavery might paradoxically be used as a metaphor for authority.[142] In a wealthy household, the slave-manager (Gr. *oikonomos*) would often have a considerable amount of authority. As a loyal and devoted servant of his master, he might even have more authority than a free person who was not as well trusted. A similar state of affairs existed in Khurasan in as-Sulamī's day, where relationships of

139. *Trois Oeuvres inédites de Mystiques musulmans: Šaqīq al-Balḫī, Ibn ᶜAṭā, Niffarī*, ed. Paul Nwyia (Beirut, 1973), 45.

140. Ibid., 60.

141. Ibid., 63.

142. Dale B. Martin, *Slavery as Salvation: the Metaphor of Slavery in Pauline Christianity* (New Haven and London, 1990), 56–57.

loyalty and intimacy with a powerful patron were also expressed through the rhetoric of servitude. By making a vocation out of service to their divine Master, as-Sulamī's Sufi women, like the *oikonomos* of late antiquity, could free themselves from the constraints that would normally have limited their role in society.

It is in this wider socio-historical context that we must understand some of the statements made by Sufi women such as ᶜĀᵓisha bint Aḥmad of Merv: "When the slave seeks glory in his servitude, his foolishness is revealed."[143] Just as the religious metaphor of slavery stands for more than humility, this statement is more than just a warning against the egoism of virtue. The Islamic culture of servitude inherited much from late antiquity, including the social stratification of slave professions and the relationship of slavery as an institution to wider, patronage-based social structures. In the Gospel of John, the Apostles of Jesus, as slaves (Gr. *douloi*) of Christ, are rhetorically transformed into the "friends" (Gr. *philoi*) of Christ, and thus become figures of religious authority.[144] Likewise, for as-Sulamī, being a "slave of God" (*ᶜabd Allāh*) was a necessary prerequisite to becoming a "friend of God" (*walī Allāh*)—in other words, a saint. Thus, the glory that ᶜĀᵓisha bint Aḥmad warns her associates to avoid is not only that of pride in one's virtue, but also the vainglory of seeking sainthood for the worldly patronage that it bestows.[145]

Further comparisons can be made between the Christian metaphor of slavery and the Islamic metaphor of servitude as understood by as-Sulamī and his contemporaries. Besides sharing a common soteriological understanding of slavery as a path to salvation, Sufis and early Christians both saw servitude as a way of overcoming the limitations of human nature (*bashariyya*). Earlier in this introduction we saw how some Middle-Period Sufis such as al-Kalābādhī attributed woman's inadequacy to the deficiencies of the female nature. Therefore, it is not surprising to find that overcoming human nature is a prominent concern for as-Sulamī's Sufi women. Commenting on the famous tradition: "He who knows himself (lit. 'his self') knows his lord" (*man ᶜarafa nafsahu ᶜarafa rabbahu*), Fuṭayma the wife of Ḥamdūn al-Qaṣṣār remarks: "When a person truly

143. *Dhikr an-niswa*, section LXXXII below.

144. Martin, *Slavery as Salvation*, 54.

145. See for example, the statements made about the fourth-century Christian ascetics of the Egyptian desert, who were "true servants [lit. "slaves"] of God. . . [through whom] the world is kept in being, and that through them too human life is preserved and honoured by God." Benedicta Ward, *The Lives of the Desert Fathers: The Historia Monachorum in Aegypto*, trans. Norman Russell (London and Oxford, 1980), 12.

knows himself [i.e., the limitations of his human nature], his only characteristic is servitude and he takes pride in nothing but his Master."[146] Even more to the point is the statement of ᶜUnayza of Baghdad: "Human forms [lit. 'the molds of human nature] are the mines of servitude" (*qawālib al-bashariyya maᶜādin al-ᶜubūdiyya*).[147]

For as-Sulamī, the spiritual path of servitude freed Sufi women from the constraints imposed on them by their physical natures.[148] As slaves of God, they could separate themselves from the ordinary masses of women who did not share the same spiritual vocation. Choosing an independent life as "career women" of the spirit, they could travel without a chaperone, mix socially with men, teach men in public assemblies, and develop intellectually in ways that were not accessible to their non-Sufi sisters. This vocational focus explains the surprising comment made by Nusiyya bint Salmān upon the birth of her son: "Oh, Lord! You do not see me as someone worthy of Your worship. So for this You have preoccupied me with a child!"[149]

As explained by al-Hujwīrī some two generations after as-Sulamī, the worldly nature of the human being has both an outward and an inward aspect. Physicality, which interacts with the world through sensation, is the outward aspect of human nature. The inward aspect of human nature is the *nafs*, which interacts with the world through the passions. The interdependency of sensation and passion is what is meant by Ibn ᶜAṭāʾ's comment (reported as a hadith by al-Hujwīrī) that "the worst of your enemies is the *nafs* that is between your two sides."[150] Overcoming the limitations of human nature requires the person to master passion and physical sensation by cultivating both outward and inward forms of servitude. Slavery to passion can be overcome by outward acts of servitude such as self-denial and altruistic service on behalf of others, while slavery to sensation can be overcome by inner acts of servitude such as invocation and complete devotion to God. This is the doctrine that lies behind the saying of Ghufayra al-ᶜĀbida as reported by Ibn al-Jawzī in *Ṣifat aṣ-Ṣafwa*: "I have sinned against You, oh God, with each of my extremities. By God, if You aid me, I will do my best to obey You with every extremity with which I have disobeyed You."[151]

146. *Dhikr an-niswa,* section LVII below.

147. Ibid., section LXXVII below.

148. This "anti-establishment" role of the slave of God is a common theme of sainthood in both Islam and Christianity. See, for example, Heffernan, *Sacred Biography*, 127–28 and Cornell, *Realm of the Saint,* 114–15.

149. *Dhikr an-niswa,* section VII below.

150. al-Hujwīrī, *The Kashf al-Mahjūb*, 206.

151. See *Ṣifat aṣ-Ṣafwa* Appendix section V below.

As a spiritual method, the practice of servitude works on the outward and inward natures of the human being at the same time. Outwardly, it cultivates the Sufi attributes of scrupulous abstinence (*waraᶜ*), patience (*ṣabr*), poverty (*faqr*), and humility (*tawāḍuᶜ*). Without these attributes, the human being is a slave to the *nafs*. In the words of Umm Ṭalq: "The *nafs* is a king if you indulge it, but it is a slave if you torment it."[152] Inwardly, the practice of servitude cultivates the attributes of fear (*khawf*), worshipfulness (*ᶜibāda*), gratitude (*shukr*), and reliance on God (*tawakkul*). These are the attributes that lead to perfection in religion (*iḥsān*), according to the words of the famous hadith: "Worship God as if you see Him; for if you do not see Him, surely He sees you."[153] It is also in respect to these inner attributes that ᶜĀᵓisha the wife of Abū Ḥafṣ of Nishapur remarks: "No state is more elevating for the slave than his awareness of his shortcomings in attaining [complete servitude]."[154]

Once women have become practitioners of servitude (*mutaᶜabbidāt*), it is no longer valid for male critics to claim that they are deficient in religion, for, as stated in the Qurᵓān, servitude is the truest form of submission to God (*islām*). Even more, because such women have overcome the sensational and passional aspects of their human natures, the highest levels of religious knowledge are now accessible to them. The limitlessness of this potential is reflected in the statement of Umm ᶜAlī, the daughter of ᶜAbdallāh ibn Ḥamshādh: "He who is confirmed in his knowledge of true servitude will soon attain the knowledge of lordship."[155] This point is even more strongly made in the words of Surayra ash-Sharqiyya: "The ultimate of what is said to be the best of knowledge is the knowledge of lordship (*rubūbiyya*) and its opposite, servitude (*ᶜubūdiyya*). Eventually, servitude vanishes and only lordship remains."[156]

For as-Sulamī, whatever limitations ordinary women may possess with respect to their religion and intellect, these have nothing to do with the spiritual and intellectual abilities of female Sufi devotees. This point is stressed time and again by as-Sulamī through his frequent mention of Sufi women who were the companions, critics, and teachers of prominent Sufi men. Apart from Fāṭima of Nishapur, who instructed Bāyazīd al-Bisṭāmī

152. *Dhikr an-niswa,* section XIX below.

153. Muslim ibn al-Ḥajjāj an-Nīsabūrī (d. 262/875), *Ṣaḥīḥ Muslim bi-sharḥ an-Nawawī* [Beirut, n.d.], vol. 1, 152–60.

154. *Dhikr an-niswa,* section XXXVI below.

155. Ibid., section LXXV below.

156. Ibid., section LXXVI below.

and Dhū an-Nūn al-Miṣrī, and Rābiᶜa al-ᶜAdawiyya, who was a teacher of the jurist Sufyān ath-Thawrī, the reader is introduced to al-Wahaṭiyya Umm al-Faḍl, a companion of Ibn Khafīf of Shiraz, whose public teaching sessions in Nishapur were attended by most of the Sufi masters in that city.[157] Another female teacher was Shaᶜwāna of the port city of al-Ubulla on the Persian Gulf, who "preached to the people and recited the Qurᵓān to them. Her sessions were attended by ascetics, worshippers, those who were close to God, and the masters of hearts and self-denial."[158]

The fact that such women transcended the social limitations of their femininity is revealed in as-Sulamī's use of the masculine term *ustādh* when referring to their teaching roles. We already have seen this in the case of Fāṭima of Nishapur, whom Dhū an-Nūn described as his "male" teacher (*ustādh*). As-Sulamī's repetition of this term in his portrait of Ḥukayma of Damascus (section XXIII) proves that it was not a linguistic anomaly. Ḥukayma, an important figure in Syrian women's Sufism, is described as the *ustādh* of the female Sufi Rābiᶜa bint Ismāᶜīl. Surprisingly, however, this term does not appear in as-Sulamī's portrait of Rābiᶜa al-ᶜAdawiyya of Basra. In this latter case, Sufyān ath-Thawrī refers to Rābiᶜa as his "mentor," using the feminine term *muᵓaddiba*.

Why is it that as-Sulamī uses only the term *ustādh* in its generic, masculine form, while he does not do so for *muᵓaddiba*? The most likely answer has to do with the relative status of these two types of teacher. The *muᵓaddib* specialized in personal training, and thus transmitted a form of knowledge that was practical in nature. The *ustādh*, however, was a specialist in matters of doctrine and in the formal Islamic sciences. The knowledge of the *ustādh* was thus more theoretical in nature and required a greater level of formal education. This is why the highly educated jurist Sufyān ath-Thawrī called Rābiᶜa al-ᶜAdawiyya a *muᵓaddiba*: since she had not acquired her knowledge through formal means, it would not have been proper for him to refer to her as an *ustādh*. Sufis, however, were more flexible in their use of this term, and often used the word *ustādh* to refer to a spiritual master. In this case, being an *ustādh* meant that one had acquired mastery of both doctrine and practice, whether one had the benefit of a formal education or not. Just as the term *rijāl* (men) might be used in hadith studies to denote authoritative transmitters of tradition, regardless of whether they were male or female, so the term *ustādh* might be used to denote authoritative teachers of Sufism.

157. Ibid., section LXVII below.
158. Ibid., section XIV below.

Thus, by calling Fāṭima of Nishapur and Ḥukayma of Damascus *ustādh*, as-Sulamī tells us that these women were masters of both practice and doctrine, and were equal in knowledge to the male Sufi masters with whom they interacted.

Institutions of Women's Sufism

The regional arrangement of as-Sulamī's portraits of Sufi women is in general agreement with the locations of Sufi schools proposed by Louis Massignon in his *Essay on the Origins of the Technical Language of Islamic Mysticism* (1922, revised in 1954).[159] Although it is difficult to identify schools of Sufi women from such a limited source, it is clear from the information provided by as-Sulamī that Basra was the site of more than one school of women's asceticism. The female ascetics of Basra and its surrounding region flourished in the late Umayyad and early ᶜAbbasid periods, roughly between the years 700 C.E. and 800 C.E. Many of these women were from non-Arab families that had recently converted to Islam and were bound to Arab tribes by formal ties of servitude (*muwālāt*).[160] As both women and the clients (*mawlāt*) of Arab patrons, they were, in a sense, socially predisposed to a spiritual path based on servitude. Among these women, Rābiᶜa al-ᶜAdawiyya, a possible convert to Islam who was a client of the Arab tribe of Banū ᶜAdī, was the most prominent.[161] However, she was by no means the earliest of them. Although Rābiᶜa has often been identified as the first Sufi woman, as-Sulamī's text, read in conjunction with that of Ibn al-Jawzī, reveals that she represented the culmination, and not the beginning, of the Basran tradition of women's spirituality.

Surprisingly, as-Sulamī did not come to this conclusion himself. For as-Sulamī, Rābiᶜa was the quintessential Sufi woman. For this reason, he opens his book of Sufi women with her portrait. Because she was so important to the paradigm of female spirituality he was trying to evoke, he uncritically assigned most of the other "Sufi" women of Basra to

159. See chapter 4, 'The First Mystical Vocations in Islam" and chapter 5, "The Schools of the Third Century A.H.," in Massignon, *Essay*, 94–214.

160. The concept of clientship (Ar. *muwālāt*) is discussed in the footnotes to as-Sulamī's notice on Rābiᶜa al-ᶜAdawiyya, section I, below.

161. On conversion and clientship in early Islam, see the footnotes to *Dhikr an-niswa,* section I below.

Rābi^{c}a's generation, ignoring the fact that many of them actually preceded her. As-Sulamī's faulty chronology is corrected by Ibn al-Jawzī, who was more systematic as a chronicler of early female asceticism. By combining as-Sulamī's portraits of the women of Basra with those of Ibn al-Jawzī, the following picture emerges:

The first school of female asceticism in Basra was founded by Mu^{c}ādha al-^{c}Adawiyya (section V), who was neither a contemporary nor a "close companion" of Rābi^{c}a al-^{c}Adawiyya as as-Sulamī claims, but actually lived a hundred years before her. That Mu^{c}ādha's circle of female ascetics constituted an actual school is indicated in the portrait of Unaysa bint ^{c}Amr al-^{c}Adawiyya (section XII), where Unaysa is described as Mu^{c}ādha's "student" (*tilmīdha*). More than Rābi^{c}a, Mu^{c}ādha al-^{c}Adawiyya was responsible for founding the way of disciplined servitude that epitomizes as-Sulamī's view of women's Sufism. Her spiritual method was highly ascetic and stressed prayer, fasting, and the performance of night-vigils. Reliance on God was also a central part of her doctrine. Her name, Mu^{c}ādha, refers to the practice of seeking God's protection (*isti^{c}ādha*) against enemies such as Satan or the *nafs*. Ghufayra al-^{c}Ābida, one of her most important disciples (section IX), also had a symbolic name: the term *ghufayra* refers to the forgiveness of sins (*ghufrān*), while *^{c}ābida* means "worshipper" or "female practitioner of servitude."

Another aspect of Basran women's asceticism was the practice of weeping (*bukāʾ*), whose frequency and intensity sometimes led to blindness. This practice appears to have reflected remorse for the sinful nature of humanity. The practice of weeping sometimes occurred in conjunction with *wara^{c}*, the systematic avoidance of anything that might be either ritually or ethically impure. Whereas weeping brings to mind the Christian concept of original sin, *wara^{c}* entails an understanding of the human body as a "sacred vessel," a metaphor that can also be found in early Christianity.[162] If the vessel of the body were to be polluted through contact with even the slightest impurity, it would be rendered unfit for worship, and hence would not be worthy to become a container for divine grace. This idea is clearly expressed in the statement of Umm al-Aswad, a disciple of Mu^{c}ādha al-^{c}Adawiyya from the Arab tribe of Banū ^{c}Adī, whom Mu^{c}ādha had nursed as a child: "I would not eat anything suspicious lest it cause me to miss either a prescribed prayer or a supererogatory invocation."[163] Through her

162. On the concept of the body as a "sacred vessel" in early Christianity, see Peter Brown, *The Body and Society: Men, Women, and Sexual Renunciation in Early Christianity* (New York, 1988), 259–84.

163. *Dhikr an-niswa,* section XL below.

practice of *wara^{c}* Umm al-Aswad sought to maintain the spiritual integrity of her body, which had been purified as a child by being fed on Mu^{c}ādha's holy breast milk: [Mu^{c}ādha said to Umm al-Aswad]: "Do not spoil the breast-feeding I have given you by eating forbidden food, for when I was nursing you I made every effort to eat only what was lawful. So make every effort after this to eat only what is lawful. Perhaps you will succeed in your service to your Lord and in your acceptance of His will."[164]

Between Mu^{c}ādha and Rābi^{c}a al-^{c}Adawiyya were several female ascetics from Basra who may have headed other schools. One was Shabaka (section VI), an ascetic who mortified herself through rigorous disciplines (*riyāḍāt*) and required her female disciples to practice their devotions in underground cells (*sarādīb*). Another was Ḥafṣa bint Sīrīn (section XXI) the sister of Muḥammad ibn Sīrīn (d. 110/728–29), the reputed founder of the Islamic science of dream interpretation. Although as-Sulamī has little to say about Ḥafṣa, a fuller picture is provided by Ibn al-Jawzī (*Ṣifat aṣ-Ṣafwa* Appendix section II), who notes her unique ability to interpret the Qurʾān. On occasion, she also lectured before male youths (*shabāb*). As-Sulamī recounts the story of a lamp that continued to illuminate Ḥafṣa's room during her devotions, even after its oil had been consumed. This appears to be the original of a similar story about Rābi^{c}a al-^{c}Adawiyya that was later made famous by Farīd ad-Dīn al-^{c}Aṭṭār (d. ca. 627/1230).[165]

The asceticism and devotion to servitude that characterized the school of Mu^{c}ādha al-^{c}Adawiyya and the divine grace and intellectual skills that characterized Ḥafṣa bint Sīrīn are combined in as-Sulamī's portrait of Rābi^{c}a al-^{c}Adawiyya (section I). In Rābi^{c}a, we encounter a Sufi master much like the men that as-Sulamī describes in *Ṭabaqāt aṣ-ṣūfiyya*. As-Sulamī's Rābi^{c}a is quite different from the highly-strung and emotional recluse portrayed by Ibn al-Jawzī. Rather, she is a rational and disciplined teacher who demonstrates her mastery of important mystical states, such as truthfulness (*ṣidq*), self-criticism (*muḥāsaba*), spiritual intoxication (*sukr*), love for God (*maḥabba*), and gnosis (*ma^{c}rifa*). Although Rābi^{c}a has often been identified as the founder of Sufi love-mysticism, this is not a particularly important aspect of her teaching for as-Sulamī. Instead, he concentrates on her intellectual abilities, detailing the spiritual advice she gives to Muslim scholars, her moral lessons to the

164. Ibid.
165. See Sells, *Early Islamic Mysticism*, 157.

jurist Sufyān ath-Thawrī, and her reputation as a specialist in *fiqh al-ᶜibādāt*, the jurisprudence of religious practice. For as-Sulamī, Rābiᶜa is more of a thinker than a lover. He reserves the role of lover for her disciple, Maryam of Basra (section III), who was noted for lecturing on love, going into ecstasies upon hearing someone speak of love, and finally dying in a swoon during a discourse on love. By downplaying love-mysticism in favor of less emotional themes, as-Sulamī's portrait of Rābiᶜa provides a more "masculine," and hence more balanced image of this major Sufi teacher.

Chronologically speaking, the next significant group of Sufi women was from Syria. Most of as-Sulamī's information on Syrian Sufi women derives from a single source, who happens to be male. This is Aḥmad ibn Abī al-Ḥawārī (d. 230/845), the husband of Rābiᶜa bint Ismāᶜīl of Damascus (section XXIX), a woman who was so similar in her spirituality to Rābiᶜa al-ᶜAdawiyya that the two have often been mistaken for one another by later authors of sacred biography.[166] Most of the early Sufi women of Syria flourished during the first half of the ninth century C.E. and were linked to the Sufis of Basra through their association with Abū Sulaymān ad-Dārānī (d. 215/830), the spiritual master of Aḥmad ibn Abī al-Ḥawārī, who came to Syria from Basra. Although many of the Sufi women of Syria were associates of ad-Dārānī, only his sisters ᶜAbda and Āmina (section LI) appear to have been his disciples. Rābiᶜa bint Ismāᶜīl, for example, was the disciple of Ḥukayma of Damascus, a spiritual master in her own right, who, as we have seen, was the only Sufi woman apart from Fāṭima of Nishapur to be called *ustādh* by as-Sulamī.

As-Sulamī's portraits of the Sufi women of Syria are clearly meant to contradict the notion that women are deficient in religion and intellect. These terms are specifically mentioned in as-Sulamī's portrait of the sisters of Abū Sulaymān ad-Dārānī, who are described as having "attained an exalted level of intellect (*ᶜaql*) and religious observance (*dīn*)."[167] In other portraits, an intellectual approach to the Sufi way is also highlighted. Lubāba al-Mutaᶜabbida of Jerusalem (sections II and XXII), a contemporary of Rābiᶜa bint Ismāᶜīl, is portrayed as a specialist in *fiqh al-ᶜibādāt*, instructing a man on what invocations to use while on pilgrimage to Mecca.[168] The name of Ḥukayma of Damascus (section XXIII), the teacher of Rābiᶜa bint Ismāᶜīl, means "Dear Sage" or "Dear Philosopher"

166. See, for example, Sirāj ad-Dīn Abū Ḥafṣ ᶜUmar ibn al-Mulaqqin (d. 804/1401–2), *Ṭabaqāt al-awliyāʾ*, Nūr ad-Dīn Shurayba ed. (Beirut, 1406/1986), 408. See also, Hodgson, *The Venture of Islam*, vol.1, 227–29; and Massignon, *Essay*, 154.

167. *Dhikr an-niswa,* section LI below.

168. Ibid.

and similarly alludes to an intellectual spiritual method. In her portrait, she is depicted as giving an exegesis of a Quranic verse according to the Sufi doctrine of love.

According to as-Sulamī, love for God (*maḥabba*), intimacy with God (*uns*), and fear of God (*khawf*), were the main doctrinal elements of Syrian women's Sufism. The Sufi women of Syria were also known for spiritual practices that have commonly been associated with early Christian ascetics. In terms of social class, they were more likely to have been of free Arab origin than the Sufi women of Basra, and at least three of them—ᶜAthāma, Ḥukayma of Damascus, and Rābiᶜa bint Ismāᶜīl—were independently wealthy.[169] Not surprisingly, philanthropy was an important aspect of their asceticism, as it had been for wealthy Christian women before them.[170] Rābiᶜa bint Ismāᶜīl spent all of her fortune on her husband and his companions, while, according to Ibn al-Jawzī, ᶜAthāma spent five hundred gold dinars on the poor of Mecca.[171]

Among Syrian Christians in the fourth century C.E., peripatetic wandering and travel for the sake of religion exemplified the ascetic path. Ibn al-Jawzī makes a similar claim for ᶜAthāma: "Saᶜīd ibn ᶜAbd al-ᶜĀzīz said: We know of no one who has made more vows to travel for the sake of religion and then has done so than ᶜAthāma."[172] Other practices that recall Christian asceticism include Muᵓnisa the Sufi's wearing of a hair shirt (section XLIII), and Umm Hārūn's frequent retreats into the countryside.[173] However, the mere similarity of such behavior with Christian antecedents does not necessarily mean that the Sufi women of Syria copied their spiritual practices from their Christian counterparts. Similar forms of asceticism had long been practiced throughout the Middle East and the Mediterranean world. Yet the fact that ninth-century Muslim authors of sacred biography such as Muḥammad ibn al-Ḥusayn al-Burjulānī and Ibrāhīm ibn al-Junayd composed works entitled *Kitāb ar-ruhbān* (Book of Monks) indicates that the early Sufis of Syria and Iraq were aware of the similarities between their own practices and those of Christian ascetics.

The most suggestive "Christian" practice of the Sufi women of Syria was the apparent spiritual marriage (known in Christian sources as

169. Ibid., sections XVI, XXIII, and XXIX below, and *Ṣifat aṣ-Ṣafwa* Appendix sections XI and XIII.

170. See, for example, the chapter on Macrina, the sister of Basil of Caesarea, in Susanna Elm, *'Virgins of God': The Making of Asceticism in Late Antiquity* (Oxford, 1996), 78–105. See also, Coon, *Sacred Fictions*, xvii.

171. *Ṣifat aṣ-Ṣafwa* Appendix section Xl below.

172. See Ibid., and Elm, *Virgins of God*, 275–76.

173. *Dhikr an-niswa,* section XXXI and *Ṣifat aṣ-Ṣafwa* Appendix section XIV below.

"syneisaktism" or *mariage blanc*) between Rābiᶜa bint Ismāᶜīl of Damascus and her husband Aḥmad ibn Abī al-Ḥawārī. In fourth-century Asia Minor and Syria, it was relatively common for unrelated male and female Christian ascetics to live together as "brother and sister," in a spiritual union that was free from sexual relations. In such relationships, the woman was expected to act as a servant of Christ by attending to her male companion.[174] A similar relationship between Rābiᶜa bint Ismāᶜīl and her husband is suggested by Ibn al-Jawzī. In *Ṣifat aṣ-Ṣafwa*, Ibn al-Jawzī states that Rābiᶜa referred to Aḥmad ibn Abī al-Ḥawārī as "brother," rejected his amorous advances, and encouraged her husband to take other wives for his sexual satisfaction. Most tellingly, she says to him: "I do not love you in the way that married couples do; instead, I love you as one of the Sufi brethren. I wanted to be with you only in order to serve you."[175] As with Rābiᶜa al-ᶜAdawiyya, Rābiᶜa bint Ismāᶜīl's conception of love left no room for anyone or anything but God. In the view of Ḥukayma, her teacher, this made Rābiᶜa the spiritual superior of her husband. This is apparent in as-Sulamī's report of Ḥukayma's criticism of Ibn Abī al-Ḥawārī for taking another wife.[176]

An important shift in emphasis occurs in as-Sulamī's portraits of Sufi women who flourished after the second half of the ninth century C.E. Previously, the pattern had been for Sufi women to be the disciples of other Sufi women, who were themselves the founders of schools of female asceticism. By the beginning of the tenth century, Sufi women could be found throughout the Muslim world from Egypt to Khurasan. However, virtually all of these women are portrayed by as-Sulamī as disciples of Sufi men. For the most part, this does not appear to reflect the placement of any restrictions on women's physical or social mobility. In Baghdad and Khurasan, the major centers of women's Sufism in the 150 years that preceded as-Sulamī's time, Sufi women mixed freely with men, traveled long distances in order to study, and occupied positions of authority and respect among their male Sufi colleagues. But they do not appear to have been spiritual masters themselves. Despite these freedoms, the fact that Sufi women no longer occupied positions of leadership indicates a relative demotion in their social status.

The most significant development in this later period was the creation of a female ethic of chivalry, whose practitioners as-Sulamī called

174. Elm, *Virgins of God*, 50–51, 206.

175. *Ṣifat aṣ-Ṣafwa* Appendix section XIII below.

176. *Dhikr an-niswa,* section XXIII below.

niswān. This unusual term is best understood in relation to its Arabic cognates, all of which come from the same root. In as-Sulamī's usage, *nisāʾ*, the most general term for women, signifies ordinary women—those who do not follow the Sufi way. *Niswa*, another term for women that has already been discussed, is the diminutive form of *nisāʾ*. This grammatical form can be used as an expression of endearment, enhancement, or even, at times, contempt.[177] As-Sulamī uses this term mainly to signify enhancement: it marks a special category of women who are distinguished by their vocation of servitude. *Niswān*, the third term for women used by as-Sulamī, is a variation of *niswa*. The *-ān* ending of this term signifies yet another level of enhancement by creating a subcategory of *niswa*—the practitioners of female chivalry.[178]

As terms used to describe Sufi women, *niswa* and *niswān* are related to their masculine counterparts, *fitya* and *fityān*. These masculine terms are commonly used in Sufi writings to denote groups of men who practice *futuwwa* (lit. "young manliness"), institutionalized chivalry.[179] As a specialist in Sufi practices and institutions, as-Sulamī was particularly noted as an expert on *futuwwa*. His *Kitāb al-futuwwa* is one of the best known of his shorter Sufi treatises and is the only example of these works to have been widely disseminated in European languages. In this work, as-Sulamī describes *futuwwa* as a spiritual method that closely complements the path of servitude followed by Sufi women:

> Know that Futuwwah means following the ordinances of perfect devotion [i.e., servitude], leaving all evil, and attaining in action and in thought the best of visible and hidden good conduct. Every condition and every moment demand from you one aspect of Futuwwah. There is no state or time without that demand. There is a Futuwwah fit for your behavior toward God, another toward the Prophet, and others toward his companions; yet others toward the pure ones of the past, your sheikh, your brotherhood, and the two angels on your shoulders who keep the accounting of your deeds.[180]

Although as-Sulamī's book of Sufi women provides no direct evidence of formal associations of *niswān* comparable to the associations that

177. See W. Wright, *A Grammar of the Arabic Language*, revised by W. Robertson Smith and M. J. de Goeje (Cambridge, 1988 reprint of 1859 first edition) 166.

178. Ibid., 168–69.

179. For a historical introduction to *futuwwa,* see Muhammad Ja'far Mahjub, "Chivalry and Early Persian Sufism," *Classical Persian Sufism: from its Origins to Rumi*, ed., Leonard Lewisohn, (London and New York, 1993), 549–81.

180. Al-Sulamī, *The Book of Sufi Chivalry*, 36.

characterized men's *futuwwa*, there is no doubt that by feminizing the term *fityān* as-Sulamī sought to impart to the practitioners of female chivalry their own corporate identity. The idea that women could practice a distinctive form of chivalry appears to have been acknowledged by Sufi masters at least a century before as-Sulamī. This is suggested in a statement by Abū Ḥafṣ of Nishapur (d. 270/883–84), who speaks of Umm ᶜAlī, the wife of the Sufi shaykh Aḥmad ibn Khaḍrawayh of Balkh (d. 240/854): "I used to dislike stories about the *niswān* until I met Umm ᶜAlī, the wife of Aḥmad ibn Khaḍrawayh. Then I learned that God Most High bestows His knowledge on whomever He wishes."[181]

Umm ᶜAlī's husband Aḥmad ibn Khaḍrawayh was a noted practitioner of *futuwwa* and, like as-Sulamī's father and grandfather, also followed the way of the *malāmatiyya*. Abū Ḥafṣ of Nishapur also had links to *futuwwa* and the *malāmatiyya*. He was a noted authority on Sufi ethics and his wives, ᶜĀᵓisha and Ṣafrāᵓ, are included among as-Sulamī's Sufi women (sections XXXVI and XXXVIII). In al-Hujwīrī's *Kashf al-maḥjūb,* Abū Ḥafṣ' discussion of the relationship between appropriate behavior (*adab*) and Sufism is highly reminiscent of as-Sulamī's description of *futuwwa*:

> All of Sufism consists of appropriate actions (*ādāb*): for every time there is an appropriate action; for every station there is an appropriate action; and for every state there is an appropriate action. He who obliges himself to perform the appropriate actions at the appropriate times has attained the rank of the "men" (*rijāl*); but he who squanders his actions is far from the nearness to God he imagines he has attained and has been rejected from the acceptance of God that he imagines he has earned.[182]

For as-Sulamī's Sufi women, *adab* was an important part of the path of servitude. In addition, *adab* is closely related to the concept of service (*khidma*), which was an essential aspect of both *futuwwa* and *taᶜabbud*. The second half of as-Sulamī's book of Sufi women contains numerous examples of women who were the personal servants (*khādimāt*) of Sufi shaykhs or combined *futuwwa* and service by acting as the servants of male *fityān*. The best example of a servant of Sufi shaykhs is Fāṭima of Baghdad (section XXXVII), who successively served the spiritual masters Abū Ḥamza al-Baghdādī (d. 289/902), Abū al-Ḥusayn an-Nūrī and Abū al-Qāsim al-Junayd. As-Sulamī also describes two women, Āmina

181. *Dhikr an-niswa,* section XLI below.
182. al-Hujwīrī, *The Kashf al-Maḥjūb*, 41–42

al-Marjiyya (section LXXX) and Fāṭima al-Khānaqahiyya (section LXXXI), who are not described as *niswān* but as *fityān*—female practitioners of male chivalry. These women earned this paradoxical designation by making a formal vow (*muta*ᶜ*ahhida*) to serve male *fityān*. From their doctrinal statements, which deal exclusively with *futuwwa* or service, and from the nickname of Fāṭima, *al-Khānaqahiyya*, "She of the Sufi Hermitage" (*khānaqah*), it is clear that both of these women served organized groups of *fityān* either individually or as part of a female auxiliary.

It is much more difficult to determine whether as-Sulamī was referring to a corporate institution, such as a Sufi sodality (sisterhood) or a *khānaqah*, when he used the term *niswān*. Clearly, this term refers to female practitioners of Sufi chivalry on the pattern of *fityān*, its masculine counterpart. But who were these *niswān*? Were they individual Sufi women who simply practiced the ethics of *futuwwa*, or were they members of a formally organized sodality that occupied its own hermitages and functioned as a corporate institution? It is impossible to give a definitive answer to this question at the present time. Evidence for the former conclusion can be found in as-Sulamī's portrait of ᶜAthāma, the niece of the early Syrian traditionist Bilāl ibn Abī ad-Dardāᵓ (section XVI). Although as-Sulamī describes ᶜAthāma as "one of the practitioners of servitude and female chivalry" (*min muta*ᶜ*abbidāt an-niswān*), it is hard to imagine that she was a member of a *fityān*-like group of women because she lived in the Umayyad period, at least one hundred years before the concept of *futuwwa* was first discussed in Sufi sources.[183] In this one case, at least, as-Sulamī appears to be projecting an institution from his own time back onto the era of a woman who embodied many of the attributes that would later come to be associated with the *niswān*. On the other hand, evidence of a possible corporate group of *niswān* can be found in as-Sulamī's portrait of Umm al-Ḥusayn the daughter of Aḥmad ibn Ḥamdān (d. 311/923– 24), where reference is made to "one of her companions among the *niswān*."[184] In addition, Amat al-ᶜAzīz (section LXV), whom as-Sulamī describes as "one of the most altruistic practitioners of female chivalry in her day" (*min aftā waqtihā fī an-niswān*), can be found instructing another woman on the ethical requirements of wearing the woolen garment of a Sufi. Although it is impossible to know

183. Although Sufi traditions trace the origins of *futuwwa* as far back as al-Ḥasan al-Baṣrī (d. 110/728), there is no verifiable evidence of the term being used before the mid-ninth century C.E. See Mahjub, "Chivalry and Early Persian Sufism," 551–52.

184. *Dhikr an-niswa,* section LXXII below.

the full context of this report, Amat al-ᶜAzīz's behavior is something that would normally be done in preparation for initiating a new disciple into the Sufi way.

Until other early sources on Sufi women come to light, we must remain in the dark about the exact meaning of the term *niswān* for as-Sulamī and his contemporaries. Although much important information has been added to our knowledge of Muslim women's spirituality by the discovery of as-Sulamī's book of Sufi women, even more remains to be uncovered. An indication of what we are looking for can be seen in *Asrār at-tawḥīd fī maqāmāt ash-shaykh Abī Saᶜīd* (The Secrets of Divine Unity in the Exploits of Shaykh Abū Saᶜīd), a twelfth-century sacred biography of one of as-Sulamī's most famous disciples, the *malāmatī* Sufi Abū Saᶜīd Abū al-Khayr (d. 440/1049). While traveling in Khurasan, Abū Saᶜīd visited Nasā, a city north of Nishapur, which was a major regional center of Sufism. Muḥammad ibn al-Munawwar, the author of *Asrār at-tawḥīd*, informs us that in Abū Saᶜīd's (and hence as-Sulamī's) day, Nasā was known as "little Syria" because, just as in the regions of Jerusalem and Damascus, more than four hundred saints were buried in its vicinity. More importantly for our purposes, however, he also implies that Nasā was like Syria because it was a center of women's spirituality:

> In this city [Nasā] there are a number of women of high spirituality who are veiled from others and of whom one finds no example in other lands. Just like the majority of the men of God, they follow the [divine] tradition: "They are beneath the veil of My coat; no one other than Me can recognize them." Although they are far from the regard of men, the effects of their life of piety, their acts of grace, and their prayers are very numerous.[185]

The metaphor of veiling that Ibn al-Munawwar uses in this passage provides a fitting postscript to as-Sulamī's book of Sufi women. Although the text of *Dhikr an-niswa al-mutaᶜabbidāt aṣ-ṣūfiyyāt* provides more information than ever before on the identities and teachings of early Sufi women, there is still too little information to write an adequate history of women's Sufism, much less a history of women in Islam. However, this work does provide enough evidence to claim that the "Islamic" position on women is not static and unchanging, but has changed repeatedly in accordance with the social and intellectual transformations that have occurred in Muslim society. As-Sulamī's book of Sufi women also

185. Ibn al-Munawwar, *Les Étapes mystiques*, 56. My translation.

demonstrates that for at least one major authority on Islamic practice (as-Sulamī himself), women were fully the equals of men in their intellect and religion, and could be full partners with men in most aspects of religious and intellectual life. However, as al-Kalābādhī's contemporaneous attempt to veil the identities of Sufi women reminds us, we still cannot say whether as-Sulamī was uniquely liberal in his opinions about women, or whether he represented a wider consensus. At the present time, the full picture remains obscure. Perhaps as-Sulamī himself would have wanted the answer to remain a mystery, for even he seems to have felt that mystery is part of a woman's nature. After unveiling no less than eighty Sufi women before the world at large, he uses one of the last traditions in his book to reestablish the sense of the mysterious by stressing the inwardness of women's spirituality: "I was informed that a professional invoker said to [ᶜĀᵓisha bint Aḥmad of Merv]: 'Do this and that and an unveiling of divine secrets will be granted to you.' She said: 'Concealment is more appropriate for women than unveiling, for women are not to be exposed.'"[186]

186. *Dhikr an-niswa,* section LXXXII below.

In the Name of Allāh, the Bestower of Grace, the Merciful.

Praise be to God, Sustainer of the Worlds from the beginning until the end.
May God preserve Muḥammad and his family and bless them profusely.

A MEMORIAL OF FEMALE SUFI DEVOTEES

By Abū ʿAbd ar-Raḥmān Muḥammad ibn al-Ḥusayn b. Muḥammad as-Sulamī (365/976–412/1021)

ذكر النّسوة المتعبّدات الصّوفيات

لأبي عبد الرّحمن محمّد بن الحسين
بن محمّد السُّلَمِي (٣٦٥ هـ - ٤١٦ هـ)

I

RĀBIᶜA AL-ᶜADAWIYYA[1]

Rābiᶜa was from Basra and was a client (*mawlāt*)[2] of the clan of Āl ᶜAtīk.[3] Sufyān ath-Thawrī (may God have mercy upon him) sought her advice on legal matters and referred such issues to her.[4] He also sought her spiritual advice and supplications. Both ath-Thawrī and Shuᶜba [ibn al-Ḥajjāj][5] transmitted Rābiᶜa's words of wisdom.

1. Rābiᶜa al-ᶜAdawiyya was born in 95/714 or 99/717–18 and died in her native city of Basra in 185/801. Rābiᶜa, Muᶜādha al-ᶜAdawiyya (see section V below), and Umm ad-Dardāᵓ, the wife of a noted ascetic and Companion of the Prophet Muḥammad, are the three great female saints of Basra. Medieval sources locate Rābiᶜa's tomb on the outskirts of Basra, not in Jerusalem or Egypt as some have claimed. For a summary of information on Rābiᶜa, see Margaret Smith and Charles Pellat, "Rābiᶜa al-ᶜAdawiyya al-Ḳaysiyya," in *Encyclopaedia of Islam Second Edition* (EI²), vol. 8, 354–56. See also, *Ṣifat aṣ-Ṣafwa* Appendix section I. Although it is somewhat outdated, the most complete work on Rābiᶜa remains that of Margaret Smith, *Rabi'a: The Life and Work of Rabi'a and Other Women Mystics in Islam* (Oxford, 1994). This is a reorganized version of Smith's original work, *Rābi'a the Mystic, A.D. 717–801, and Her Fellow Saints in Islam* (Cambridge, 1928). For a translation of Farīd ad-Dīn al-ᶜAṭṭār's (d. ca. 627/1230) influential notice on Rābiᶜa in *Tadhkīrat al-awliyāᵓ* (Memorial of the Saints), See Michael A. Sells, *Early Islamic Mysticism: Sufi, Qurᶜan, Miᶜraj, Poetic and Theological Writings* (Mahwah, New York, 1996), 151–70.

2. From the time of the Islamic conquests through the end of the Umayyad caliphate (634–750 C.E.), a non-Muslim could only convert to Islam if he or she were sponsored by an Arab patron, who either adopted the convert into his or her clan or maintained the convert in a state of clientship (*muwālāt*), which was often formalized by a contract of mutual assistance (*tanāṣur*). This client was known as a *mawlā* (fem. *mawlāt*). The same term was also used to designate a freed slave who remained tied to a network of mutual obligations between herself and her former master's clan. Since Rābiᶜa was a *mawlāt* of the clan of Āl ᶜAtīk, this meant that she was either a freed slave of that clan or was the client of a member of Āl ᶜAtīk who sponsored her conversion to Islam. In either case, it appears likely that her origin was both non-Arab and non-Muslim. On the use of the term *mawlā* in pre-Islamic and early Islamic times, see Jacob Lassner, *The Shaping of ᶜAbbāsid Rule* (Princeton, 1980), 96–98; and Mahmood Ibrahim, *Merchant Capital and Islam* (Austin, Texas, 1990), 59–60 and 182–83.

3. Āl ᶜAtīk was a subclan of ᶜAdī ibn Qays, a clan of the Quraysh tribe of Mecca.

4. Sufyān ibn Saᶜīd ath-Thawrī was born in Kufa in 97/715–16 and died in Basra in 161/777–8. He was one of the most important figures of the formative period of Islamic law. He was highly regarded for his knowledge of hadith and wrote a commentary on the Qurᵓān (See idem, *at-Tafsīr,* Imtiyāz ᶜAlī ᶜArshī ed. [Beirut, 1983].). His school of jurisprudence was popular among early Sufis, and his teaching sessions were open to both men and women. Margaret Smith calls him "the founder of the school of Sufi tradition" (See idem, *An Early Mystic of Baghdad: A Study of the Life and Teachings of Ḥārith b. Asad al-Muḥāsibī, A.D. 781–857* [London, 1977 reprint of 1935 first edition], 72–73). Sources indicate that he disapproved of the corruption of political figures. He was said to have always been fleeing for his life and wrote notes on his shirt because he could not carry his books with him. Toward the end of his life he was exiled to Basra. Among his sayings is the following: "The scholar is the doctor of religion and money is the disease of religion. When the doctor himself contracts the disease, how can he cure another?" The most detailed account of Sufyān ath-Thawrī's life can be found in Abū Nuᶜaym al-Iṣfahānī, *Ḥilyat al-awliyāᵓ wa ṭabaqāt al-aṣfiyāᵓ,* Abū Hājir as-Saᶜīd ibn Basyūnī Zaghlūl, ed. (Beirut, reprint of 1357/1938 edition), vol. 6, 356–93 and vol. 7, 3–143. See also, Jamāl ad-Dīn Abū al-Faraj ibn al-Jawzī, *Ṣifat aṣ-Ṣafwa,* Maḥmūd Fākhūrī and Muḥammad Rawwās Qalᶜanjī eds. (Beirut, 1406/1986), vol. 3, 148–52.

5. Abū Bisṭām Shuᶜba ibn al-Ḥajjāj (d. 160/776–77 or 165/781–82) was a hadith transmitter and

(١)

منهنّ رابعة العدوية

كانت من أهل البصرة، وكانت مولاة لآل عتيك. وكان سفيان الثوري، رحمة الله عليه، يسألها عن مسائل و [يردها] [إليها]، ويرغب في موعظتها ودعائها. وروى عن رابعة من حكمتها الثوري وشُعْبة.

Muḥammad ibn ᶜAbdallāh b. Akhī Mīmī[6] personally reported from Aḥmad ibn Isḥāq b. Wahb that his father [Wahb al-Bazzāz] reported through ᶜAbdallāh ibn Ayyūb al-Muqriᵓ (the Qurᵓān Reciter) through Shaybān ibn Farrūkh, that Jaᶜfar ibn Sulaymān[7] related: Sufyān ath-Thawrī took me by the hand and said about Rābiᶜa: "Take me to the mentor. For when I am apart from her, I can find no solace." When we entered her abode, Sufyān raised his hand and said, "Oh God, grant me safety!" At this, Rābiᶜa wept. "What makes you weep?" he asked. "You caused me to weep," she replied. "How?" he asked. She answered, "Have you not learned that true safety from the world is to abandon all that is in it? So how can you ask such a thing while you are still soiled with the world?"

Abū Jaᶜfar Muḥammad ibn Aḥmad b. Saᶜīd ar-Rāzī[8] reported from al-ᶜAbbās ibn Ḥamza[9] through Aḥmad ibn Abī al-Ḥawārī[10] through al-ᶜAbbās ibn al-Walīd al-Mashriqī that Shaybān al-Ubullī related: I heard Rābiᶜa say: "For everything there is a fruit (*thamara*), and the fruit of the knowledge of God (*maᶜrifa*) is in orienting oneself toward God at all times (*iqbāl*)."[11]

companion of Sufyān ath-Thawrī. He was from the Iraqi city of al-Wāsiṭ but lived in Basra. His origin was Persian and, like Rābiᶜa, he was the *mawlā* of an Arab clan. When he died, Sufyān ath-Thawrī said: "Hadith has died with the death of Shuᶜba." See al-Iṣfahānī, *Ḥilyat al-awliyāᵓ,* vol. 6, 144–209.

6. This person cannot be identified in the published Sufi sources contemporary with as-Sulamī. It is possible that his name is a misspelling of "Akhmīmī," a term used to describe the inhabitants of Akhmīm (ancient Panopolis), the city in Upper Egypt that was the birthplace of Dhū an-Nūn al-Miṣrī.

7. Jaᶜfar ibn Sulaymān aḍ-Ḍubᶜī (d. 178/794–95) was a major hadith transmitter and source of information on Rābiᶜa. See, for example, Abū Ṭālib al-Makkī, *Qūt al-qulūb fī muᶜamalat al-Maḥbūb wa waṣf ṭarīq al-murīd ilā maqām at-tawḥīd* (Beirut, reprint of Būlāq edition of 1302/1884–85), vol. 2, 57. See also al-Iṣfahānī, *Ḥilyat al-awliyāᵓ,* vol. 6, 287–96.

8. I was unable to find any biographical information on this individual. His name indicates that he was from the Persian city of Rayy. Nūr ad-Dīn Shurayba, the editor of as-Sulamī's *Ṭabaqāt aṣ-ṣūfiyya,* reports only that Abū Jaᶜfar ar-Rāzī transmitted a false tradition about ᶜAlī ibn Abī Ṭālib (d. 41/661), the Prophet Muhammad's son-in-law and fourth caliph. In this tradition, ᶜAlī is depicted as ostentatiously wearing four rings on his fingers. See Abū ᶜAbd ar-Raḥmān as-Sulamī, *Ṭabaqāt aṣ-ṣūfiyya,* Nūr ad-Dīn Shurayba ed. (Cairo, 1406/1986), np. 8–9.

9. Al-ᶜAbbās ibn Ḥamza b. ᶜAbdallāh b. Ashūs of Nishapur (d. 288/901) was an eloquent preacher and traditionist. He transmitted reports from Aḥmad ibn Abī al-Ḥawārī. See Ibid., np. 25.

10. Aḥmad ibn Abī al-Ḥawārī (d. 230/845) was a famous Sufi of Damascus. He was a specialist in self-denial and scrupulousness. Al-Iṣfahānī cites him as a major source of information about Christian asceticism and love mysticism. For information about his wife, see section XXIX below. See also the notices on him in as-Sulamī, *Ṭabaqāt aṣ-ṣūfiyya,* 98–102 and al-Iṣfahāni, *Ḥilyat al-awliyāᵓ,* vol. 10, 5–33. See also, ᶜAbd al-Karīm ibn Hāwāzin al-Qushayrī, *ar-Risāla al-Qushayriyya fī ᶜilm at-taṣawwuf,* Maᶜrūf Zurayq and ᶜAlī ᶜAbd al-Ḥamīd Bilṭarjī eds. (Beirut, 1410/1990), 410; ᶜAlī ibn ᶜUthmān al-Jullābī al-Hujwirī, *The Kashf al-Mahjūb: The Oldest Persian Treatise on Sufism,* Reynold A. Nicholson, trans. (London, 1976 reprint of 1911 original), 118-119. See also, Louis Massignon, *Essay on the Origins of the Technical Language of Islamic Mysticism,* Benjamin Clark, trans. (Notre Dame, Indiana, 1997 translation of 1922 original), 152–58.

11. On its surface, this aphorism may appear problematical from a doctrinal point of view. Two terms are involved: *maᶜrifa,* which literally means "knowledge" but in a Sufi context is usually translated as "gnosis," and *iqbāl,* which means "turning one's face toward God" or "orienting oneself toward God." According to the understanding of *maᶜrifa* most common to Sufism, orienting oneself toward God would

أخبرنا محمد بن عبد الله بن أخي ميمي بنفسه، قال: حدّثنا أحمد بن إسحاق بن وهب، قال: حدّثني أبي، قال: حدّثنا عبد الله بن أيوب المقرئ، قال: حدّثنا شيبان بن فرّوخ، قال: حدّثنا جعفر بن سليمان، قال: أخذ بيدي سفيان الثوري وقال: مُرَّ بِي إلى المؤدبة التي لا أجِدُنِي أستَرِيحُ إذا فارقتها.

فلما دخلنا عليها رفع سفيان يدَهُ، وقال: اللهمّ إنّي أسألُكَ السّلامة. فبَكَتْ رابعة. فقال لها: ما يُبْكيك؟ قالت: أنتَ عَرّضْتَني للبُكاء! فقال لها: وكيف؟ فقالت: أمَا علِمْتَ أنّ السّلامة من الدّنيا تركُ ما فيها، فكيف وأنت مُتلطّخ بِها؟

أخبرنا أبوجعفر محمد بن أحمد بن سعيد الرّازي، قال: حدّثنا العبّاس بن حمزة، قال حدّثنا أحمد بن أبي الحواري، قال: حدّثنا العباس بن الوليد المشرقي، قال: حدّثنا شيبان الأُبُلي، قال: سمعت رابعة تقول: لكلّ شئ ثمرة، وثمرة المعرفة الإقبال.

Also on his authority, Rābiᶜa said: "I ask God's forgiveness for my lack of truthfulness in saying, 'I ask God's forgiveness.'"

Also on his authority, Rābiᶜa was asked: "How is your love for the Prophet (may God bless and preserve him)?" To which she replied, "Verily, I love him. But love for the Creator has turned me away from love for created things."

[Shaybān al-Ubullī] also said: One day, Rābiᶜa saw Rabāḥ [al-Qaysī][12] kissing a young boy. "Do you love him?" she asked. "Yes," he said. To which she replied, "I did not imagine that there was room in your heart to love anything other than God, the Glorious and Mighty!" Rabāḥ was overcome at this and fainted. When he awoke, he said, "On the contrary, this is a mercy that God Most High has put into the hearts of His slaves."[13]

I heard Abū Bakr ar-Rāzī[14] report from Abū Salama al-Baladī that Maymūn ibn al-Aṣbagh related through Sayyār[15] from Jaᶜfar [ibn Sulaymān]: Muḥammad ibn Wāsiᶜ[16] came upon Rābiᶜa while she was staggering like one inebriated. "What causes you to stagger?" he asked. "Last night I became intoxicated with love for my Lord and woke up inebriated from it," she replied.

normally precede gnosis, thus making *maᶜrifa* the "fruit" of *iqbāl* and not the other way around. If, however, *maᶜrifa* is translated as "knowledge of God," with the same meaning as the phrase *al-ᶜilm bi-llāh,* Rābiᶜa's statement would make sense as it is. The above translation of Rābiᶜa's aphorism follows the interpretation of ᶜAbd ar-Raḥmān ibn Aḥmad al-Jāmī (d. 899/1492) in idem, *Nafaḥāt al-uns min ḥaḍarāt al-quds,* Mehdi Tawhidipur, ed. (Tehran, 1337/1918–19), 616.

12. Abū al-Muhājir Rabāḥ ibn ᶜAmr al-Qaysī (d. 180/796) of Basra was an ascetic and hadith transmitter who was known for his fear of God and weeping. He practiced mortification of the flesh in ways that were more representative of Christian asceticism than of the Islamic variety. Al-Iṣfahānī, for example, reports that Rabāḥ used to put a heavy iron collar on his neck when he performed his nightly devotions. He also advocated vows of chastity, acts of contrition, and pious visits to cemeteries. According to Massignon, Rabāḥ introduced the early Sufi doctrines of divine friendship (*khulla*) and the superiority of saints to prophets *(tafḍīl al-walī*). Because of copyists' errors, he is sometimes listed as "Riyāḥ." See al-Iṣfahānī, *Ḥilyat al-awliyāʾ,* vol. 6, 192-197 and Ibn al-Jawzī, *Ṣifat aṣ-Ṣafwa,* vol. 3, 367–70. See also, Smith, *Rabi'a,* 33–34, idem, *An Early Mystic,* 73–74; and Massignon, *Essay,* 150–52.

13. Although it contradicts his reputation for chastity, some heresiographers, such as the Hanbalite scholar al-Khushaysh an-Nisāʾī (d. 253/867), accused Rabāḥ al Qaysī of belonging to a group of "spirituals" (*rūḥāniyya*) who belived that their friendship with God allowed them to take liberties with the moral teachings of Islam. According to al-Khushaysh, such practices included licentiousness with women and young boys. See Carl W. Ernst, *Words of Ecstasy in Sufism* (Albany, New York, 1985), 100, 118–22.

14. Abū Bakr Muḥammad b. ᶜAbdallāh b. ᶜAbd al-ᶜAzīz b. Shādhān ar-Rāzī was from the Iranian city of Rayy (near modern Tehran) and died in Nishapur in 376/986–87. He traveled widely in Iran and Central Asia, and was a major source of Sufi traditions for as-Sulamī. See idem, *Ṭabaqāt aṣ-ṣūfiyya,* np. 18–19.

15. This individual may be Abū al-Ḥakam Sayyār ibn Dīnār (or ibn Wardān) al-ᶜAnbarī, a weeper (*bakkāʾ*) who was an associate of Mālik ibn Dīnār (d. 128/745). See Ibn al-Jawzī, *Ṣifat aṣ-Ṣafwa,* vol. 3, 13–14.

16. Abū ᶜAbdallāh Muḥammad ibn Wāsiᶜ b. Jābir (d. ca 120/738) was a noted hadith transmitter, Qurʾān reciter, and ascetic from Khurasan who settled in Basra. His self-mortification included

وبإسناده، قالت رابعة: أستغفرُ الله مِنْ قِلّة صِدقِي في "أستغفر الله".

وبإسناده، قيل لها: كيف حبُّك للرّسول صلّى الله عليه وسلّم؟ فقالت: إنّي لأحبُّه، ولكنْ شَغَلَني حُبُّ الخَالِق عن حُبِّ المخلُوقِين.

وقال: رأت رابعة يوما رباحا وهويقبّل صبيا صغيرا. فقالت

أتُحِبُّه؟ قال: نعم. فقالت: ما كنت أحْسبُ أنّ في قلبك موضع محبّة لغير الله عزّ وجلّ. فخرّ ربّاح مغشيا عليه. فلمَّا أفاق قال: بَلْ رحمةٌ جعلها اللّه تعالى في قُلوب عباده.

سمعتُ أبا بكر الرّازي يقول: سمعتُ أبا سلمة البلدي يقول: حدّثنا ميمون بن الأصبغ، قال: حدّثنا سيّار، عن جعفر، قال: دخل محمد بن واسع، على رابعة وهي تتمايلُ، فقال لها: ممّا تمايُلُكِ؟ فقالت: سكرت من حبِّ ربّي الليلة، فأصبحتُ وأنا منه مخمورة.

In a quarter of Baghdad named Qaṭīᶜat ad-Daqīq, I heard Muḥammad ibn ᶜAbdallāh b. Akhī Mīmī report from Aḥmad ibn Isḥāq b. Wahb al-Bazzāz (the Cloth Merchant) through ᶜAbdallāh ibn Ayyūb al-Muqriᵓ through Shaybān ibn Farrūkh that Jaᶜfar ibn Sulaymān said: I heard Rābiᶜa al-ᶜAdawiyya say that Sufyān ath-Thawrī asked her, "What is the best way for the slave (*ᶜabd*) to come close to God, the Glorious and Mighty?" She wept and replied: "How can the likes of me be asked such a thing? The best way for the slave to come close to God Most High is for him to know that he must not love anything in this world or the Hereafter other than Him."

Also on [Jaᶜfar ibn Sulaymān's] authority it is reported that ath-Thawrī said in Rābiᶜa's presence, "How sorrowful I am!" "Do not lie!" she said. "Say instead, 'How little is my sorrow!' If you were truly sorrowful, life itself would not please you."

Also on his authority Rābiᶜa said: "My sorrow is not from feeling sad. Rather, my sorrow is from not feeling sad enough."

Also on his authority: In Basra, Rābiᶜa came across a man who had been arrested and crucified for immorality. She said: "Upon my father! With that tongue you used to say, 'There is no god but God!'" Sufyān said: "Then she mentioned the good works that the man had done."

Also on his authority: Ṣāliḥ al-Murrī[17] said in her presence, "He who persists in knocking at the door will have it opened for him."[18] "The door is already open," she replied. "But the question is: Who wishes to enter it?"

the wearing of rough wool and chains. He was a disciple of al-Ḥasan al-Baṣrī (d. 110/728) and died as a defender of the faith in Khurasan. He is said to have stated: "I never saw anything without seeing God therein." He was also a companion of Mālik ibn Dīnār and could only have known Rābiᶜa in the early part of her career. See Ibn al-Jawzī, *Ṣifat aṣ-Ṣafwa,* vol. 3, 266–71 and al-Iṣfahānī, *Ḥilyat al-awliyāᵓ,* vol. 2, 345–57. See also al-Qushayrī, *ar-Risāla,* 277, and al-Hujwīrī, *The Kashf al-Maḥjūb,* 91–92. See also, Massignon, *Essay,* 114, 147.

17. Abū Bishr Ṣāliḥ ibn Bashīr al-Murrī (d. 176/792–93) was a preacher, Qurᵓān reciter, and transmitter of early Muslim traditions. He had his own mosque in Basra where he taught Quranic studies. He was formerly the slave of a woman of the Banū Murra bedouins. After she freed him, he remained a *mawlā* of her clan. See al-Iṣfahānī, *Ḥilyat al-awliyāᵓ,* vol. 6, 165–77 and Ibn al-Jawzī, *Ṣifat aṣ-Ṣafwa,* vol. 3, 350–52. On his knowledge of the Qurᵓān see also, ᶜAbdallāh ibn al-Mubārak al-Marwazī (d. 181/797), *Kitāb az-zuhd wa yalīhī Kitāb ar-raqāᵓiq,* Ḥabīb ar-Raḥmān al-ᶜAẓmī, ed. (Beirut, n.d.), 88.

18. This is a paraphrasis of the famous saying of Jesus from the Sermon on the Mount: "Ask, and it shall be given you; seek, and ye shall find; knock, and it shall be opened unto you; for everyone that asketh receiveth; and he that seeketh findeth; and to him that knocketh it shall be opened." *New Testament, King James Version,* Matthew 7:7–8.

سمعتُ محمد بن عبد الله بن أخي ميمي، ببغداد، في قطيعة الدّقيق، يقول: أخبرنا أحمد بن اسحاق بن وهْب البزّاز، قال: حدّثنا عبد اللّه بن أيّوب المقرئ، قال: حدّثنا شيبان بن فروخ، قال: حدّثنا جعفر بن سليمان، قال: سمعتُ رابعة العدوية، وقال لها سفيان الثوري: ما أقرب ما تقرّب به العبد إلى الله عزّ وجلّ؟ فبكت وقالت: مثلي يُسْألُ عن هذا؟ أقرب ما تقرّب العبد به إلى اللّه تعالى أن يعلم أنّه لا يحبُّ من الدّنيا والآخرة غيرَهُ.

وبإسناده، قال الثوري بين يَديّ رابعة: وا حُزْنَاهُ! فقالت: لا تكْذبْ، قُلْ: وا قِلَّةَ حُزْنَاه. لوكُنتَ محزونا ما هنأ لك العيشُ.

وبإسناده، قالت رابعة: ما حُزْنِي أنّي حَزِنْتُ، ولكنّ حُزْنِي أنّي لم أحْزَنْ.

وبإسناده، قال: مرّت رابعة على رجُل بالبصرة أُخذَ على فاحشَة فصُلب. فقالت: بأبي ذلك اللّسان الذي كنت تقول به: لا إله إلاّ اللّه. قال سفيان: ذكرَتْ محَاسِن أعماله.

بإسناده، قال صالح المرّي بين يديها: من أكثر قرْعَ الباب يُفْتَحُ له. فقالت: البابُ مفتوحٌ، ولكنّ الشّأن فِيمَنْ يَرغَبُ أنْ يدخُلَهُ.

II

LUBĀBA AL-MUTAᶜABBIDA[19]
(Lubāba the Devotee)
From Jerusalem

Lubāba was a specialist in the ways of gnosis (*maᶜrifa*) and self-denial (*mujāhadāt*).

Abū Jaᶜfar Muḥammad ibn Aḥmad b. Saᶜīd ar-Rāzī reported from al-ᶜAbbās ibn Ḥamza through Aḥmad ibn Abī al-Ḥawārī that Muḥammad ibn Rawḥ[20] related: Lubāba the Worshipper said: "I am ashamed lest God see me preoccupied with other than Him."

Lubāba also said: "The more I observe self-denial, the more comfortable I become with its practice. Thus, when I get tired from human encounter, I find intimacy in the remembrance of God. And when human discourse tires me, I take my rest in dedication to the worship of God and fulfilling His service."

A man said to her: "This is the question.[21] I want to perform the pilgrimage to Mecca, so what invocation should I make during this period?" She said: "Ask God Most High for two things: that He will be pleased with you, so that He will make you attain the station of those who find their satisfaction in Him, and that He will magnify your reputation among His friends (*awliyāʾ*)."[22]

19. See also, section XXII below.

20. In *Ḥilyat al-awliyāʾ* al-Iṣfahānī lists this individual as "Aḥmad ibn Rawḥ." He gives no dates for either his birth or his death, citing only some lines of poetry in which Ibn Rawḥ speaks about the necessity of turning toward God in misfortune. Ibid., vol. 10, 166.

21. This question is posed in the form of a *masʾala,* or query on a point of Islamic law. Several of the women discussed in this work, such as Lubāba al-Mutaᶜabbida and Rābiᶜa al-ᶜAdawiyya, are depicted by as-Sulamī as specialists in the field of *fiqh al-ᶜibādāt,* the study of legal doctrines pertaining to worship. Although such issues would seldom come up in court, they were highly important to the spiritual life of the community.

22. *Walī* (pl. *awliyāʾ*) as used in the Qurʾān means "manager," "guardian," "protector" or "intercessor." In Sufi discourse it also means "intimate" or "friend," as in *walī Allāh,* "friend of God." This latter term is often translated in English to mean a Muslim "saint" who is Allah's "friend" and is thus able to protect or intercede for others as Allah's deputy or vicegerent.

(٢)

لبابة المتعبّدة
من أهل بيت المقدس

وكانت من أهل المعرفة، والمُجاهَدات.

أخبرنا أبوجعفر محمد بن أحمد بن سعيد الرّازي، قال: حدّثنا العبّاس بن حمزة، قال: حدّثنا أحمد بن أبي الحواري، قال: حدّثنا محمد بن روح، قال: قالت لبابة المتعبّدة: إنّي لأستحْيي من الله تعالى أن يراني مشتغلةً بغيره.

وقالت لبابة: مازلتُ مجتهدةً في العبادة حتّى صرتُ أستروحُ بها. فإذا تعِبْتُ من لقاء الخلق آنسَني ذِكرُهُ، وإذا أعيَاني حديثُ الخلق روّحني التّفرّغ لعبَادة الله، والقيام إلى خدمته

وقال لها رجل: هوذى (ذا)، أُريدُ أن أحجَّ، فماذا أدعوفي الموسم؟ فقالت: سل الله تعالى شيئين: أن يرضى عنك، ويُبلِّغَكَ منزل الرّاضين عنه، وأن يُخملَ [يُحْمِلَ] ذِكرك فيما بين أوليائه.

III

MARYAM OF BASRA
From the Natives of Basra

Maryam was a contemporary of Rābiᶜa [al-ᶜAdawiyya] and survived her. She was also her companion and served her. She used to lecture on the subject of love (*maḥabba*), and whenever she listened to discourses on the doctrine of love, she went into ecstasy.

It was said: One day she attended the session of a preacher. When he started to speak about love, her spleen ruptured and she died during the session.

Muḥammad ibn Aḥmad b. Saᶜīd ar-Rāzī reported from al-ᶜAbbās ibn Ḥamza through Aḥmad ibn Abī al-Ḥawārī that ᶜAbd al-ᶜAzīz ibn ᶜUmayr[23] related: Maryam of Basra would remain standing in worship from the beginning of the night, saying, "Gracious is God toward His servants" [Qurᵓān 42 (*ash-Shūrā*), 19], and did not go beyond this verse until daylight.

Maryam said: "I have never been preoccupied with my sustenance, nor have I exhausted myself in seeking it from the day when I heard the statement of God the Glorious and Mighty: 'For in heaven is your sustenance, as is that which you are promised' [Qurᵓān 61 (*adh-Dhāriyāt*), 22]."[24]

23. ᶜAbd al-ᶜAzīz ibn ᶜUmayr (fl. 200/815–16) was originally from Khurasan, but lived in Basra. He was a contemporary of the Syrian Sufi Aḥmad ibn Abī al-Ḥawārī and was noted for his aphorisms on asceticism. See Ibn al-Jawzī, *Ṣifat aṣ-Ṣafwa*, vol. 4, 234.

24. This anecdotal form of Qurᵓān commentary (*tafsīr al-Qurᵓān*) is typical for traditionists in early Islam. When used by Sufis, it serves as the basis for a particular interpretation of a point of *fiqh al-ᶜibādāt*. In this account, Maryam of Basra validates the practice of *tawakkul,* leaving all initiative to God, by referring her audience to the Qurᵓān's promise of future sustenance for those who trust in God. As-Sulamī also uses this type of commentary as a form of pro-Sufi apologetics, demonstrating that the roots of Sufism come from the Quranic roots of Islam itself. On Sufyān ath-Thawrī's use of this exegetical method, see C. H. M. Versteegh, *Arabic Grammar and Quranic Exegesis in Early Islam* (Leiden, 1993), 111–14.

(٣)

مريم البصرية
من أهل البصرة

في أيام رابعة، وعاشت بعدها. وكانت تصحبُها وتخدمُها. وكانت تتكلّمُ في المحبّة، فإذا سمِعَتْ بعلوم المحبّة طاشت.

وقيل: إنّها حضرت في مجالس بعض الواعظين. فتكلّم في المحبّة، فانشقّت مرارتها، فماتت في المجلس.

أخبرنا محمد بن أحمد بن سعيد الرّازي، قال: حدّثنا عبّاس بن حمزة، قال: حد ثنا أحمد بن ابي الحواري، قال: حدّثنا عبد العزيز بن عمير، قال: قامت مريم البصرية المتعبّدة من أوّل اللّيل، فقالت: " الله لطيف بعباده " ثم لم تُجَوِّزْ به حتّي أصبحت.

وقالت مريم: ما اهْتَمَمْتُ بالرّزق ولا تَعِبْتُ في طَلَبِه منذ سمعتُ اللّه عزّ وجلّ يقول: "وفي السّماء رزقكم وما توعدون ".

IV

MUʾMINA THE DAUGHTER OF BAHLŪL[25]
From the Female Worshippers of Damascus

Muʾmina was one of the most important female gnostics (*ʿārifāt*) of her age. I found this in the handwriting of my father, who related: It was reported that Muʾmina bint Bahlūl said: "This world and the Hereafter are not pleasurable except through God or through contemplation of the effects of His artifice and His power. He who is denied closeness to God experiences intimacy through these effects. How desolate is the hour in which God is not mentioned!"

[My father] also related: Muʾmina was asked, "From whence did you acquire these spiritual states (*aḥwāl*)?" She replied, "By following God's commands according to the Sunna of the Prophet Muḥammad (may God bless and preserve him), by magnifying the rights of the Muslims, and by rendering service to the righteous and the virtuous."

I heard Abū al-Mufaḍḍal ash-Shaybānī [report from Ibrāhīm ibn al-Azhar through Abū Hāshim ar-Rāzī through Ibn Abī al-Ḥawārī][26] who said: I heard Muʾmina bint Bahlūl (the quintessential female ascetic of Damascus) say: "Oh most Beloved! This world and the Hereafter are not pleasurable except through You. So do not overwhelm me with the loss of You and the punishment that results from it!"

25. I have been unable to determine whether Muʾmina was the daughter of the famous Bahlūl al-Majnūn (Bahlūl the Madman). Although most accounts place Bahlūl in either Kufa or Baghdad, it is possible that his daughter may have moved to Damascus. Bahlūl was a contemporary of the ʿAbbasid caliph Hārūn ar-Rashīd (r. 170/786–193/809). See Ibn al-Jawzī, *Ṣifat aṣ-Ṣafwa,* vol. 2, 516–18. In this work, Ibn al-Jawzī cites only a single aphorism from Muʾmina bint Bahlūl: "Bliss is only to be found in intimacy with God and in living in accordance with His decree." See Ibid., vol. 2, 527.

26. This passage is missing from the aṭ-Ṭanāḥī edition.

(٤)

مؤمنة بنت بهلول

من عابدات دمشق

كانت من العارفات الكبار.

وجدت بخطّ أبي، قال: حُكي عن مؤمنة بنت بهلول، أنّها قالت: ما طابت الدّنيا والآخرة إلاّ باللّه، أوبالنّظر إلى آثار صُنعه وقدرته. ومن مُنع من القُرْبِ أنِسَ بالأثر. وما أوحشَ ساعةً لا يُذكر اللّه فيه (فيها).

قال: سُئِلَتْ مؤمنةُ: من أين استفدت هذه الأحوال؟ قالت: من اتّباع أمر اللّه، علىَ سنّة رسول اللّه صلى اللَه عليه وسلّم، وتعظيم حقوق المسلمين، والقيام بخدمة الأبرار الصّالِحين.

سمعتُ أبا المفضّل الشيباني، يقول: سمعتُ ابراهيم بن الأزهر، يقول: سمعتُ أبا هاشم الرّازي، يقول: سمعتُ بن أبي الحواري، يقول: سمعتُ مؤمنة بنت بهلول -- وكانت زاهدة دمشق -- تقول: قرّة عيني، ما طابت الدّنيا والآخرة إلاّ بك. فلا تجمع عليّ فَقْدَكَ والعذاب.

V

MU^c^ĀDHA BINT ^c^ABDALLĀH AL-^c^ADAWIYYA[27]

Mu^c^ādha was a contemporary of Rābi^c^a [al-^c^Adawiyya] and was her close companion.[28]

She did not lift up her gaze toward the sky for forty years. She did not eat during the day and did not sleep at night. For this she was told, "You are causing yourself harm." To which she replied, "No. I have postponed one time for the other. I have postponed sleep from night until day and have postponed food from day until night."

I found this in the handwriting of my father (may God have mercy upon him).[29] It says: A woman used to take care of Mu^c^ādha al-^c^Adawiyya,[30] who used to stay up all night praying. When overcome by the need for sleep, she would get up and wander around the house, saying, "Oh, soul! Eternal sleep is ahead of you. If I were to die, your repose in the grave would be a long one, whether it be sorrowful or happy." She would remain that way until daylight.

27. See also, *Ṣifat aṣ-Ṣafwa* Appendix section I below. The earliest notice on Mu^c^ādha al-^c^Adawiyya is in Muḥammad ibn Sa^c^d (d. 230/845), *aṭ-Ṭabaqāt al-kubrā* (Beirut, 1405/1985) vol. 8, 483. Apart from the biographical information reproduced above, the only account of Mu^c^ādha given by Ibn Sa^c^d depicts her as sitting with her legs drawn up (*muḥtabiyya*) and discoursing to a group of women who surround her.

28. Mu^c^ādha al-^c^Adawiyya could not have been Rābi^c^a al-^c^Adawiyya's contemporary, as as-Sulamī claims, because she was a figure of the early Umayyad period. Her husband, Ṣila ibn Ushaym al-^c^Adawī, died in battle in the year 75/694–95. As-Sulamī does not cite a chain of transmission (*isnād*) for his notice on Mu^c^ādha, saying only that he obtained his information from his father. Ibn al-Jawzī reports from other, more authenticated sources that Mu^c^ādha al-^c^Adawiyya transmitted traditions from the Prophet Muḥammad's wife ^c^Ā'isha. Mu^c^ādha died in either 83/702 or 101/719–20, around the time of Rābi^c^a al-^c^Adawiyya's birth. In passing on as-Sulamī's erroneous information, Margaret Smith (*Rabi'a,* 173–74) relies on Jāmī (idem, *Nafaḥāt al-uns,* 617).

29. As-Sulamī's father, al-Ḥusayn ibn Muḥammad as-Sulamī, died around the year 345/956–57, when Abū ^c^Abd ar-Raḥmān as-Sulamī was still a young man. This explains why as-Sulamī states that he found this information about Mu^c^ādha al-^c^Adawiyya "in the handwriting of my father" rather than receiving it orally. See Nūr ad-Dīn Shurayba's introduction to as-Sulamī, *Ṭabaqāt aṣ-ṣūfiyya,* 16–17.

30. This woman probably was Unaysa bint ^c^Amr. See section XXXIX below.

(٥)

مُعاذة بنت عبد اللّه العدوية

وكانت من أقران رابعة. وكانت تأنس بها.

ولم ترفع بصرها إلى السّماء أربعين سنةً. وكانت لا تأكل بالنّهار، ولا تنام باللّيل. فقيل لها: أضررت بنفسك! فقالت: لا! أخّرتُ من وقتٍ إلى وقتٍ: أخّرتُ النّوم من الليل إلى النّهار، والأكل من النّهار إلى الليل.

وجدتُ بخطّ أبي رحمه اللّه، قال: كانت امرأةٌ تخدمُ مُعاذة العدوية. وكانت هي تحيي اللّيل صلاةً، فإذا غلبها النّوم قامت فجالت في الدّار، وهي تقول: يا نفسُ، النّومُ أمامَك. لوقدْ متُّ لَطالَتْ رقدتُكِ في القَبْر على حَسْرَةٍ أوسُرُورٍ. ولا تزالُ كذلك حتّى تُصْبِحَ.

VI

SHABAKA OF BASRA

Shabaka was a companion of her brother[31] and like him specialized in the way of scrupulousness (*wara*ᶜ).

There were underground cells (*sarādīb*)[32] in her house for her female students and disciples, where they learned the ways of self-denial and spiritual practice.

She used to say: "Souls are purified by acts of worship (*riyāḍāt*). When they are purified, they find peace in worship, just as before they were burdened by it." Abū Saᶜīd ibn al-Aᶜrābī also mentioned this statement in *Kitāb aṭ-ṭabaqāt.*[33]

31. Neither corroborating evidence for Shabaka nor information about her brother could be found in the sources consulted for this work.

32. The Swedish Islamicist Tor Andrae noted that "during the earliest period of Islam certain ascetics arranged for a cell or subterranean chamber to be built in or under their own houses, where, periodically, they practiced a life of quasi-eremitism." Idem, *In the Garden of Myrtles: Studies in Early Islamic Mysticism,* Birgitta Sharpe, trans. (Albany, New York, 1987 translation of 1947 original), 10. Although Louis Massignon does not mention the Persian term *sardāb* (subterranean vault, cellar) in *Essay,* he does discuss the *maṭmura* (Pers. *shikāft,* underground storehouse). First used as cells by Nestorian Christian ascetics, underground storehouses were also used by early Sufis in Khurasan. See Ibid., 107 and n. 103.

33. Abū Saᶜīd Aḥmad ibn al-Aᶜrābi (d. 341/952–53) was from Basra but died in Mecca, where he served as Imam of the Masjid al-Ḥarām. He was a companion of al-Junayd, ᶜAmr ibn ᶜUthmān al-Makkī, and Abū al-Ḥusayn an-Nūrī. He was a respected traditionist and was known for his knowledge of both Prophetic hadith and accounts of the Sufis. Both as-Sulamī and al-Iṣfahānī transmitted traditions from Ibn al-Aᶜrābī's *Kitāb ṭabaqāt an-nussāk* (Categories of the Ascetics). See as-Sulamī, *Ṭabaqāt aṣ-ṣūfiyya,* 427–30, and al-Iṣfahānī, *Ḥilyat al-awliyā*ʾ, vol. 2, 25. See also Ali Hassan Abdel-Kader, *The Life, Personality and Writings of Al-Junayd: A Study of a Third/Ninth Century Mystic* (London, 1976), x-xii; and Manuela Marin, "Abū Saᶜīd ibn al-Aᶜrābī et le Développement du Soufisme en al-Andalus," *Revue du Monde musulman et de la Méditerranée,* 63–64 (1992), 28–38.

(٦)

شبكة البصرية

كانت صاحبة أخيها ذي ورع.

وكانت في بيتها سراديبُ لتلامذتها وللمريدات، تعَلّمُهُنّ طُرُقَ المجاهدات والمعاملة.

وكانت تقول: تُطَهَّرُ النّفُوس بالرِّياضات، وإذا طَهُرَتْ استراحَتْ إلى العبادة، كما كانت قبلَ ذلك تَتَعنّى فيها. كذلك ذكره أبوسعيد بن الأعرابي، في كتاب الطبقات.

VII

NUSIYYA BINT SALMĀN

Nusiyya was the wife of Yūsuf ibn Asbāṭ.[34] She once said to Yūsuf ibn Asbāṭ: "You will be asked by God on my behalf whether you have provided me with any food other than that which is lawful, and whether you might be suspected of any wrongdoing for my sake."

[Yūsuf ibn Asbāṭ] said: When Nusiyya gave birth to a son she said: "Oh, Lord! You do not see me as someone worthy of Your worship. So for this You have preoccupied me with a child!"

34. Yūsuf ibn Asbāṭ ash-Shaybānī (d. 199/814–15) was an ascetic preacher and traditionist who specialized in the way of humility (*tawāḍuʿ*). When asked, "What is the limit of humility?" he replied, "It is that when you leave your house you see everyone you meet as better than you." He transmitted hadith from Sufyān ath-Thawrī and others. It is said that he buried his books because he was dissatisfied with the quality of his memory. Although as-Sulamī does not count him as a Sufi, he is mentioned as such by al-Kalābādhī in *Kitāb at-taʿarruf,* 11. See also, as-Sulamī, *Ṭabaqāt aṣ-ṣūfiyya,* np. 36; al-Iṣfahānī, *Ḥilyat al-awliyāʾ,* vol. 8, 237–43; Ibn al-Jawzī, *Ṣifat aṣ-Ṣafwa,* vol. 4, 261–66; and Smith, *An Early Mystic,* 75.

(٧)

نُسيَة بنت سَلْمان

وكانت امرأة يوسف بن أسباط.

قالت ليوسف بن أسباط: اللّه سائِلُكَ عنّي، لا تُطْعِمُني إلاّ حلالاً، ولا تَمُدّ يَدَكَ إلى شُبْهةٍ بِسَبَبِي.

قال: وولدتْ ولداً، فقالت: يا رَبِّ، لمْ تَرَني أهلاً لِخِدْمَتِكَ فشغلتني بالولَدِ!

VIII

RAYḤĀNA THE ENRAPTURED[35]

From the Ascetics of Basra

Rayḥāna was a contemporary of Ṣāliḥ al-Murrī.[36] The following verses were written beneath her collar:

You are my Intimate Companion, my Aspiration, and my Happiness,
And my heart refuses to love anything but You.

Oh, my Dear, my Aspiration, and Object of my desire,
My yearning is endless! When will I finally meet You?

My request is not for Heaven's pleasures;
I desire only to encounter You!

35. See also, *Ṣifat aṣ-Ṣafwa* Appendix section X below, where she is called "Rayḥāna al-Majnūna" (Rayḥāna the Possessed).

36. This would put the date of Rayḥāna's death in the second half of the second/eighth century.

(٨)

رَيْحَانَة الوَالِهَة
من متعبّدات البصَرة

كانت في أيّام صالح المُرّي.

كانت كتَبَتْ مِنْ وَراءِ جَيْبِها :

أنت أُنْسِي وهِمَّتِي وسُروري أبَى القلبُ أن يُحِبَّ سِواكا
يا عزيزي وهِمّتي ومُرادي طال شوقي متى يكون لقاكا
ليس سُؤْلي من الجِنان نعيمٌ غيرَ أنّي أُريدُ أنْ ألقاكا

IX

GHUFAYRA AL-ᶜĀBIDA[37]
(Ghufayra the Worshipper)
From the Natives of Basra

Ghufayra was a companion of Muᶜādha al-ᶜAdawiyya.[38] Ibrāhīm ibn al-Junayd[39] reported from Muḥammad ibn al Ḥusayn [al-Burjulānī][40] that Yaḥyā ibn Bisṭām related: Ghufayra the Worshipper wept until she became blind. A man said to her: "How devastating is blindness!" To which Ghufayra replied: "Being veiled from God is worse. And the blindness of the heart from understanding the intent of God's commands is even greater!"

37. See also, *Ṣifat aṣ-Ṣafwa* Appendix section V below.

38. This would put the date of Ghufayra's death in the middle Umayyad period, around the year 100/718–19.

39. Abū Isḥāq Ibrāhīm ibn ᶜAbdallāh b. al-Junayd (d. before 270/883–84) was an ascetic who lived in the Iraqi city of Sāmarrā. According to the medieval biographer an-Nadīm (ca. 380/990), he was the author of several works on Sufism, including a *Kitāb ar-ruhbān* (Book of Monks and Ascetics), much like that of his predecessor Muḥammad ibn al-Ḥusayn al-Burjulānī (see below). See as-Sulamī, *Ṭabaqāt aṣ-ṣūfiyya,* np. 84. See also, Massignon, *Essay,* 160; and Abū al-Faraj Muḥammad an-Nadīm, *Kitāb al-fihrist,* Ibn ᶜAlī ibn Zayn al-ᶜĀbidīn al-Ḥāʾirī al-Mazandarānī, ed. (Beirut, 1988), 237.

40. Muḥammad ibn al-Ḥusayn al-Burjulānī of Baghdad (d. 238/852) was a specialist in the way of asceticism and self-denial. Like Sufyān ath-Thawrī's student ᶜAbdallāh ibn al-Mubārak, he wrote a book entitled *Kitāb az-zuhd wa ar-raqāʾiq* (Book of Asceticism and Spiritual Practices). He also wrote a work entitled *Kitāb ar-ruhbān* (Book of Monks and Ascetics). In it he said: "These monks speak words of wisdom, although they are misguided unbelievers. Why is this? Because their legacy of hunger is attractive to you." See al-Iṣfahānī, *Ḥilyat al-awliyāʾ,* vol. 10, 150–51, where al-Burjulānī appears under the name of "Muḥammad ibn Isḥāq." See also, as-Sulamī, *Ṭabaqāt aṣ-ṣūfiyya,* np. 227; Smith, *An Early Mystic,* 42; Andrae, *In the Garden of Myrtles,* 8-12 and 32; and an-Nadīm, *Kitāb al-fihrist,* 236. Massignon (*Essay,* 160) gives a somewhat different interpretation of al-Burjulānī's *Kitāb ar-ruhbān,* seeing this work as being primarily about Muslim ascetics. This is corroborated by the present account, which is clearly taken from al-Burjulānī. Al-Burjulānī was a major source for both as-Sulamī and Ibn al-Jawzī.

(٩)

غُفَيْرة العَابِدة

من أهل البصرة

صَحِبَتْ معاذة العدوية.

ذكر إبراهيم بن الجنيد، عن محمد بن الحسين، عن يحيى بن بسطام، قال: بَكَتْ غُفَيْرة العابدة حتّى عَميَتْ. فقال رجلٌ: ما أشَدَّ العَمَى؟ فقالت غُفَيْرة: الحجابُ عن اللّه أشَدّ، وعمى القلب عن فهم مرادِ اللّه في أوامِره أشدّ وأشدّ.

X

ᶜĀFIYYA THE INFATUATED
From the Tribe of ᶜAbd al-Qays
From the Natives of Basra

ᶜĀfiyya was constantly enraptured (*wāliha*) and lost in the love of God (*hāʾima*). Most of her time was spent in remembrance of God and she seldom associated with anyone.

Ibrāhīm ibn al-Junayd mentioned that she would spend all night awake, and during the day she would seek refuge from human contact in cemeteries. She used to say: "The lover is never weary from confiding in his Beloved, and nothing is of interest to him other than the Beloved. Oh, desire! Oh, desire! Oh desire!" (three times).[41]

41. This account implies that ᶜĀfiyya was a contemporary of Ibrāhīm ibn al-Junayd. It is therefore likely that she also lived in the second half of the third/ninth century.

(١٠)

عَافِيَة المُشْتاقة

من عبد القيس
من أهل البصرة

وكانت والهةً هائمةً، كثيرة الذِّكر. قلّ ما [قلّما] كانت تأنس إلى أحد.

ذكر إبراهيم بن الجنيد أنّها كانت تحيي اللّيل، وتأوي بالنّهار إلى المقابر، وتقول: المحبُّ لا يسْأمُ من مناجاة حبيبه، ولا يهُمُّهُ سواهُ. وا شوقاهُ! وا شوقاهُ! ثلاثًا.

XI

UMM ᶜABDALLĀH
the Daughter of Khālid ibn Maᶜdān[42]

Umm ᶜAbdallāh was the mother of Ismāᶜīl ibn ᶜAyyāsh.[43] Muḥammad ibn Ismāᶜīl b. ᶜAyyāsh related that he heard his father say: I heard my mother Umm ᶜAbdallāh say: "Were I certain that God Most High would grant me Heaven, I would have increased my self-denial and service to Him. Truly, [the best legacy][44] for slaves is excellence in their service to their masters."

42. Khālid ibn Maᶜdān was a noted hadith transmitter and early Sufi from Syria. He was an associate of the founder of the Syrian school of jurisprudence, Abū ᶜAmr ᶜAbd ar-Raḥmān al-Awzāᶜī (d. 151/768 or 157/774). According to al-Iṣfahānī, Ibn Maᶜdān defined Sufism as "The exertion of effort for the sake of witnessing the Object of Worship." He had two daughters, Umm ᶜAbdallāh and ᶜAbda. Both transmitted traditions from al-Awzāᶜī. See al-Iṣfahānī, *Ḥilyat al-awliyāʾ*, vol. 5, 210–21.

43. Ismaᶜīl ibn ᶜAyyāsh (d. 181/797) was a student of Sufyān ath-Thawrī and was considered one of the greatest hadith transmitters of his time. He was born in the Syrian city of Hims. See as-Sulamī, *Ṭabaqāt aṣ-ṣūfiyya*, np. 392.

44. Although this phrase was left as a lacuna in the aṭ-Ṭanāḥī edition, it is legible in the original manuscript.

(١١)

أمّ عبد اللّـه بنت خالد بن معدان

كانت أمَّ إسماعيل بن عيّـاش.

ذكر محمد بن اسماعيل بن عيّاش، قال: سمعتُ أبي يقول: سمعتُ أمّي أمّ عبد اللّـه تقول: لوتَيَـقّـنْـتُ أنّ اللّـهَ تعالى يُدْخِلُـنـي الجنّةَ ما ازددتُ إلاّ اجتهاداً وخِدْمـةً [فلأرثَنّه] أحسن على العبيد من حسَن الخدمة لمواليهم.

XII

UNAYSA BINT ᶜAMR AL-ᶜADAWIYYA[45]

Unaysa was a native of Basra and was a student (*tilmīdha*) of Muᶜādha al-ᶜAdawiyya.[46]

I heard my grandfather Ismāᶜīl ibn Nujayd[47] report from Musaddad ibn Qaṭan through Muḥammad ibn al-Ḥusayn [al-Burjulānī] that ᶜAbd ar-Raḥmān ibn Jabala related: Unaysa bint ᶜAmr was a servant of Muᶜādha al-ᶜAdawiyya. She used to say: "My spirit has never resisted anything that I compelled it to do more strongly than the avoidance of eating that which is permissible and earning a living."

45. See also, section XXXIX below. Either as-Sulamī or the copyist of the Riyadh manuscript included two notices on Unaysa bint ᶜAmr al-ᶜAdawiyya.

46. This would put the date of Unaysa's death in the middle Umayyad period, around the year 100/718-19.

47. Ismāᶜīl ibn Nujayd (d. 366/976-7) was the grandfather of as-Sulamī on his mother's side. He was a noted Sufi and traditionist. He was a companion of Abū ᶜUthmān al-Ḥīrī (298/910) and met Abū al-Qāsim al-Junayd (d. 298/910). He was adept at concealing the onset of spiritual states and was noted for his Sufi aphorisms. See as-Sulamī, *Ṭabaqāt aṣ-ṣūfiyya,* 454–57 and al-Qushayrī, *ar-Risāla,* 435–36.

(١٢)

أُنَيْسة بنت عمرو العدوية

كانت من أهل البصرة. تلميذة معاذة العدوية.

سمعتُ جدّي إسماعيل بن نجيد، يقول: سمعتُ مسدّد بن قطن، يقول: حدّثنا محمد بن الحسين، قال: حدّثنا عبد الرحمن بن جبلة، قال: كانت أنيْسَة بنت عمرو تَخْدُم مُعاذة العدوية، وكانت تقول: ما رُضتُ نفسي على شئ فأبَتْ عليَّ إبَاءَها إيّاي على أكل الحلال والكسْبِ.

XIII

UMM AL-ASWAD[48] BINT ZAYD [YAZĪD] AL-ᶜADAWIYYA OF BASRA[49]

Muᶜādha [al-ᶜAdawiyya] was Umm al-Aswad's wet-nurse.[50] Musaddad ibn Qaṭan reported from Muḥammad ibn al-Ḥusayn [al-Burjulānī] through Yaḥyā ibn Bisṭām that ᶜImrān ibn Khālid related: Umm al-Aswad bint Zayd told me that she was asked about the statement of God the Glorious and Mighty: "So forgive with gracious forgiveness" [Qurᵓān 15 (*al-Ḥijr*), 85]. Commenting on this verse, she said: "Acceptance without blame."[51]

48. See also, section XL below. The notice on Umm al-Aswad in Ibn al-Jawzī's *Ṣifat aṣ-Ṣafwa* is a verbatim copy of section XL. See Ibid., vol. 4, 32.

49. Umm al-Aswad and her brother al-Aswad ibn Yazīd ibn Qays (d. 75/694–95) were the niece and nephew of ᶜAlqama ibn Qays an-Nakhaᶜī (see note 58 below), an important traditionist of the second generation after the Prophet Muḥammad. Al-Aswad was older than his uncle ᶜAlqama and died in Kufa, nearly a generation before the latter. He was an extreme ascetic and was said to have mortified his flesh so severely from fasting and worship that it became "green and yellow." ᶜAlqama worried that al-Aswad would be harmed by his ascetic practices. It is said that he lost the sight of one eye because of his fasting. Al-Aswad's contemporaries called him "one of the monks" (*rāhib min ar-ruhbān*) of his time. See al-Iṣfahānī, *Ḥilyat al-awliyāᵓ*, vol. 2, 102–5; and Ibn al-Jawzī, *Ṣifat aṣ-Ṣafwa*, vol. 3, 23–24. On the controversy over the use of the term "monk" (*rāhib*) in Islam, see Andrae, *In the Garden of Myrtles*, 9–14; and Massignon, *Essay*, 98–104.

50. This information puts the date of Umm al-Aswad's death in the middle Umayyad period, around the year 100/718–19.

51. Umm al-Aswad's commentary on this verse refers to the concept of humility (*tawāḍuᶜ*) discussed above in the footnote on Yūsuf ibn Asbāṭ. She implies that to know one's human nature is to acknowledge the existence of faults in oneself and others. Thus, one must always be tolerant of one's fellow human beings.

(١٣)

أُمّ الأسود بنت زيد العدوية
بصرية

وكانت معاذة قد أرضعتها.

ذكر مسدّد بن قطن، عن محمد بن الحسين، عن يحيى بن بسطام، عن عمران بن خالد، قال: حدّثتْني أمّ الأسود بنت زيد، وسُئلت عن قول اللّه عزّ وجلّ "فاصْفحْ الصَّفحَ الجميلَ" قالت: رضا بلا عتابٍ.

XIV

SHAᶜWĀNA[52]

Shaᶜwāna used to live in al-Ubulla. She was a remarkable person, and had a beautiful and melodious voice. She preached to the people and recited the Qurʾān to them. Her sessions were attended by ascetics, worshippers, those who were close to God, and the masters of hearts and self-denial.

She was one of those known for self-denial, who fear God, who weep, and influence others to weep.

Musaddad ibn Qaṭan reported through Muḥammad ibn al-Ḥusayn [al-Burjulānī] through Abū Muᶜādh that Abū ᶜAwn [Muᶜādh ibn al-Faḍl] related: Shaᶜwāna wept until we feared that she would become blind. So we said to her, "We are afraid that you might become blind." She wept and replied: "'We are afraid?' By God! Becoming blind in this world from weeping is more desirable to me than being blinded by Hellfire in the Hereafter!"

Shaᶜwāna used to say: "Can an eye be separated from its Beloved and yearn to be united with Him without weeping? This is not right!"

52. See also, *Ṣifat aṣ-Ṣafwa* Appendix section IX below. According to Ibn al-Jawzī, Shaᶜwāna was a contemporary of the famous Sufi al-Fuḍayl ibn ᶜIyāḍ (d. 187/803). See also, Zaynab bint Yūsuf Fawāz al-ᶜĀmilī, *ad-Durr al-manthūr fī ṭabaqāt rabbāt al-khudūr* (Beirut, reprint of the Būlāq edition of 1312/1894–95), 256.

(١٤)

شعْوانـــة

كانت تَنْزلُ الأُبُـلَّـة. وكانت عجيبة، حسنة الصّوت، طيّبة النّغمة، تعـظُ الناس، وتقرأُ لهم، ويحضُرها الزّهّـاد والعُبَّـادُ والـمتقَرِّبة، وأربابُ القُـلوَب والـمجاهدات.

وكانت هي من الـمجتهدات الخائفات الباكيات الـمبكيات.

ذكر مسدّد بن قطن، عن محمد بن الحسين، حدّثنا أبومعاذ، قال: حدّثنا أبوعون، قال: بَكَتْ شعوانة حتّى خفْنا عليها العَمَى. فقلنا لها: إنّا نخافُ عليك العَمَى. فبكتْ وقالت: خفْنا ! أعْمَى والّله في الدّنيا من البُكاء أحبُّ إلَيَّ من أعْمَى في الآخرةَ من النّار.

وكانت شعْوانة تقول: عَيْـنٌ فارقتْ حبيبها، واشتاقت إلى لقائه بغير بكاء؟ لايحسُنُ!

XV

SAᶜĪDA BINT ZAYD
The Sister of Ḥammād ibn Zayd[53]

Saᶜīda was one of the female gnostics of Basra. She was similar to Rābiᶜa [al-ᶜAdawiyya]. She frequently practiced self-denial, and was always in a meditative state (*tafakkur*).

It was reported that she used to say: "When one reflects upon the bounties that God has bestowed on him, and how little he is thankful for them, he becomes ashamed of asking for more because of how much he has attained thus far."

53. Abū Ismāᶜīl Ḥammād ibn Zayd (d. 177/793–94) was a traditionist and opponent of Abū Ḥanīfa (d. 150/767), the founder of the Ḥanafī school of jurisprudence. Ḥammād advocated a literal interpretation of the Prophet Muḥammad's Sunna and did not accept the Ḥanafī school's practice of deriving new laws from the Sunna by analogy. When Abū Ḥanīfa died, he said: "Praise be to God who has swept the innards of the earth with him!" Ḥammād died in the latter half of the second/eighth century. See al-Iṣfahānī, *Ḥilyat al-awliyāᵓ*, vol. 6, 257–67; and Ibn al-Jawzī, *Ṣifat aṣ-Ṣafwa*, vol. 3, 321–25, where he is called "ᶜAbd al-Wāḥid ibn Zayd." He also appears under this name in Massignon, *Essay*, who attributes to Ḥammād ibn Zayd the use of the term *ᶜishq* (ardent desire) for the love of God and the founding of the anchoritic community of Muslim ascetics at Abadan (formally ᶜAbbādān) in present day Iran. See Ibid., 147–48. See also note 77 below.

(١٥)

سعيدة بنت زيد

أخت حمّاد بن زيد

كانت من عارفات البصريين. وكانت تُشَبَّه برابعة. وكانت كثيرة الاجتهاد، دائمة التفكُّر.

رُويَ عنها أنّه [أنّها] كانت تقول: من تفكّر في نعم اللّه عليه، وتقصيره في شُكرِهِ استحيا [استحيى] من السّؤال مع كثير ما عليه من النّوال.

XVI

ʿATHĀMA THE DAUGHTER [NIECE?] OF BILĀL IBN ABĪ AD-DARDĀʾ[54]

ʿAthāma was a devotee and practitioner of female chivalry (*min mutaʿabbidāt an-niswān*). She was stricken by blindness but bore it patiently.

The ascetic Abū al-Fatḥ Yūsuf ibn ʿUmar [al-Qawwās] of Baghdad[55] reported from Jaʿfar ibn Muḥammad b. Nuṣayr [al-Khuldī][56] through Aḥmad ibn Muḥammad b. Masrūq[57] through Muḥammad ibn al-Ḥusayn al-Burjulānī through al-Ḥusayn ibn ʿAbd al-ʿAzīz b. al-Wazīr al-Judhāmī that ʿAbdallāh ibn Yūsuf of Damascus related: ʿAthāma the daughter of Bilāl b. Abī ad-Dardāʾ lost her eyesight. One day she was engaged in worship and her son came into the house after finishing his prayers. She said, "Have you prayed, my son?" "Yes," he said. And she replied:

> "Oh ʿAthāma, why are you so distracted?
> "Your house must have been invaded by a trickster!

54. See also, *Ṣifat aṣ-Ṣafwa* Appendix section XI below. Bilāl ibn Abī ad-Dardāʾ (d. 96/714–15) was the son of Abū ad-Dardāʾ ʿUwaymir ibn Zayd (d. 32/652), a noted Companion of the Prophet Muḥammad. He transmitted hadith from his father and was appointed as a judge in Syria. According to Ibn al-Jawzī, ʿAthāma's son was named Muḥammad ibn Sulaymān b. (the son of) Bilāl ibn Abī ad-Dardāʾ. If this is true, as-Sulamī's version of ʿAthāma's name would indicate that she had married her own brother. It is thus likely that ʿAthāma was either the niece of Bilāl ibn Abī ad-Dardāʾ or that her husband Sulaymān was his nephew. See as-Sulamī, *Dhikr an-niswa,* aṭ-Ṭanāḥī ed., np. 46. See also al-Qushayrī, *ar-Risāla,* np. 365. On Abū ad-Dardāʾ see Smith, *An Early Mystic,* 63; and Massignon, *Essay,* 108.

55. Abū al-Fatḥ Yūsuf ibn ʿUmar al-Qawwās al-Baghdādī (d. 385/995) was known for his asceticism and uncompromising honesty (*ṣidq*). He was also known for his piety and goodness. It was said that his supplications were answered by God. See as-Sulamī, *Ṭabaqāt aṣ-ṣūfiyya,* np. 84.

56. Jaʿfar ibn Muḥammad b. Nuṣayr al-Khuldī (d. 348/959–60) was born and died in Baghdad. He was a companion of al-Junayd and Abū al-Ḥusayn an-Nūrī. He is said to have written over 150 Sufi poems. He also wrote a well-known hagiographical work entitled *Ḥikāyāt al-awliyāʾ* (Stories of the Saints). The Riyadh manuscript of "Sulamiyyāt" from which the present work is taken also contains a work entitled *Kitāb al-muntakhab min ḥikāyāt aṣ-ṣūfiyya* (Selections from the Tales of the Sufis). This may be an abridged version of al-Khuldī's work. Another portion of al-Khuldī's work can be found in the partially incomplete section on Sufis in an-Nadīm's *Kitāb al-fihrist,* 235–38. See also as-Sulamī, *Ṭabaqāt aṣ-ṣūfiyya,* 434–39; al-Iṣfahānī, *Ḥilyat al-awliyāʾ,* vol. 10, 381–82; and Ibn al-Jawzī, *Ṣifat aṣ-Ṣafwa,* vol. 2, 468–69. See also, Abdel-Kader, *al-Junayd,* xii-xiii, and al-Hujwirī, *The Kashf al-Maḥjūb,* 156–57.

57. Aḥmad ibn Muḥammad b. Masrūq (d. 299/911–12) was from the Iranian city of Ṭūs (near modern Mashhad) but lived and died in Baghdad. He was one of the most important early Sufis and

(١٦)

عثامة بنت بلال بن أبي الدّرداء

من مُتعبِّدات النِّسوان. أُصيبتْ في عينها فصبَرَتْ على ذلك

أخبرنا أبوالفتح يوسف بن عمر الزّاهد ببغداد، قال: حدّثنا جعفر بن محمد بن نُصير، قال أحمد بن محمد بن مسروق، حدّثنا محمد بن الحسين البرجُلاني، حدّثني الحسين بن عبد العزيز بن الوزير الجُذامي، حدّثني عبد اللّه ابن يوسف الدّمشقي، أنّ عَثامة بنت بلال بن أبي الدّرداء كُفَّ بصرُها، وكانت متعبّدة، فدخل عليها ابنُها يومًا وقد صلّى، فقالت: صلّيْتُمْ يا بُنَيَّ؟ قال: نعم، فقالت:

أَعَثامَ مالَكِ لاهِيَة ... حَلَّتْ بدارِكِ داهِيَهْ

"Weep so that you may complete your prayers on time,
"If you are to weep at all today!

"And weep while the Qurᵓān is being recited,
"For once you too, used to recite it.

"You used to recite it with reflection,
"While tears streamed down from your eyes.

"I shall lament for you with fervent love,
"For as long as I shall live!"

was a companion of al-Ḥārith ibn Asad al-Muḥāsibī (d. 243/857) and Sarī as-Saqaṭī (d. 253/867). He said: "He who does not guard his intellect with his intellect from his intellect, is destroyed by his intellect." See as-Sulamī, *Ṭabaqāt aṣ-ṣūfiyya,* 237–41 and al-Iṣfahānī, *Ḥilyat al-awliyāᵓ,* vol. 10, 213. See also, al-Hujwirī, *The Kashf al-Maḥjūb,* 146–47.

عثامة بنت بلال بن أبي الدّرداء

إِبكِي الصّلاة لوَقْتِها   إنْ كُنْتِ يومًا باكِيَهْ
وابكِي القرآنَ إذَا تُلِيَ   قد كُنتِ يومًا تاليَهْ
تَتْلِينَهُ بتفَكُّرٍ   ودُموعِ عَيْنٍ جاريَهْ
لَهْفِي عليكِ صبابةً   ما عِشْتُ طولَ حَيَاتِيَهْ

XVII

UMM SAᶜĪD THE DAUGHTER OF ᶜALQAMA AN-NAKHAᶜĪ[58]

Umm Saᶜīd was one of the ascetics of Basra. Abū al-Fatḥ al-Qawwās related from Jaᶜfar ibn Muḥammad b. Nuṣayr [al-Khuldī] through Ibn Masrūq through Muḥammad ibn al-Ḥusayn [al-Burjulānī] through Isḥāq ibn Manṣūr as-Salūlī that Umm Saᶜīd an-Nakhaᶜiyya related that she heard Dāwūd aṭ-Ṭāᵓī[59] say: "Your grace[60] [oh God] has put an end to my worries and came between me and my insomnia.[61] And my longing to gaze upon You banished my desires." Umm Saᶜīd used to serve Dāwūd aṭ-Ṭāᵓī.

Her path of servitude followed that of aṭ-Ṭāᵓī. She used to weep ceaselessly, following Dāwūd aṭ-Ṭāᵓī's example.

58. ᶜAlqama ibn Qays an-Nakhaᶜī (d. before 110/728) was an early ascetic of Kufa. He is counted among the "Followers" (*at-Tābiᶜūn*), those who transmitted traditions from the Companions of the Prophet Muḥammad. He is said to have married outside of his own clan as a sign of humility. ᶜAlqama's mother, known as Umm ᶜAlqama, related hadith from the Prophet's wife ᶜĀᵓisha, which she passed on to her son. See Ibn Saᶜd, *aṭ-Ṭabaqāt al-kubrā,* vol.8, 490. See also al-Iṣfahānī, *Ḥilyat al-awliyāᵓ,* vol. 2, 98–102; and Massignon, *Essay,* 112.

59. Abū Sulaymān Dāwūd ibn Nuṣayr aṭ-Ṭāᵓī (d. 165/781) was also from Kufa. He is often counted among the Sufis, although he was not seen as such by as-Sulamī. At the beginning of his career, he was a jurist and studied under Abū Ḥanīfa. Later in life, he renounced the study of law, threw his books into the Euphrates river, and turned to asceticism. See al-Qushayrī, *ar-Risāla,* 422–23; al-Iṣfahānī, *Ḥilyat al-awliyāᵓ,* vol. 7, 335–67; Ibn al-Jawzī, *Ṣifat aṣ-Ṣafwa,* vol. 3, 131–46. See also, al-Hujwirī, *The Kashf al-Maḥjūb,* 109–10.

60. The original phrase, "Your grace" (*mannuka*), was replaced by aṭ-Ṭanāḥī with "concern for You" (*hammuka*) following modern editions of al-Iṣfahānī's *Ḥilyat al-awliyāᵓ,* al-Khaṭīb al-Baghdādī's *Tārīkh Baghdād,* and Ibn al-Jawzī's *Ṣifat aṣ-Ṣafwa.*

61. The phrase, "came between me and . . ." (*ḥāla baynī wa bayna*) in the original manuscript was changed by aṭ-Ṭanāḥī to "caused me to ally myself with" (*ḥālafa baynī wa bayna*), following a modern edition of Ibn al-Jawzī's *Ṣifat aṣ-Ṣafwa.*

(١٧)

أمّ سعيد بنت علقمة النّخعية

كانت من زُهّـاد البصرة.

أخبرنا أبوالفتح القوّاس، حدّثنا جعفر بن محمد بن نُصير، حدّثنا بن مسروق، حدّثنا محمد بن الحسين، حدّثنا إسحاق بن منصور السَّلولي، حدّثتني أم سعيد النّخعية: أنّها سمعت داود الطّائي يقول: مَنُّكَ عطّل عليَّ الهُمُوم، وحالَ بيني وبين السُّهاد. وشوقي إلى النّظر إليك أوبق منّي الشهوات. وكانت أم سعيد تخدُم داودَ الطّائي.

وكانت أمةً طائيةً. وكانت أبداً تبكي بِبُكاءِ داود.

XVIII

KURDIYYA BINT ᶜAMR[62]

Kurdiyya was either from Basra or al-Ahwāz. She used to serve Shaᶜwāna.[63] She said: "Once I spent the night at Shaᶜwāna's. When I fell asleep, she kicked me and said, 'Get up, oh, Kurdiyya! This is not the abode of sleep! Verily, sleep is reserved for cemeteries!'"

It was said to Kurdiyya: "What blessings did you attain from serving Shaᶜwāna?" She replied, "Since serving her I have never loved the world; I have never preoccupied myself with my sustenance; I have never exalted in my sight any of the greats of the world out of greed for what they possess; and I have never shortchanged any Muslim in the least."

62. See also, Ibn al-Jawzī, *Ṣifat aṣ ṣafwa,* vol. 4, 41–42.

63. This information puts the date of Kurdiyya's death in the first part of the third/ninth century.

(١٨)

كردية بنت عمرو

وكانت من أهل البصرة أوالأهواز.

وكانت تخدُمُ شعوانة. قالت: بتُّ ليلةً عند شعوانة، فنمتُ فركضَتْنِي، وقالت: قومِي يا كُردية، ليس هذاَ دارَ النّومِ، إنّما النّومُ فَي القُبور.

وقيل لكُردية: ما الذي أصابَكِ من بركاتِ خدمة شعوانة؟

قالت: ما أحبَبْتُ الدّنيا منذُ خدَمْتُها، ولا اهتمَمْتُ لِرزْقي، ولا عظُمَ في عيني أحدٌ من أربابِ الدّنيا لطَمَعٍ لي فيه، وما استقصرتُ أحداً من المسلمين قطُّ.

XIX

UMM ṬALQ[64]

Umm Ṭalq was one of the female devotees and specialists in the ways of self-denial and gnosis.

Musaddad reported from Muḥammad ibn al-Ḥusayn [al-Burjulānī] through Yaḥyā ibn Bisṭām that Salama al-Afqam related that he heard ᶜĀṣim al-Jaḥdarī[65] say: Umm Ṭalq used to say: "Whenever I prevent my lower soul from attaining its desires, God makes me a ruler over it."

Umm Ṭalq also said: "The lower soul is a king if you indulge it, but it is a slave if you torment it."

64. See also, *Ṣifat aṣ-Ṣafwa* Appendix section VII below. The earliest mention of Umm Ṭalq is in Ibn Saᶜd, *aṭ-Ṭabaqāt al-kubrā,* vol. 8, 486. In this work, a certain Ibn ar-Rūmī (Son of the Roman) is depicted as visiting Umm Ṭalq and observing that the roof of her house is extremely low. By way of explanation she notes that the caliph ᶜUmar ibn al-Khaṭṭāb (r. 13/634–23/644) told his governors not to erect tall buildings, lest "the evil of your days come when you erect tall buildings." See also, al-Iṣfahānī, *Ḥilyat al-awliyā*ᵓ, vol. 3, 63–66; Ibn al-Jawzī, *Ṣifat aṣ-Ṣafwa,* vol. 3, 258; and Smith, *An Early Mystic,* 189–90.

65. Abū al-Mujashshir ᶜĀṣim al-Jaḥdarī (d. before 130/748–49) was a famous Qurᵓān reciter from Basra. His companionship with Umm Ṭalq puts the date of her death in the later Umayyad period, around the first quarter of the second/eighth century. See al-Makkī, *Qūt al-qulūb,* vol. 1, 45. See also, as-Sulamī, *Dhikr an-niswa,* aṭ-Ṭanāḥī ed., np. 49.

(١٩)

أمّ طلق

من المتعبّدات المجتهدات العارفات.

ذكر مسدّد، عن محمد بن الحسين، عن يحيى بن بسطام، عن سلمة الأفقم، قال: سمعتُ عاصم الجحدري يقول: كانت أمّ طلق تقول: ما ملّكتُ نفسي ما تشتهي منه، جعل اللّهُ لي عليها سلطانًا.

وقالت أمّ طلق: النّفس ملِكٌ إن تنعَّمْتَها، ومملوكٌ إن أتْعَبْتَهَا.

XX

ḤASNĀ BINT FAYRŪZ

Ḥasnā was one of the female devotees of Yemen and a specialist in the way of desire. She was endowed with great spiritual states.

Abū al-Faḍl Muḥammad ibn Ibrāhīm b. al-Faḍl al-Muzakkī related from Muḥammad ibn Ismāᶜīl al-Ismāᶜīlī through Aḥmad ibn Abī al-Ḥawārī of Damascus through Muḥammad ibn Abī Dāwūd al-Azdī, who reported that ᶜAbd ar-Razzāq[66] said: There was a woman in Yemen who was called Ḥasnā bint Fayrūz and she used to say: "Oh, God! How long will you keep Your friends buried in the ground and under the earth? Why don't You bring about the Day of Resurrection so that You can fulfill that which You have promised them?"

66. This individual may be the ascetic ᶜAbd ar-Razzāq aṣ-Ṣanᶜānī (d. 211/826), who gave counsel to the caliph Hārūn ar-Rashīd in Mecca. See al-Hujwirī, *The Kashf al-Maḥjūb,* 98.

(٢٠)

حسنا بنت فيروز

من متعبّدات اليمن والمشتاقين. وكانت كبيرة الحال.

أخبرنا أبوالفضل محمد بن إبراهيم بن الفضل المُزكّي، قال محمد بن إسماعيل الإسماعيلي، قال: حدّثنا أحمد بن أبي الحواري الدمشقي، قال: حدّثنا محمد بن أبي داود الأزدي، قال: حدّثنا عبد الرزّاق، قال: كانت باليمن امرأةٌ يُقالُ لها: حسنا بنت فيروز، وكانت تقول: إلهي، حتّى متى تدَعُ أولياءَك تحت التّراب والثّرى؟ ألا تُقيمُ القيامةَ حتّى تُنْجِزَ ما وعدتَهُمْ.

XXI

ḤAFṢA BINT SĪRĪN[67]
The Sister of Muḥammad ibn Sīrīn[68]

Ḥafṣa was one of the female devotees of Basra. Like her brother, Muḥammad ibn Sīrīn, she was a specialist in the ways of asceticism and scrupulousness. She used to manifest exemplary signs and miracles.

I heard Muḥammad ibn Ṭāhir al-Wazīrī report from al-Ḥusayn ibn Muḥammad b. Isḥāq through Sacīd ibn cUthmān al-Ḥannāṭ[69] of Baghdad through Sayyār ibn Ḥātim that Hishām ibn Ḥassān[70] related: Ḥafṣa bint Sīrīn used to light her lamp at night, and then would rise to pray in her prayer area. At times, the lamp would go out, but it would continue to illuminate her house until daylight.

67. See also, *Ṣifat aṣ-Ṣafwa* Appendix section II below. The earliest account of Ḥafṣa bint Sīrīn can be found in Ibn Sacd, *aṭ-Ṭabaqāt al-kubrā,* vol. 8, 484.

68. Abū Bakr Muḥammad ibn Sīrīn (d. 110/728–29) is reputed to be the earliest master of dream interpretation in Islam. He was also known for his weeping and fasting. According to Massignon, he was the first to transmit the so-called "Hadith of Suffering" (*Ḥadīth al-Ibtilā'*): "When God loves one of His slaves, He tests him with suffering." He would refer people to his sister for commentaries on the Qur'ān. See al-Hujwirī, *The Kashf al-Maḥjūb,* 92–93; al-Iṣfahānī, *Ḥilyat al-awliyā',* vol. 2, 263–82. See also, Massignon, *Essay,* 110; and *EI²,* vol. 3, 947–48.

69. Abū cUthmān Sacīd ibn cUthmān al-Ḥannāṭ (d. 294/906–7) was a disciple of the Egyptian Sufi Dhū an-Nūn al-Miṣrī (d. 245/859) and an important transmitter of esoteric traditions. The name *al-Ḥannāṭ* means "seller of herbs and perfumes used to prepare bodies for burial." See Ibn cArabī, *La vie merveilleuse de Dhū-l-Nūn l'Égyptien,* Roger Deladrière trans. and ed. (Paris, 1988), 379–80.

70. Abū cAbdallāh Hishām ibn Ḥassān al-Firdawsī (d. 148/765) was a traditionist and ascetic who would spend his nights in devotion and weeping. He was the main source for information about Ḥafṣa bint Sīrīn. In *Ṣifat aṣ-Ṣafwa,* Ibn al-Jawzī reports nearly the same story about Hishām ibn Ḥassān that he gives for Ḥafṣa. In his notice on Hishām, the latter's servant states: "What sin has this one committed? Whom has he killed? For he weeps the entire night!" See *Ṣifat aṣ-Ṣafwa* Appendix section II below and idem, *Ṣifat aṣ-Ṣafwa,* vol. 3, 312.

(٢١)

حفصَة بنت سيرين
أخت محمد بن سيرين

من متعبّدات البصرة

وكانت مثل أخيها محمد بن سيرين في الزّهد والورع. وكانت صاحبة آيات وكرامات.

سمعتُ محمد بن طاهر الوزيري، يقول: سمعتُ الحسين بن محمد بن إسحاق، يقول: سمعتُ سعيد بن عثمان الحنّاط البغدادي، قال: أخبرنا سيّار بن حاتم، عن هشام بن حسّان، قال: كانت حفصة بنت سيرين تُسْرِجُ سراجَها من الليل، ثمّ تَقومُ وتُصلّي في مُصَلاّها. فربّما طَفِئَ السِّراجُ وتُضيءُ [يُضيءُ] لها البيتُ حتّى تُصبِحَ.

XXII

LUBĀBA AL-ᶜĀBIDA[71]
(Lubāba the Worshipper)
From the Natives of Syria

Lubāba was a specialist in the ways of scrupulousness (*waraᶜ*) and reclusiveness (*nusuk*).

Aḥmad [ᶜAbdallāh] ibn Muḥammad of Antioch[72] reported from Aḥmad ibn Abī al-Ḥawārī that Aḥmad ibn Muḥammad[73] related: Lubāba said, "I am ashamed lest God see me preoccupied with other than Him after having known Him."

He also related that she said: "Knowledge of God bequeaths love for Him; love for Him bequeaths longing for Him; longing for Him bequeaths intimacy with Him; and intimacy with Him bequeaths constancy in serving Him and conforming to His laws."

71. See also, section II above, where she is called "Lubāba the Devotee" (*al-mutaᶜabbida*).

72. This individual is probably Abū Muḥammad ᶜAbdallāh ibn Khubayq al-Anṭākī, who was a follower of the Sufi way of an-Nūrī (d. 295/908) and an advocate of ethical scrupulousness (*waraᶜ*). In *Ḥilyat al-awliyāʾ*, al-Iṣfahānī records an account transmitted by Ibn Khubayq through Aḥmad ibn Abī al-Ḥawārī about a Sufi woman who appears to be Lubāba. As-Sulamī seems to have confused Ibn Khubayq, who lived in the fourth/tenth century, with the earlier Aḥmad ibn ᶜĀṣim al-Anṭakī (d. 220/835), who was a source for Ibn Abī al-Ḥawārī. In *Ṭabaqāt aṣ-ṣūfiyya,* as-Sulamī claims that Ibn Khubayq was a companion of both Yūsuf ibn Asbāṭ (d. 199/814–15) and the Sufi disciples of an-Nūrī. This appears to be impossible, since nearly a century separates these two masters. On Ibn Khubayq al-Anṭākī, see as-Sulamī, *Ṭabaqāt aṣ-ṣūfiyya,* 141-145; al-Qushayrī, *ar-Risāla,* 408; al-Iṣfahānī, *Ḥilyat al-awliyāʾ*, vol. 10, 168–89; and Ibn al-Jawzī, *Ṣifat aṣ-Ṣafwa,* vol. 4, 280–81. In *at-Taᶜarruf,* al-Kalābādhī mentions a third Anṭākī, Abū Muḥammad ᶜAbdallāh ibn Muḥammad al-Anṭākī, whose name most closely matches that given in the text. He provides no other information on this individual, however, merely listing him with the other two Anṭākīs as the author of a work on Sufi practice. Ibid., 12.

73. This individual may be Abū ᶜAbdallāh Aḥmad ibn ᶜĀṣim al-Anṭākī (d. 220/835). Known as the "Spy of Hearts" (*jasūs al-qulūb*), he wrote *Kitāb dawāʾ dāʾ an-nufūs* (Cure for the Disease of Souls). He said: "That which brings you nearest to God is the abandonment of secret sins, because if you fail inwardly, both your outward and your inward acts are voided." He also said: "The most harmful act of disobedience is being obedient out of ignorance; this is more harmful to you than being disobedient out of ignorance." See Smith, *An Early Mystic,* 77–79. See also, as-Sulamī, *Ṭabaqāt aṣ-ṣūfiyya,* 137–40; and al-Iṣfahānī, *Ḥilyat al-awliyāʾ*, vol. 9, 280–97.

(٢٢)

لبابة العابدة
من أهل الشّام

كانت من أهل الورع والنُّسْكِ.

ذكر أحمد بن محمد الأنطاكي، عن أحمد بن أبي الحواري، قال: سمعتُ أحمد بن محمد، يقول: قالت لُبابة: إنّي لأ ستحيي من اللّه تعالى أن يراني مشغولةً بغيرهِ بعد أن عرفتُهُ.

قال: وقالت: المعرفة للّه تورثُ المحبّة لَهُ، والمحبّةُ للّه تورثُ الشّوقَ إليه، والشّوقُ إليهِ يورثُ الأُنسَ بهِ، والأُنسُ بهِ يورثُ المَداومةَ على خِدمَتِهِ وموافقتِهِ.

XXIII

ḤUKAYMA OF DAMASCUS
From the Noble Women of Syria

Ḥukayma was Rābiᶜa [bint Ismāᶜīl's][74] teacher (*ustādh*)[75] and companion. Abū Jaᶜfar Muḥammad ibn Aḥmad b. Saᶜīd ar-Rāzī reported from al-ᶜAbbās ibn Ḥamza that Aḥmad ibn Abī al-Ḥawārī related that his wife Rābiᶜa [bint Ismāᶜīl] said to him: I entered Ḥukayma's room while she was reading the Qurᵓān and she said to me, "Oh, Rābiᶜa! I have heard that your husband is taking another wife." "Yes," I said. "How could he?" she replied. "Given what I have been told about his good judgment, how could his heart be distracted from God by two women? Have you not learned the interpretation of this verse: 'Except one who comes to God with a sound heart' [Qurᵓān 26 (*ash-Shuᶜarāᵓ*), 89]?" "No," I said. Ḥukayma said, "It means that when one encounters God, there should be nothing in his heart other than Him." Abū Sulaymān [ad-Dārānī][76] said: "In thirty years I have not heard an account more excellent than this."

Rābiᶜa said: "When I heard her words I went out, staggering, into the streets. I was embarrassed lest men see me and assume that I was inebriated."

Aḥmad [ibn Abī al-Ḥawārī] said: "By my father! This is true intoxication!"

74. On Rābiᶜa bint Ismāᶜīl, the wife of Aḥmad ibn Abī al-Ḥawārī, see section XXIX below.

75. The word used in this account for "teacher" (*ustādh*) is in the masculine rather than the feminine form. This grammatical novelty indicates that for as-Sulamī, Ḥukayma of Damascus had attained the status of the "men" (*rijāl*) of the Sufi tradition. The same term is also used to describe Fāṭima of Nishapur, in section XXX below.

76. Abū Sulaymān ad-Dārānī (d. 215/830) lived for a time in Basra, but spent the latter part of his life in the village of Dārāyā, near Damascus. He was influential in establishing the Sufi doctrine of hope (*rajāᵓ*) and fear (*khawf*), linking the fear of God to self-discipline (*mujāhada*) and hope with the contemplation of God (*mushāhada*). He was the spiritual master of Aḥmad ibn Abī al-Ḥawārī. See Smith, *An Early Mystic,* 76–77; and Massignon, *Essay,* 152–54. See also, as-Sulamī, *Ṭabaqāt aṣ-ṣūfiyya,* 75–82; al-Iṣfahānī, *Ḥilyat al-awliyāᵓ,* vol. 9, 254–80; Ibn al-Jawzī, *Ṣifat aṣ-Ṣafwa,* vol. 4, 223–34; and al-Hujwirī, *The Kashf al-Maḥjūb,* 112–13.

(٢٣)

حُكَيمة الدِّمشقية
من سادات نساء الشّام

وكانت أستاذ رابعة وصاحبتها.

أخبرنا أبوجعفر بن محمد بن أحمد بن سعيد الرّازي، قال: حدّثنا العبّاس بن حمزة، قال: حدّثنا أحمد بن أبي الحواري، قال: قالت رابعة: دخلتُ على حُكيمة وهي تقرأ في المصحف، فقالت لي: يا رابعة، بلغني أنَّ زوجَك يتزوّجُ عليك. قُلتُ: نعم. قالت: كيف يرضى مع ما يبلُغُني من عقله أن يشتغلَ قلبُهُ عن اللّه تعالى بامرأتين؟ أما بلغك تفسيرُ هذه الآية: "إلاَّ من أتى اللّهَ بقلب سليمٍ"؟ قلتُ: لا. قالت: هو أن يَلقى اللّه تعالى وليس في قلبه أحدٌ غيرُهُ. قال أبوسليمان: ما سمعتُ منذ ثلاثين سنةً حديثًا أرفعَ من هذا.

قالت رابعة: فلمّا سمعتُ كلامَها خرجتُ وأنا أتمايَلُ في الزُّقاق، فاستحييت من الرّجال، لايرون أنّها [أنّني] سكرانة.

قال أحمدُ: بِأبي هذا هوالسّكر!

XXIV

RĀBIᶜA AL-AZDIYYA
From the Natives of Basra

Rābiᶜa was one of the greatest companions of the Sufis of Basra and was a specialist in the way of scrupulousness.

ᶜAbd al-Wāḥid ibn Zayd[77] was her companion and transmitted reports about her.

Abū Jaᶜfar [ar-Rāzī] reported from al-ᶜAbbās [ibn Ḥamza] through Aḥmad [ibn Abī al-Ḥawārī] that Bikr [ibn ᶜAbdallāh][78] b. Muḥammad of Basra related: ᶜAbd al-Wāḥid ibn Zayd asked Rābiᶜa al-Azdiyya to marry him. She refused and kept away from him, and he was greatly distressed. However, he bore her refusal patiently until one day she gave him permission to see her. When he entered her house she said, "Oh lustful one! What did you see in me that aroused your desire? Why don't you ask a lustful person like yourself to marry you?"[79]

77. Given ᶜAbd al-Wāḥid ibn Zayd's advocacy of solitude and world-renunciation, it is ironic that he was noted for dreams of slave girls and houris. In a dream reported by Ibn al-Jawzī, Ibn Zayd sees a beautiful slave-girl dressed in green silk, whose sandals and ankle bracelets praise and magnify God. She entices him to buy her, saying that her price is the love of God and that God will never reject the money of the one who asks for her hand. It is this "lustfulness" that Rābiᶜa al-Azdiyya criticizes in the above account. See Ibn al-Jawzī, *Ṣifat aṣ-Ṣafwa,* vol. 3, 321–24. See also, Massignon, *Essay,* 147–48.

78. This name is missing from the aṭ-Ṭanāḥī edition.

79. By making Rābiᶜa al-Azdiyya the object of ᶜAbd al-Wāḥid ibn Zayd's affections, as-Sulamī corrects a mistake in al-Makkī's *Qūt al-qulūb,* where Ibn Zayd asks Rābiᶜa al-ᶜAdawiyya to marry him. The widespread popularity of *Qūt al-qulūb* has caused this mistaken version to become better known than the original. See al-Makkī, *Qūt al-qulūb,* vol. 2, 57. See also, Smith, *Rabi'a,* 29–31.

(٢٤)

رابعة الأزدية

من أهل البصرة

كانت من كبار أصحابهم وورعيهم.

صحبها عبد الواحد بن زيد وحكى عنها.

أخبرنا أبوجعفر، قال: حدّثنا العبّاس، قال: حدّثنا أحمد، قال: حدّثنا بكر بن عبد اللّه بن محمد البصري، قال: خطب عبد الواحد بن زيد رابعة الأزدية فحجبته، فاغتمّ، فتحمّل عليها حتّى أذنته. فلمّا دخل قالت: ياشهواني، أيّ شئ رأيت فيَّ من آلة الشهوةِ؟ ألاَ خطبْتَ شهوانيةً مثلَكَ.

XXV

ᶜAJRADA THE BLIND[80]

From the Natives of Basra

ᶜAjrada was one of the masters of self-denial. Sayyār reported from Jaᶜfar ibn Sulaymān [aḍ-Ḍubᶜī],[81] who said: I heard one of our women (either my mother or someone else) relate: ᶜAjrada the Blind did not break her fast for sixty years. She would only sleep for part of the night, and when she awoke she would say: "Oh my! Daytime cuts us off from intimate discourse with our Lord and returns us to the human discourse of which we are most worthy, both in our hearing and our speech."[82]

80. See also, *Ṣifat aṣ-Ṣafwa* Appendix section IV below.

81. Since Jaᶜfar ibn Sulaymān aḍ-Ḍubᶜī lived in the generation after ᶜAjrada, this would put the date of her death in the latter half of the second/eighth century.

82. In this statement ᶜAjrada refers to the practice of nightly vigils (*qiyām al-layl*). This time of intimate discourse with God, uninterrupted by the affairs of the world, is seen by her as a gift for which the heedless human being is unworthy. Her statement is also an example of rhetorical inversion, which implicitly contrasts the nightly intimacies of invocation with the night-long parties for which the ruling classes of the ᶜAbbasid period were famous.

(٢٥)

عجردة العمّـية
من أهل البصرة

من أرباب المجاهدات

ذكر سيّار عن جعفر بن سليمان، قال: سمعتُ نسا ءنا ، أمي أوغيرها تقول: لم تـُفْطرْ عجردة العمّـية ستّين سنة ً ، ولم تنمْ بالليل إلاّ هُدوًّهُ. وكانـــت إذا صَحَتْ قالت: أوه! قطع بنا النّهــــار عن مناجاة سيّدنا ، وردّنـا إلى ما نَستَحِقُّــه من كــلام المخلوقين، سماعًا وقولاً.

XXVI

UMM SĀLIM AR-RĀSIBIYYA[83]

From the Natives of Basra

Umm Sālim was one of the greatest masters of self-denial (*ijtihād*). Muḥammad ibn Sulaym b. Hilāl ar-Rāsibī said: Umm Sālim ar-Rāsibiyya fulfilled the requirements of *iḥrām* [i.e., the Ḥajj pilgrimage to Mecca] from Basra seventeen times.[84]

Another person mentioned that Umm Sālim said when she made the intention to perform the Ḥajj in a state of *iḥrām:* "A slave should not seek his Lord unless he resolves to see himself fulfill all of his service to God. For if the slave delays fulfilling his service near to his goal, it is as if he has failed to fulfill all of it."[85]

83. See also, *Ṣifat aṣ-Ṣafwa* Appendix section XVI below. Although as-Sulamī lists Umm Sālim as a native of Basra, Ibn al-Jawzī includes her among the "bedouins and country-folk." She may have come from a village near Basra. Neither gives a date for her death.

84. The verb *aḥrama* in Arabic means to declare something sacred, sacrosanct, inviolable, or taboo. The verbal noun *iḥrām* thus refers to a state of taboo or ritual consecration. To perform the Ḥajj pilgrimage to Mecca, each pilgrim must enter a state of *iḥrām:* to purify oneself with a full bath and to put on the "garment of consecration" (*libās al-iḥrām*), which consists of two white linen or woolen sheets for men and a plain linen or woolen garment for women, and to refrain from sexual relations and bodily adornment for the period of the pilgrimage. One must also devote oneself entirely to thoughts of God and the requirements of the Ḥajj. Because gender distinctions are effaced in this state of consecration, women are allowed to leave their faces uncovered and to mix among men while performing the rites of the pilgrimage. It has also been observed that the absence of face veiling during the Ḥajj has to do with the elimination of class distinctions; face veiling was associated with upper-class Christian women of Najran in southern Arabia during pre-Islamic times. See the notices on the upper-class martyrs Elizabeth and Ruhm (d. ca. 518–22 C.E.) in Sebastian P. Brock and Susan Ashbrook Harvey eds. and trans., *Holy Women of the Syrian Orient* (Berkeley and Los Angeles, 1987), 105–7 and 111–15.

85. The meaning of this statement is that every resolution to serve God must be made with as much seriousness as the vow to perform the Ḥajj pilgrimage. Once a person has consecrated himself to God, the vow must be carried out, even if it results in one's death. Muslims believe that those who die on the Ḥajj pilgrimage enter heaven as a reward for their efforts. A tradition of the Prophet Muḥammad states: "Required of women is a holy war (*jihād*) without fighting: the Ḥajj and the *ᶜumra* (off-season pilgrimage)." See Abū ᶜAbdallāh Muḥammad ibn Māja al-Qazwīnī, *Sunan Ibn Māja,* Maḥmūd Fuᵓād ᶜAbd al-Bāqī, ed. (Beirut, n.d.), vol. 2, 968.

(٢٦)

أمّ سالم الرّاسبِيَة
من أهل البصرةَ

كانت من المجتهدات الكِبار.

ذكر محمد بن سليم بن هِلال الرّاسبيّ، قال: أحرمتْ أمّ سالم الرّاسبية من البصرة سبع عشرة مرّةً.

وذكر غيْرُهُ أنّها كانت تقول إذا قصدت الحجّ محرمة: ما ينبغي للعبد أن يقْصُدَ سيّدَهُ إلاّ بعقْدٍ يَرى على نفسه آثارَ خدْمَته، فإنّ العبْد إذا تعطّل عن آثارَ الخِدمَةِ عن قريبٍ يتَعَطّل عَنها.

XXVII

ᶜUBAYDA BINT ABĪ KILĀB[86]

From the Natives of Basra

ᶜUbayda used to live in aṭ-Ṭufāwā [a bedouin village near Basra]. She was sound in judgment (*ᶜāqila*)[87] and practiced the way of self-denial (*mujtahida*). She was an excellent preacher.

Dāwūd ibn al-Muḥabbir (Son of the Ink-Maker)[88] related: After ᶜUbayda bint Abī Kilāb died, Basra never produced a woman better than she was.

It was reported that she said: "When one perfects his consciousness of God and knowledge of Him, nothing is more beloved to him than meeting his Lord and coming near to Him."

86. See also, *Ṣifat aṣ-Ṣafwa* Appendix section VI below. ᶜUbayda was a contemporary of Mālik ibn Dīnār (d. 128/745), and thus was a figure of the late Umayyad period.

87. The person who possesses sound judgment (*rajul ᶜāqil,* fem. *marʾa ᶜāqila*) is considered competent to provide testimony in an Islamic court of law. As-Sulamī uses this term to indicate that ᶜUbayda bint Abī Kilāb was fully the equal of a man in her judgment.

88. Dāwūd ibn al-Muḥabbir, who appears to be a figure of the third/ninth century, is mentioned by Massignon as the author of a *Kitāb al-ᶜaql* (Book of the Intellect). See idem, *Essay,* np. 147.

(٢٧)

عبيدة بنت أبي كلاب
من أهل البصرة

وكانت تنزِلُ الطّفاوة.

عاقلة مجتهدة، جيّدة المواعظ.

حكى داود بن المحبّر، قال: لمّا ماتت عبيدة بنت أبي كلاب، ما خلّفَتْ البصرةُ امرأة أفضلَ منها.

وحكي عنها أنّها قالت: من صحّ تقواهُ ومعرفتُه لا يكون عليه شئ أحبّ من لقاء ربّه والقدوم عليه.

XXVIII

HIND BINT AL-MUHALLAB
From Basra

Musaddad [ibn Qaṭan] reported from Muḥammad ibn al-Ḥusayn [al-Burjulānī] through Abū ᶜUmar aḍ-Ḍarīr (The Blind),[89] who related: I heard their client (*mawlā*) Abū Salama al-ᶜAtakī say: Hind bint al-Muhallab said: "If you are granted a blessing from God, hurry toward it with thankfulness before it disappears."

89. This *isnād* indicates that Hind bint al-Muhallab lived at the beginning of the third/ninth century.

(٢٨)

هند بنت المهلّب

بصرية

حكى مسدّد، عن محمد بن الحسين، عن أبي عمر الضّرير، قال: سمعتُ أبا سلمة العَتَكي مولاهم، يقول: قالت هند بنت المهلّب: إذا رأيتم النّعمة مستَدرّة فبادروها بالشّكر قبل حلول الزّوال.

XXIX

RĀBIᶜA [RABĪᶜA] BINT ISMĀᶜĪL[90]
The Wife of Aḥmad ibn Abī al-Ḥawārī[91]

Rābiᶜa was one of the great women of Syria. She was extremely rich and spent all of her wealth on Aḥmad [ibn Abī al-Ḥawārī] and his companions.

Abū Jaᶜfar ar-Rāzī reported from al-ᶜAbbās ibn Ḥamza that Aḥmad ibn Abī al-Ḥawārī related: Rābiᶜa said to me one day: "I used to pray to God Most High that someone like you or your companions would consume my fortune."

I heard Abū Bakr ibn Shādhān [ar-Rāzī] report from Yūsuf ibn al-Ḥusayn [ar-Rāzī][92] that Aḥmad ibn Abī al-Ḥawārī related: Rābiᶜa said to us: "Take that wash basin away from me! For I see written on it: 'Hārūn [ar-Rashīd], the Commander of the Believers[93] has died.'"

Aḥmad said: We looked into the matter, and found that Hārūn had indeed died on that day.[94]

90. See also, *Ṣifat aṣ-Ṣafwa* Appendix section XIII below. Rābiᶜa bint Ismāᶜīl's name has also been rendered as "Rayiᶜa" (see Roded, *Women in Islamic Biographical Collections,* 94). A more probable alternative, however, is "Rabīᶜa." Rabīᶜa was the name of one of the two branches of the "northern" or Qays Arabs of Syria, the region where Rābiᶜa bint Ismāᶜīl lived. The Rabīᶜa allied themselves with the Qaḥṭān or Yemeni Arabs against the other northern branch, the Muḍar. Rabīᶜa and Qaḥṭān were closely associated with the sedentary and urbanized peoples of Syria and Iraq and their members were often patrons of non-Arab Muslim converts. Rābiᶜa's burial place is in Jerusalem, on the Mount of Olives next to the tomb of the female Christian saint Pelagia of Antioch. Later writers have often confused her with Rābiᶜa al-ᶜAdawiyya of Basra. See, for example, Sirāj ad-Dīn Abū Ḥafṣ ᶜUmar ibn al-Mulaqqin (d. 804/1401–2), *Ṭabaqāt al-awliyāʾ,* Nūr ad-Dīn Shurayba ed. (Beirut, 1406/1986), 408. See also, Marshall G. S. Hodgson, *The Venture of Islam: Conscience and History in a World Civilization* (Chicago, 1977), vol. 1, 227-229; and Massignon, *Essay,* 154. For another notice on Rābiᶜa bint Ismāᶜīl, see al-ᶜĀmilī, *ad-Durr al-manthūr,* 203.

91. Aḥmad ibn Abī al-Ḥawārī died in 230/845 (see note 10 above).

92. Abū Yaᶜqūb Yūsuf ibn al-Ḥusayn ar-Rāzī (d. 304/916–17) was a disciple of Dhū an-Nūn al-Miṣrī (d. 245/859) and studied under Aḥmad ibn Ḥanbal (d. 241/855), the founder of the Ḥanbalī school of Islamic jurisprudence. He was a noted stylist in the Arabic language and a great traveler, visiting Iraq, Syria, and Egypt. See al-Iṣfahānī, *Ḥilyat al-awliyāʾ,* vol. 10, 238–43; and Ibn al-Jawzī, *Ṣifat aṣ-Ṣafwa,* vol. 4, 102–3. See also, Abdel-Kader, *al-Junayd,* 32–34.

93. "Commander of the Believers" (*Amīr al-Muʾminīn*) was the official title of the caliphs of Islam.

94. Hārūn ar-Rashīd, the fifth ᶜAbbasid caliph, died in the year 193/809.

(٢٩)

رابعة بنت اسماعيل

امرأة أحمد بن أبي الحواري

كانت من كبار نساء الشام. وكانت موسرة، فأنفقت جميع ملكها على أحمد وأصحابه.

أخبرنا أبوجعفر الرازي، قال: حدّثنا العبّاس بن حمزة، قال: حدّثنا أحمد بن أبي الحواري، قال: قالت رابعة يوما لأحمد بن أبي الحواري: كنتُ أدعوالله تعالى أن يأكُلَ مالي مثلُكَ ومثلُ أصحابِكَ.

سمعتُ أبا بكر بن شاذان، يقول: سمعتُ يوسف بن الحسين، يقول: سمعتُ أحمد بن أبي الحواري، يقول: قالت لنا رابعة: نحّوا عنّي ذلك الطّسْت، فإنّي أرى عليه مكتوبا: مات أمير المؤمنين هارونُ.

قال أحمدُ: فنظروا، فإذا هومات في ذلك اليوم.

Muḥammad ibn Aḥmad b. Saᶜīd reported from al-ᶜAbbās ibn Ḥamza that Aḥmad ibn Abī al-Ḥawārī related: I heard Rābiᶜa say: "Sometimes I see spirits (*al-jinn*) in the house coming and going. At times they are houris (*al-ḥūr al-ᶜayn*),[95] who veil themselves from me with their sleeves." She said this swearing with her hand upon her head.

[Aḥmad ibn Abī al-Ḥawārī] said: I heard Rābiᶜa say: "I never look at blowing snow without thinking of the dispersal of the pages of destiny; I never look at a swarm of locusts without thinking of the gathering of souls at the Resurrection; and I never hear the muezzin without thinking of the Caller of Souls on Judgment Day."

And on the same authority Aḥmad said: Once I called for Rābiᶜa and she did not answer. After an hour had passed she answered me: "What prevented me from answering you was that my heart was filled with happiness from God Most High. For this reason, I could not answer you."

95. The Arabic noun *ḥūr,* rendered in English as "houris," is the plural of both *aḥwar* (masc.) and *hawrāʾ* (fem.), which denote a person distinguished by *ḥawar,* intense whiteness of the eye and lustrous black of the iris. In a more general sense, *ḥawar* signifies whiteness, or as a moral attribute, purity. Hence, the compound expression *ḥūr ᶜayn,* used in this passage and in the Qurʾān, signifies "pure beings" or "companions pure" that are pleasing to the eye. *ᶜAyn* may also be understood as "the essence of the soul." Some early Qurʾān commentators, such as al-Ḥasan al-Baṣrī (d. 110/728) interpreted *al-ḥūr al-ᶜayn* as meaning "the righteous among women." See, for example, Qurʾān 56 (*al-Wāqiᶜa*), 22–23: "And with them will be their companions pure, most beautiful of eye, like unto pearls still hidden in their shells." See also Muhammad Asad, *The Message of the Qurʾān* (Gibraltar, 1984), 831 and n. 8.

أخبرنا محمد بن أحمد بن سعيد، قال: حدّثنا العبّاس بن حمزة، قال: حدّثنا أحمد بن أبي الحواري، قال: سمعتُ رابعة تقول: رُبّما رأيتُ الجنَّ في البيت يجيئون ويذهبون. ورُبّما كانت الحُورالعينُ تَسْتَتِرُ منّي بأكمَامِهِنَّ. وقالت بيدها على رأسها.

قال: وسمعتُ رابعة تقول: ما رأيتُ الثّلجَ إلاّ تذكّرتُ تَطايُرَ الصُّحُف، ولا رأيتُ الجرادَ إلاّ ذكرتُ الحشْرَ، ولا سمِعْتُ مؤذّنًا إلاّ ذكرتُ منادىَ يوم القيامة.

وبإسناده، قال أحمد: دعوتُ رابعة مرّةً فلم تُجبْني. فلمّا كان بعد ساعة أجابتني وقالت: إنّما منعني أن أُجيبَكَ، لأنّ قلبيَ كان امتلأ فرحًا باللّهِ تعالى، فلم أقدِرْ أنْ أجيبَكَ.

XXX

FĀṬIMA OF NISHAPUR[96]

Fāṭima was a woman from one of the oldest families of Khurasan. She was one of the greatest female gnostics. Abū Yazīd al-Bisṭāmī[97] praised her and Dhū an-Nūn [al-Miṣrī][98] sought her advice on doctrinal matters. She used to spend time devoted to worship in Mecca. Possibly, she also went to Jerusalem and then returned to Mecca. There was no other woman like her in her time.

It is related that she once sent Dhū an-Nūn a gift. Dhū an-Nūn sent it back to her and said: "Accepting the gifts of Sufi women is a sign of humiliation and weakness." Fāṭima replied: "There is no Sufi in this world more lowly than one who doubts another's motives."[99]

96. See also, Ibn al-Jawzī, *Ṣifat aṣ-Ṣafwa,* vol. 4, 123–24; Ibn ᶜArabī, *Dhū-l-Nūn l'Egyptien,* 236–37; and al-ᶜĀmilī, *ad-Durr al-manthūr,* 367–68.

97. Abū Yazīd (or Bāyazīd) Ṭayfūr ibn ᶜĪsā b. Surūshān al-Bisṭāmī (d. 261/875 or 264/877–78) was the grandson of a convert from Zoroastrianism and the son of one of the notables of Bistam in northern Iran. Al-Junayd said about him: "Bāyazīd holds the same rank among us as Gabriel does among the angels." Al-Hujwirī calls him one of the "Ten Imams of Sufism." He was a master of the station of love (*maḥabba*) and a founder of the *malāmatiyya,* or "path of blame." He was also known for his ecstatic utterances (*shāṭaḥāt*). He was an ascetic for over 30 years, but later abandoned this discipline, saying: "Those who are most veiled from God are three: First is the ascetic who is veiled by his asceticism, second is the worshipper who is veiled by his devotion, and third is the scholar who is veiled by his knowledge." See as-Sulamī, *Ṭabaqāt aṣ-ṣūfiyya,* 67–74; al-Hujwirī, *The Kashf al-Maḥjūb,* 106-108; Abdel-Kader, *al-Junayd,* 31–32, and al-Qushayrī, *ar-Risāla,* 395–97. See also, al-Iṣfahānī, *Ḥilyat al-awliyā',* vol. 10, 33–42; and *EI*², vol. 1, 162–63.

98. Abū al-Fayḍ Dhū an-Nūn Thawbān ibn Ibrāhīm al-Miṣrī (d. 246/861) was of Nubian descent and was from the town of Akhmīm (ancient Panopolis) in Egypt, about 350 miles south of Cairo. Like Abū Yazīd al-Bisṭāmī, he followed the path of blame. According to al-Hujwirī, "the people of Egypt were lost in doubt as to his true state, and did not believe in him until he was dead." However, late in life he was favored by the ᶜAbbasid caliph al-Mutawakkil (r. 232/847–247/86). He is reputed to be one of the first to discuss the doctrine of spiritual states (*aḥwāl*) and spiritual stations (*maqāmāt*) in Sufism. He is said to have recited the following verses on his death-bed: "Oh Ultimate Goal of all lovers, grant me a favored place among Your visitors! For I care not for bygones, so long as You are my only Companion in the two abodes!" According to Ibn al-Jawzī, he died in Giza and was taken by boat to al-Fusṭāṭ out of fear that bridges would collapse from the number of people attending his funeral. He was buried in the graveyard of Ahl al-Maᶜāfir in Old Cairo. See as-Sulamī, *Ṭabaqāt aṣ-ṣūfiyya,* 15–26; al-Qushayrī, *ar-Risāla,* 433–34, al-Iṣfahānī, *Ḥilyat al-awliyā',* vol. 9, 331–95 and vol. 10, 1–4. See also, al-Hujwirī, *The Kashf al-Maḥjūb,* 100–103; Ibn al-Jawzī, *Ṣifat aṣ-Ṣafwa,* vol. 4, 315–21; Smith, *An Early Mystic,* 80–82; and *EI*², vol. 2, 242–43.

99. Literally, "investigates the cause." This means that the person who rejects such a gift is needlessly suspicious or lacking in thankfulness, as in the English expression, "One who looks a gift-horse in the mouth."

(٣٠)

فاطمة النيسابورية

كانت من قدماء نساء خراسان. وكانت من العارفات الكبار. أثنى عليها أبويزيد البسطامي. وسألها ذوالنّون عن مسائل. وكانت مجاورة بمكة. وربّما دخلت بيت المقدس، ثم رجعت إلى مكة. لم يَكُن في زمانها في النّساء مثلُها.

ذُكِرَ أنّها بعثت مرّةً إلى ذي النّون برفقٍ، فردَّهُ وقال: في قَبُول أرفاق النّسوانَ مذلّة ونُقصانٌ. فقالتْ فاطمة: ليس في الدّنيا صوفيّ أخَسُّ مِمَّن يرى السّبب.

Abū Yazīd al-Bisṭāmī said: "In all of my life, I have only seen one true man and one true woman. The woman was Fāṭima of Nishapur. Whenever I informed her about one of the stages of spirituality, she would take the news as if she had experienced it herself."

Dhū an-Nūn said to her when they were together in Jerusalem: "Advise me." So she said to him: "Make truthfulness obligatory and mortify yourself in your actions and your words. God Most High has said: 'And when a matter is resolved, it would be best for them if they were true to God' [Qurʾān, 47 (*Muḥammad*), 21]."

Aḥmad ibn Muḥammad ibn Miqsam reported with certification[100] (*ijāzatan*) from Abū Muḥammad al-Ḥusayn ibn ʿAlī b. Khalaf from Ibn Malūl (a very aged shaykh who met Dhū an-Nūn al-Miṣrī), who related: I asked [Dhū an-Nūn], "Who is the most excellent person you have ever seen?" To which he replied, "I have never seen anyone more excellent than a woman I saw in Mecca who is called Fāṭima of Nishapur. She used to discourse wonderfully on matters pertaining to the meaning of the Qurʾān."

I asked Dhū an-Nūn about her and he said: "She is a saint from among the friends of God, the Glorious and Mighty. She is also my teacher (*ustādhī*)."

[Dhū an-Nūn said]: "I heard her say: 'When God ignores a person, he will wander aimlessly in every city square and will prattle constantly with every tongue. When God does not ignore a person, He silences him except for the truth and compels him to hold Him in reverence and sincerity.'"

[Dhū an-Nūn] said: Fāṭima of Nishapur said: "Today, the person who speaks the truth and the person who is aware of God finds himself in a wave-tossed sea. He calls upon his Lord with the prayer of the drowning man and asks his Lord to be saved and rescued."

Fāṭima said: "One who acts for the sake of God while desiring to witness Him is a gnostic (*ʿārif*), whereas one who acts in the hope that God will notice him is the sincere believer (*mukhliṣ*)"

Fāṭima (may God have mercy on her) died in Mecca in the year 223/838 while on her way to perform the lesser pilgrimage (*ʿumra*).

100. An *ijāza* is a written certificate given by a teacher of oral traditions (*riwāya*) to his or her pupil. This certificate entitles the pupil to transmit the traditions that are stipulated in the *ijāza* to his or her own students.

وقال أبويزيد البسطامي: ما رأيتُ في عمري إلاّ رجلاً وامرأةً. فالمرأة كانت فاطمة النّيسابورية. ما أخبرتها عن مقام من المقامات إلاّ وكان الخبرُ لها عيانًا.

وقال لها ذوالنّون: عظيني، وقد اجتمعا ببيت المقدس، فقالت له: الْزم الصِّدق، وجاهدْ نفسَكَ في أفعالكَ وأقوالكَ، لأنّ اللّه تعالى قال: «فإذا عَزم الأمرَ فلوصدقوا اللّه لكان خيرا لهم.»

أخبرنا أحمد بن محمد بن مقسم، إجازةً، قال: سمعتُ أبا محمد الحسين بن علي بن خلف، قالَ: سمعتُ بن ملول -- وكان شيخا كبيرا رأى ذا النّون المصري -- قال: فسألتُه: مَن أجَلُّ ممَّن رأيتَ؟ فقال: ما رأيتُ أحداً أجلّ من امرأةٍ رأيتُها بمكّة، يُقال لَها: فاطمة النّيسابورية، كانت تتكلّم في فهم القرآن، في تعجيبٍ منها.

فسألتُ ذا النّون عنها، فقال لي: هي وليةٌ من أولياء اللّه عزّ وجلّ، وهي أستاذي.

وسمعتها تقول: من لم يكن اللّه منه على بالٍ فإنّه يتخطّى في كلّ ميدانٍ، ويتكلّم بكلّ لسانٍ. ومن كان اللّه منه على بالٍ أخرَسَهُ إلاّ عن الصّدق، وألزمَهُ الحياء منه والإخلاص.

قال: وقالت فاطمة النّيسابورية: الصّادق والمتّقي اليوم في بحرٍ يضطربُ عليه أمواجُهُ، ويدعوربّهُ دعاء الغريق، يسأل ربّهُ الخلاص والنّجاة.

وقالت فاطمةُ: مَن عملَ للّه على المُشاهدة فهوعارفٌ ومن عَمِل على مُشاهَدةِ اللّه إيّاهُ فهوالمَخلِصُ.

وماتت فاطمةُ رحمةُ اللّه عليها بمكّة، في طريق العمرة، سنة ثلاثٍ وعشرين ومائتين.

XXXI

UMM HĀRŪN OF DAMASCUS[101]

Umm Hārūn was one of the great women of Syria. Abū Sulaymān ad-Dārānī used to say: "I never thought that in Syria there would be a woman such as Umm Hārūn."[102]

Abū Jaᶜfar ar-Rāzī (may God have mercy on him) reported from al-ᶜAbbās ibn Ḥamza through Aḥmad ibn Abī al-Ḥawārī, who said: I said to Umm Hārūn, "Do you desire death?" "No," she said. "Why?" I asked. She replied, "If I were disobedient to a human being, I would not want to encounter him. So how could I desire to encounter God when I have disobeyed Him?"

Also on his authority [Aḥmad ibn Abī al-Ḥawārī] said: Umm Hārūn was leaving her village, when a man shouted out to a boy, "Take him!" Umm Hārūn fell to the ground. She hit her head on a rock, and blood appeared on her veil. Abū Sulaymān [ad-Dārānī] said: "He who wishes to see one who is truly thunderstruck should look at Umm Hārūn!"[103]

101. See also, *Ṣifat aṣ-Ṣafwa* Appendix section XIV below; and al-ᶜĀmilī, *ad-Durr al-manthūr,* 70.

102. Umm Hārūn's association with Abū Sulaymān ad-Dārānī and Aḥmad ibn Abī al-Ḥawārī indicates that she lived in the first half of the third/ninth century.

103. When Umm Hārūn heard the man shout "Take him!" she thought that God had commanded the Angel of Death to take her soul. Accounts about Umm Hārūn indicate that she was in such fear of God that she expected her death at any moment.

(٣١)

أمّ هـارون الدِّمَشْقِيـة

من كِبار نِسـاء الشّامَ

كان أبوسليمان الدّراني يقـول: ما كنتُ أرى أن يكـون بالشّـام مثـلُ أمّ هارون.

أخبرنا أبوجعفر الرّازي، رحمـه اللـّـه، قال: حدّثنا العبّاس بن حمـزة، قـال: حدّثنا أحمد بن أبي الحواري، قـال: قلتُ لأمّ هـارون: أتُحبّيـن المـوت؟ قالت: لا. قلتُ: ولِمَ؟ قالت: لوعصيتُ آدميًا ما أحببْتُ لَقاءَهُ، فكيف أحِبُّ لقاء اللّـهِ وقد عَصَيتُهُ.

وبإسناده قال: خرجت أمّ هارون منْ قريتها، فصاح رجلٌ بصبيٍّ: خُـذوهُ. قال: فسقطت أمّ هارون، فوقعت على حجرٍ، فظهر الدّمُ على مقنعَتها. فقال أبوسليمان: من أحَبَّ أن ينظُرَ إلى صَعْق ٍصحيحٍ فليَنْظُر إلَى أمّ هارون.

XXXII

BAḤRIYYA[104]
(The Woman of the Sea)

Baḥriyya was one of the female gnostics of Basra. She was a companion of Shaqīq [al-Balkhī][105] and his contemporary. Once she stopped to see Shaqīq and said: "Teach me a tradition that has neither been recorded by pens nor polluted by inaccuracy, and is near in time to its informant." Shaqīq was shocked by her words and exclaimed, "Look at what this one is saying!"

Abū Jaᶜfar ar-Rāzī reported from al-ᶜAbbās ibn Ḥamza through Aḥmad ibn Abī al-Ḥawārī, who said: An old woman from the people of Basra told me that she heard Baḥriyya say: "When the heart abandons its desires, it becomes habituated to knowledge and pursues it, bearing everything which this entails."

104. See also, *Ṣifat aṣ-Ṣafwa* Appendix section VIII below, where she is called "Baḥriyya the Worshipper."

105. Abū ᶜAlī Shaqīq ibn Ibrāhīm al-Azdī (d. 194/810) was from the city of Balkh in Khurasan (present-day Afghanistan). He was knowledgeable in all of the Islamic sciences including the exegesis of the Qurʾān. He was a companion of Ibrāhīm ibn Adham (d. 160/777) and was said to have given a vast amount of wealth away in alms. In his youth he was a merchant and traveled widely in the land of the Turks. Sources indicate that he was in the region of Baghdad in the year 158/775. It was probably around this time that he associated with Baḥriyya. See as-Sulamī, *Ṭabaqāt aṣ-ṣūfiyya,* 61–66; al-Iṣfahānī, *Ḥilyat al-awliyāʾ,* vol. 8, 58–83; al-Qushayrī, *ar-Risāla,* 397–98; Ibn al-Jawzī, *Ṣifat aṣ-Ṣafwa,* vol. 4, 159–60. See also, al-Hujwirī, *The Kashf al-Maḥjūb,* 111–12; Smith, *An Early Mystic,* 75.

(٣٢)

بحــرية

كانت من عارفات البصريين.

صحبت شقيقا، وكانت من أقرانه.

وقفَت يوما على شقيق، فقالت: أخبِرْني عن عِلْم لم تُسَطِّرْهُ الأقلام، ولم تُدَنِّسْهُ الأوهَام، جديدُ العهدِ بالعَلاَّم. فتحيَّر من كلاَمها، وقال: انظُروا ما تقول هذه!

أخبرنا أبوجعفر الرّازي، حدّثنا العبّاس بن حمزة، حدّثنا أحمد بن أبي الحواري، قال: حدّثتني عجوزٌ من أهل البصرة، قالت: سمعتُ بحرية تقول: إذا ترك القلبُ الشّهوات ألِفَ العِلم واتّبَعَه، واحتمل كلّ ما يَرِدُ عليه.

XXXIII

FĀṬIMA AL-BARDAᶜIYYA[106]

Fāṭima used to live in Ardabīl [a city in the ᶜAbbasid province of Adharbayjan]. She was one of the female gnostics who speak words of ecstasy (*al-mutakallimāt bi-ash-shaṭḥ*).

I heard Abū al-Ḥasan as-Salāmī[107] say: A shaykh asked Fāṭima al-Bardaᶜiyya about the statement of the Prophet (may God bless and preserve him) relating [a saying] from his Lord: "I am the Companion of the one who remembers Me." After he had argued with her about the meaning of the tradition for some time, she said: "No. Complete remembrance of God means that you witness yourself being remembered by the One you are remembering, while maintaining constant remembrance of Him. Therefore, your remembrance is annihilated in remembrance of Him whereas His remembrance of you persists beyond place and time."

106. A Persian translation of this notice can also be found in Jāmī, *Nafaḥāt al-uns,* 619–20. Fāṭima al-Bardaᶜiyya most likely flourished around the middle of the fourth/tenth century.

107. There is some question about the actual name of Abū al-Ḥasan as-Salāmī (d. 374/985). Whatever it may have been, he was a widely-traveled traditionist of Khurasan. He recorded traditions from Iraq, Khurasan, Transoxania, Bukhara, and Samarqand. He was particularly interested in unusual stories and oddities. He died in Bukhara. See as-Sulamī, *Ṭabaqāt aṣ-ṣūfiyya,* np. 28.

(٣٣)

فاطمة البردعية

كانت تنزل أردبيل. وكانت من العارفات المتكلّمات بالشّطح.

سمعتُ أبا الحسن السّلامي، يقول: سألتْ فاطمة البردعية بعض المشايخ، عن قول النبيّ صلى اللّه عليه وسلّم، حاكيا عن ربّه: «أنا جليسُ من ذكرني». فَفَاوضَها ساعةً. فقالت: لا، ولكن أتمُّ الذّكر أن تشهَدَ ذكرَ المذكور لك مع دوام ذكرِكَ له، فيَفنى ذِكرُكَ في ذِكرِهِ، ويَبقَى ذكرُهُ لك حين لا مكان ولا زمان.

XXXIV

ᶜĀᵓISHA OF DĪNAWAR

Muḥammad ibn al-Faḍl[108] reported (with certification) that Aḥmad ibn Muḥammad al-Kawkabī said: I asked ᶜĀᵓisha of Dīnawar about what advice Ibrāhīm ibn Shaybān[109] had entrusted to her. She said: "I went to see him when I wanted to perform the Ḥajj pilgrimage. I said to him, 'Entrust me with something that will sustain me along the way.' He said, 'After taking your first step past the threshold of your house, do not think of taking another step until you become aware that your grave will be in it.'" She said: "That was what sustained me along the way."

ᶜĀᵓisha said: "I was present at [Ibrāhīm ibn Shaybān's] death[110] and said: 'Entrust me with something.' He said: "Take blessings from all that the Sufi shaykhs give you."

108. Muḥammad ibn al-Faḍl al-Balkhī (d. 319/931) was born in Balkh but was forced to move to Samarqand (in present-day Uzbekistan) because of his beliefs. He was one of the major shaykhs of Khurasan. He was a strong believer in asceticism. He said: "The people who know the most about God are the strongest in self-denial and its requirements; they are also the best in following the Sunna of His Prophet, may God bless and preserve him." See as-Sulamī, *Ṭabaqāt aṣ-ṣūfiyya,* 212–16; al-Iṣfahānī, *Ḥilyat al-awliyāᵓ,* vol. 10, 232–33; al-Qushayrī, *ar-Risāla,* 398–99; and Ibn al-Jawzī, *Ṣifat aṣ-Ṣafwa,* vol. 4, 165.

109. Abū Isḥāq Ibrāhīm ibn Shaybān al-Qirmīsīnī (d. 337/948-9) was the paramount Sufi of the region of al-Jabal, south of the Caspian Sea in Iran. He was a specialist in the Sufi doctrines of spiritual states (*aḥwāl*) and complete reliance on God (*tawakkul*). Like Ibrāhīm al-Khawwāṣ (d. 291/904), another specialist in *tawakkul,* he was a disciple of the North African Sufi Muḥammad ibn Ismāᶜīl al-Maghribī (d. 299/911). He said: "The knowledge of extinction in God (*fanāᵓ*) and continued existence through God (*baqāᵓ*) revolves around the sincere belief in the oneness of God and correct worship. Anything other than this is error and heresy." He also said: "*Tawakkul* is a secret between God and the slave. No one else should attain the knowledge of this secret." Ibrāhīm ibn Shaybān was the spiritual master of ᶜĀᵓisha ad-Dīnawariyya. See as-Sulamī, *Ṭabaqāt aṣ-ṣūfiyya,* 402–5; and al-Iṣfahānī, *Ḥilyat al-awliyāᵓ,* vol. 10, 361–62.

110. The fact that ᶜĀᵓisha of Dīnawar was present at Ibrāhīm ibn Shaybān's death indicates that she was one of his closest disciples. This particular tradition cannot have been transmitted through Muḥammad ibn al-Faḍl because he died before Ibn Shaybān.

(٣٤)

عائشة الدِّينَوَرية

أخبرنا محمد بن الفضل، إجازةً، قال: سمعتُ أحمد بن محمد الكوكبي، قال: سألتُ عائشة الدِّنورية عمَّا أوصاها به إبراهيم بن شيبان. قالت: دخلتُ عليه وأنا أُريدُ الحجّ. فقلتُ: أوصِنِي بشيءٍ يحملُني في الطّريق. فقال: إذا خرجت من عتبَة دارك، ووضَعت قدماً، فلاَ تأمُلي أنّكِ ترفعين الآخَر حتّى يكون قبرُكِ هناك. قالَت: فكان ذلك الذي حملنِي في الطّريق.

قالت: وحضرتُه عند وفاتِه، فقلتُ: أوصِنِي بشيءٍ. قال: تبرّكِي بكُلّ ما يدفعهُ إليكِ الشّيوخ.

XXXV

AMAT AL-ḤAMĪD[111] BINT AL-QĀSIM

Amat al-Ḥamīd was a companion of Abū Saᶜīd al-Kharrāz.[112] She used to serve him and transmitted traditions about him.

Abū Bakr ibn al-Mufīd al-Jarjarāʾī reported with certification from Amat al-Ḥamīd bint al-Qāsim[113] that Abū Saᶜīd al-Kharrāz said: "Those who have attained are a folk whose hearts have entered the treasuries of lights, and have prostrated themselves in the presence of the Omnipotent."

Amat al-Ḥamīd said: I said to Abū Saᶜīd al-Kharrāz, "Advise me." He said: "Keep a watchful eye on God Most High in your innermost soul, follow His commands outwardly, strive to fulfill the needs of your fellow Muslims, and maintain service to them. Through this you will arrive at the station of the virtuous (*abrār*) if God the Glorious and Mighty wills it."

111. *Ama* (slave) is the feminine form of the Arabic word *ᶜabd. Amat al-Ḥamīd* (Slave-Girl of the Praiseworthy) is thus the feminized version of the name *ᶜAbd al-Ḥamīd* (Slave of the Praiseworthy).

112. Abū Saᶜīd Aḥmad ibn ᶜĪsā al-Kharrāz (d. 277/890–91) was a companion of al-Junayd and fellow disciple of al-Junayd's uncle Sarī as-Saqaṭī (d. 253/867). He is said to have been the first to discuss the doctrine of *fanāʾ*, extinction in God, and *baqāʾ*, existence through God. He supported himself as a shoemaker (*kharrāz*). Al-Junayd said about him: "He remains at his bench year after year, and never forgets to mention God between each two stitches." Al-Hujwirī mentions a Sufi school named after al-Kharrāz and quotes extensively from the latter's writings on *fanāʾ* and *baqāʾ*. Al-Kharrāz said on this subject: "*Fanāʾ* is annihilation from the consciousness of personhood (*ᶜubūdiyya*), whereas *baqāʾ* is persistence in the contemplation of God-hood (*ilāhiyya*)." See al-Hujwirī, *The Kashf al-Maḥjūb,* 143, 241–46; Abdel-Kader, *al-Junayd,* 41; and Massignon, *Essay,* 203–05. See also, as-Sulamī, *Ṭabaqāt aṣ-ṣūfiyya,* 228–32; al-Qushayrī, *ar-Risāla,* 409; and al-Iṣfahānī, *Ḥilyat al-awliyāʾ,* vol. 10, 246–49. Al-Kharrāz is also cited numerous times by al-Kalābādhī in *at-Taᶜarruf.* Ibn al-Jawzī, *Ṣifat aṣ-Ṣafwa,* vol. 2, 435–38, mentions that al-Kharrāz used to teach his female disciples from behind a curtain (*īzār*).

113. It is unusual for a woman to issue an *ijāza* for the transmission of a body of traditions, as was done in this case. This means that Amat al-Ḥamīd was an especially close disciple of Abū Saᶜīd al-Kharrāz and that her traditions about his sayings were highly regarded.

(٣٥)

أمة الحميد بنت القاسم

صحبت أبا سعيد الخرّاز، وكانت تخدمُـه وتحكي عنه.

أخبرنا أبوبكر المفيد الجرجرائي، إجازة ً، قال: سمعتُ أمة الحميد بنت القاسم، تقول: سمعتُ أبا سعيد الخرّاز، يقول: الواصلون قومٌ أدخِلَتْ قلُوبُهم خَزائنُ الأنوار، فأناختْ بين يديّ الجبّار.

وقالت أمة الحميد: قلتُ لأبي سعيد الخرّاز: أوصني. فقال لي: راقِبِي اللّه تعالى في سِرِّك، واتّبِعي أوامِرَهُ على ظَاهِرك، واجتَهدي في قضاء حَوائِجِ المسلمِين، والقيَام بخدمتهم، تَصِلي بذلك إلى مقام الأبرار. إن شاء اللّه عزّ وجلّ.

XXXVI

ʿĀʾISHA THE WIFE OF ABŪ ḤAFṢ OF NISHAPUR[114]

I found this in the handwriting of Abū Jaʿfar Aḥmad ibn Ḥamdān:[115] ʿĀʾisha the wife of Abū Ḥafṣ asked her husband about the practice of weeping (*bukāʾ*). Abū Ḥafṣ said: "The weeping of the truthful person (*ṣādiq*) is that he sheds tears and cries for his weeping because he is not truthful enough in his weeping. He hopes, thereby, that God Most High may be satisfied with his weeping. This is because his shedding of tears for his lack of truthfulness in weeping is of greater value to him than all of the weeping that he did at the beginning of his spiritual path. No state is more elevating for the slave than his awareness of his shortcomings in attaining it."

114. Abū Ḥafṣ ʿAmr ibn Salama al-Ḥaddād of Nishapur (d. 270/883–84) was the Sufi master of his time in Khurasan. Al-Hujwirī cites him as a specialist in virtuous conduct (*muʿāmalāt*) and opens his section on this subject with the following quotation from Abū Ḥafṣ: "All of Sufism consists of appropriate actions (*ādāb*): for every time there is an appropriate action (*adab*); for every station there is an appropriate action; and for every state there is an appropriate action. He who obliges himself to perform the appropriate actions at the appropriate times has attained the rank of the "men" (*rijāl*); but he who squanders his actions is far from the nearness to God he imagines he has attained and has been rejected from the acceptance of God that he imagines he has earned" (my translation). Although al-Hujwirī reproduces this statement in Arabic, he claims that Abū Ḥafṣ did not speak the Arabic language, but miraculously became fluent in it as a student of al-Junayd in Baghdad. This may either be an example of hiding one's true state on Abū Ḥafṣ' part (an action of the *malāmatiyya*), or an expression of Persian nativism on al-Hujwirī's part. *Kashf al-Maḥjūb* was the first work on Sufism to be written in the Persian language. See Ibid., 41–42, 123–25. Other sources maintain that Abū Ḥafṣ was a Muʿtazilite, a follower of theological rationalism, and that he composed works on scholastic theology. See Abdel-Kader, *al-Junayd,* 28–31; and Sara Sviri, "Ḥakīm Tirmidhī and the *Malāmatī* Movement in Early Sufism," in Leonard Lewisohn ed., *Classical Persian Sufism: from its Origins to Rumi* (London and New York, 1993), 596–99. See also as-Sulamī, *Ṭabaqāt aṣ-ṣūfiyya,* 115–22; al-Iṣfahānī, *Ḥilyat al-awliyāʾ,* vol. 10, 229–30; and Ibn al-Jawzī, *Ṣifat aṣ-Ṣafwa,* vol. 4, 118–20.

115. Abū Jaʿfar Aḥmad ibn Ḥamdān, also known as Ibn Sinān (d. 311/923–24) was one of the most important Sufi shaykhs of Nishapur. According to as-Sulamī, "his house was one of asceticism (*zuhd*) and scrupulousness (*waraʿ*)." He was known for his statements on asceticism and his knowledge of hadith. See as-Sulamī, *Ṭabaqāt aṣ-ṣūfiyya,* 332–34.

(٣٦)

عائشة
امرأة أبي حفص النّيسابوري

وجدتُ بخطّ أبي جعفر أحمد بن حمدان: سألتْ عائشة امرأة أبي حفص، أبا حفصٍ عن البُكاء. فقال أبوحفص: بكاءُ الصّادق أن يبْكي، ويبْكي على بُكائه أنّه غيرُ صادقٍ في بُكائه، لعلّ اللّهَ تعالى أن لا [ألاّ] يرضى منه ذَلك البكاء، فبُكاؤُهُ على قلّة صدقه في بُكائه أنفعُ لهُ من ابتِداءِ بُكَائِه، لأنّه لا يُرفَعُ للعبدِ حالٌ إلاّ بنُقصانِه عندَهُ.

XXXVII

FĀṬIMA

Nicknamed Zaytūna (Olive)

Fāṭima was a servant of Abū Ḥamza [al-Baghdādī],[116] [Abū al-Qāsim] al-Junayd,[117] and [Abū al-Ḥusayn] an-Nūrī.[118] She was one of the friends of God *(awliyāʾ)*.

I heard Abū al-Faraj al-Warthānī relate that Mufaḍḍal ibn Dāwūd of Baghdad said that he heard Fāṭima, known as Zaytūna, the servant of al-Junayd, an-Nūrī, and Abū Ḥamza say: "I visited Abū al-Ḥusayn an-Nūrī on a bitterly cold day. I said to him, 'Should I bring you something to eat?' 'Yes,' he said. 'What would you like?' I asked. He said, 'Bread and buttermilk.' He was sitting in front of a fire and turning its burning coals with his hands. He ate the bread and drank from the buttermilk and his hand was darker than the ashes. The buttermilk started running down his hand and cleaned the blackness from it. I looked at him and said, 'Oh, Lord! How filthy are Your friends! Not one of them is clean!'

116. Abū Ḥamza al-Baghdādī al-Bazzāz (d. 289/902) was one of the principal scholastic theologians (*mutakallimūn*) of the Sufis and a specialist in Qurʾān recitation. Although he is said to have been the first to occupy a "chair" for the teaching of Sufism in Baghdad, his doctrines were often controversial. He was an associate of Sarī as-Saqaṭī and an-Nūrī. He was the preacher of the Ruṣāfa mosque of Baghdad and was also allowed to preach in the Prophet's mosque in Medina. He visited Basra often and died in Medina. See as-Sulamī, *Ṭabaqāt aṣ-ṣūfiyya,* 295–98; al-Qushayrī, *ar-Risāla,* 395. See also, al-Hujwirī, *The Kashf al-Maḥjūb,* 154; and Smith, *An Early Mystic,* 29–31.

117. Abū al-Qāsim al-Junayd ibn Muḥammad al-Khazzāz (d. 298/910) of Baghdad was one of the greatest Sufis of all time. The head of the so-called "Baghdad school" of Sufism, he is often called the "Master of the Way" (*Shaykh aṭ-Ṭarīqa*) and appears in the spiritual lineages of most contemporary Sufi orders. Highly trained in theology and the Law, he is credited with defining the Sufi conception of *tawḥīd,* Divine oneness. He is considered to be the greatest advocate of "sober" Sufism, and warned his followers against giving too much importance to Sufi states and the performance of miracles. He also believed that Sufism should be strictly linked to the teachings of the Qurʾān and the Sunna. See Abdel-Kader, *al-Junayd,* 1–8, 35–103; al-Hujwirī, *The Kashf al-Maḥjūb,* 128–30, 188–89; and EI^2, vol. 2, 600–601. See also, as-Sulamī, *Ṭabaqāt aṣ-ṣūfiyya,* 155–63; al-Qushayrī, *ar-Risāla,* 430-431; al-Iṣfahānī, *Ḥilyat al-awliyāʾ,* vol. 10, 255–78; and Ibn al-Jawzī, *Ṣifat aṣ-Ṣafwa,* vol. 2, 412–24.

118. Abū al-Ḥusayn (or Abū al-Ḥasan) Aḥmad ibn Muḥammad al-Baghawī an-Nūrī (d. 295/ 907) was originally from the region of Merv in Khurasan but lived in Baghdad. Like al-Junayd, he was the disciple of al-Junayd's uncle, Sarī as-Saqaṭī. His name, *an-Nūrī,* means "The Illuminated One." Besides teaching a Sufi doctrine of knowledge based on divine illumination, he was also an advocate of *īthār,* giving preference to another over oneself. See EI^2, vol. 8, 139–40; Abdel-Kader, *al-Junayd,* 40–41; al-Hujwirī, *The Kashf al-Maḥjūb,* 130–32, 189–95; Smith, *An Early Mystic,* 31–34; and Annemarie Schimmel, "Abū'l-Ḥusayn al-Nūrī: '*Qibla of the Lights*,'" in Lewisohn ed., *Classical Persian Sufism,* 59–64. See also, as-Sulamī, *Ṭabaqāt aṣ-ṣūfiyya,* 164–69; al-Qushayrī, *ar-Risāla,* 438–39; al-Iṣfahānī, *Ḥilyat al-awliyāʾ,* vol. 10, 249–55; and Ibn al-Jawzī, *Ṣifat aṣ-Ṣafwa,* vol. 2, 439–40. Carl Ernst discusses an-Nūrī's trial for heresy in idem, *Words of Ecstasy,* 97–101.

(٣٧)

فاطمة
المُلَقّبة بزيتونة

خادمة أبي حمزة، والجنيد، والنّوري. وكانت من الأولياء.

سمعتُ أبا الفرج الورثاني، يقول: سمعتُ مفضّل بن داود البغدادي، يقول: سمعتُ فاطمة المعروفة بزيتونة خادمة الجنيد والنّوري وأبي حمزة، تقول: أتيتُ أبا الحسين النّوري، في يوم شديد القُرّ. فقلتُ له: أجيك (أجيئك) بشئ تأكلُه؟ قال: نعم. قلت: ما تريدُ؟ قال: خبْزٌ ولبنٌ. وكان بين يديه نارٌ يُقَلّبُها بيده. فأكل من ذلك الخبز واللبن، ويدُه أسودُ من الرّماد. فجعل اللبنُ يَسيلُ على يَده، ويغْسلُ ذلك السّوادَ عنه. فنظرتُ إليه، وقُلتُ: ياربّ ما أقذرَ أولياءَك! ما فيهم أحدٌ نظيفٌ!

"Then I left him and passed by the headman of the quarter where I lived. Suddenly, a woman grabbed me and said, 'The parcel that was here, you stole it!' The headman of the quarter took me to the Amīr. When the news of this reached an-Nūrī, he hurriedly came to look for me. When we went before the Sulṭān an-Nūrī said to him, 'Do not go against her, for she is a friend of God!' The Sulṭān replied, 'What else can I do, since someone is present to accuse her?' Then a black slave-girl appeared with the missing parcel. 'We have found the parcel,' she said.

An-Nūrī took me by the hand and we left the Ṣulṭān. 'Why did you say, "How uncivilized and filthy are God's friends?"' he asked. 'I repent before God most High for that statement of mine!' I replied."

ثمّ خرجتُ من عنده، فجُزتُ على صاحب الرّبع. فإذا بامرأةٍ تعلّقَتْ بي، وقالت: الرّزمة التَي كانت ها هُنا أخذتيها. فحملني صاحبُ الرّبع إلى الأمير. وبلغ ذلك النّوري، فأسرع في طلبي، فلمّا صِرنا بين يدي السُّلطان قال النّوري: لا تتعرّضْ لها فإنّها وليّةٌ للّه. فقال: ما حيلتي ومعها مَنْ يُطالِبُها؟

فإذا بجاريةٍ سوداء معها الرّزمة، قالت: قد وجدنا الرّزمة.

فأخذ النّوري بيدي، وأخرجني من عند السّلطان، وقال: لمَ تقولين: ما أوحشَ أولياءكَ وأقذرَهم؟ فقلتُ: تُبتُ إلى اللّه تعالى من قولي هذا.

XXXVIII

ṢAFRĀʾ OF RAYY

[Another Wife of Abū Ḥafṣ of Nishapur]

Abū Ḥafṣ an-Nīsābūrī married Ṣafrāʾ in Rayy.[119] She was one of the Muslim elite.

Abū Ḥafṣ lived with her for a time. When he wanted to leave Rayy, he said to her: "If you want me to divorce you and pay back your dowry I shall do so,[120] for I am leaving and I do not know when I shall be able to see you again."

She replied, "I prefer not to do that. Instead, allow me to remain married to you, so that the blessings of this marriage will accrue to me, and that I will be in your thoughts and your prayers."

When Abū Ḥafṣ was about to leave her, she said: "Teach me a lesson that I may keep as a memento from you."

He said to her: "Know that the people who are most knowlegeable about God are those who are the most in fear and in awe of Him. The one with the most love for God is he who chooses serving Him over any other activity. He does not stir but for God's sake, and does not seek anything but His satisfaction."

Ṣafrāʾ then said to Abū Ḥafṣ "Advise me." He said: "I advise you to remain in the house, to stay close to the prayer-niche (*miḥrāb*), to recite what you have memorized from the Qurʾān, to remain silent, to avoid that which does not concern you, and to maintain that which is of benefit to the people to the extent of your ability."[121]

119. This seems to have been a temporary marriage that occurred while Abū Ḥafṣ was visiting Rayy for an extended period. It was not uncommon for Muslim men in the premodern period to take another wife at such times. Proper etiquette might also include the provision of a house and a slave-girl by the host for the visitor's personal use.

120. The phrase rendered here as "I shall do so" (*ḥatta afʿala*) is not written with dots in the original manuscript. Aṭ-Ṭanāḥī read it as "until I return" (*ḥatta uqfila*), assuming that Abū Ḥafṣ an-Nīsābūrī intended to return to his wife at some unspecified date in the future. However, neither the context of the discussion nor Ṣafrāʾ's reply bears out this interpretation.

121. Abū Ḥafṣ' advice to Ṣafrāʾ can be interpreted in two different ways. In one respect, he can be seen as continuing to exercise his rights over her as a husband. Because Ṣafrāʾ refused to divorce him, she would not be free of the marriage bond and the obligations that it entailed. In another respect, she remained under the authority of Abū Ḥafṣ as his Sufi disciple. From a Sufi point of view, one could just as easily see his advice to stay home, pray, recite the Qurʾān, and stay out of trouble as a way for Ṣafrāʾ to realize through her behavior the goals described in the answer to her first question: "One does not stir but for God's sake, and does not seek anything but His satisfaction." This example illustrates the danger of automatically ascribing gender-based interpretations to the actions of those who follow a spiritual vocation.

(٣٨)

صفراء الرّازية

تزوّجها أبوحفص النّيسابوري، بالرّيّ.

وكانت من سادات المسلمين.

وأقام أبوحفص عندها مُدّةً. فلمّا أراد أن يخرج من الرّيّ قال لها: إن أردت أن أُطلّقكِ وأدفعَ إليكِ مهركِ حتّى أفعلَ، فإنّي خارجٌ ولا أدري متى أصل إليك.

فقالت: لا أختارُ ذلك، ولكن دعني أكونُ في حبالتِكَ، وتَلحَقُنِي بركات ذلك، وأكون في ذِكْرِكَ ودُعَائِكَ.

وقالت لأبي حفص وقتَ خُروجِه من عندها. عَلِّمْنِي كلمةً أحفظُها عنكَ.

فقال لها: اعلَمي أنّ أعْرَفَ النّاس باللّه أشدُّهُم خوفًا منه وخَشْيةً له. وأكثرَهُم محبّةً لَهُ مَنْ آثر خدمتَه على جميع حركاته، ولا يتحرّك إلاّ له، ولا يسعى إلاّ في مرضاته.

وقالت لأبي حفص: أوصني. فقال: أُوصيك بلُزومِ البيت، والدُّنُوِّ من المحْراب، والقراءة من القرآن ما تحفّظْتهِ، ومُلازَمةِ الصَّمتِ، وتركِ ما لا يعنيكِ، والقيامِ بمنافعِ النّاس على حَسبِ الطّاقة.

XXXIX

UNAYSA BINT ᶜAMR

Unaysa was a companion of Muᶜādha al-ᶜAdawiyya.[122] Muḥammad ibn al-Ḥusayn al-Burjulānī reported from ᶜAbd ar-Raḥmān ibn ᶜAmr ibn Jabala[123] that Dalāl the daughter of al-Mudill related: Unaysa bint ᶜAmr was the servant of Muᶜādha al-ᶜAdawiyya. Muᶜādha used to say: "Spiritual practice requires three things: sincerity, correctness, and the Sunna of the Prophet."

122. This infomation places the date of Unaysa's death in the early Umayyad period, around the end of the first/seventh century.

123. This may have been Abū ᶜAbd ar-Raḥmān ibn Jabala of Merv (d. 221/836). He was an important traditionist who transmitted reports from Shuᶜba and others. See as-Sulamī, *Ṭabaqāt aṣ-ṣūfiyya,* np. 441.

(٣٩)

أنيسة بنت عمرو

صحبت معاذة العدوية.

حكى محمد بن الحسين البرجلاني، عن عبد الرحمن بن عمروبن جبلة، عن دلال بنت المُدلّ، قالت: كانت أنيسة بنت عمروخادمة معاذة العدوية. وكانت تقول: العمل يَجبُ أن يكون معه ثلاثة أشياء: الإخلاص والصّواب والسّنّة.

XL

UMM AL-ASWAD BINT ZAYD AL-ᶜADAWIYYA[124]

Muᶜādha al-ᶜAdawiyya was Umm al-Aswad's wet-nurse. Umm al-Aswad related: Muᶜādha al-ᶜAdawiyya said to me: "Do not spoil the breast-feeding I have given you by eating forbidden food, for when I was nursing you I made every effort to eat only what was lawful. So make every effort after this to eat only what is lawful. Perhaps you will succeed in your service to your Lord and in your acceptance of His will."

Umm al-Aswad used to say: "I would not eat anything suspicious lest it cause me to miss either a prescribed prayer or an extra invocation."

124. See also, *Ṣifat aṣ-Ṣafwa,* vol. 4, 32. Umm al-Aswad was a figure of the middle Umayyad period, flourishing at the end of the first/seventh century.

(٤٠)

أمّ الأسود بنت زيد العدوية

كانت معاذة العدوية أرضعتها.

قالت أمّ الأسود: قالت لي معاذة العدوية: لا تُفسدي رضاعي بأكل الحرام، فإنّي جهدتُ جُهدي حين أرضعتُك أن لا آكلَ إلاّ حلالا، فاجتهدي بعد ذلك أن لا تأكلين [تأكُلي] إلاّ حلالاً، لعَلّكِ تُوفَّقين لخدمةِ سيّدك، والرّضا بقضائه.

وكانت أمّ الأسود تقول: ما أكلتُ شُبهةً إلاّ فاتَتْني فريضةٌ أوورْدٌ من أورادي.

XLI

UMM ᶜALĪ [FĀṬIMA]
The Wife of Aḥmad ibn Khaḍrawayh of Balkh[125]

Umm ᶜAlī was one of the daughters of the leaders and the high elites. She was very rich and spent all of her wealth on the Sufis. She helped Aḥmad [ibn Khaḍrawayh] in all matters pertaining to his spiritual practice.[126]

She met both Abū Ḥafṣ an-Nīsābūrī and Abū Yazīd al-Bisṭāmī. She consulted Abū Yazīd on doctrinal matters.[127]

It was reported that Abū Ḥafṣ said: "I used to dislike stories about the practitioners of female chivalry until I met Umm ᶜAlī, the wife of Aḥmad ibn Khaḍrawayh. Then I learned that God Most High bestows His knowledge on whomever He wishes."

Abū Yazīd al-Bisṭāmī said: "Whoever practices Sufism should do so with the spiritual motivation (*himma*) of Umm ᶜAlī, the wife of Aḥmad ibn Khaḍrawayh, or with a state similar to hers."

It was reported that Umm ᶜAlī said: "God Most High calls humanity to Him through charity and kindness, but they do not respond to Him. Then He afflicts them with misfortune in order to bring them back to Him through misfortune, because He loves them."

125. Abū Ḥāmid Aḥmad ibn Khaḍrawayh al-Balkhī (d. 240/854) followed the path of blame (*malāmatiyya*) and wore the dress of a soldier. He was famed as a specialist in Sufi chivalry (*futuwwa*). He said: "Kill your lower soul (*nafs*) so that God may bring it back to life." He also said: "He who serves the Sufis is honored by three things: humility, good conduct, and generosity." See as-Sulamī, *Ṭabaqāt aṣ-ṣūfiyya,* 103–6; al-Qushayrī, *ar-Risāla,* 410; al-Iṣfahānī, *Ḥilyat al-awliyāᵓ,* vol. 10, 42-43; Ibn al-Jawzī, *Ṣifat aṣ-Ṣafwa,* vol. 4, 147–48.

126. According to al-Hujwirī, Umm ᶜAli was the daughter of the Emir of Balkh. When she wished to leave her former life and embrace Sufism, she asked Aḥmad ibn Khaḍrawayh to petition her father for her hand in marriage. When he refused, she sent another letter to Ibn Khaḍrawayh, saying: "Oh Aḥmad, I thought you would have been too manly to attack those who travel on the way to God. Be a guide, not a brigand!" Idem, *The Kashf al-Maḥjūb,* 119–20.

127. Al-Hujwirī is one of the first to recount the following well-known story of Umm ᶜAlī's encounter with al-Bisṭāmī: When Aḥmad went to visit Bāyazīd she accompanied him, and on seeing Bāyazīd she removed her veil and talked to him without embarrassment. Aḥmad became jealous and said to her: "Why dost thou take this freedom with Bāyazīd?" She replied: "Because you are my natural spouse, but he is my religious consort; through you I come to my desire, but through him to God. The proof is that he has no need of my society, whereas to you it is necessary." She continued to treat Bāyazīd with the same boldness, until one day he observed that her hand was stained with henna and asked her why. She answered: "Oh Bāyazīd, so long as you did not see my hand and the henna I was at my ease with you, but now that your eye has fallen on me our companionship is unlawful." Ibid., 120. In *Ḥilyat al-awliyāᵓ* al-Iṣfahānī reports a very different story: Umm ᶜAlī asked Aḥmad ibn Khaḍrawayh to take back his bride-price so that she could marry al-Bisṭāmī. Upon arriving before Bāyazīd, she unveiled her face. When asked by her husband why she had done so, she replied, "When I looked at Abū Yazīd I lost all sense of self. But when I look at you [Aḥmad], I return to my awareness of self." Ibid., vol. 10, 42.

(٤١)

أمّ علـــي
امرأة أحمد بن خضرويه البلخي

كانت من بنات الرؤساء والأجِلّة.

وكانت موسِرةً، فأنفقت مالَها كلّها [كلّه] على الفُقراء، وساعدت أحمد على ما هوعليه.

لقيت أبا حفص النّسابوري، وأبا يزيد البسطامي. وسألت أبا يزيد عن مسائل.

حُكيَ عن أبي حفص النّيسابوري أنّه قال: مازلْتُ أكْرَهُ حديث النّسْوان حتّى لقَيتُ أمّ علي، زوجة أحمد بن خضرويه. فعلَمتُ أنّ الله تعالى يجعل معرفته حيث يشاء.

وقال أبويزيد البسطامي: من تصَوّفَ فليتصوّفْ بهمّةٍ كهمّةِ أمّ علي، زوجة أحمد بن خضرويه، أوحالٍ كحالِها.

حكي عن أمّ علي أنّها قالت: دعا الله تعالى الخلق إليه بأنواع البرّ واللّطف، فما أجابوه. فصبّ عليهم أنواع البلاء، ليردّهم بالبلاء إليه، لأنّه أحبّهم.

Umm ᶜAlī said: "I have never mentioned my poverty (*faqr*) without also mentioning my sufficiency (*istighnāᵓ*) in my Lord and my wealth (*ghinā*) in Him, for He relieves me of the circumstances of poverty. Thus, I say: "How can anyone be poor who has a master like God?"

She said: "Transcending a need is easier than being humiliated by it."

She said to a woman who came to see her from Balkh: "What are your needs?" The woman answered, " I came so that I could be closer to God by serving you." Umm ᶜAlī replied, "Why don't you become closer to me by serving your Lord?"

وقالت أمّ علي: ما ذكرتُ فقري قطّ إلاّ ذكرتُ استغنائي بربّـي وغنا ه، فيُزيل عنّي مواقف الفقر، وأقولُ: [لا] يكون فقيرا من له سيّد مثلُـه.

وقالت: فوتُ الحاجةِ أيسَـرُ من الذُلّ فيـــهـا .

وقالت وجاءتها امرأة من أهل بلخ، فقالت لها: ما حاجـتُـك؟ قالت: جئتُ لأتقرّب إلى اللّـه بخدمتك. فقالت لها: لمَ لا تتقرّبين إليّ بخدمَةِ ربّكِ .

XLII

FĀṬIMA BINT ᶜABDALLĀH
Known as Juwayriyya (The Little Slave)

Fāṭima was a companion of Abū Saᶜīd al-Kharrāz [of Baghdad].[128] ᶜAlī ibn Saᶜīd al-Muqriᵓ reported that Aḥmad ibn al-Ḥusayn al-Mālikī heard Fāṭima bint ᶜAbdallāh, known as Juwayriyya, the student (*tilmīdha*) of Abū Saᶜīd al-Kharrāz, say: "The first feeling of distress that befalls the gnostic cuts him off from everything. This is a sign of God's consideration for them, for He purifies them of all worldly affairs through their distress."

Also based on [Aḥmad ibn al-Ḥusayn's] authority she said: "I heard Abū Saᶜīd al-Kharrāz say: 'It is in the nature of the lover's (*muḥibb*) relationship with his Master, that when affection (*mawadda*) for Him is established in his consciousness (*ḍamīr*), it purifies his heart for fondness (*kalaf*) toward Him, for infatuation (*shaghaf*) in his love (*ḥubb*) for Him, for delirium (*hadhayān*) because of his remembrance (*dhikr*) of Him, and prevents him from opening himself up to anything else.'"

[Abū Saᶜīd al-Kharrāz also said]: "It is in the nature of one whose heart is touched by desire (*shawq*) that he forgets his destiny in this world and the Hereafter, he loses control over himself, and, unlike Majnūn, he finds no satisfaction in service. He becomes delirious, wasted, dazed, and confused in his infatuation for his Master."

Also based on [Ibn al-Ḥusayn al-Mālikī's] authority, Fāṭima bint ᶜAbdallāh said: I heard Abū Saᶜīd say: "It is in the nature of the gnostic (*ᶜārif*) to be seen at times as infatuated and cut off from the world; he performs no action that is not for the sake of his Lord. At other times, he can be seen among humankind, as if he is one of them. However, his station is concealed from them; he has ceased all inner turmoil, and is attached in his spiritual motivation (*himma*) to the source of his ecstasy."

128. This information puts the probable date of Fāṭima bint ᶜAbdallāh's death at the beginning of the fourth/tenth century.

(٤٢)

فاطمة بنت عبد اللّـه
المعروفة بجُوَيْرية

صاحبة أبي سعيد الخرّاز.

سمعتُ علي بن سعيد المقرئ، يقول: سمعتُ أحمد بن الحسين المالكي، قال: سمعتُ فاطمة بنت عبد اللّـه، المعروفة بجُويرية تلميذة أبي سعيد الخرّاز، تقول: أوّلُ همٍّ يَردُ على العارف يقطعُه عن كلّ شيء. إنّما ذلك نظرٌ من اللّـه لهم، ليُطهِّرهم عن كلّ شيء بذلك.

وبإسناده قالت: سمعتُ أبا سعيد الخرّاز، يقول: من شأن المُحبِّ لمولاه إذا تمكّنت مودّتُهُ في ضميره، أن يُطهِّر قلبَهُ للكلفِ به، والشَّغَفِ بحُبِّه، والهذيان بذكره، ويمنعَه من الاتّساع.

ومن شأن من قد باشرَ قلبُه شيئًا من الشّوق أن ينسى حظّه من الدّنيا والآخرة، ويفقد تدبيرَ نفسه، ولا يجدَ طعمَ الخدمة كما وجده المجنون، يكون بمولاه كلِفًا دنِفًا هائمًا متَحيِّراً.

وبإسناده قالت: سمعتُ أبا سعيد، يقول: من شأن العارف أن تراه مرّةً والهًا مُنقطعًا، لا فعلَ فيه لغير سيّده. وتارةً تراه مع الخلق، كأنّه واحدٌ منهم، قد خفِيَ عليهم مكانُه، إلاّ أنّه ساكنٌ من هيجانه، متّصلُ الهمّة بواجده.

XLIII

MUʾNISA THE SUFI

Muʾnisa was one of the female devotees of Syria. She was tough and stern.

I heard Muḥammad ibn ʿAbdallāh al-Ḥāfiẓ report from al-Ḥusayn ibn Muḥammad ibn Isḥāq through Abū ʿUthmān al-Ḥannāṭ[129] that Muḥammad ibn Yaʿqūb b. Yūsuf related: I asked Muʾnisa aṣ-Ṣūfiyya the female devotee: "Why do you wear this hair?"[130] Is it out of fear of God or love for Him?" "To learn how to endure suffering," she replied.

129. Abū ʿUthmān al-Ḥannāṭ (d. 294/906–7) was a disciple of Dhū an-Nūn al-Miṣrī (see note 69 above). His position in the *isnād* indicates that Muʾnisa flourished in the middle of the third/ninth century.

130. This account probably refers to Muʾnisa aṣ-Ṣūfiyya's practice of wearing a hair shirt (Ar. *masūḥ*). Massignon (*Essay,* 99) mentions this as one of the practices learned by Sufis from Christian ascetics.

(٤٣)

مؤنسة الصّوفية

كانت من متعبّدات الشّام. وكانت جلدة نكدة.

سمعتُ محمد بن عبد اللّه الحافظ يقول: سمعتُ الحسين بن محمّد بن إسحاق، يقول: سمعتُ أبا عثمان الحنّاط، يقول: سمعتُ محمد بن يعقوب بن يوسف، يقول: سألتُ مؤنسة الصّوفية المتعبّدة: لِمَ لبستِ هذا الشعرِ، أخوفًا منه، أوْ حبّا له؟ فقالت: مكابدةً.

XLIV

FAKHRAWAYH BINT ᶜALĪ
From the Natives of Nishapur

Fakhrawayh was the wife of Abū ᶜAmr ibn Nujayd [the grandfather of as-Sulamī].[131]

I heard my grandfather Abū ᶜAmr ibn Nujayd say: "What I gained from my companionship with my wife Fakhrawayh was no less than what I gained from my companionship with Abū ᶜUthmān [Saᶜīd al-Ḥīrī of Nishapur].[132]

I also heard my grandfather say: I heard Fakhrawayh say: "A weak spiritual state [leads to] grave danger, a vast pretense, and insufficient honesty!"[133]

Once Fakhrawayh said to Abū ᶜAlī ath-Thaqafī[134] (may God have mercy on him): "When a person speaks with knowledge, he puts his heart and his spirit at ease. Then he magnifies himself because of the excellence of his speech. But when he puts knowledge to use, his spirit and his heart become weary, and he belittles himself because he is aware of the lack of sincerity in his behavior."

Abū ᶜAlī wept at this statement and said: "I will say only what the Caliph ᶜUmar ibn al-Khaṭṭāb (may God be pleased with him) said: "This woman is superior in understanding to ᶜUmar!"

131. Fakhrawayh bint ᶜAlī was not the grandmother of as-Sulamī, but another wife of Abū ᶜAmr ibn Nujayd.

132. Abū ᶜUthmān Saᶜīd ibn Ismāᶜīl al-Ḥīrī (d. 298/910) was originally from Rayy. His first Sufi master was Yaḥyā ibn Muᶜādh ar-Rāzī (d. 258/872). Then he went to the city of Kirman and joined the master of *futuwwa* Shāh ibn Shujāᶜ al-Kirmānī (d. before 300/912–13). Al-Ḥīrī traveled to Nishapur with Shāh ibn Shujāᶜ and stayed there, becoming a disciple of Abū Ḥafṣ al-Ḥaddād an-Nīsābūrī (d. 270/883), whose daughter he married. He was given a formal lectureship in Sufism at a mosque in Nishapur and was the Sufi shaykh of as-Sulamī's grandfather. Al-Hujwirī states that al-Ḥīrī attained three Sufi stations (*maqāmāt*) through his teachers: the station of hope for God's blessings through Yaḥyā ibn Muᶜādh, the station of jealousy for God's love from Shāh ibn Shujāᶜ, and the station of God's affection through Abū Ḥafṣ. See al-Hujwirī, *The Kashf al-Maḥjūb,* 132–34. See also, as-Sulamī, *Ṭabaqāt aṣ-ṣūfiyya,* 170–75; al-Qushayrī, *ar-Risāla,* 407; al-Iṣfahānī, *Ḥilyat al-awliyāᵓ,* vol. 10, 244–46; Ibn al-Jawzī, *Ṣifat aṣ-Ṣafwa,* vol. 4, 85–88. On al-Ḥakīm at-Tirmidhī's (d. ca. 295/908) letter to al-Ḥīrī, in which he criticizes the latter's concern with the lower soul (*nafs*), see Sviri, "Ḥakīm Tirmidhī and the *Malāmatī* Movement," 610–12.

133. The original of this statement in Arabic is written as an equational sentence, without a verb. It should thus be understood as the semantic equivalent of a mathematical equation: weak spirituality = danger to the soul + pretensiousness + dishonesty.

134. Abū ᶜAlī Muḥammad ibn ᶜAbd al-Wahhāb ath-Thaqafī (d. 328/940) was a native of Nishapur. Like Abū ᶜUthmān al-Ḥīrī, he was a disciple of Abū Ḥafṣ an-Nīsābūrī. He started his career as a specialist in Islamic jurisprudence but later turned to Sufism. He was known for his aphorisms about the dangers of the lower soul and the pitfalls of the Sufi path. Given the high level of his scrupulousness in Sufi practice, his praise of Fakhrawayh is particularly meaningful. See as-Sulamī, *Ṭabaqāt aṣ-ṣūfiyya,* 361–65; and al-Qushayrī, *ar-Risāla,* 302.

(٤٤)

فخرويه بنت علي

من أهل نيسابور

كانت زوجة أبي عمروبن نجيد.

سمعتُ جدّي أبا عمروبن نُجيد، يقول: كانت فائدتي من صُحبة فخرويه لم تكُن دون فائدتي من صُحبةِ أبي عثمان.

وسمعتُ جدّي يقول: سمعتُ فخرويه تقول: حالٌ ضعيفٌ، وخطرٌ عظيمٌ، ودعوى عريضٌ [عريضةٌ]، وصدقٌ قليلٌ.

وقالت فخرويه مرّةً لأبي علي الثقفي، رحمه اللّه: إنّ الإنسان إذا تكلّم بالعلم يُريحُ قلبَهُ ونفسَهُ، ويعظم في نفسه؛ لاستحسانه كلامه. وإذا استعمل العلم أتعبَ نفسَه وقلبه، ويصغر في نفسه؛ لعلمه بقلّة إخلاصه في معاملته.

فبكى أبوعلي [ثمّ قال]: لا أقول لكِ إلاّ ما قال عمر بن الخطّاب، رضي اللّه عنه: امرأةٌ أفقهُ من عمر.

It was reported that Fakhrawayh said: "One who makes as his reason for attaining to his Lord anything other than the obligation of obeying God and following His Messenger (may God bless and preserve him) has lost the way to Him."

She died in the year 313/925–26.

فخرويه بنت علي

وحُكي عنها أنّها قالت: مَنْ جَعَلَ السّبَبَ إلى الوصول إلى ربِّه غيرَ ملازمةِ طاعتِهِ، واتّباع رسوله صلى اللّه عليه وسلّم، فقد أخطأ السّبيل إليه.

ماتت سنة ثلاث عشرة وثلاثمائة.

XLV

FĀṬIMA BINT AḤMAD AL-ḤAJĀFIYYA

Fāṭima was a companion of Zakarīyā ash-Shukhtanī.[135] She met Abū ᶜUthmān [Saᶜīd al-Ḥīrī of Nishapur].

I heard my grandfather (may God have mercy on him) say: I heard Fāṭima al-Ḥajāfiyya say: "Whenever I hear someone calling to a person, 'Oh, crazy one!' I reply, 'At your service!' thinking that I am the one meant by it. For no one is more clearly insane than he who supports his enemies and makes enemies of his friends. The ego and Satan are two of our enemies, yet we support and obey them, whereas the Qurʾān and the Sunna are abodes of safety and security for us, yet we reject them."

One day, Fāṭima said to Abū al-ᶜAbbās ad-Dīnawārī[136] while he was speaking on a subject pertaining to intimacy (*uns*): "How fluent is your description of that which you lack! [If you experienced what you described or witnessed what you speak of, you would be mute!]"[137]

135. Zakarīyā ash-Shukhtanī was from Shukhtan, a village in the region of Nishapur. Although no date can be found for his death, he is known to have been a disciple of Abū ᶜUthmān al-Ḥīrī. See al-Qushayrī, *ar-Risāla,* 233–34.

136. Abū al-ᶜAbbās Aḥmad ibn Muḥammad ad-Dīnawārī (d. after 340/951–52) ended his days in Samarqand. He stayed in Nishapur for a time and was a popular preacher on the subject of gnosis (*maᶜrifa*). It appears that Fāṭima bint Aḥmad's attacks on his sincerity may have played a part in his sudden departure for Samarqand. As-Sulamī cites a report in which someone asks him: "What has made you leave for Samarqand while the people of Nishapur turn toward you and love you?" In response, ad-Dīnawārī recited the following lines of poetry: "When destiny's final contract is decreed for you, Only destiny itself can annul its decree. So why should you remain in the abode of humiliation, While the abode of glory lies in destiny's expanse?" See as-Sulamī, *Ṭabaqāt aṣ-ṣūfiyya,* 475–78.

137. This sentence is missing in the aṭ-Ṭanāḥī edition.

(٤٥)

فاطمة بنت أحمد الحجافية

صحبت زكريّا السّخني. ولقيت أبا عثمان.

سمعتُ جدّي، رحمه اللّـه، يقول: سمعتُ فاطمة الحجافية، تقول: ما قال أحمد [أحدُ] لأحد: يا أحمقُ، إلاّ قلتُ: لبّيك، ظننتُ أنّه يعنيني به. فلا أحدَ أظهر حُمقا ممّن يوالي عَدُوَّه، ويُعادي عدُوَّه، ويُعادي وليَّه! النّفسُ والشّيطانُ عدوّان، ونحنُ نُواليهما ونُطيعُهما. والكتاب والسّنة مواضع نجاتِنا وخلاصِنا، وقد أعرضنا عنهُما.

وقالت فاطمة يومًا لأبي العبّاس الدِّينَوَري، وهويتكلّم في شئ من الأنْس: ما أحسنَ وصفكَ عمّا أنتَ غائبٌ عنهُ! لوذُقْت شيئا مِمّا تصِفُهُ أوشاهدت شيئا مِمّا تنطِقُ بِهِ لَخَرَسْتَ.

XLVI
DHAKKĀRA
(The Invoker)

Dhakkāra was one of the enraptured worshippers of God (*al-ᶜābidāt al-wālihāt*). Abū Ḥafṣ ᶜUmar ibn Masrūr, the ascetic from Baghdad, reported from Aḥmad ibn al-Ḥusayn b. Muḥammad b. Sahl al-Wāᵓiẓ (the Preacher)[138] through Muḥammad (i.e., ibn Jaᶜfar) through Ibrāhīm ibn al-Junayd[139] through Muḥammad ibn al-Ḥusayn [al-Burjulānī] that ᶜAbbās al-Iskāf (the Shoemaker) related: A madwoman (*majnūna*) called Dhakkāra used to live among us.[140] One holiday she saw me holding a piece of *fālūdaj* [a Persian sweet made of starch, honey, and water] in my hand. "What do you have?" she asked. "*Fālūdaj*" I replied. She said: "I am embarrassed to be regarded disapprovingly by God Most High. Shall I explain to you how to make real *fālūdaj* so that you may go home and make it if you are able to do so?" "Certainly," I said.

She said: "Take the sugar of the divine gift, the starch of purity, the water of modesty, the butter of self-awareness, and the saffron of recompense, and strain them in the sieves of fear and hope. Then place under the mixture a tripod of sorrow, hang the sauce-pots of grief, seal it with the lid of contemplation, light beneath it the fire of sighs, and spread it out over caution until it is touched by the fragrant breeze of the night-vigil. When you take a bite of it, you will become one of the wise and will be liberated from vain fantasies. It will bring you near to people's hearts, the ploys of the clever will become distasteful to you, you will be protected from 'the evil of the Whisperer, who withdraws' [Qurᵓān 114 (*an-Nās*), 4], and the Houris will wait on you in Paradise with goblets of heavenly wine."

Then she recited the following verse:

> The lover's aspirations wander in the angelic realm,
> The outer heart complains but the inner heart is mute!

138. Abū al-Fatḥ Aḥmad ibn al-Ḥasan b. Muḥammad b. Sahl al-Mālikī (d. 330/941–42) was originally from Egypt but had a career as a preacher in Basra. He was a well-known traditionist who was a major source for both as-Sulamī and al-Iṣfahānī. Nūr ad-Dīn Shurayba, the editor of as-Sulamī's *Ṭabaqāt aṣ-ṣūfiyya,* erroneously gives his death date as 430/1039, eighteen years after as-Sulamī's own death. Since an *isnād* in *Ṭabaqāt aṣ-ṣufiyya* shows a separation of three generations between this individual and Abū Yazīd al-Bisṭāmī (d. 261/875), a death date of 330/941–42 seems much more likely. See Ibid., 68 and np. 68.

139. Little is known about this individual, other than that he followed al-Burjulānī in composing a *Kitāb ar-ruhbān.* He also composed works on the love of God (*maḥabba*), the fear of God (*khawf*), and pious scrpulousness (*waraᶜ*). See An-Nadīm, *Kitāb al-fihrist,* 237.

140. The dates of the identifiable transmitters in this *isnād* indicate that Dhakkāra flourished in the first half of the third/ninth century.

(٤٦)

ذكّـــارة

من العابدات الوالـهـات.

أخبرنا أبوحفص عُمر بن مسرور الزّاهد ببغداد، قال: حدّثنا أحمد بن الحسن بن محمد بن سهل الواعظ، حدّثنا محمد -- يعني بن جعفر -- قال: حدّثنا إبراهيم بن الجنيد، قال: حدّثني محمد بن الحسين، قال: حدّثنا عبّاس الإسكاف، قال: كانت عندنا مجنونةٌ يقال لها: ذكّارة. فنظرت إليّ يومَ العيد وفي يدي قطعة فالوذج فقالت: ما معك؟ قلتُ: فالوذج. فقالت: إنّي لأستحيي أن يراني اللّهُ تعالى حيثُ يكرَهُ. ألا أصِفُ لكَ فالوذجًا تذهبْ فتعْمَلْهُ إن قدرتَ عليه؟ قلتُ: بلى.

قالت: خُذْ سكّر العطاء ونشاستج الصّفاء وماء الحياء، وسمْنَ المراقبة، وزعفران الجزاء، وصفّه بمناخل الخوف والرّجاء، وانصبْ تحتَهُ ديكدان الحزن، وركّبْ ظناجير الكمد، واعقدهُ باسطام الاعتبارَ، وأوقد تحتَهُ نيران الزّفيرَ، وابسُطهُ على الحذر حتّى يضْربَهُ نسيم هواء التهَجّد. فإذا أكلت منهُ لُقمةً تصيرُ من الأكياس، وتبرأ من الوسواس، وحبّبك إلى صدور النّاس، وتُبغّض إليك ريط الأكياس، ويكفيك من شرّ الوسواس الخنّاس، وتدورُ عليك الحُورُ العينُ في الفردوس بالكأس. ثم أنشدت تقول:

هِمَمُ المُحبِّ تَجولُ في الملَكوت
والقلبُ يشكووالفؤادُ صمُوت [سكوت]

XLVII

ᶜĀᵓISHA THE DAUGHTER OF ABŪ ᶜUTHMĀN SAᶜĪD B. ISMĀᶜĪL AL-ḤIRĪ OF NISHAPUR

Of all the children of Abū ᶜUthmān [al-Ḥīrī], ᶜĀᵓisha was the most ascetic and scrupulous. She was the best among them in her spiritual state and in conforming to the requirements of the moment.[141] She was also known for her prayers being answered.

I heard her daughter Umm Aḥmad bint ᶜĀᵓisha[142] say: My mother said to me: "Oh daughter, do not take pleasure in that which perishes, and do not anguish over that which vanishes. Rather, take pleasure in God, and be anxious about falling out of God's favor."

I also heard her say: My mother said to me: "Commit yourself to good conduct (*adab*) both outwardly and inwardly; for whenever one transgresses the bounds of conduct outwardly, he is punished outwardly, and whenever one transgresses the bounds of conduct inwardly, he is punished inwardly."

[As-Sulamī] said: ᶜĀᵓisha said: "When one feels lonely in his solitude, this is because of his lack of intimacy with his Lord."

She also said: "He who shows contempt for God's slaves shows his lack of knowledge of the Master. For he who loves the Craftsman glorifies the Craftsman's handiwork."

She died in the year 346/957–58.

141. As-Sulamī's student al-Qushayrī (fl. 438/1046) defined "the moment" (*al-waqt*) as follows: "The Sufi is 'the son of his moment.' In other words, he is only concerned with what concerns him in his present state, firmly maintaining what is required from him at the present moment" (idem, *ar-Risāla,* 55–56). In the tradition about ᶜĀᵓisha bint Abī ᶜUthmān given above, as-Sulamī similarly links the mastery of the moment to the maintenance of one's present state. For a detailed description of this concept see Gerhard Böwering, "Ideas of Time in Persian Sufism," in Lewisohn, ed., *Classical Persian Sufism,* 199–233.

142. On Umm Aḥmad, see section LXIII below.

(٤٧)

عائشة بنت أبي عثمان سعيد بن إسماعيل الحيري النّيسابوري

كانت من أزهدِ أولادِ أبي عُثمان وأورعِهم، وأحسَنِهم حالاً ووقتًا.

وكانت مُجابةَ الدّعوةِ.

سمعتُ ابنتها أمّ أحمد بنت عائشة تقول: قالت لي أمّي: يا ابنتي لا تفرحي بفاني [بفان]، ولاتجزعي من ذاهِب، وافرحي باللّه، واجزعي من سُقُوطِك عن عفواللّه.

وسمعتُها تقول: قالت لي أمّي: الْزَمي الأدَب ظاهراً وباطنًا، فما ساء أحدُ الأدب ظاهراً إلاّ عوقِب ظاهراً، وما ساء أحدُ الأدَب باطِنًا إلاّ عوقب باطنًا.

قال: وقالت عائشة: من استوحش بوحدتِه فذلك لقِلّةِ أنسِه بربِّه.

وقالت: من تهاونَ بالعبيد فهولقلّة معرفته بالسيِّد. فمن أحبّ الصّانعَ عظّم صُنعَهُ.

ماتت سنة ستّ وأربعين وثلاثمائة.

XLVIII

FĀṬIMA UMM AL-YUMN
The Wife of Abū ᶜAlī ar-Rūdhbārī[143]

Fāṭima was one of the greats. She was a master of spiritual states and the understanding of Sufi doctrine and was an eloquent speaker.

I heard one of our companions say: Fāṭima, the wife of Abū ᶜAlī ar-Rūdhbārī, used to say: "How could I not desire to obtain that which You [God] possess, since 'to You is my return [Qurᵓān 2 (*al-Baqara*), 156]?' How could I not love You, since whatever good I have comes only from You? And how can I not yearn for You, since You have made me yearn for You?"

It was also reported that she said: "No action benefits the slave as much as seeking one's sustenance from lawful sources."

Fāṭima also said: "The ascetic seeks his fortune because he seeks relief from seeking the world and its burdens and nothing more."

[As-Sulamī] said: Fāṭima went out of al-Fusṭāṭ[144] when the people were leaving to perform the Ḥajj pilgrimage. When the camels passed by her, she wept and cried, "Oh my weakness!" Then immediately thereafter she recited:

> I said: 'Do not interfere in my pursuit of your caravans,
> For I will be at your service as obediently as slaves are.'
>
> How is it that my predicament does not move the men,
> For they know that I have no recourse but through them?[145]

143. Abū ᶜAlī Aḥmad ibn Muḥammad b. al-Qāsim ar-Rūdhbārī (d. 322/934) was a native of Baghdad but lived and died in Egypt, where he introduced the doctrines of his teachers al-Junayd and an-Nūrī. He was said to have been of royal Persian descent. He was trained in the Law, proficient in hadith, and well-versed in the doctrines of Sufism. He said: "The seeker (*murīd*) is he who desires for himself naught but what God desires for him; the one who is sought (*murād*) desires nothing in the two worlds but God." See as-Sulamī, *Ṭabaqāt aṣ-ṣūfiyya,* 354–60; al-Qushayrī, *ar-Risāla,* 416–17; al-Iṣfahānī, *Ḥilyat al-awliyāᵓ,* vol. 10, 356–57; Ibn al-Jawzī, *Ṣifat aṣ-Ṣafwa,* vol. 2, 454–55. See also, Abdel-Kader, *al-Junayd,* 47; and al-Hujwirī, *The Kashf al-Maḥjūb,* 157.

144. The term *al-Miṣr,* given in the manuscript, was used since pre-Islamic times to refer to the populated areas of Egypt in the Nile valley. More specifically, it refers to the city of Old Cairo, then called al-Fusṭāṭ. Modern Cairo was founded by the Shi'ite Fatimid dynasty in 358/969.

145. This poem describes the frustration felt by Fāṭima Umm al-Yumn at being unable to perform the Ḥajj pilgrimage whenever she wished. As a woman, she could not go on the pilgrimage without the permission of her husband and could not travel in the pilgrims' caravan without a proper male escort. A hadith transmitted from the Prophet Muḥammad states: "A woman cannot travel for three days or more without the company of her father, her brother, her son, her husband, or her closest male relatives." Ibn Mājja, *Sunan,* vol. 2, 968.

(٤٨)

فاطمة أمّ اليمن
امرأة أبي علي الرّوذباري

وكانت من الأجلّة. صاحبة حال وفهم وكلام حسن.

سمعتُ بعض أصحابنا يقول: كانت فاطمة امرأة أبي علي الرّوذباري، تقول: كيف لا أرغب في تحصيل ما عندك وإليك مرجعي؟ وكيف لا أحبّك وما لقيتُ خيرا إلاّ منْكَ؟ وكيف لا أشتاق إليك وقد شوّقتني إليك؟.

وحكي عنها أنّها قالت: لا يَنْتَفِعُ العبدُ بشيء من أفعالِه كما يَنْتَفِعُ بطلَب قوتِه من حلال.

وقالت فاطمة: الزّاهد طالبُ حظّه؛ لأنّه يطلبُ الاستراحة من طلبِ الدّنيا وتعَبِها، لا غيرُ.

قال: وخرجَتْ يومًا من المصر وقْتَ خروج الحاجّ، والجمال تمرُّ بها، وهي تبكي وتقول: وا ضعفتاه ! وتنشُدُ على أثرِه.

فقلتُ دعوني واتِّباعي ركابكُم   أكُنْ طوْعَ أيديكم كما يفعل العبد
وما بالُ رغمي لا يهونُ عليهِم   وقد علِمُوا أن ليس لي منهُم بدُّ

Fāṭima also used to say: "If this is the sorrow of one who is prevented from reaching the House of God, imagine the sorrow of one who is prevented from attaining to Him!"

وتقول: هذه حسرةُ من انقطعَ عن الوصول إلى البيتِ، فكيف ترى حسْرةَ من انقطعَ عن الوصولِ إليه.

XLIX

ᶜAMRA OF FARGHANA

ᶜAmra was the unique one of her age in ethical conduct (*khuluq*), spiritual states (*ḥāl*), and clairvoyance (*firāsa*).

In Merv [a city in northern Khurasan], Abū Manṣūr Muḥammad ibn Aḥmad b. ᶜAbdān related that ᶜĀᵓisha, the wife of Aḥmad ibn [Muḥammad] as-Sarī[146] used to say: ᶜAmra al-Farghāniyya said: "The legacy of silence is wisdom and contemplation. One who accustoms himself to retreat in the pursuit of knowledge inherits intimacy with God without loneliness."

ᶜAmra said: "One who dedicates himself to the service of the actualized Sufis (*aḥrār*) and chivalrous youths (*fityān*) inherits glory and dignity in the eyes of mankind. It also leads him to divine guidance, and makes him attain the rank of the friends of God."

ᶜAmra was asked: "Is the way of the gnostic in harmony with the way of the ascetic?" She replied: "If the one who is alive is in harmony with the one who is dead, then the gnostic is in harmony with the ascetic!"

ᶜAmra was asked: "How did Moses (peace be upon him) know that what he heard was the speech of God Most High?" She said: "Because that speech annihilated all of his human characteristics, and afterwards made human discourse hateful to him."

146. Abū Bakr Aḥmad ibn Muḥammad as-Sarī (d. 352/963) was a Shi'ite (*rāfiḍī*) traditionist from Kufa. Sunni Muslims doubted the veracity of his reports because he would criticize the Companions of the Prophet Muḥammad. See as-Sulamī, *Ṭabaqāt aṣ-ṣūfiyya*, np. 109. ᶜAmra al-Farghāniyya would have been a contemporary of this individual. See also, section LII below.

(٤٩)

عمرةُ الفَرغَانِيـة

كانت واحدة وقتها، خلُقًا وحالاً وفراسةً.

سمعتُ أبا منصور محمد بن أحمد بن عبدان، بمرو، يقول: سمعتُ عائشة امرأة أحمد بن السرّي، تقول: قالت عمرة الفرغانية: ميراثُ الصّمت الحكمة والتّفكُـر. ومن أنِسَ بالخُلوة مع العِلم أورثَـه ذلك أُنسًا من غيرِ وحشةٍ.

وقالت عمرة: من خَدم الأحْرار والفتيان أورثه ذلك عزًا عندَ الخلق ومهابةً في أعْيُنِهِم، ودلّـهُ ذلك على رُشْدِهِ، وبلّغهُ درجاتِ الأولياءِ.

وسئلت عمرةُ: هل يُوافِقُ العَارِفُ الزّاهِد؟

فقالت: إن وافق الحيّ الميّت وافق العارف الزّاهد.

وسئلت: كيف عرف موسى عليه السّلام أنّ الذي يسمعه كلامُ اللّه تعالى؟

قالت: لأنّ ذلك الكلام أفنى عنه أوصافَه، وبغّض إليهِ بعد ذلك كلامَ الخلقِ.

L

ZUBDA AND MUḌGHA[147] (Essence and Embryo) The Sisters of Bishr ibn al-Ḥārith al-Ḥāfī (the Barefoot)[148]

Zubda and Muḍgha were both known for their states of scrupulousness and asceticism.

Aḥmad ibn Ḥanbal[149] said: "If one wants to know how far he is from the ways of the scrupulous, he should visit the sisters of Bishr al-Ḥāfī. He should listen to their counsel and observe their ways."

Zubda, the sister of Bishr, said: "The heaviest thing for the slave is sinfulness, and the lightest is repentence. So why does one not relinquish that which is heavy for that which is light?"

Muḍgha, the sister of Bishr, said to a client (*mawlā*) of her family who visited her: "How strange it is that you are not guided toward God, and are not seeking the way to Him!"

147. See also, *Ṣifat aṣ-Ṣafwa* Appendix section XV below. Bishr al-Ḥāfī also had a third sister named Mukhkha (Marrow).

148. Abū Naṣr Bishr ibn al-Ḥārith al-Ḥāfī (d. 226/840 or 227/841–42) was born in Merv and lived a life of celibacy and asceticism in Baghdad. He was a student of Yūsuf ibn Asbāṭ (d. 199/814–15), followed the legal school of Sufyān ath-Thawrī (d. 161/777–78), and had an ambiguous relationship with Aḥmad ibn Ḥanbal (see below). Abū Ṭālib al-Makkī mentions that Bishr was a specialist in jurisprudence and that Ibn Ḥanbal would refer questions about Sufi practice to him and his sisters. Although he is not specifically identified as such, Bishr may also be considered one of the founders of the *malāmatiyya*, the path of blame. He said that the Sufi should count it good fortune to be neglected by the public and have his true state concealed from them; for when people contend for superiority, it means ruin. The unusual names of his sisters follow the *malāmatī* pattern. See as-Sulamī, *Ṭabaqāt aṣ-ṣūfiyya,* 39-47; al-Qushayrī, *ar-Risāla,* 404–6; al-Iṣfahānī, *Ḥilyat al-awliyā*ʾ, vol. 8, 336–60; and Ibn al-Jawzī, *Ṣifat aṣ-Ṣafwa,* vol. 2, 325–36. See also, Smith, *An Early Mystic,* 79–80; al-Hujwirī, *The Kashf al-Maḥjūb,* 105-106; al-Makkī, *Qūt al-qulūb,* vol. 1, 131; Massignon, *Essay,* 159–60; and *EI*², vol. 1, 1244–46.

149. Aḥmad ibn Ḥanbal (d. 241/855) was a traditionist and jurist who is credited with founding the Ḥanbalī school of jurisprudence. He advocated a strict interpretation of the Qurʾān and Sunna and was opposed to many aspects of Sufi doctrine. However, he associated with a number of Sufis, including Bishr al-Ḥāfī, whose asceticism and scrupulousness he admired. See Smith, *An Early Mystic,* 80–81; and *EI*², vol. 1, 272–77. See also, al-Iṣfahānī, *Ḥilyat al-awliyā*ʾ, vol. 9, 161–233; and Ibn al-Jawzī, *Ṣifat aṣ-Ṣafwa,* vol. 2, 336–59.

(٥٠)

زُبدة ومُضغة

أختــا بشــر الحـافي

كانتا جميعًا من الورع والزّهد بحال.

قال أحمد بن حنبل: من أحَبّ أن يعرِفَ بُعْـدَهُ عن سُبُلِ الورعين فلْيَدْخُـلْ على أُختَـيْ بشر الحافي، ويَسْمَعْ من مسائِلهِـما، ويُبصِرْ طريقتَهما.

قـالت زبدة أخت بشـر: أثقلُ شئ على العَبْد الذنـوب، وأخـفّـه عليـه التّوبـة. فمالَـهُ لا يدفَـعُ أثقـلَ شـئ بأخفِّ شـئٍ.

وقـالت مضـغـة أخت بشر لمولاةٍ دخلت عليـها: أعْجَبُ ما فيكِ أنّكِ لا تهـتدين إلى اللّــه، ولستِ تَطلُبين الطّريق إليه !

LI

ᶜABDA AND ĀMINA[150]

The Sisters of Abū Sulaymān ad-Dārānī[151]

Both ᶜAbda and Āmina attained an exalted level of intellect (*ᶜaql*) and religious observance (*dīn*).

ᶜAbda, the sister of Abū Sulaymān [ad-Dārānī] said: "Asceticism bequeaths peacefulness in the heart, and generosity of spirit in respect to one's wealth."

ᶜAbda also said: "The intelligent person (*ᶜāqil*) is one who protects the interests of his brothers, not one who follows his brothers' desires."

Aḥmad ibn Abī al-Ḥawārī related that Abū Sulaymān [ad-Dārānī] said: I heard my sister Āmina say: "The Sufis (*fuqarāʾ*) are all dead, except for the one whom God revives through the glory of satisfaction with his portion in life (*qanāᶜa*) and contentment (*riḍā*) in his poverty (*faqr*)."[152]

150. See also, *Ṣifat aṣ-Ṣafwa* Appendix section XII below. ᶜAbda and Āmina flourished in the first half of the third/ninth century. Like their brother Abū Sulaymān ad-Dārānī, they lived in the region of Damascus.

151. See note 76 above.

152. In the context of early Sufism, poverty (*faqr*) meant both poverty in the material sense and emptiness for God's presence. It is important not to Christianize this concept by thinking only of the spiritual meaning of poverty in the Gospels, nor to anachronistically refer to the later Sufi meaning of the concept, which down-played the idea of material poverty. The majority of as-Sulamī's Sufi women were extreme ascetics by the standards of later generations. It was felt that their spiritual poverty was both reinforced and proven by their material austerities.

(٥١)

عبدة وآمنة
أختا أبي سُليمان الداراني

كانتا من العَقل والدّين بمحلٍّ عظيم.

قالت عبدة أختُ أبي سليمان: الزّهدُ يورِثُ الرّاحة في القلب، وسخَاء النّفس بالمال.

وقالت عبدة: العاقلُ من يحفَظُ صلاح إخوانِه، لا مَن يتبعُ مُرادَهُم.

وحكى أحمدُ بن أبي الحواري، عن أبي سليمان، قال: سمعتُ أختي آمنة تقول: الفقراءُ كُلُّهُم أمْواتٌ إلاّ من أحياهُ اللّه بِعِزِّ القناعة، والرّضا بفقْرِه.

LII

ᶜĀᵓISHA OF MERV
The Wife of Aḥmad ibn as-Sarī[153]

ᶜĀᵓisha visited Abū ᶜUthmān [al-Ḥīrī]. Then Abū ᶜUthmān invited her to stay with him in his house.[154]

I heard ᶜĀᵓisha say: "One who is not attentive to the first *takbīra*[155] of the congregational prayer is the least attentive to the prayer itself."

Abū Muḥammad said that he heard ᶜĀᵓisha say: "The intellect (*ᶜaql*) of the gnostic is the mirror of his heart (*qalb*); his heart is the mirror of his spirit (*nafs*); his soul (*rūḥ*) is the mirror of his intellect; his quintessence (*sirr*) is the mirror of his soul; divine acceptance (*tawfīq*) is the light of the mirror; and the sharpness of his insight (*baṣīra*) reveals to him the difference between error and correctness."

I heard Abū Manṣūr Muḥammad ibn Aḥmad b. ᶜAbdān al-Marwazī say that he heard ᶜĀᵓisha say: "I have never eaten a morsel that satisfied me unless it was in the company of a Sufi, or while following the way of a Sufi, or while watching a Sufi."

I also heard [Muḥammad ibn Aḥmad al-Marwazī] say that he heard ᶜĀᵓisha say: "Whenever one of the practitioners of Sufi chivalry (*fityān*) from anywhere seeks me out, I sense the light of his intention in my inner soul until he arrives. If I am successful in serving him and fulfilling his needs, that light becomes fully mine, but if I cut short my service to him, the light goes out."

153. On Aḥmad ibn Muḥammad as-Sarī, see note 146 above.

154. Since ᶜĀᵓisha was married to Aḥmad ibn as-Sarī, it would be very unusual for her to live apart from her husband, in the home of her Sufi shaykh, without a compelling reason to do so. Equally noteworthy is as-Sulamī's silence on the cause of her action. Could it have been that ᶜĀᵓisha, as a Sunni, rejected the Shiᶜite sympathies of her husband and considered him a heretic? As a noted scholar and religious figure, Abū ᶜUthmān al-Ḥīrī would have been able to act as her guardian (*wakīl*) in a case of separation for religious reasons.

155. The term *takbīra* refers to the phrase *Allāhu akbar* ("God is most great") which is recited at the beginning of the Muslim prayer.

(٥٢)

عائشة المروزية
امرأة أحمد بن السّري

دخلت على أبي عثمان، وأنزلها أبوعثمانَ في داره.

سمعتُ عائشة تقول: من لم يَحرِصْ على التّكبيرةِ الأولى في الجماعة فهوعلى الصّلاةِ أقَلُّ حِرْصًا.

سمعتُ أبا محمد يقول: سمعتُ عائشة تقول: عقلُ العارف مرآةُ قلبه، وقلبُهُ مرآةُ نفسه، وروحُهُ مرآةُ عقله، وسرُّهُ مرآةُ رُوحِه، والتّوفيقُ نورُ المرآة، ودقّةُ البصيرة في المِرآة يُظْهِرُ لَهُ الخطأ من الصّوابِ.

سمعتُ أبا منصور محمد بن أحمد بن عبدان المروزي، يقول: سمعتُ عائشة تقول: ما أكلتُ أكلةً قطّ أتهنّى بها إلاّ أكلةً مع فقيرٍ، أوفي مُتابعةِ فقير، أوفي مُشاهدتِهِ.

وسمعتُهُ يقول: سمعتُ عائشة تقول: ما قصدني أحدٌ من الفتيان من موضعٍ إلاّ وجدتُ في سِرّي نوراً بقصده، إلى أن يصلَ إليَّ. فإنْ وُفّقْتُ لخدمَته، والقيام بواجبه، تمّ لي ذلك النّورَ، وإن قصّرتُ في خدمتِه طفِئ ذلك النّورُ.

LIII

FĀṬIMA BINT AḤMAD IBN HĀNĪʾ

From Nishapur

Fāṭima was a companion of Abū ᶜUthmān [al-Ḥīrī][156] and spent much of her wealth on him and his companions.

Abū ᶜUthmān used to say: "Fāṭima's open-handedness towards the Sufis was the same as the open-handedness of the practitioners of Sufi chivalry (*fityān*). She never sought anything in return for it, neither from this world nor from the Hereafter."

Fāṭima asked Abū ᶜUthmān: "What is the way to the knowledge of God the Glorious and Mighty?" He replied: "Through complete forgetfulness of yourself and humankind, and through the renunciation of everything but God, until you attain the reality of the knowledge of God."

Fāṭima said: "The world is a snare for the insane. No one stumbles into it except he who has neither good sense (*ᶜaql*) nor good fortune (*tawfīq*)."

156. This information places Fāṭima in the first half of the fourth/tenth century.

(٥٣)

فاطمة بنت أحمد بن هانئ
نيسابورية

صحبت أبا عثمان فأنفقت عليه وعلى أصحابهِ مالا كثيراً.

وكان أبوعثمان يقول: إرفاق فاطمة للفقراء إرفاق الفِتيان، لا تطلُب به عِوضًا في الدّنيا والآخرة.

وسألت فاطمة أبا عثمان: كيف السّبيل إلى معرفة الّله عزّ وجلّ؟ فقال لها: بنسيانك نفسك والخلقِ، وإنكاركِ كلَّ شيءٍ سوى الّله، حتّى تبلُغي إلى حقيقةِ معرَفةِ الّلَه.

وقالت فاطمة: الدّنيا شبكة للحمقى، لا يقعُ فيها إلاّ من لا عقلَ لهُ ولا توفيقَ.

LIV

UMM ᶜABDALLĀH
The Wife of Abū ᶜAbdallāh as-Sijzī[157]

[As-Sulamī said]: I heard my grandfather say: I heard Umm ᶜAbdallāh say: "One who belittles the Sufis has neither ambition for God nor a true spiritual state."

I heard her say: "Being in the company of one's spiritual brethren in this world is the consolation for being in the abode of materiality."

[My grandfather] said that he heard her say: "Life is in meeting the person who opens your heart to encountering God and guides you toward the acceptance of God and the avoidance of the world and its people."

157. Abū ᶜAbdallāh as-Sijzī (d. 271/884–85) was one of the great shaykhs of Khurasan and a master of Sufi chivalry (*futuwwa*). He was a disciple of al-Junayd's student Abū Ḥafṣ al-Ḥaddād an-Nīsābūrī (d. 270/883–84). He said: "He who does not sanctify his knowledge does not sanctify his acts; he who does not sanctify his acts does not sanctify his body; he who does not sanctify his body does not sanctify his heart; he who does not sanctify his heart does not sanctify his intentions; all of Sufism is built on one's intentions." When asked the meaning of *futuwwa,* he said: "It means accepting the excuses of humankind and your own shortcomings; seeing their perfections and your imperfections; and having compassion for all creatures, in their goodness and evil. The perfection of *futuwwa* is that you not busy yourself with humankind at the expense of God, the Glorious and Mighty." See as-Sulamī, *Ṭabaqāt aṣ-ṣūfiyya,* 254–55; and al-Iṣfahānī, *Ḥilyat al-awliyāʾ,* vol. 10, 350–51.

(٥٤)

أمّ عبد اللّـــه

امرأة عبد اللّـــه السِّـجــزي

سمعتُ جدّي يقـــول: سمعـتُ أمّ عبد اللّـه تقول: من احتقـر الفُـقَـراء لايكون له همّةٌ باللّــه، ولا حالٌ صحيحا [صحيح].

وسمعتُها تقول: صُحْبـةُ الإخوان في الدّنيا نعيمُ دار الدّنيا.

قال: وسمعتُـها تقول: العيش في لقاء من شرح صـدرك بلقائه، ويدُلّـكَ على الإقبال على اللّـه، والإعراض عن الدّنيا وأهلِها.

LV

ḤABĪBA AL-ᶜADAWIYYA
From the Natives of Basra

Ḥabība was one of the great female gnostics.[158] Muḥammad ibn Aḥmad b. Saᶜīd ar-Rāzī reported from al-ᶜAbbās ibn Ḥamza through Aḥmad ibn Abī al-Ḥawārī that Abū Muḥammad al-Makkī related: When Ḥabība performed her nightly prayer, she would stand on the roof of her house. She would enfold herself tightly in her wrap, put her blouse under her veil, and say: "My God! The stars have set, everyone's eyes are closed, the rulers have locked the gates of the city, and every lover is alone with his beloved; this is when I devote myself to You."[159]

And just before dawn she would say: "The night has slipped away and the day is drawing near. If only You had accepted my worship, I would be at peace, or if You had reciprocated it, I would be consoled. Upon Your glory! Thus shall persist my devotion and Your devotion as long as You allow me to remain alive. Even if You were to drive me away from Your door, I would not leave, because my heart has become aware of Your kindness and generosity!"

158. The following *isnād* indicates that Ḥabība al-ᶜAdawiyya lived in the first part of the third/ninth century. She most likely belonged to the generation after Rābiᶜa al-ᶜAdawiyya.

159. This passage is similar to a tradition recounted in the Andalusian Sufi Abū Madyan's *Bidāyat al-murīd,* where God speaks of His worshippers to the Prophet David: "When night falls, when darkness overcomes [the light], when the bedcovers are spread out, when the family is at rest, and when every lover is left [alone] with his beloved—then they arise, pointing their feet toward Me, turning their faces to Me, and speak intimate words, adoring Me by virtue of My grace" Vincent J. Cornell ed. and trans., *The Way of Abū Madyan: Doctrinal and Poetic Works of Abū Madyan Shuᶜayb ibn al-Ḥusayn al-Anṣārī (c. 509/1115–16–594/1198)* (Cambridge, 1996), 74. The original version of this tradition can be found in al-Makkī, *Qūt al-qulūb,* vol. 2, 60.

(٥٥)

حبيبة العدوية

من كبار العارفات. وكانت من أهل البصرة.

أخبرنا محمد بن أحمد بن سعيد الرّازي، قال: حدّثنا العبّاس بن حمزة، حدّثنا أحمد بن أبي الحواري، قال: حدّثنا أبومحمد المكّي، قال: كانت حبيبة إذا صلت العتمة قامت على السّطح وشدّت مئزرها، وبدرعها في خمارها، وتقول: إلهي، غارت النّجوم، ونامت العيون، وغلّقت الملوك أبوابَها، وخلا كلّ حبيبٍ بحبِيبِه، وهذا مقامي بين يديك.

وإذا كان السّحَر قالت: إلهي، هذا اللّيل قد أدبر، وهذا النّهار قد أقبل، فليت شعري، قبلتَ منّي فأُهنى، أم رددتها فأُعزّى؟ وعِزّتك، لهذا دأبي ودأبُكَ أبداً ما أبقَيْتَني، لوانتَهَرْتَني من بابكَ ما بَرِحتُ، لما وقع في قلبي من جُودِك وكرمِكَ.

LVI

FĀṬIMA OF DAMASCUS

Fāṭima was unique in her age. She used to rebuke the Sufi shaykhs. I heard ᶜAlī ibn Aḥmad of Tarsus[160] say: When Abū al-Ḥasan al-Mālikī entered Damascus, he lectured at the Umayyad mosque of Damascus and spoke well. Fāṭima attended his session and said to him: "Oh, Abū al-Ḥasan! You spoke very eloquently, and you have perfected the art of rhetoric. Have you perfected the art of silence?" Abū al-Ḥasan became silent, and did not utter a word after that.

160. Abū Bakr ᶜAlī ibn Aḥmad aṭ-Ṭarsūsī (d. 364/974–75) was a Sufi traditionist who was a source for both as-Sulamī and Abū Naṣr as-Sarrāj (d. 378/988–89), the author of *Kitāb al-lumaᶜ*. He was from the Syrian city of Tarsus and died in Mecca. See Abū Naṣr as-Sarrāj, *Kitāb al-lumaᶜ fi'l-Taṣawwuf,* R. A. Nicholson, ed. (London, 1963 reprint of 1914 first edition), xxi.

(٥٦)

فاطمة الدّمشقية

كانت واحدة وقتها.

وكانت تتناكر على المشايخ.

سمعتُ علي بن أحمد الطّرسوسي يقول: لمّا دخل أبوالحسين المالكي دمشق تكلّم في جامع دمشق، وأحسن الكلام. فحضرتْ مجلسَهُ فاطمة، وقالت له: يا أبا الحسن: تكلّمت فأحسَنْتَ، وأنت تُحسِنُ أن تتكلّمَ، هل تُحْسِنُ أن تسْكُتَ؟ فسكت أبوالحسن، ولم يتكلّم بَعد ذلك.

LVII

FUṬAYMA
The Wife of Ḥamdūn al-Qaṣṣār[161]

Fuṭayma attained a high rank in her spiritual state and was very highly regarded.

It was reported that Fuṭayma said: "The ethical rules of the Sufi in his relationship with others include: When a person seeks him he accepts him; when a person is away from him he does not forget about him; when a person associates with him he shapes his conduct; and when a person refuses to asssociate with him he will not force him to be his companion."

Fuṭayma was asked about the sage (*al-ᶜāqil*). She said: "The sage is he who revives your heart when you sit with him."

Fuṭayma also said: "When a person truly knows himself, his only characteristic is servitude (*ᶜubūdiyya*),[162] and he takes pride in nothing but his Master."

Fuṭayma also said: "The fulfillment of the heart is in rejection of the world and the destruction of the heart is in reliance on humankind."

Fuṭayma also said: "When one reflects on the bestowal of God's bounties upon him, maintaining his gratitude for them should preoccupy him from everything else."

161. Abū Ṣāliḥ Ḥamdūn ibn Aḥmad b. ᶜAmmāra al-Qaṣṣār (d. 271/884) introduced the *malāmatiyya* to Nishapur. He was an expert in both theology and jurisprudence and followed the legal school of Sufyān ath-Thawrī. He was asked to preach to the people of Nishapur but refused, saying: "My heart is still attached to the world, so my words will make no impression on the hearts of others. To speak unprofitable words is to despise theology and deride the sacred Law. Speech is permissible to him alone whose silence is injurious to religion, and whose speaking would remove the injury." According to al-Hujwirī, a Sufi sect known as the Qaṣṣārīs continued to follow Ḥamdūn's way after his death. See al-Hujwirī, *The Kashf al-Maḥjūb,* 125–26, 183–84; and Sviri, "Ḥakīm Tirmidhī and the *Malāmatī* Movement," 596–99. See also, as-Sulamī, *Ṭabaqāt aṣ-ṣūfiyya,* 123–29; al-Qushayrī, *ar-Risāla,* 426; al-Iṣfahānī, *Ḥilyat al-awliyāᵓ,* vol. 10, 231–32; Ibn al-Jawzī, *Ṣifat aṣ-Ṣafwa,* vol. 4, 122–23

162. Literally, the Arabic word *ᶜubūdiyya* means "slavery." It describes the state of being a slave (*ᶜabd*) of God. When used by the Sufis, it may also refer to service, as when the virtues of pious behavior are seen as one's service to the Lord. In the value system of the premodern Islamic world, the relationships between master and slave, master and servant, and master and disciple were often culturally intertwined.

(٥٧)

فُطيمة

امرأة حمدون القصّار

كانت كبيرة الحال، عظيمة القدر.

حكي عن فطيمة أنّها قالت: من أخلاق الصّوفي في المُعاشرة: أنّ مَنْ قصَدَهُ قبِلَهُ، ومن غاب عنهُ لا يفتقِدُه، ومن عاشره تخلّق معه، ومن كره عشرتَهُ لم يُجبرهُ على صُحْبَتِهِ.

وسئلت فُطيمة عن العاقل: قالت: من يحيا قلبُكَ بمُجالستِهِ.

وقالت فُطيمة: من عرف نفسَهُ لم يَتّسِمْ إلاّ بالعبُودية، ولا يفتخِرُ إلاّ بمولاهُ.

وقالت فُطيمة: عِمارةُ القلب بالإعراض عن الدّنيا، وخرابُ القلب بالاستعانة بالخلق.

وقالت فُطيمة: من أبصرَ نِعَمَ اللهِ عليه شَغَلَهُ القيامُ بشكرها عن كلّ شيءٍ.

LVIII

AMAT ALLĀH[163] AL-JABALIYYA

Amat Allāh was from the mountains of Damaghan [south of the Caspian Sea in northern Iran] and a village called Nūqābadh. Her husband was ᶜAbdallāh al-Jabalī. He was a companion of Abū Yazīd al-Bisṭāmī.[164] She was known for signs of sanctity and miracles. She was also clairvoyant (*ṣāḥiba firāsāt*). Her village was one parasang [a pre-Islamic Persian measure of distance—about three and and a half miles] from Bisṭām.

She used to inform her husband through her clairvoyance about Abū Yazīd and his actions. She would say: "At this moment Abū Yazīd is doing this or that."

[As-Sulamī] said: Once ᶜAbdallāh al-Jabalī visited Abū Yazīd and informed him of Amat Allāh's clairvoyance. Abū Yazīd was sitting on his stool and making his ablution. Then Abū Yazīd took a piece of white cloth, wetted it, and slapped it down on the stool. He said to ᶜAbdallāh: "Tell your wife to inform you of this if she is really truthful and ask her what is on the stool." As soon as ᶜAbdallāh left, Abū Yazīd removed the white cloth from the stool. When ᶜAbdallāh arrived home and asked the woman about what Abū Yazīd had told him, she said, "There is nothing there." ᶜAbdallāh said, "Now I know that she is a liar!"

Abū Yazīd intended by this to veil her from her husband.

I heard ᶜAlī ibn Muḥammad report from Muḥammad ibn ᶜAlī that Abū ᶜImrān related that he heard Abū Yazīd say: "My attention was on ᶜAbdallāh but it was brought to fruition in his wife."

This woman also said to her husband ᶜAbdallāh: "What would you say if your Lord asks you tomorrow, 'With what did you return to Me?'" He replied, "I would say to Him, 'I trusted in You to provide this fried bread." She said: "I would be ashamed of myself before God Most High to answer His question with fried bread!"

163. This is the feminine form of the name *ᶜAbdallāh* (Slave of God).

164. This information indicates that Amat Allāh and her husband flourished around the end of the third/ninth century.

(٥٨)

أمة اللّـه الجبلية

كانت من جبال دامغان، من قرية يقال لها: نوقابذ. وهي امرأة عبد اللّـه الجبلي، صاحب أبي يزيد البسطامي. كانت لها آيات وكرامات. وكانت صاحبة فراسات. وقريتها على فرسخ من بسطام.

وكانت تخبر زوجها عن أبي يزيد، وعن أفعاله وتقول: أبويزيد الساعة يفعل كذا وكذا.

قال: فقدمِ مرّةً على أبي يزيد، فأخبرَهُ بذلك. وكان أبويزيد على كرسيّه يتوضّأ، فأخذَ أبويزيد بياضا فبلّه وضرب به على كرسيّه، وقال له: قُل لها إن كانت صادقة تُخْبرُ بذلك، وإيشٍ [أيّ شئ] على الكرسي. فلمّا خرج عبد اللّـه أخذ أبويزيد البياضَ من الكرسي. فجاء عبد اللّـه فسأل المرأةَ عن ذلك، فقالت: ليس هناك شئ. قال عبد اللّـه: الآن علمتُ أنّها كاذبِة.

وأراد أبويزيد بذلك أن يستُرَها عن زوجها.

سمعتُ علي بن محمد، يقول: سمعتُ محمد بن علي، يقول: سمعتُ أبا عمران يقول: سمعتُ أبا يزيد يقول: كانت همّتي في عبد اللّـه فظهرت في امرأته.

وقالت هذه المرأة لزوجها عبد اللّـه: إنْ قال لك ربُّك غداً: بأيشٍ [بأيّ شئٍ] رجعت إليّ؟ فقال: أقول له: كنتُ أثقُ بك في أمْرِ هذا الرّغيف. فقالت: إنّي أستحيي من اللّـه تعالى أن أجيبَه عنَ سؤالِه برغيف.

LIX

QUSAYMA THE WIFE OF ABŪ YAᶜQŪB OF TINNĪS[165]

Qusayma was one of the greatest practitioners of female chivalry (*min kibār an-niswān*) in her day. She was a companion of Abū ᶜAbdallāh ar-Rūdhbārī[166] and other Sufi shaykhs who were even greater than him.

I heard ᶜAlī ibn Aḥmad of Tarsus say: One day Abū ᶜAbdallāh ar-Rūdhbārī came to Qusayma's house. When he saw that the door was locked, he said to his companions, "Break the lock!" so they broke it. Then Abū ᶜAbdallāh entered the house and said, "Take everything that is in it!" So they took everything that was in the house, including the cooking-pots and the porcelain dishes. Then they sold the contents of the house, bought food from the proceeds, and sat down for an invocation session.

When [Qusayma's husband] Abū Yaᶜqūb returned, he entered the house and saw that nothing was there. However, he showed little concern and sat down.

After a while Qusayma came. Her husband greeted her and said, "Shaykh Abū ᶜAbdallāh took everything and emptied the house!"

She came in and joined the middle of the circle of invocation. She was wearing a walnut-brown garment from Basra. She took it off and placed it in front of the Sufis, and then went back into the house. Abū Yaᶜqūb said to her, "The only thing we had left was what you were wearing, and you just gave it away to them!" She said, "Oh, wet-eyed one! When someone like Shayh Abū ᶜAbdallāh ar-Rūdhbārī delights us with his presence, do we keep anything for ourselves after that?"

165. Tinnīs is a town on the eastern edge of the Nile Delta in Egypt.

166. Abū ᶜAbdallāh Aḥmad ibn ᶜAṭāʾ ar-Rūdhbārī (d. 369/979–80) was the nephew (son of the sister) of Abū ᶜAlī ar-Rudhbārī. He lived and died at Ṣūr (Tyre) in the south of present-day Lebanon. For information on his mother Fāṭima bint Aḥmad, see section LXI below. See also as-Sarrāj, *Kitāb al-lumaᶜ*, xviii–xix.

(٥٩)

قسيمة

امرأة يعقوب التِّنِّيسي

وكانت من كبار النّسوان في وقتها. صحبت أبا عبد اللّه الرّوذباري، ومَنْ فَوقَهُ من المشايخ.

سمعتُ علي بن أحمد الطرسوسي، يقول: جاء أبوعبد اللّه الرّوذباري يومًا إلى بيت قُسَيْمَة. فرأى الباب مقفولا، فقال: اكسروا القفل، فكسّروا. فدخل أبوعبد اللّه البيت، فقال: خذوا كلّ ما فيه، فأخذوا كلّ ما فيه، حتّى القدر والخزف، فباعوه وأخذوا طعاما، وقعدوا للسّماع.

فجاء أبويعقوب، فدخل البيت، فلم ير شيئًا، فتغيّر قليلاً ثمّ قَعَد.

وجاءت قُسيمة بعد ساعة. فاستقبلها زوجُها، وقال: الشيخُ أبوعبد اللّه، وقد أخذ كلّ ما في البيتٍ، وفرّغ البيت!

فجاءت ودخلت وسط الحلقة وعليها كساء جوزيّ بصريّ، فطرحته فيما بينهم. ودخلت البيت. فقال لها أبويعقوب: لم يكن لنا إلاّ ما عليك، فطرحتيه إليهم!

فقالت: يا سخين العين، ينبسط علينا مثل الشيخ أبي عبد اللّه الروذباري، فنُبْقى لأنفسِنا بعد ذلك شيئًا؟

LX

MARHĀ᾿ OF NISIBIS[167]

Marhā᾿ was a companion of Abū ᶜAlī ibn al-Kātib,[168] Abū ᶜAbdallāh ibn Jāmār, Abū Bakr ad-Duqqī,[169] Abū al-Ḥusayn al-Baṣrī,[170] Abū ᶜAbdallāh ar-Rūdhbārī, and ᶜAyyāsh ibn ash-Shāᶜir (Son of the Poet). She was comparable to al-Wahaṭiyya in spiritual rank.[171]

She used to say: "Poverty is a garment of glory when the Sufi attains realization through it."

167. Nisibis is a town in northern Mesopotamia, between the Euphrates and Tigris rivers. In pre-Islamic times it occupied the border between the Byzantine and Persian empires. See J. B. Drury, *History of the Later Roman Empire from the Death of Theodosius I to the Death of Justinian* (New York, 1958), vol. 2, 94 and 122.

168. Abū ᶜAlī al-Ḥasan ibn Aḥmad b. al-Kātib (d. 345/956–57) was one of the great Egyptian Sufis of his time. He was a disciple of Abū ᶜAlī ar-Rūdhbārī and advocated complete withdrawal from the world for the sake of God. He said: "The aroma of the breeze of love emanates from the lovers. Even if they conceal it, its traces are apparent on them, and even if they hide it, it reveals who they are." See as-Sulamī, *Ṭabaqāt aṣ-ṣūfiyya,* 386–88; al-Qushayrī, *ar-Risāla,* 426; al-Iṣfahānī, *Ḥilyat al-awliyā᾿,* vol. 10, 360; and Ibn al-Jawzī, *Ṣifat aṣ-Ṣafwa,* vol. 4, 323.

169. Abū Bakr Muḥammad ibn Dāwūd ad-Dīnawarī ad-Duqqī (d. 359/970) was originally from Dīnawār in Khurasan, but resided in Baghdad and settled in Damascus, where he died. He discoursed on the difference between poverty and Sufism. He said: "Poverty is but one of the Sufi states. The true Sufi occupies himself with everything that is most important to him other than his own soul; he is thus protected from performing blameworthy acts." He was a major source of Sufi traditions for as-Sarrāj. See idem, *Kitāb al-lumaᶜ*, xvi. See also, as-Sulamī, *Ṭabaqāt aṣ-ṣūfiyya,* 448–50; and al-Qushayrī, *ar-Risāla,* 412.

170. This is probably Abū al-Ḥasan ᶜAlī ibn Ibrāhīm al-Ḥuṣrī al-Baṣrī (d. 371/981–82). He was a native of Basra but lived in Baghdad, where he was a disciple of the famous ecstatic Sufi Abū Bakr ash-Shiblī (d. 334/946). He was considered the paramount shaykh of his time in Baghdad and was a noted poet. See as-Sulamī, *Ṭabaqāt aṣ-ṣūfiyya,* 489–93; and al-Qushayrī, *ar-Risāla,* 406.

171. See section LXVII below. The list of Marhā᾿ an-Naṣībiyya's Sufi associates indicates that she traveled widely, from Iraq to Syria and Egypt.

(٦٠)

مرهاء النّصيبية

صحبت أبا علي بن الكاتب، وأبا عبد اللّـه بن جامار، وأبا بكر الدُّقّـي، وأبا الـحسين البَصري وأبا عبد اللّـه الروذباري، وعيّاش بن الشاعر.

وكانت هي تُباهي الوهطية.

وكانت تقول: الفقر لباسُ عِزٍّ إذا تحقّق الفقيرُ فيـه.

LXI

FĀṬIMA BINT AḤMAD
The Mother of Abū ᶜAbdallāh ar-Rūdhbārī[172]

Fāṭima was the sister of Abū ᶜAlī ar-Rūdhbārī. She was one of the greatest practitioners of female chivalry (*niswān*) and was also a gnostic (*min al-ᶜārifāt*).

She used to say: "My son Abū ᶜAbdallāh is not a Sufi. Instead, he is a righteous man (*rajul ṣāliḥ*). But my brother Abū ᶜAlī[173] is a real Sufi."

She was also known for her signs of sanctity and miracles.

172. Although the manuscript states that Fāṭima was the wife (lit. "woman") of Abū ᶜAbdallāh ar-Rūdhbārī, this is clearly a mistake, probably made by the copyist. It is well-established that Abū ᶜAbdallāh ar-Rūdhbārī's mother was the sister of Abū ᶜAlī ar-Rūdhbārī.

173. "My brother Abū ᶜAbdallāh" in the original manuscript must also be a copyist's error.

(٦١)

فاطمة بنت أحمد

امرأة أبي عبد اللّه الروذباري

وكانت أخت أبي علي الرّوذباري. وكانت من كبار النّسوان. ومن العارفات.

وكانت تقول: ابني أبوعبد اللّه ليس بصوفي، إنّما هورجل صالح. وكان أخي أبوعبد اللّه صوفيا.

ولها آيات وكرامات.

LXII

MAYMŪNA[174]
The Sister of Ibrāhīm al-Khawwāṣ[175]

Maymūna was the half-sister of Ibrāhīm al-Khawwāṣ from his mother. She was under [i.e., married to] Ḥāmid al-Aswad (the Black).

I heard Abū Bakr ar-Rāzī report from Jaᶜfar al-Khuldī that Ibrāhīm al-Khawwāṣ related: My sister, who was married to Ḥāmid al- Aswad, said to me: "I lost my respect for my husband Ḥāmid after I saw him entering the mosque and sitting down without performing the prayer of respect for the mosque."[176]

I heard Muḥammad ibn ᶜAbdallāh report that Abū al-Khayr al-Aqṭaᶜ[177] related: Ibrāhīm al-Khawwāṣ visited his sister Maymūna, who was his half-sister from his mother, and said to her, "Today, I feel a tightness in my chest." She replied: "When one's heart is constricted, the world and what is in it also becomes constricted. Did you not notice that God Most High has said: 'To such a degree that the Earth seemed constricted for them, for all its spaciousness, and their very souls seemed straitened to them' [Qurᵓān 9 (*at-Tawba*), 118]? They had plenty of room on the Earth, but when their souls became constricted then the world and all that was in it became constricted too."

174. See also, Ibn al-Jawzī, *Ṣifat aṣ-Ṣafwa,* vol. 2, 527. Ibn al-Jawzī transmits one tradition that is not reported here: Aḥmad ibn Sālim said: Someone knocked on the door of Ibrāhīm al-Khawwāṣ. "Who do you want?" asked his sister. "Ibrāhīm al-Khawwāṣ," he replied. "He has left," she said. "When will he return?" the caller asked. "If somone's soul is in the hands of another," she answered, "who could know when he will return?"

175. Abū Isḥāq Ibrāhīm al-Khawwāṣ (d. 291/904), originally from the royal town of Sāmarrā, north of Baghdad, was a companion of al-Junayd and a disciple of Abū ᶜAbdallāh al-Maghribī (d. 299/911-12). He is one of the early masters of *tawakkul,* the complete reliance on the will of God. He said: "*Tawakkul* has three degrees: patience in the face of adversity, satisfaction with what God provides, and love for God." See as-Sulamī, *Ṭabaqāt aṣ-ṣūfiyya,* 284–87; al-Qushayrī, *ar-Risāla,* 411; al-Iṣfahānī, *Ḥilyat al-awliyāᵓ,* vol. 10, 325–26; Ibn al-Jawzī, *Ṣifat aṣ-Ṣafwa,* vol. 4, 98–102. See also, al-Hujwirī, *The Kashf al-Maḥjūb,* 153–54.

176. This account, along with the above tradition related by Ibn al-Jawzī, implies that Maymūma may have divorced her husband and gone to live with her brother.

177. Abū al-Khayr al-Aqtaᶜ (d. 340/952) was originally from North Africa, but lived in at-Tīnāt, on the Syrian coast near Antioch. He was known for clairvoyance and other miracles, and was a master of *tawakkul.* He was called "al-Aqṭaᶜ" (The Amputated One) because his right hand was amputated when he was falsely accused of belonging to a gang of thieves. See as-Sulamī, *Ṭabaqāt aṣ-ṣūfiyya,* 370–72; al-Qushayrī, *ar-Risāla,* 394; al-Iṣfahānī, *Ḥilyat al-awliyāᵓ,* vol. 10, 377–78; Ibn al-Jawzī, *Ṣifat aṣ-Ṣafwa,* vol. 4, 282–85.

(٦٢)

ميمونة
أخت إبراهيم الـخوّاص

وكانت أخته لأمّه. وكانت تحت حامد الأسود.

سـمعتُ أبا بكر الرّازي يقـول: سـمعتُ جعـفر الـخُـلـدي، يقول: سـمعتُ إبراهيم الـخواص، يقول: قالت لي أختي -- وكانت تحت حامد الأسود --: ما احـتـشـمتُ من زوجي حـامد، بعد مـا رأيتـه يدخُلُ الـمسـجدَ ويقـعُدُ، ولا يُصلي تحيّـةَ الـمسجدِ.

سمعتُ محمد بن عبد اللـّه، يقول: سمعتُ أبا الـخير الأقطع، يقول: دخل إبراهيم الـخواص على أخته ميمونه -- وكانت أختَه لأمّه -- وقـال لها: إنّي اليومَ ضيّقُ الصّدر.

فـقالت: من ضـاق قلبُـه ضاقت عليـه الدّنيا بما فـيـهـا، ألا ترى أنّ اللّــه تعـالى يقـول:«حـتّى إذا ضـاقت عليـهم الأرضُ بما رحُـبَتْ وضـاقت عليـهم أنفُسُهُم.»

لقد كان لـهم في الأرض مُتّسَعٌ، ولكن لـمّا ضاقت عليـهم أنفسُهُم ضاقت عليهم الدّنيا بما فيها.

LXIII

UMM AḤMAD BINT ᶜĀʾISHA
The Grand Daughter of Abū ᶜUthmān al-Ḥīrī[178]

Umm Aḥmad remained inside her home for fifty years and never left her house. She was unique in her age and was known for her spiritual motivation (*himma*), her spiritual state (*ḥāl*), and her moral conduct (*khuluq*).

I heard her say: "Knowledge (*ᶜilm*) is the life of humanity, spiritual practice (*ᶜamal*) is its conveyance, intellect (*ᶜaql*) is its ornament, and gnosis (*maᶜrifa*) is its illumination and insight."

She also said: "All actions are defective. The only one who fully knows the defects of his soul is one who has been freed of all defects."

She also said: "If one is satisfied with the defects of one's soul and does not cure them with the right cure, God will bequeath to him false pretenses."

178. In the manuscript Umm Aḥmad is mistakenly listed as the daughter of Abū ᶜUthmān al-Ḥīrī. See section XLVII above. As his grand daughter, she would have flourished in the first half of the fourth/tenth century.

(٦٣)

أمّ أحمد بنت عائشة
بنت أبي عثمان الحِيري

لزمت البيت خمسين سنةً، لم تخرُجْ من بيتِها. وكانت واحدةَ وقتِها: همّةً وحالاً وخُلُقًا.

سمعتُها تقول: العلمُ حياةُ الخلق، والعملُ مطيّتُه، والعقلُ زينتُه، والمعرفةُ نورُهُ وبصيرتُهُ.

وقالت: الأفعال كلّها معيوبةٌ. ولا يعرف عيوبَ نفسِه إلاّ المبرّءون من العيوب.

وقالت: من رضِيَ بعيُوب نفسِه ولم يُداوها بدَوائِها أورثَهُ اللّه الدّعاوي الباطلة.

LXIV

ᶜAWNA OF NISHAPUR

ᶜAwna was an emaciated ascetic and was extreme in her self-denial. It was said that her prayers were answered.

I heard Abū Aḥmad al-Ḥasnawī say: I heard ᶜAwna say: "I repent my prayers and my fasting as the fornicator repents his fornication and the thief repents his theft."[179]

179. This tradition indicates that ᶜAwna lived in the generation before as-Sulamī, at the end of the fourth/tenth century.

(٦٤)

عونة النّيسابورية

كانت زاهدة صفيقة، وكثيرة المجاهدات. كان يُقالُ: إنّها مُجابةُ الدعوةِ.

سمعتُ أبا أحمد الحسنوي، يقول: سمعتُ عونة تقول: أنا أتوبُ من صلاتي وصِيَامي، كما يَتُوبُ الزّاني من زناهُ، والسّارق من سَرِقتِه.

LXV

AMAT AL-ᶜAZĪZ[180]

Also Known as Hawra (the Foolhardy)

Hawra was one of the female Sufis (*aṣ-ṣūfiyyāt*), gnostics (*al-ᶜārifāt*), and masters of spiritual states (*arbāb al-aḥwāl*). She was one of the most altruistic practitioners of female chivalry in her day (*min aftā waqtihā fī an-niswān*).

I heard Abū Naṣr ibn Abī Isḥāq b. Abī Bishr b. Mārawayh say: A woman visited Hawra. The woman was wearing a *jubba* [a long outer garment, open in the front, with wide sleeves] and a blouse made of wool. Hawra said to her: "The person who wears wool must be the purest person of his age, the best person in morals, the noblest of humankind in his actions, the sweetest person in his nature, the most generous of them in spirit, and the most open-handed in his liberality. Just as he is distinguished from humanity in general by his clothing, he must also be distinguished from them in his spiritual characteristics."

180. *Amat al-ᶜAzīz* is the feminine form of *ᶜAbd al-ᶜAzīz* (Slave of the Glorious). This person should not be confused with the famous philanthropist, Amat al-ᶜAzīz (d. 216/831), the wife of the ᶜAbbasid caliph Hārūn ar-Rashīd. Also known as Zubayda, she was originally the slave of ar-Rashīd's father al-Hādī (r. 169–70/785–86) and distinguished herself by building roads, wells, and even a school for women in the city of Mecca. Zubayda was an associate of the jurist Sufyān ath-Thawrī (d. 161/777–78) and the Sufi Bahlūl al-Majnūn and was said to have kept a hundred slave-girls whose sole occupation was chanting the Qur'ān in successive relays. See Nabia Abbot, *Two Queens of Baghdad: Mother and Wife of Hārūn al-Rashīd* (Chicago, 1946), 137–264.

(٦٥)

أمةُ العزيز

المعروفة بهورة

كانت إحدى الصّوفيات والعارفات، وأرباب الأحوال. وكانت من أفتى وقتها في النّسوان.

سمعتُ أبا نصر بن أبي اسحاق بن أبي بشر بن مارويه، يقول: دخلت امرأة عليها، وعليها جُبّة صوف وقميص صوف. فقالت لها: من لبس الصّوف يجب أن يكون أصفى النّاس وقتًا، وأحسنَ النّاس خُلُقًا، وأكرمَ الخلق حركةً، وأعذبَ النّاس طبعًا، وأسخاهم يداً، كما تمَيّز عن الخلق بلِباسِهِ، كذلك يتميّزُ عنهم بأوصافِهِ.

LXVI

QURASHIYYA OF NASĀ[181]

Qurashiyya was one of the greatest of those called to God. She experienced sudden spiritual states (*ṣāḥibat aḥwāl*).

It was reported that she said: "God Most High has created heaven for those who worship Him and fear Him, not for those who disobey Him and put worldly hopes in Him."

It was also reported that she said: "Enduring silence is easier than making excuses for lies."

One day she said to [Abū al-Qāsim] an-Naṣrābādhī:[182] "How fine are your words and how ugly are your morals!"

It was reported that one day an-Naṣrābādhī said to her, "Be quiet!" She replied, "I will be quiet when you are quiet!"

On another day an-Naṣrābādhī said to her, "Don't attend my teaching sessions!" She replied, "We won't come if you don't invite us!"

Qurashiyya said: "Nothing drives me crazy like doubts. If I had attained the realization of anything, I would have become silent. My fires would have been extinguished, and God's blessings would have been revealed in me."

181. See also, section LXXVIII below where Qurashiyya is called "Jumᶜa bint Aḥmad ibn Muḥammad b. ᶜUbayd Allāh, known as Umm al-Ḥusayn al-Qurashiyya." She was also called "al-Maḥmiyya al-ᶜUthmāniyya" because her family (the Maḥmīs) were descended from the third caliph of Islam, ᶜUthmān ibn ᶜAffān (r. 23–35/644–56). The Maḥmīs were one of the most important families of Shāfiᶜite jurists in Nishapur. See Richard W. Bulliet, *The Patricians of Nishapur: A Study in Medieval Islamic Social History* (Cambridge, Massachusetts, 1972), 91–92.

182. Abū al-Qāsim Ibrāhīm ibn Muḥammad an-Naṣrābādhī (d. 367/977–78) was as-Sulamī's spiritual master. He was learned in many disciplines, including sacred biography (*siyar*) and history. Al-Hujwirī said: "He was like a king in Nishapur, save that the glory of kings is in this world, while his was in the next world." He was a companion of Abū ᶜAlī ar-Rūdhbārī and Abū Bakr ash-Shiblī (d. 334/946) and discoursed on the Divine Realities. He resided in Nishapur between the years 340/951 and 365/976. Later, he moved to Mecca, where he died. See as-Sulamī, *Ṭabaqāt aṣ-ṣūfiyya,* 484–88; and al-Hujwirī, *The Kashf al-Maḥjūb,* 159–60. See also, Bulliet, *Patricians of Nishapur,* 150.

(٦٦)

قُرشية النّسوية

كانت من المدعيات [المدعوات] الكبار، وكانت صاحبة أحوال ٍ.

حكي عنها أنّها قالت: خلق اللّهُ تعالى الجنّة لمن يعبُدُهُ ويخافُهُ، لا لِمَنْ يعصيه [يعصاه] ويتمنّى عليه.

وحكي عنها أنّها قالت: مُكابدة الصّمت أيْسَرُ من اعتذا رٍ بِكَذِبٍ.

وقالت يومًا للنّصراباذي: ما أحْسَنَ أقوالَكَ وأوْحَشَ أخلاقَكَ !

وحُكي أنّ النّصراباذي قال لها يومًا: اسْكُتِي. فقالت: اسكُتْ حتّى أسْكُتَ.

وقال لها يوما: لا تحضُري. فقالت: لا تَدْعُنَا حتّى لا نحضُرك.

وقالت قُرشية: ما هيّمَتْني إلاّ الظّنون. لوتحقّقتُ في شئٍ لخَرسْتُ وخمدتُ، وظهرت عليّ بركاتُهُ.

LXVII

AL-WAHAṬIYYA UMM AL-FAḌL

Al-Wahaṭiyya was unique in her age in her speech, her knowledge, and her spiritual state. She was a companion of most of the spiritual masters in her time, and at the end of her life she joined Shaykh Abū ᶜAbdallāh ibn Khafīf [in Shiraz].[183] She visited Nishapur and met there [as-Sulamī's maternal grandfather] Abū ᶜAmr ibn Nujayd and [Abū al-Qāsim] an-Naṣrābādhī. The shaykh and imam Abū Sahl Muḥammad ibn Sulaymān (may God have mercy on him)[184] used to attend her teaching sessions and listen to her lessons, as did a group of Sufi shaykhs, such as Abū al-Qāsim ar-Rāzī,[185] Muḥammad al-Farrāᵓ,[186] ᶜAbdallāh al-Muᶜallim [the Teacher], and others from their generation.

I heard al-Wahaṭiyya say: "Beware not to be occupied with seeking peace of mind, assuming that you are pursuing knowledge; for the one who seeks knowledge is one who acts on it. Acting on one's knowledge is not in the amount of fasting, almsgiving, and praying that one does. Rather, acting on one's knowledge is in sincerely dedicating one's actions to God with correct intention and the awareness that God Most High is observing him, even if he is not observant toward His Lord and witnessing Him at all times."

I heard her say: "Among the requirements of the actualized Sufi is not to beg, not to aggrandize oneself through anything, not to reject a windfall when it is not from a doubtful source, and not to put off one time for another or for any time at all."

183. Abū ᶜAbdallāh Muḥammad ibn Khafīf of Shiraz (d. 371/982) was considered by as-Sulamī to be the greatest shaykh of his age. He was a master in both the exoteric and the esoteric sciences. He was personally known to as-Sulamī and gave him certificates for the transmission of oral traditions. See as-Sulamī, *Ṭabaqāt aṣ-ṣūfiyya,* 462–66; al-Qushayrī, *ar-Risāla,* 420–21; al-Iṣfahānī, *Ḥilyat al-awliyāᵓ*, vol. 10, 385–89. See also, al-Hujwirī, *The Kashf al-Maḥjūb,* 158.

184. Abū Sahl Muḥammad ibn Sulaymān as-Saᶜlūkī (d. 369/980) was a traditionist and specialist in the Shāfiᶜī school of Islamic jurisprudence. After studying in Iraq and occupying an important position in Isfahan, he moved to Nishapur in 337/949. He was the pre-eminent teacher of Shāfiᶜī law in Nishapur and was also important in the introduction of Ashᶜarite theology in that city. He followed the Sufi way and was a teacher of as-Sulamī. The vizier Ṣāḥib ibn al-ᶜAbbād said about him: "I have never seen the like of him- and he has never seen the like of himself." See Bulliet, *Patricians of Nishapur,* 115–17.

185. Abū al-Qāsim Jaᶜfar ibn Aḥmad al-Muqriᵓ (the Qurᵓān Reciter) ar-Rāzī (d. 378/988–89) was an eminent Sufi and transmitter of hadith. He lived and died in Nishapur. He said: "Sufi chivalry (*futuwwa*) is to see the excellence of other people through your own shortcomings." See as-Sulamī, *Ṭabaqāt aṣ-ṣūfiyya,* 509–12.

186. Abū Bakr Muḥammad ibn Aḥmad b. Ḥamdūn al-Farrāᵓ (d. 370/980–81) was an eminent Sufi and hadith transmitter of Nishapur. He was personally known to as-Sulamī. He said: "Concealing virtuous acts is better than concealing evil acts; for through their concealment you can attain salvation." See as-Sulamī, *Ṭabaqāt aṣ-ṣūfiyya,* 507–8. See also, as-Sarrāj, *Kitāb al-lumaᶜ*, xvi.

(٦٧)

الوهطية أمّ الفضـــــل

كانت واحدة وقتها، لسانًا وعلمًا وحالاً. صحبت أكثر مشايخ الوقت. ورحلت في آخر عُمرها إلى الشيخ أبي عبد اللّه بن خفيف. ودخلت نيسابور، ولقيت بها أبا عمروبن نُجيد، والنصراباذي. وكان الشيخ الإمام أبوسهل محمد بن سليمان، رحمه اللّه، يحضُرها ويسمعُ كلامها، وكذلك جماعة مشايخ الفقراء، مثل أبي القاسم الرّازي، ومحمد الفرّاء، وعبد اللّه المعلّم، ومَن في طبقتهم.

سمعتُ الوهطية تقول: احذروا ألاّ يكون شغلكم طلب راحات النّفوس. وتوهّمون [تتوهّمون] أنّكم في طلبِ العلم، وطالبُ العلمِ هوالعاملُ به! وليس العملُ بالعلم كثرة الصّوم والصّدقة والصّلاة، وإنّما العملُ بالعلَم إخلاصُ العمَل للّه؛ بصحّة النّيّة، ومراقبة نظر اللّه تعالى إليه، إن لم يكَن هوناظراً إلى ربِّه، ومشاهداً له.

وسمعتُها تقول: مِن آلة الصوفي المتحقّق ألاّ يطلبَ، ولا يتشرّف إلى شيءٍ، ولا يرُدُّ فتوحا، إذا كان من وجهٍ غير متّهم، ولا يدّخر من وقتٍ إلى وقتٍ، أولوقتٍ.

I heard her say: "The master of reality (*ṣāḥīb ḥaqīqa*) does not return to temporary spiritual states (*aḥwāl*) after attaining realization (*taḥaqquq*); rather, all of the states occur through his agency."

I heard her say: "The reality of love (*maḥabba*) is that the lover is mute before all but his Beloved and deaf to all but His speech, for the Prophet (may God bless and preserve him) has said: 'Your love for a thing makes you blind and deaf.'"

I heard a trustworthy person relate about al-Wahaṭiyya: I asked her to define Sufism and she said: "Sufism means rejecting all worldly means of support (*naqḍ al-asbāb*) and ending all worldly attachments (*qaṭᶜ al-ᶜalāʾiq*)."

وسمعتُها تقول: لا يكون لصاحبِ حقيقةٍ رجوعٌ إلى الأحوال إلاّ بعد التحقّق، بل تكون الأحوال كلّها تبعًا لهَ.

وسمعتُها تقول: حقيقةُ المحبّة أن يخرُس المحبُّ إلاّعن محبوبه، ويصمّ إلاّ عن سماعٍ كلامه، كما قال النبيّ صلى اللّه عليه وسلّم: «حبُّك الشّيئَ يُعمي ويُصِمّ».

سمعتُ الثقة يحكي عنها، قال: سألتها عن التصوف، فقالت: نقضُ الأسباب وقطع العلائق.

LXVIII

ZIYĀDA BINT AL-KHAṬṬĀB OF ṬAZAR

Ṭazar Qūmīs is a village in the mountains five leagues from Damaghan. Ziyāda was the mother of Ismāᶜīl ibn Ibrāhīm al-Quhistānī. Her father al-Khaṭṭāb was one of Abū Yazīd [al-Bisṭāmī's] greatest companions.[187] She was famous for her miracles and well known for her signs of sanctity. She used to report stories and traditions from her father al-Khaṭṭāb. Her son Ismāᶜīl reported traditions about her.

187. Al-Iṣfahānī lists Ziyāda's father as "Khaṭṭāb al-ᶜĀbid" (Khaṭṭāb the Worshipper), but gives almost no information about him. The fact that he was a disciple of Abū Yazīd al-Bisṭāmī (d. 261/875) indicates that Ziyāda flourished at the beginning of the fourth/tenth century. See al-Iṣfahānī, *Ḥilyat al-awliyāʾ*, vol. 10, 144.

(٦٨)

زيادة بنت الخطّـاب الطّزرية

طزر قومس. وهي قرية في الجبال، من دامغان على خمس فراسخ. وكانت أمَّ إسماعيل بن إبراهيم القُهستاني. وأبوها خطّاب. صحب أبا يزيد، وهومن كبار أصحابِه. لها الكَرامات المشهورة، والآيات المعروفة. وكانت تروي الحكايات والحَديث عن أبيها الخطّاب. روى عنها ابنُها إسماعيل.

LXIX

MALIKA THE DAUGHTER OF AḤMAD IBN ḤAYYAWAYH

Malika was the wife and paternal cousin of al-Ḥasan ibn ᶜAlī b. Ḥayyawayh.[188] Her father [Aḥmad ibn Ḥayyawayh] was the ruler of Damaghan. She experienced spiritual states (*ṣāḥibat ḥāl*).

Her husband al-Ḥasan took her with him on the pilgrimage to Mecca and took her to visit [Abū Bakr] ash-Shiblī. When ash-Shiblī saw her he said to al-Ḥasan, "You are a man and this is a woman, but she is greater than you in her spiritual state."

Al-Ḥasan said: "This statement did not enter my heart until we reached Medina, the City of the Messenger of God (may God bless and preserve him). She had with her only a few dirhams [a silver coin based on the Persian *drahm*] left over from our Ḥajj allowance, and nothing else. She saw some people from sub-Saharan Africa sitting by the head of the Prophet [i.e., at the Prophet's tomb], so she passed out all of the money to them." I remonstrated with her about this two times, saying: 'Only some of that money would have been enough for those blacks, or even less than that!' She replied: 'How long will you go on with your words, oh Ḥasan? It is as if you see nothing but blacks!'"

188. Al-Ḥasan ibn ᶜAlī ibn Ḥayyawayh was personally known to as-Sulamī. No other information about him is given in *Ṭabaqāt aṣ-ṣūfiyya*. This indicates that Malika and her husband flourished at the end of the fourth/tenth century. Ibid., 69.

(٦٩)

مَلِكة بنت أحمد بن حيّويه

امرأة الحسن بن علي بن حيّويه، وبنت عمّه. كان أبوها رئيس دامغان. وكانت صاحبة حال.

حملها زوجُها الحسن إلى الحجّ، وأدخلها على الشّبلي. فلمّا رآها الشّبلي قال للحسن: أنت رجلٌ وهذه امرأة، لكنّها أكبرُ منكَ حالاً.

قال الحسن: فلم يدخُل ذلك في قلبي، حتّى دخلنا مدينة رسول اللّه صلّى اللّه عليه وسلّم. قال: وكان معها دُرَيْهمات من نفقته، لم يبق لنا غيرها. فرأت قومًا من السّودان قُعوداً عند رأس النّبي صلّى اللّه عليه وسلّم، فنثرت عليهم تلك الدراهم. فكلّمتُها في ذلك مرّتين، وقُلت لها: كان يكفي لأولئك السّودان ببعض ذلك، أوأقلُّ من ذلك. فقالت لي: إلى متى تقول يا حسن؟ كأنّك لم ترَ غير السّودان!

LXX

FĀṬIMA BINT ᶜIMRĀN[189]

From the Natives of Damaghan

Fāṭima was great in her spiritual state (*ḥāl*), strong in her ecstasy (*wajd*), and frequent in her self-denial (*ijtihād*). She was a companion of Abū ᶜAbdallāh az-Zāhid (The Ascetic) at Damaghan.

I heard ᶜAlī ibn Muḥammad report that al-Ḥasan ibn ᶜAlī related: Abū Muḥammad of Mosul came to see us. He met Fāṭima[190] and said, "This is the Rābiᶜa [al-ᶜAdawiyya] of her age!"

Her prayers were known to be answered. She was dedicated to the care of Sufis and strangers until the day she died (may God have mercy on her).

189. Part of this account is duplicated in Ibn al-Jawzī, *Ṣifat aṣ-Ṣafwa,* vol. 4, 107.

190. The fact that three generations separate as-Sulamī from his subject suggests that Fāṭima bint ᶜImrān probably flourished in the middle of the fourth/tenth century.

(٧٠)

فاطمة بنت عمران

من أهل دامغـــــــان

كانت كبيرة الـحال، شديدة الوجد، كثيـرة الاجتهاد. صحبت أبا عبد الـلّـه الزّاهد، بدامغان.

سمعتُ علي بن محمّد، يقول: سمعتُ الحسن بن علي، يقول: قدِمَ علينا أبومحمد الـموصلي، فلقيَ فاطمة، فقال: هذه رابعةُ وقتِـها.

وكانت مستجابةَ الدّعوة، مقيمةً على تعهُّد الفقراء والغُرباء، إلى أن ماتـــت، رحمها الـلّـه.

LXXI

ᶜABDŪSA BINT AL-ḤĀRITH

From the Natives of Damaghan

ᶜAbdūsa served the Sufis of her country for thirty years. A man once asked her, “What is your spiritual state?” “Asking about one’s spiritual state is folly,” she replied.

(٧١)

عبدوسة بنت الحارث

من أهل دامغـــــــان

كانت خادمة الفقراء في بلدتها ثلاثين سنةً.

سألها رجلٌ فقال: ما حالُكِ؟

فقالت: السّؤالُ عن الحالِ مُحالٌ.

LXXII

UMM AL-ḤUSAYN THE DAUGHTER OF AḤMAD IBN ḤAMDĀN[191]

Umm al-Ḥusayn was the mother of Abū Bishr al-Ḥulwānī.[192] I heard one of her companions among the practitioners of female chivalry say that she heard Umm al-Ḥusayn say: "One who desires to be recognized for the way of poverty (*faqr*) should choose dirt for a bed, hunger for food, anxiety for happiness, rejection for acceptance, and debasement for glory."

It was reported to me that Umm al-Ḥusayn said: "Verily, the only price that God Most High has put on the souls of the believers is Heaven. Thus, He made their hearts a place for contemplating Him. Therefore, do not sell your souls for worldly displays, and make sure that the place for the contemplation of God Most High is protected from whatever displeases Him."

191. Abū Ja^c^far Aḥmad ibn Ḥamdān ibn Sīnān (d, 311/923–24) was one of the great traditionists and Sufi shaykhs of Nishapur. He was a companion of Abū ^c^Uthmān al-Ḥīrī and Abū Ḥafṣ al-Ḥaddād of Nishapur. His family was known for their asceticism and scrupulousness. He said: "The beauty of a man is in the excellence of his speech; the perfection of a man is in the sincerity of his actions." See as-Sulamī, *Ṭabaqāt aṣ-ṣūfiyya,* 332–34.

192. Abū Bishr Muḥammad ibn Aḥmad (d. 387/997), called "al-Ḥalāwī" by as-Sulamī in *Ṭabaqāt aṣ-ṣūfiyya,* was the grandson of Aḥmad ibn Ḥamdān. He moved from Nishapur to Mecca, where he spent twenty years until his death. He was one of the most important Sufis of his day in the holy city. See Ibid., 332.

(٧٢)

أمّ الحسين بنت أحمد بن حمدان

والدة أبي بشر الحلواني [الحلاوي].

سمعْتُ بعضَ من صحبَتْها من النّسوان، تقول: سمعْتُ أمّ الحسين، تقول: من أحبّ أن تصحِّ لَه طريقةُ الفقر فليخترْ من الفُرُش التُّراب، ومن الأطعمة الجوع، ومن السّرور الهمّ، ومن القبُول الردّ، ومن العِزّ الذُّلّ.

وحُكي عنها أنّها قالت: إنّ اللّه تعالى لم يجعل لأنفُس المؤمنين ثمنًا إلاّ الجنّة، وجعل قلُوبَهم محلاً لنظره، فلا تبيعوا أنفسكم بالدّون من العُرُوض، وطالعوا موضع نظر اللّه تعالى أن يكون مصُونًا عمّا لا يرضاهُ.

LXXIII

UMM KULTHŪM
Also Known as Khāla (Auntie)

Umm Kulthūm was the companion of Abū ᶜAlī ath-Thaqafī and ᶜAbdallāh ibn Munāzil.[193] Abū al-Qāsim an-Naṣrābādhī used to honor her and allowed her to be close to him.

I heard Umm al-Ḥusayn al-Qurashiyya[194] say: I went out with Umm Kulthūm to the mountains and she said to me, "Take me back to the lowlands, for my chest is tight." When we left the mountains I asked her, "Why did your chest tighten?" She said, "The vision of divine power nearly caused me to forget God the Powerful."

I heard Auntie Umm Kulthūm say: "Ecstasy (*wajd*) is beyond description, because it is the secret of God Most High manifested in the slave. If God wills it to be manifested, it is manifested, and if He wills it to be hidden, it is hidden. Thus, when one pretends to experience ecstasy, his pretentiousness will become apparent on him."

193. Abū Muḥammad ᶜAbdallāh ibn Munāzil (d. 329/941) was a well-known leader of the *malāmatiyya* in Nishapur. As-Sulamī states that he followed a unique spiritual method. He was a disciple of Ḥamdūn al-Qaṣṣār (d. 271/884). He was also learned in the exoteric sciences of Islam and transmitted hadith. He said: "When one banishes the shade of his soul from his soul, people live in his shade." See as-Sulamī, *Ṭabaqāt aṣ-ṣūfiyya,* 326–29; and al-Qushayrī, *ar-Risāla,* 435.

194. See sections LXVI and LXXVIII for information on this individual.

(٧٣)

أمّ كلثوم
المعروفة بخالة

كانت صحبت أبا علي الثّقفي، وعبد اللّه بن مُنازل. وكان أبوالقاسم النّصراباذي يُكْرِمُها ويُقَرِّبُها.

سمعتُ أمّ الحسين القُرشية، تقول: خرجتُ معها إلى الجبَل. فقالت لي: رُدّيني إلى البلد، فقد ضاق صدري. فلمّا انصرفنا سألتُها: بماذا ضاق صدرُكِ؟

فقالت: كادت رؤية القدرةِ أن تشغلَ عن القادر.

سمعتُ أُمّ كلثوم الخالة، تقول: الوجدُ لا تصحُّ عنها [عنه] العبارة؛ لأنّه سرّ اللّه تعالى في العبْد، إذا شاء أن يُظهرَهُ أظهَرَهُ، وإذا شاء أن يُخفيَهُ أخفاهُ. والمتكلّفُ فيه ظاهرٌ عليه تَكلّفُهُ.

LXXIV

ᶜAZĪZA AL-HARAWIYYA

ᶜAzīza was sagacious, pious, and scrupulous. She was eloquent and experienced spiritual states (*ṣāḥibat lisān wa ḥāl*). She moved to Nishapur and died there. She was a companion of ᶜAbd ar-Raḥmān ibn Shahrān in Herat [a city of Khurasan, now in present-day Afghanistan].

I heard ᶜAzīza say:[195] "The ascetic (*zāhid*) seeks out the King for his needs, but the King seeks out the gnostic (*ᶜārif*) for His fellowship."

I heard her say: Sufyān [ath-Thawrī] used to say: "God Most High mentioned four things in one place. He said: 'It is God who created you. Next, He provided for your sustenance. Next, He will cause you to die. Then, He will bring you back to life' [Qurʾān 30 (*ar-Rūm*), 40]. Insofar as another person cannot increase the span of your life, he cannot increase your sustenance. So why suffer?"[196]

I heard Umm al-Ḥusayn al-Qurashiyya say: I heard ᶜAzīza al-Harawiyya say: "The ascetic and the person who seeks close proximity to God look down at other people from the perspective of the aggrandizement and glorification of their egos. For this reason, other people appear insignificant to their eyes."

195. This notice indicates that ᶜAzīza al-Harawiyya was a contemporary of as-Sulamī, and flourished in the latter half of the fourth/tenth century.

196. This Quranic exegesis probably comes from Sufyān ath-Thawrī's *Tafsīr.*

(٧٤)

عزيزة الهروية

كانت كيّسة ديّنة ورعة. صاحبَةَ لِسانٍ وحالٍ. وردت نيسابور، وماتت بها. صحبت عبد الرحمن بن شهران بهراة.

سمعتُ عزيزة، تقول: الزّاهِدُ لِزِم المَلِكَ لِحاجتِه، والعارفُ لِزمَهُ المَلِكُ لِمُجالَسَتِه.

وسمعتُها تقول: كان سُفيان يقول: ذكر اللّهُ تعالى أربعةَ أشياءَ في موضعٍ واحدٍ، فقال: «اللّهُ الّذي خلقَكُم ثمّ رزقكُم ثمّ يُميتُكُم ثمّ يُحْيِيكُم». كما لا يقدر أحدٌ أن يزيدَ في عُمرِك، كذلك لا يُمكنُه أن يزيدَ في رزقِك. فَفِيمَ التّعَبُ؟

سمعتُ أمّ الحسين القرشية، تقول: سمعتُ عزيزة الهروية، تقول: الزّاهدُ والمُتقرّبُ، في عُلوّ نفسِه وارتفاعِها ينظُرُ إلى النّاس، لذلك يتصاغرون في عينِه.

LXXV

UMM ᶜALĪ THE DAUGHTER OF ᶜABDALLĀH IBN ḤAMSHĀDH[197]

Umm ᶜAlī was one of the great women of Nishapur. She attained an exalted spiritual state and was highly esteemed. She was a companion of Abū al-Qāsim an-Naṣrābādhī and other Sufi shaykhs. The Sufi shaykhs used to honor her and recognized her status.

I heard Umm ᶜAlī say: "Abandoning a sense of shame without first experiencing an expansion of the heart (*inbisāṭ*) bequeaths rejection by God."

I also heard her say: "The totality of created things conspire to alienate humankind from their Fashioner."

It was reported that she said: "One who is confirmed in his knowledge of true servitude will soon attain the knowledge of lordship."

197. Although Umm ᶜAlī's father cannot be located in the sources consulted for this work, her brother Abū Manṣūr Muḥammad ibn ᶜAbdallāh ibn Ḥamshādh (d. 388/998) was a well-known preacher who maintained his own school (*madrasa*) in Nishapur. See as-Sulamī, *Dhikr an-niswa,* aṭ-Ṭanāḥī ed., np. 116. See also, Bulliet, *Patricians of Nishapur,* 250.

(٧٥)

أمّ علي بنت عبد اللّـه بن حمشاذ

من كبار نســـاء نيســـابور، رفيعة الحال، عظيمة القدر. صَحِبَتْ أبا القاسم النّصرابـاذي، وغـيرَهُ من المشـايخ. كـان المشـايـخ يُكْرِمُونَـها ويعْرِفُون مَحَلَّها.

سمعْتُ أمّ علي تقـول: طَرْحُ الحِشْمَـة من غيرِ انْبسـاطٍ مُتَقَدِّمٍ يُورِثُ الطّردَ.

وسمعتها تقول: الأكْوانُ كلُّها أسبابٌ لقطع العبيدِ عن مُكوِّنِها.

وحُكي عنها أنّها قالت: مَنْ صحَّ له عِلمُ حقيقةِ العُبُودية فإنّه عن قريبٍ يَصِلُ إلى عِلم الرُّبُوبيـةِ.

LXXVI

SURAYRA ASH-SHARQIYYA

Surayra was noble in spirit, great in her spiritual state, far-sighted, and very unusual among her contemporaries. There were no women like her in her age. She was a companion of Abū Bakr al-Fārisī.[198]

I heard Umm al-Ḥusayn al-Qurashiyya say: I heard Surayra say: "The greatest cause of divine disapproval is the inability to understand."

[Umm al-Ḥusayn] said: I heard Surayra say: "The ultimate of what is said to be the best of knowledge is the knowledge of lordship and its opposite, servitude. Eventually, servitude vanishes and only lordship remains."

[Umm al-Ḥusayn] said: I heard her say: "Correctness in the confirmation of one's spiritual state (*iqrār*) is that one has been emptied of all ignorance. Correctness in gnosis (*maʿrifa*) is that one's knowledge of God has been cleansed of all traces of anthropomorphism. Correctness in spiritual practice (*ʿamal*) is that one is purified from attributing partners to God."

[Umm al-Ḥusayn] said: I heard Surayra say: "Adversity and good fortune are both from a single source. However, the truthful person is revealed by his fortitude when adversity befalls him."

198. Abū Bakr aṭ-Ṭamastānī al-Fārisī (d. 340/951) was a major Sufi shaykh from the region of Fars, in southwestern Iran. He spent the latter part of his life in Nishapur and was noted for his aphorisms. He said: "The entire world is but one lesson; each person learns it according to how much of it is revealed to him." He also said: "Sufism is struggle; when the struggle ceases, it is no longer Sufism." See as-Sulamī, *Ṭabaqāt aṣ-ṣūfiyya,* 471–74; al-Qushayrī, *ar-Risāla,* 423; al-Iṣfahānī, *Ḥilyat al-awliyāʾ,* vol. 10, 382.

(٧٦)

سُريرة الشرقيــة

كانت شريفة النّفس، عظيمة الحال، بعيدة المرمى، غريبة الوقت فيما بين أقرانِها. لم يكُن في وقتِها من النّساء مثلُها. صحِبَتْ أبا بكر الفارسي.

سمعتُ أمّ الحسين القرشية، تقول: سمعتُ سُريرة، تقول: أكثرُ سببِ الإنكار العجزُ عن الإدارك.

قالت: وسمعتُها تقول: المنتهى فيما يُقال من دقائق العلوم: علمُ الرّبوبية والعبُودية. ثمّ تتلاشى العبودية، وتبقى الرّبوبية.

قالت: وسمعتها تقول: صحّةُ الإقرار أن يكونَ عن الجهل خاليا، والمعرفةُ أن تكُون عن التّشبيهِ نَقِية، والعمل أن يكون عن الشّركِ صافيا.

قالت: وسمعتُها تقول: البلاءُ والنّعمةُ كلّها من معدنٍ واحدٍ، إلاّ أنّ الصّادقَ مَن يَتبَيَّنُ في الثّبات عند نُزولِ البَلاء.

LXXVII

ᶜUNAYZA OF BAGHDAD

She served Abū Muḥammad al-Jarīrī.[199] She was one of the wittiest female Sufis and was full of spirit. She experienced great spiritual states.

I heard one of our companions say: I said to ᶜUnayza: "Advise me." She said: "Be there for God today as you want Him to be there for you tomorrow."

Someone else reported to me that she said: "One who loves God never tires of His service. On the contrary, he takes pleasure in it."

It was also reported that she said: "The gnostic (*ᶜārif*) is neither one who describes God nor one who passes on information about Him."[200]

It was also reported that she said: "Knowledge of God (*ᶜilm*) bequeaths awe, whereas gnosis (*maᶜrifa*) bequeaths reverence."

She said: "Human forms are the mines of servitude."

199. There is some question about the exact name of Abū Muḥammad al-Jarīrī (d. 311/923–24). He was one of the foremost disciples of al-Junayd and succeeded al-Junayd after the latter's death. Like his shaykh, he was learned in the Law as well as in theology and Sufi doctrine. He died while making the pilgrimage to Mecca. See as-Sulamī, *Ṭabaqāt aṣ-ṣūfiyya,* 259–64; al-Qushayrī, *ar-Risāla,* 402–3; al-Iṣfahānī, *Ḥilyat al-awliyāʾ,* vol. 10, 347–48; Ibn al-Jawzī, *Ṣifat aṣ-Ṣafwa,* vol. 2, 252. See also, Abdel-Kader, *al-Junayd,* 43–44 (where he is called "Jurayrī"); and al-Hujwīrī, *The Kashf al-Maḥjūb,* 148–49.

200. The meaning of this statement is that the true knower of God is neither a theologian, who defines God through His attributes, nor a purveyor of traditions, who merely passes on information about God. True knowledge of God goes beyond mere description.

(٧٧)

عُنيزة البغدادية

كانت من ظراف الصوفيات

خدمت أبا محمد الجريري. وكانت من ظراف [ظرفاء] الصّوفيات، ظريفة النّفس، كبيرة الحال.

سمعْتُ بعض أصحابنا يقول: قُلتُ لِعُنَيْزة: أوصيني. فقالت: كُنْ لِلّه اليوم، كما تُحِبُّ أن يكُونَ لكَ غداً.

وحُكيَ لي عن غيرِه، أنّها قالت: مَنْ أحَبَّهُ لم يتعَبْ في خِدمَتِه، بل يتَلَذّذُ بها.

وحُكِيَ عنها أنّها قالت: العارفُ لا يكُونُ واصِفًا ولا مُخبْراً.

وحُكِيَ عنها أنّه [أنها] قالت: العِلمُ يُورثُ الخَشية، والمعرفةُ تورثُ الهيبةَ.

وقالت: قوالِبُ البشرية معادِنُ العبُودية.

LXXVIII

JUM^{c}A BINT AḤMAD IBN MUḤAMMAD B. ^{c}UBAYD ALLĀH[201]

Also Known as Umm al-Ḥusayn al-Qurashiyya

Jum^{c}a was unique in her age for her knowledge (*^{c}ilm*) and spiritual states (*ḥāl*). She spent her wealth on the Sufis of her time. She was a companion of Abū al-Qāsim an-Naṣrābādhī, Abū al-Ḥusayn al-Khiḍrī, and other shaykhs. She performed the pilgrimage to Mecca many times.

I heard Jum^{c}a say: Once, I visited shaykh Abū al-Ḥusayn al-Khiḍrī in Baghdad. "With whom do you keep company?" he asked. "An-Naṣrābādhī," I replied. "What did you memorize of his words?" he asked. I said: [an-Naṣrābādhī] says, "If one's spiritual lineage is solid, his knowledge is perfected." At hearing this, al-Khiḍrī became silent.

When I returned to Nishapur, an-Naṣrābādhī was pleased with my answer and said, "This is appropriate for one who visits another shaykh. Excellence in both knowledge and practice flows through my hands." I replied: "For the one who brags about his knowledge: Knowledge is not something that people brag about. All of this is but empty words and utterances. Rather, knowledge consists of what God Most High addressed to His Prophet (may God bless and preserve him): 'Know that there is no god but God' [Qur$^{\circ}$ān 47 (*Muḥammad*), 19]. All of humanity was meant to speak, but only the Prophet (may God bless him) was meant to possess knowledge, because of his exalted spiritual state and the greatness of his status."

I also heard Jum^{c}a say: "One who has no beginnings to consume him will have no endings to sustain him."

201. See also, section LXVI above. Umm al-Ḥusayn al-Qurashiyya's father Aḥmad ibn Muḥammad ibn ^{c}Ubayd Allāh was the head of the Maḥmīs, one of the great aristocratic families of Nishapur. In his children's biographies he is referred to as "The Great" (*al-Akbar*) or "Chief" (*ra$^{\circ}$īs*). He was probably headman of the district of Rukhkh, where he and his relatives possessed large landholdings. See Bulliet, *Patricians of Nishapur,* 89–92, 100.

(٧٨)

جُمعة بنت أحمد
بن محمد بن عبيد اللّه
المعروفة بأمّ الحسين القرشية

هي واحدة وقتها في العلم والحال. وهي المنفِقَةُ على الفُقَراء في وقتها.

صَحِبَت أبا القاسم النّصراباذي، وأبا الحسين الخِضْري، وغيرهما من المشايخ.

حجّتْ حججا.

سمعتُها تقول: دخلتُ ببغداد على الشيخ أبي الحسين الخضري، فقال لي: من صحبْت؟ قُلتُ: النّصراباذي. فقال لي: أيش [أيّ شئ] تحفظ [تحفظين] مَن كلامه؟ قلتُ: إنّه يقول: مَنْ صَحَّتْ نِسْبَتُهُ كَمُلَتْ مَعْرِفَتُهُ. فَسَكَت الخِضْري.

فلمّا رجَعْتُ رضي النّصراباذي ذلك، وقال: جَرى بين يَديَّ فضلُ العلْم والعَمَل. فقُلتُ لِمَنْ تكلّم فيه: ليس العلمُ ما يتكلّم به النّاس، هذا كلُّه كلامٌ ونُطقٌ. العِلمُ ما خاطَب اللّهُ به نبيّه صلى اللّه عليه [وسلّم]، فقال: «فاعلم أنّه لا إله إلاّ اللّه». وكلّ النّاس أمِرُوا بالقول والنّبيّ صلّى اللّه عليه بالعِلم، لِعُلوّ حَالِه، وعَظِيم مَحَلّه.

وسمعتُها تقول: مَن لم تكُنْ لهُ أوائِل تُفنيهِ لم تكنْ لهُ أواخِرُ تُبقيهِ.

LXXIX

UMM AL-ḤUSAYN AL-WARRĀQA
(Umm al-Ḥusayn the Copyist)
From Iraq

Umm al-Ḥusayn was eloquent in speech. She was also a specialist in self-denial (*mujtahida*) and scrupulousness (*wāriᶜa*).

I heard her say: "The blind person does not 'see' a substance unless he touches it."[202]

I also heard her say: [Abū Bakr] ash-Shiblī[203] said: "If you allow God to escape you, at least do not allow His command to pass you by."

202. This saying refers to the Sufi concept of *dhawq* (taste, flavor), or direct experience.

203. Abū Bakr Dulaf ibn Jaḥdar ash-Shiblī (d. 334/945) of Baghdad was a high ᶜAbbasid official until he was converted to Sufism and became a disciple of al-Junayd. He was noted for his use of symbolic allusions (*ishārāt*) and ecstatic utterances (*shaṭaḥāt*). At times he was accused of being a madman. He said to one accuser: "You think I am mad, and I think you are sensible; may God increase my madness and your sense!" He was highly esteemed by as-Sulamī and his tomb in the Aᶜẓamiyya quarter of Baghdad is still one of the most popular in the city. Umm al-Ḥusayn was not a contemporary of ash-Shiblī, but of as-Sulamī. Her information about ash-Shiblī very likely came from a written work which she copied. See *EI²*, vol. 9, 432–33; Abdel-Kader, *al-Junayd,* 44–45; and al-Hujwirī, *The Kashf al-Maḥjūb,* 155-156. See also, as-Sulamī, *Ṭabaqāt aṣ-ṣūfiyya,* 338–48; al-Qushayrī, *ar-Risāla,* 419–20; al-Iṣfahānī, *Ḥilyat al-awliyā',* vol. 10, 366–75; and Ibn al-Jawzī, *Ṣifat aṣ-Ṣafwa,* vol. 2, 456–61. On ecstatic utterances in general, see Carl W. Ernst, *Words of Ecstasy.*

(٧٩)

أمّ الحسين الورّاقة
من العراق

حسنة الكلام، مجتهدة ورعة.

سمعتُها تقول: ليس للأعمى من رُؤيةِ الجوهر إلاّ مسُّهُ.

وسمعتُها تقول: قال الشّبلي: إن فاتكُم اللّهُ فلا يفوتَنّكُم أمرُهُ.

LXXX

ĀMINA AL-MARJIYYA

Āmina swore herself (*mutaᶜahhida*) to the service of the Sufis. She was chaste and virtuous, and of high spiritual motivation.

I heard her say: "The friends of God are not gratified by food, but are gratified by acts of devotion above and beyond those required (*al-kifāyāt*)."[204]

Āmina also said: "In service to the Sufis is the illumination of the heart and the rectification of the quintessence of one's soul."

204. Religious obligations in Islam are divided into two categories: (1) *farḍ ᶜayn,* obligations that are required of all Muslims, and (2) *farḍ kifāya,* obligations that are required only of a sufficient number of the Muslim community. As religious specialists, the "friends of God" or Sufi saints are particularly devoted to *kifāyāt,* acts above and beyond those required by the Law.

(٨٠)

آمنة المرجيّة

متعهّدة للفقراء.

كانت صائنة مستورة، رفيعة الهمّة.

سمعتها تقول: الأولياءُ لا تُشْبِعُهُم الأقواتُ، ولكن تُشْبِعُهم الكِفايات.

وقالت: خدمةُ الفقرا [الفقراء] فيه نورُ القلب وصلاحُ السِّرّ.

LXXXI

FĀṬIMA AL-KHĀNAQAHIYYA
(Fāṭima of the Hermitage)

Fāṭima was one of the practitioners of Sufi chivalry (*fityān*) in her age. She swore herself (*muta^c^ahhida*) to the service of the Sufis and held them in high esteem.

It was reported that she said: "Sufi chivalry (*futuwwa*) is to maintain service to others without discrimination."

It was also reported that she said: "The sight of chivalrous youths (*fityān*) brings joy to the hearts of the gnostics and separation from them brings sorrow."

(٨١)

فاطمة الخانقهية

من فتيان وقتها.

كانت متعهّدة ً للفُقَراء، مُحْتَرِمَة ً لهُم.

حُكيَ عنها أنّها قالت: الفُتُوة هي القيام إلى الخدمة من غير تمييزٍ.

وحُكيَ عنها أنّها قالت: سُرورُ قُلُوب العارفين برؤية الفتيان، وغمُّها بُمفارقتهم.

LXXXII

ᶜĀᵓISHA BINT AḤMAD AṬ-ṬAWĪL OF MERV

The Wife of ᶜAbd al-Wāḥid as-Sayyārī[205]

ᶜĀᵓisha was one of the most excellent of the Sufis and specialists in self-denial. No one exceeded her spiritual state in her time, and no path in Sufism equaled hers in subtlety. She spent more than five thousand dirhams on the Sufis (*fuqarāᵓ*).

I was informed that a professional invoker said to her: "Do this and that and an unveiling of divine secrets will be granted to you." She said: "Concealment is more appropriate for women than unveiling, for women are not to be exposed."

I heard ᶜĀᵓisha say: "One who has not tasted the food of poverty (*faqr*) will not have the virtues of poverty revealed to him."

It was said to her: "So-and-so does not approve of your gift. He said, 'Dishonor is in accepting gifts from the practitioners of female chivalry (*niswān*).'" She replied: "When the slave seeks glory in his servitude, his foolishness is revealed."[206]

205. ᶜAbd al-Wāḥid ibn ᶜAlī as-Sayyārī (d. 375/985) was a Sufi of Nishapur. He was the nephew on his mother's side of the Sufi master Abū al-ᶜAbbās al-Qāsim as-Sayyārī (d. 342/953–54). A native of Merv, al-Qāsim as-Sayyārī was a disciple of Abū Bakr al-Wāsiṭī (d. 331/942), a companion of al-Junayd. Al-Wāsiṭī and as-Sayyārī are credited by as-Sulamī and others with bringing the way of al-Junayd to Khurasan. Al-Hujwirī mentions that the Sayyārīs comprised a tightly-knit Sufi community that adhered closely to their founder's doctrines. They maintained doctrinal continuity through an exchange of letters between their centers at Merv and Nasā. See idem, *The Kashf al-Maḥjūb*, 157–58, 251–60. See also as-Sulamī, *Ṭabaqāt aṣ-ṣūfiyya*, 440–47.

206. Note the similarity of this account with that of Fāṭima of Nishapur and Dhū an-Nūn al-Miṣrī in section XXX above.

(٨٢)

عائشة بنت أحمد الطّويل المروزية
زوجة عبد الواحد السّيّاري
رحمهم اللّـه

كانت من الأفاضل والمجتهدين. لم يكن في وقتها أحسنُ حالاً منها، ولا ألطف طريقةً في التصوّف. أنفقت على الفقراء أكثر من خمسة آلاف درهم.

بلغني أنّ بعض المدّعين قال لها: افعلي كذا وكذا ليقَع لكِ كشفٌ.

فقالت: "السّتر أولى للنّساء من الكشف؛ لأنّهنّ عوراتٌ".

وسمعتها تقول: من لم يستلِذّ طعمَ الفقر لا يُكشَفُ له عن فضائل الفقر.

وقيل لها: إنّ فلانا لم يقبل رفقك، وقالت: في قبول أرفاق النسوان مذلة.

فقالت: إذا طلب العبدُ التّعزّزَ في العبودية فقد أظهر رُعُونَتَهُ.

May God have mercy on all of the Sufis mentioned in this work.

The End.

Praise be to God, Sustainer of the Worlds.
May God bless and preserve His Messenger Muḥammad
and his pure family.

By the hand of the powerless slave [c]Abd as-Sayyid ibn Aḥmad al-Khaṭīb (may God forgive him, his parents, and all of the believing men and women with His mercy).

The completion of [this manuscript] was approximately ten nights before the middle of the month of Ṣafar in the year 474 (July 17, 1081).

It was completed on a Saturday. On the same day it was put by the Judge and Imam, the Judge of Judges, Aḥmad ibn Sulaymān al-Kāshānī in the school (*madrasa*) of the Shaykh, the Imam and Preacher Muḥammad ibn Ḥamza (may God have mercy on him).

آخره الحمدُ للّـه ربّ العالَـمين

والصّلاة والسلام على رسوله محمد وآله الطيبين.

على يد العبد الضّعيف عبد السيد بن أحمد الخطيب. غفر اللّـه له ولوالديه مع جميع المؤمنين والمؤمنات برحمته.

وكان الفراغ منه لعشر ليال خلت منه للنصف من صفر سنة أربع وسبعين وأربعمائة.

وكان الفراغ منه يوم السّبت ووضع ذلك اليوم القاضي الإمام قاضي القضاة أحمد بن سليمان الكاشاني في مدرسة الشيخ الإمام الخطيب محمد بن حمزة بن أحمد رحمه اللّـه.

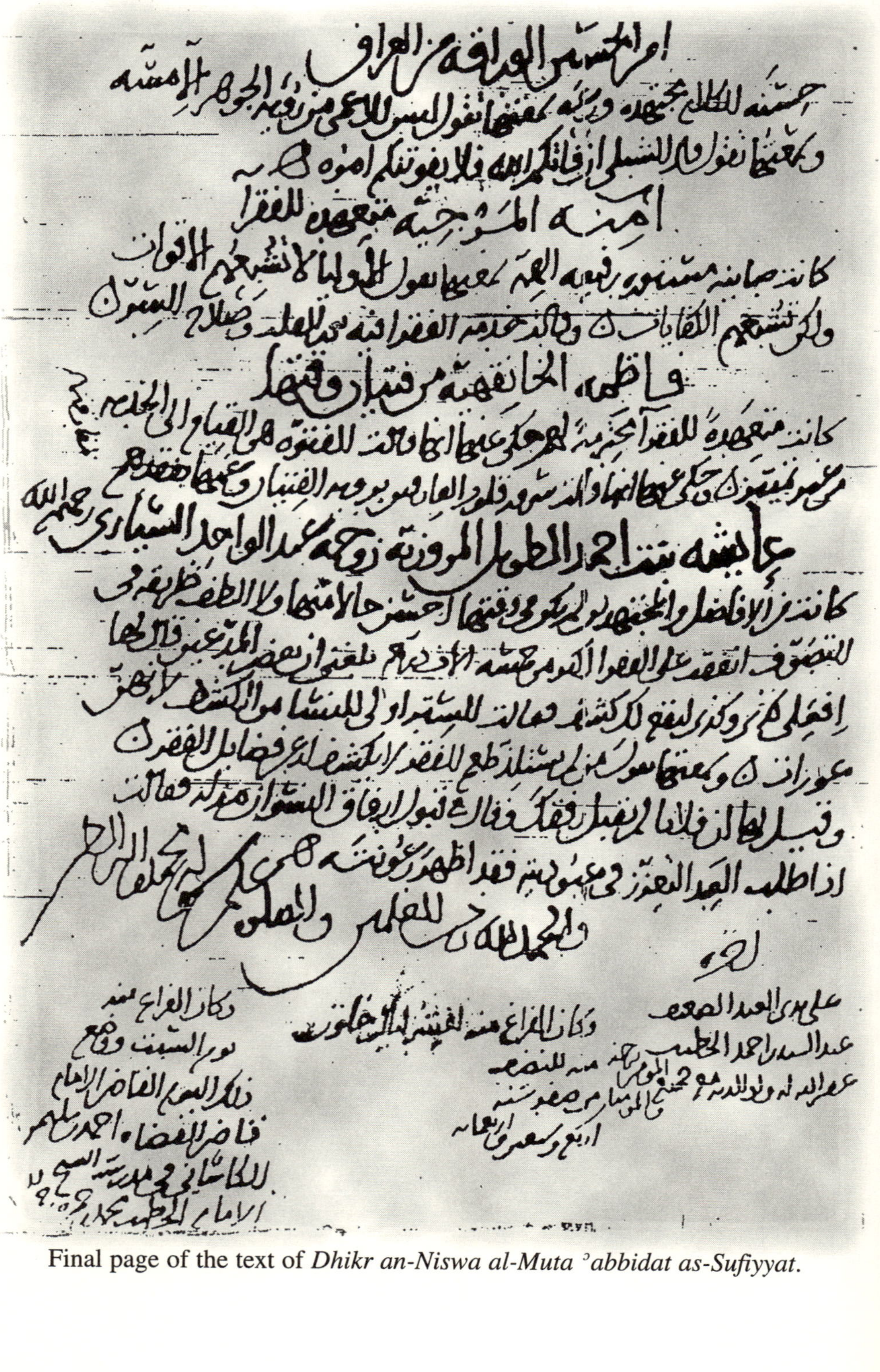

ام الحسين الوراقة من العراق

حسنة الكلام مجتهدة ورعة سمعتها تقول [illegible]

وسمعتها تقول قال الشبلي ان فاتكم الله فلا يفوتنكم امره

امنة المرجية متعبدة للفقرا

كانت صاحبة مستورة رفيعة الهمة سمعتها تقول الاوليا لا تشبعهم الاقوال

ولكن تشبعهم الكفايات [illegible]

فاطمة الخانقهية [illegible]

[illegible]

عايشه بنت احمد الطويل المروزية زوجة عبد الواحد السياري رحمهم الله

[illegible]

والحمد لله رب العالمين والصلوة [illegible]

Final page of the text of *Dhikr an-Niswa al-Muta ʾabbidat as-Sufiyyat.*

Appendix

ENTRIES ON AS-SULAMĪ'S EARLY SUFI WOMEN FOUND IN *ṢIFAT AṢ-ṢAFWA*

by Jamāl ad-Dīn Abū al-Faraj ibn al-Jawzī[1]
(d. 597/1201)

1. The sixteen sections in this Appendix were taken from Jamāl ad-Dīn Abū al-Faraj ibn al-Jawzī, *Ṣifat aṣ-Ṣafwa,* Maḥmūd Fākhūrī and Muḥammad Rawwās Qal^{c}anjī eds. (Beirut, 1406/ 1986), vols. 2 and 4. Notices which reproduce as-Sulamī's text exactly or contain only a line or two of information are not reproduced here, but are mentioned in the footnotes to as-Sulamī's *Dhikr an-niswa al-muta^{c}abbidāt aṣ-ṣūfiyyāt,* above.

Notices of the Elect among the Female Worshippers (*ᶜābidāt*) of Basra:

I

MUᶜĀDHA BINT ᶜABDALLĀH AL-ᶜADAWIYYA[2]

Muᶜādha was nicknamed Umm aṣ-Ṣahbāᵓ (Mother of the Redhead). Muḥammad ibn al-Fuḍayl reported from Ubayy who said: At the break of day Muᶜādha used to say: "This is the day in which I shall die." So she did not sleep until evening. And when night fell she said: "This is the night in which I shall die." So she continued without sleep until morning. During the winter, she would wear only thin garments so that the cold would prevent her from falling asleep.

Al-Ḥakam ibn Sinān al-Bāhilī said: A woman who used to take care of Muᶜādha al-ᶜAdawiyya said: "Muᶜādha used to stay up all night praying. When overcome by the need for sleep, she would get up and wander around the house, saying, "Oh, Self! Eternal sleep is ahead of you. If I were to die, your repose in the grave would be a long one, whether it be sorrowful or happy!" She would remain that way until daylight.

ᶜAbd ar-Raḥmān ibn ᶜAmr al-Bāhilī reported from Dalāl the daughter of Abū al-Mudill that Āsiya the daughter of ᶜAmr al-ᶜAdawī related: Muᶜādha al-ᶜAdawiyya used to pray six hundred prostrations (*rakᶜāt*) every day and night. She would read her nightly portion of the Qurᵓān in the standing position. She used to say: "How astonished I am to see an eye that sleeps when it is aware of the long sleep that will come in the darkness of the grave!"

Al-Ḥasan ibn ᶜAlī b. Muslim al-Bāhilī said: I heard Abū as-Sawwār al-ᶜAdawī[3] say: "The people of Banū ᶜAdī are the most rigorous ascetics in this land! Here is Abū aṣ-Ṣahbāᵓ,[4] who did not sleep during the night and did not eat during the day, and here is his wife Muᶜādha bint ᶜAbdallāh, who did not look up at the sky for forty years!"

2. Ibn al-Jawzī, *Ṣifat aṣ-Ṣafwa,* vol. 4, 22–24.

3. Abū as-Sawwār Ḥassān ibn Ḥārith al-ᶜAdawī of Basra was a traditionist and commentator on the Qurᵓān who transmitted reports from the fourth caliph, ᶜAlī ibn Abī Ṭālib (d. 40/ 661). In *Ḥilyat al-awliyāᵓ,* al-Iṣfahānī cites a report where Muᶜādha al-ᶜAdawiyya criticizes Abū as-Sawwār for trying to prevent women from attending the mosque of the Banū ᶜAdī in Basra. Neither al-Iṣfahānī nor ibn al-Jawzī gives a date for his death. See al-Iṣfahānī, *Ḥilyat al-awliyāᵓ,* vol. 2, 249–51; and Ibn al-Jawzī, *Ṣifat aṣ-Ṣafwa,* vol. 3, 230–31. See also, Arberry, *A Sufi Martyr,* 46.

4. This was the nickname (*kunya*) of Ṣila ibn Ushaym al-ᶜAdawī (d. 75/694–95), the husband of Muᶜādha al-ᶜAdawiyya. He was a famous second-generation Muslim and hadith transmitter who died as a defender of the faith (*mujāhid*) in either Iraq or Sijistān. See al-Iṣfahānī, *Ḥilyat al-awliyāᵓ,* vol. 2, 237–42.

(١)

معاذة بنت عبد اللّه العدوية

و تكنّى أمّ الصّهباء محمد بن فضيل قال: حدّثنا أبي قال: كانت معاذة العدوية إذا جاء النّهار قالت: هذا يومي الذي أموت فيه، فما تنام حتّى تمسي وإذا جاء اللّيل قالت: هذه ليلتي التي أموت فيها فلا تنام حتّى تصبح و إذا جاء البرد لبست الثياب الرّقاق حتّى يمنعها البردُ من النّوم.

الحكم بن سنان الباهلي قال: حدّثتني امرأة كانت تخدم مُعاذة العدوية قالت: كانت تُحيي اللّيل صلاة فإذا غلبها النوم قامت فجالت في الدّار و هي تقول: يا نفسُ، النّوم أمامك لو قد متّ لَطَالَت رقدتُكِ في القبر على حَسْرة أو سرور. قالت: فهي كذلك حتّى تُصبَح.

قال عبد الرحمن بن عمرو الباهلي: و حدّثتنا دلال ابنة أبي المدل قالت: حدّثتني آسية بنت عمرو العدوية قالت: كانت مُعاذة العدوية تُصَلي في كلّ يومٍ و ليلةٍ ستمائة ركعةٍ و تقرأ جزءَها من الليل تقومُ به. و كانت تقول: عجبتُ لعينٍ تنامُ و قد عرفت طول الرُّقادِ في ظُلَمِ القُبُور.

الحسن بن علي بن مسلم الباهلي قال: سمعتُ أبا السّوار العدوي يقول: بنو عدى أشدُّ أهْلِ هذه البلدة اجتهاداً، و هذا أبو الصّهباء لا ينام ليلَهُ و لا يُفطر نهارَهَ، و هذه امرأتُه مُعاذة ابنة عبد اللّه لم ترفعْ رأسَها إلى السّماء أربعينَ عامًا.

Zuhayr as-Salūlī reported from a man from the Banū ᶜAdī that a woman from the same tribe whom Muᶜādha Bint ᶜAbdallāh had nursed related that Muᶜādha said to her: "Oh daughter, be cautious and hopeful of your encounter with God, the Glorious and Mighty, for I have seen that when the hopeful person meets God, he is made worthy by his devoted servitude, and I have seen the God-fearing person hoping for safety on the day when humanity stands before the Lord of the Worlds!" Then she cried until she was overcome by weeping.

Ḥammād ibn Salama[5] said: Thābit al-Bunānī[6] reported that Ṣila ibn Ushaym was in a battle with his son, and he said to him: "Oh my son, go forward and fight so that I might claim you as a reward in the hereafter!" The son charged the enemy and fought until he was killed. Then his father went forward and fought until he was killed as well. Later, the women gathered around his wife Muᶜādha al-ᶜAdawiyya and she said to them: "Welcome. If you are here to congratulate me, then you are welcome. But if you have come with something else in mind, then return to your homes."

Salama ibn Ḥassān al-ᶜAdawī said: Al-Ḥasan [al-Baṣrī?][7] reported that Muᶜādha did not sleep after that until she died.

5. Abū Salama Ḥammād ibn Salama (d. 168/784–85) was a *mawlā* of the Banū Tamīm tribe and lived in Basra. He was a God-fearing ascetic and seldom laughed. According to Ibn al-Jawzī, "If someone told him that he would die tomorrow, he would not be able to continue doing anything." He was devoted to the study of the Qurʾān and died while praying in a mosque. See Ibn al-Jawzī, *Ṣifat aṣ-Ṣafwa,* vol. 3, 621–23; and al-Iṣfahānī, *Ḥilyat al-awliyāʾ,* vol. 6, 249–57. His maternal uncle, Ḥamīd aṭ-Ṭawīl (the Tall) ibn Tarkhān al-Khuzaᶜī (d. 142/759–60) was a student of Ḥasan al-Baṣrī (see below) and compiled a volume of the latter's sermons. See Massignon, *Essay,* 122.

6. Abū Muḥammad Thābit ibn Aslam al-Bunānī of Basra (d. 127/744–45) was a *mawlā* of the tribe of Banū Saᶜd ibn Luʾayy and was a famous transmitter of traditions about the Prophet Muḥammad and the early generations of Muslims. He transmitted hadith from Anas ibn Mālik (d. 91/710) and was personally acquainted with many of the *Tābiᶜūn,* the followers of the Companions of the Prophet. See Ibn al-Jawzī, *Ṣifat aṣ-Ṣafwa,* vol. 3, 260–63; and al-Iṣfahānī, *Ḥilyat al-awliyāʾ,* vol. 2, 318–33. See also, Smith, *An Early Mystic,* 70; and as-Sulamī, *Ṭabaqāt aṣ-ṣūfiyya,* np. 207.

7. Abū Saᶜīd al-Ḥasan ibn Abī al-Ḥasan Yasār al-Baṣrī (d. 110/728) was one of the most famous early Muslim ascetics. His mother was a *mawlāt* and servant of the Prophet Muḥammad's wife Umm Salama. Among his known works are collections of sermons (*mawāᶜiẓ*), short commentaries on the Qurʾān (*tafsīr*), sayings (*riwāyāt*), and responses to questions on dogma and morals (*masāʾil*). He was an important figure in the formation of the doctrines of Sunni Islam and based his mystical practice on self-reflective contemplation (*fikr, tafakkur*). He said: "Self-reflection is the mirror that makes you see what is both good and bad in yourself." See Massignon, *Essay,* 119–38; Smith, *An Early Mystic,* 68–70; and Smith, *Rabi'a,* 30–31 and 56–57. See also al-Iṣfahānī, *Ḥilyat al-awliyāʾ,* vol. 2, 131–61; and Ibn al-Jawzī, *Ṣifat aṣ-Ṣafwa,* vol. 3, 233–39.

عن زهير السلولي، عن رجل من بني عدى، عن امرأة منهم أرضعتها مُعاذة ابنة عبد اللّه قالت: قالت لي معاذة: يا بنية كوني من لقاء اللّه عز وجلّ على حذر و رجاء، و إنّي رأيت الرّاجي له محقوقا بحسن الزُّلفى لديه يومَ يلقاه، و رأيتُ الخائفَ له مؤمِلاً للأمان يومَ يقوم النّاسُ لربِّ العالمين ثم بكت حتّى غلبها البكاءُ.

حماد بن سلمة قال: أنبأ ثابت البُناني أنّ صلة بن أُشَيْم كان في مغزًى له و معه ابنٌ له، فقال: أي بُنيّ تقدّمْ فقاتِل حتّى أحتسبك. فحمَل فقاتَلَ حتى قُتِلَ ثمّ تقدّم فقُتلَ فاجتمعت النّساء عَند امرأته معاذة العدوية فقالت: مرحبا، إن كنتُنّ جئتُنّ لتهنئنني، فمرحبًا بكُنّ وإن كُنْتُنّ جئتُنّ بغير ذلك فارْجِعْنَ.

سلمة بن حسّان العدوي قال: أنبأ الحسن أنّ مُعاذة لم توسد [تَتَوَسَّدْ] فِراشًا بعد أبي الصهباء حتّى ماتَت.

ᶜImrān ibn Khālid reported that Umm al-Aswad bint Zayd al-ᶜAdawiyya,[8] whom Muᶜādha had nursed, said: Muᶜādha told me after her husband and her son had been killed: "By God, my daughter! My desire to continue living in this world is neither for the sake of luxury nor of relaxation. By God, I desire to continue living only so that I may get closer to My Lord the Glorious and Mighty through acts of worship, in the hope that He would grant me the pleasure of joining Abū aṣ-Ṣahbā᾽ and his son in heaven."

Rawḥ ibn Salama al-Warrāq said: I heard Ghufayra the Worshipper[9] say: I heard that when Muᶜādha al-ᶜAdawiyya was near death, she first cried and then laughed. "What made you cry and then laugh?" she was asked. "What is the purpose of laughing and then crying?" She replied: "As for the crying that you just saw, I cried because I was thinking of being separated from my fasting, my prayers and my remembrance of God. As for the smiling and laughing that you saw, it was because I saw Abū aṣ-Ṣahbā᾽ coming into the entrance hall of the house wearing two green garments. He was among a group of people the likes of which I swear I have never seen before in this world. So I laughed with him and from there I could not see myself making it to the next prayer." Rawḥ said: And she died before time of the next prayer.

Muᶜādha lived in the time of ᶜĀ᾽isha [the wife of the Prophet Muḥammad] and transmitted hadith from her.[10] Al-Ḥasan al-Baṣrī, Abū Qulāba[11] and Yazīd ar-Rishq [ar-Raqqāshī?][12] transmitted reports on her authority.

8. See as-Sulamī, *Dhikr an-niswa,* sections XIII and XL above.

9. See section V below, and as-Sulamī, *Dhikr an-niswa,* section IXabove.

10. ᶜĀ᾽isha, the daughter of the caliph Abū Bakr aṣ-Ṣiddīq and the wife of the Prophet Muḥammad, died on 17 Ramaḍān, 58 A. H. (13 July, 678 C.E.). For an example of a tradition transmitted from ᶜĀ᾽isha through Muᶜādha al-ᶜAdawiyya, see Abū Zakarīyā Yaḥyā ibn Sharaf an-Nawawī, *Riyāḍ aṣ-ṣāliḥīn min kalām Sayyid al-Mursalīn* (Gardens of the Righteous Made from the Words of the Lord of Messengers), ᶜAbdallāh Aḥmad Abū Zayna, ed. (Kuwait and Beirut, 1389/1970), "Bāb istiḥbāb ṣawm thalāthat ayyām min kulli shahr" (section on the desirability of fasting three days out of every month), 369–70.

11. Abū Qulāba ᶜAbdallāh ibn Zayd al-Jarmī (d. 104/723) was an early authority on Islamic doctrine who lived most of his life in Basra but died in Syria after gaining the favor of the Umayyad caliph ᶜUmar ibn ᶜAbd al-ᶜAzīz (r. 99–101/717–20). Ḥammād ibn Zayd (d. 177/793–94) transmitted accounts from him (see as-Sulamī, *Dhikr an-niswa,* section XV above). Al-Iṣfahānī describes Abū Qulāba's practice of Sufism as: "Purity in compassion and eloquence in morals." According to Massignon, he advocated a purely Islamic form of spirituality, opposing "pristine religiosity" (*ḥanīfiyya samḥa*) to "monkery" (*rahbāniyya*). See al-Iṣfahānī, *Ḥilyat al-awliyā᾽,* vol. 2, 282–89; and Ibn al-Jawzī, *Ṣifat aṣ-Ṣafwa,* vol. 3, 238–39. See also Massignon, *Essay,* 136.

12. This individual is probably Yazīd ibn Ābān ar-Raqqāshī, a disciple of al-Ḥasan al-Baṣrī. Ar-Raqqāshī was a severe ascetic and weeper (*bakkā᾽*) who was said to have fasted continuously for forty-two years. He transmitted the famous Prophetic hadith which states: "My community will divide into seventy-two sects, each of which will be in hellfire except for one." When asked which one this would be, ar-Raqqāshī replied, "The one in the majority." See al-Iṣfahānī, *Ḥilyat al-awliyā᾽,* vol. 3, 50–54; and Ibn al-Jawzī, *Ṣifat aṣ-Ṣafwa,* vol. 3, 289–90.

عمران بن خالد قال: حدّثتني أمّ الأسود بنت زيد العدوية و كانت مُعاذة قد أرضَعَتْها قالت: قالت لي معاذة -لمّا قُتل أبو الصّهباء و قُتلَ و لَدُها: «و اللّه يا بُنَيّة ما محبّتي للبقاء في الدّنيا للذيذ عَيْشٍ ولا لرَوحِ نَسيمٍ، ولكن و اللّه أحبُّ البقاءَ لأتقرّبَ إلى ربّي عزّ و جلّ بالوسائلِ لعلّه يجمَعُ بيني و بين أبي الصّهباء و ولدِه في الجنّة» .

روح بن سلمة الورّاق قال: سمعتُ غفيرة العابدة تقول: بلغني أنّ معاذة العدوية لما احْتَضَرَهَا الموتُ بكَتْ ثم ضحكَت. فقيل لها ممّ بَكيت ثم ضَحكْت؟ فَممّ البكاءُ و ممّ الضّحكُ؟ قالت أمّا البُكاءُ الذي رأيتُم فإنّي ذكرتُ مُفارَقةَ الصّيامِ والصّلاةِ و الذّكر فكان البكاءُ لذلك، وأمّا الذي رأيتم من تَبَسُّمي و ضَحكي فإنّي نظرتُ إلى أبي الصّهباء قد أقْبَل في صحْنِ الدّار و عليه حُلّتان خُضْراوان و هو في نَفَرٍ و الله ما رأيتُ لهم في الدّنيا شبهًا فضحكتُ إليه و لاأُرانِي أُدْرِكُ بعد ذلك فرضًا.

قال فماتت قبل أن يَدْخُلَ وقتُ الصّلاةِ.

أدركت معاذة عائشة و روت عنها. و روى عن معاذة الحسن البصري وأبوقلابة. و يزيدالرّشك.

II

ḤAFṢA BINT SĪRĪN[13]

ᶜĀṣim al-Aḥwal[14] said: We used to visit Ḥafṣa bint Sīrīn. She would pull her garment in such-and-such a way and would veil her face with it. So we admonished her: "May God have mercy upon you. God has said: 'Such elderly women as are past the prospect of marriage, there is no blame on them if they lay aside their outer garments, provided they make not a wanton display of their beauty' (Qurᵓān 24 [*an-Nūr*], 60]." This refers to the garment known as the *jilbāb* [a loose outer garment for women that is pulled over the head]. "Is there anything else after that?" she asked. We answered: "But it is best for them to be modest" (Ibid.). Then she replied: "This part of the verse is what confirms the use of the veil (*ḥijāb*)."

Hishām ibn Ḥassān said: Ḥafṣa said to us: "Oh assembly of youths (*shabāb*), give of yourselves while you are still youths. For I see true spiritual practice only among the youths!" [Hishām] said: Ḥafṣa mastered the art of Qurᵓān recitation by the age of twelve, and she died when she was ninety.

Hishām related that Ḥafṣa used to enter her mosque [i.e., private place of worship] and would pray the noon (*ẓuhr*), afternoon (*ᶜaṣr*), sunset (*maghrib*), evening (*ᶜīshā*), and morning (*ṣubḥ*) prayers. She would remain there until the full light of day; then she would make a single prostration and leave. At this time she would perform her ablution and sleep until the time for the noon prayer. Then she would return to her place of worship and perform the same routine as before.

Mahdī ibn Maymūn said: "Ḥafṣa remained in her place of worship for thirty years, not leaving it except to answer the call of nature or to get some sun."

Hishām [ibn Ḥassān] reported that whenever [Ḥafṣa's brother Muḥammad] Ibn Sīrīn was faced with a difficult question about the discipline of Qurᵓān recitation he would say to his questioners: "Go and ask Ḥafṣa how she recites."

13. Ibn al-Jawzī, *Ṣifat aṣ-Ṣafwa,* vol. 4, 24–26.

14. Abū ᶜAbd ar-Raḥmān ᶜĀṣim ibn Sulaymān al-Aḥwal (d. 141/758-9 or 142/759–60) was a *mawlā* of the tribe of Banū Tamīm. He was appointed judge for the Iraqi city of al-Madāᵓin (near Baghdad) by Abū Jaᶜfar al-Manṣūr (r. 136–58/754–75), who was the first ᶜAbbasid caliph to fill his provincial administration with *mawālī.* Before that, he was in charge of weights and measures in the city of Kufa. He was a close companion of Muḥammad ibn Sīrīn. See al-Iṣfahānī, *Ḥilyat al-awliyāᵓ,* vol. 3, 120–22; and Ibn al-Jawzī, *Ṣifat aṣ-Ṣafwa,* vol.3, 301. On al-Manṣūr and the *mawālī,* see Lassner, *The Shaping of ᶜAbbasid Rule,* 91–115.

(٢)

حفصة بنت سيرين

عن عـاصم الأحول قال: كنّاندخـل على حفصة بنت سـيرين و قد جَعلت الجلباب هكذا۔ وتنقبّـت به فنقول لها: رحمَـك اللّه قال اللّه: «و القواعدُ من النّساء اللاّتــي لا يرجون نكاحـًا فليْـــس عليهنّ جُنــاحٌ أن يضعْن ثِـيَابَـهُـنّ غيرَ مُـتبرّجات بزينةٍ » و هــو الـجلبـابُ. قال فتقــول لنا: أيّ شيئ بعـد ذلك؟ فنقــول: «وأَن يَـستَـعْـفِـفْنَ خيرٌ لهُــنّ» فتقــول هو إثباتُ الـحِجــابِ.

هشــام بن حسان قــال: كانت حفصــة تقول لنا: يا معشـَر الشّبّاب خُذوا من أنفُسكُـم و أنتُـم شبَـابٌ فإنّي مـا رأيْتُ العملَ إلاّ في الشّبّـــاب. قال: قَـرأَتْ القرآنَ و هي ابنةُ اثنتيْ عشرةَ سنةً و ماتت و هي ابنةُ تسعين.

عن هشــام أنّ حـفـصــة كـانت تدخــُل في مـسـجـدها فـتـُصلّي فيـــه الظّـهـر والعصـر والـمغرب و العشـاء و الصّبـح ثمّ لا تـزال فيه حتّى يرتفـع النّهـارُ وتـركَع ثـمّ تخرُج فيكـون عنـد ذلك وضـــوءَها ونومَــها، حتّى إذا حضرت الصّلاةَ عادت إلى مسجـدِها إلى مِثلِـها.

عن مـهدي بن مـيمـون قال: مكثـتْ حفصة في مُـصَلاّها ثلاثين سنةً لا تخرجُ إلاّ لِـحاجةٍ أو لقائلـةٍ.

عن هشام أنّ ابن سيرين كان إذا أُشكِل عليـه شيئٌ من القراءة قال اذهبوا فَسَلوا [فاسألوا] حفصة كيف تقرأ.

Hishām ibn Ḥassān said: Al-Hudhayl the son of Ḥafṣa used to gather firewood in the summertime. He would peel it, and then take the reeds and split them. Ḥafṣa said: "I used to feel cold. When winter came, al-Hudhayl would bring a brazier and put it behind me while I was in my place of worship. Then he would sit down and kindle a fire that did not produce harmful smoke with the firewood peelings and the reeds that he had split into strips. In this way he would make me warm. We would remain with that fire as long as God permitted." She added: "One would have as much of it as one wanted."

Ḥafṣa said: "Sometimes I wanted to go to al-Hudhayl and say: 'Oh my son, return to your family!' Then I would remember what he desired by serving me, so I left him alone."

Ḥafṣa said: "When my son al-Hudhayl died, God blessed me with much patience. However, I had a lump in my throat which would not go away."

Ḥafṣa said: "One night while I was reciting the Sura of the Bee (*an-Naḥl*), I came upon this verse: 'Nor sell the convenant of Allah for a miserable price. For with Allah is a reward far better for you, if you only knew. What is yours must vanish; What is Allah's will endure. And We will certainly bestow, on those who patiently persevere, their reward according to the best of their actions' (Qurʾān 16 [*an-Naḥl*], 95-96)." She said: "I repeated this verse, and God made what I had found in my throat disappear."

Hishām [ibn Ḥassān] said: Al-Hudhayl used to own a she-camel heavy with milk. Ḥafṣa said: "He used to send me milk in the morning, and I would say to him, 'Oh my son! You know that I cannot drink it because I am fasting.' He would reply, 'Oh Umm Hudhayl! The best milk is that which is left overnight in the camel's udder, so [if you cannot drink it youself] serve the milk to whomever you please.'"

Hishām ibn Ḥassān [reporting from a certain Ibrāhīm] said: Ḥafṣa bought a slave-girl, whom I assumed to be from Sind.[15] The slave-girl was asked: "What is your opinion of your mistress?" Ibrāhīm mentioned some words in Persian, to the effect that the slave-girl answered: "Ḥafṣa is a righteous woman, but she must have committed a grave sin because she spends the entire night weeping and praying."

15. The region of Sind is in present-day Pakistan.

هشام بن حسان قال: كان الهُذَيْل بن حفصة يجمع الحطب في الصّيف فيُقشّرُهُ و يأخُذ القصبَ فيُفْلقُهُ. قالت حفصة و كنت أجد قرّةً فكان إذا جاء الشّتاء جاء بالكانون فيضعه خلفي وأنا في مصلايَ ثمّ يقعُد فيُوقد بذلك الحطب المقشّر و ذاك القصب المفلّق وُقودا لا يُؤذي دخّانه ويُدفِئني. نمكث بذلك ما شاء الّله. قالت: و عند من يكفيه لو أراد ذلك.

قالت: و ربّما أردتُ أنصَرفُ إليه فأقول يا بنيّ ارْجِعْ إلى أهلكَ ثمّ أذكُر ما يُريدُ فأدعُه. قالت حفصة: فلما مات رزق الّله عليه من الصّبْر ما شاءَ أن يرزُقَ غير أنّي كُنت أجدُ غُصّةً لا تذهب. قالت فبينا أنا ذات ليلة أقرأ سورة النّحل إذْ أتيتُ على هذه الآية: « و لا تشتروا بعهد الّله ثمنًا قليلاً إنّ ما عند الّله خيرٌ لكُم إنْ كنتُم تعلمون، ما عندكُم يَنْفُذُ و ما عند الّله باقٍ ولَنَجْزيَن الذين صبَروا أجرَهم بأحسن ما كانوا يعملون [قرآن: سورة النّحل: آية ٩٥-٩٦] » قالت: فأعدْتُها فأذهَبَ الّله ما كنتُ أجدُ. قال هشام: و كانت له لقحَة.قالت حفصة: كان يبْعث إليّ بحلبَة بالغداة فأقول: يا بنيّ إنّك تعلمُ أنّي لا أشربه، أنا صائمة . فيقول: يا أمّ الهُذيل إنّ أطيبَ اللّبن ما بات في ضروع الإبِل، اسقِيه مَن شِئْتِ.

عن هشام بن حسان قال: اشترت حفصة جارية أظنّها سنديّة فقيل لها: كيف رأيْت مولاتَك؟ فذكر ابراهيم كلامًا بالفارسية تفسيرُه أنّها امرأةٌ صالحةَ إلاّ أنّها أذنبَت ذنبًا عظيما فهي الليل كلَّه تبكي و تُصلّي.

ᶜAbd al-Karīm ibn Muᶜāwiyya said: It was mentioned to me about Ḥafṣa that she would recite half of the Qurʾān every night and would fast every day, not breaking her fast except for the two canonical feast days (*al-ᶜīdayn*)[16] and the Days of *Tashrīq.*[17]

Hishām ibn Ḥassān said: I have seen al-Ḥasan [ibn Sīrīn] and I have seen [his father Muḥammad] ibn Sīrīn, but I have never seen anyone who was more endowed with reason (*aᶜqil*) than Ḥafṣa.

Hishām ibn Ḥassān reported about Ḥafṣa: She used to own a burial-shroud, and whenever she made the Ḥajj pilgrimage, she would wear it as her pilgrimage garment. During the last ten days of Ramaḍān, she would also wear it while performing her night vigils.

Hishām ibn Ḥassān said: [Ḥafṣa's sister] Umm Sulaym bint Sīrīn reported to me: "At times, the house of Ḥafṣa bint Sīrīn was illuminated for her."

Hishām also related: Ḥafṣa bint Sīrīn used to light her lamp at night, and then would rise to pray in her place of worship. Sometimes, the oil in the lamp would go out, but the lamp would continue to illuminate her house until daylight.

16. The canonical feast days in Islam are the feast day that marks the end of the fasting month of Ramaḍān (*ᶜĪd al-Fiṭr*) and the feast day that celebrates the end of the Ḥajj pilgrimage to Mecca and the sacrifice of the Prophet Abraham (*ᶜĪd al-Aḍḥā*).

17. The "Days of Tashrīq" (*ayyām tashrīq*) are the three days of the Hajj pilgrimage that follow the ᶜĪd al-Aḍḥā sacrifice. From the 11th to the 13th of the month of Dhū al-Ḥijja, the pilgrims gather at Mīnā, where they sacrificed on the 10th, and each day throw stones or date pits (*jimār,* sing. *jamra*) at the pillars that commemorate Satan's attempt to corrupt the Prophet Ismāᶜīl. Because the state of *iḥrām* is lifted from pilgrims after the ᶜĪd sacrifice, Muslims are not encouraged to fast on the Days of *Tashrīq.* See, for example, *Sunan ibn Māja,* "Bāb mā jāʾa fī an-nahyi ᶜan ṣiyām ayyām at-tashrīq" (section on what has been transmitted concerning the prohibition of fasting on the Days of Tashrīq), vol. 1, 548; and "Bāb ramā al-jimār ayyām at-tashrīq" (section on the throwing of stones during the Days of Tashrīq), vol. 2, 1014. According to at-Tirmidhī, however, fasting on these days was allowed by some Companions of the Prophet after the latter's death. See Abū ᶜĪsā Muḥammad ibn ᶜĪsā at-Tirmidhī (d. 297/909–10), *al-Jāmiᶜ aṣ-ṣaḥīḥ,* Muḥammad Fuʾād ᶜAbd al-Bāqī, ed. (Cairo, 1396/1976), "Bāb mā jāʾa fī karāhiyat aṣ-ṣawm fī ayyām at-tashrīq" (section on what has been transmitted concerning the disapproval of fasting on the Days of Tashrīq), vol. 3, 134–35.

عبد الكريم بن معاوية قال: ذُكِر لي عن حفصة أنّها كانت تقرأ نصْف القرآن في كلّ ليلةٍ وكانت تَصومُ الدّهر و تُفْطِرُ العِيدَيْن وَأيّام التّشريق.

عن هشام عن حفصة قال: قد رأيتُ الحسن و ابن سيرين و ما رأيتُ أحداً أرى أنّه أعقَلُ من حفصة.

عن هشام عن حفصة قال: كان لها كُفْنٌ مُعَدٌّ فإذا حَجَّتْ و أحرمَت لبِسَتْهُ و كانت إذا كانت العشر الأواخر من رمضان قامت من اللّيل فلَبِسَتْهُ.

عن هشام قال: حدّثتني أمّ سليم بنت سيرين قالت: رُبّما نُوّرَ لحفصة بنت سيرين بيتُها.

عن هشام قال: كانت حفصة بنت سيرين تسرج سراجها من اللّيل ثمّ تقوم في مُصلاّها فربّما طفئ السِّراج فيضيئ لها البيتُ حتّى تصبِح.

III

RĀBIʿA AL-ʿADAWIYYA[18]

ʿAbdallāh ibn ʿĪsā said: I entered Rābiʿa al-ʿAdawiyya's house and saw light upon her face. She also used to weep frequently. Once a man read in her presence a verse from the Qurʾān in which Hellfire was mentioned. Upon hearing it, Rābiʿa shrieked, then passed out.

[ʿAbdallāh ibn ʿĪsā said]: I visited Rābiʿa while she was sitting on a mat made of the skin of a striped mullet (a type of fish). A man was discussing something with her. As I listened, I began to hear the sound of Rābiʿa's tears falling on the dried mullet skin like pouring rain. Then she became agitated and cried out. At that point, we got up and left.

Masmaʿ ibn ʿĀṣim [al-Jaḥdarī] and Rabāḥ al-Qaysī said: We observed Rābiʿa when a man came to her with forty dinars [a gold coin based on the late Roman and Byzantine *denarius*] and said: "Use this money to fulfill some of your needs." Rābiʿa wept, then raised her head towards the sky and said: "God knows that I am ashamed to petition Him for the goods of the world because He alone possesses them. How could I ever wish to take them from someone who does not possess them?"

Muḥammad ibn ʿAmr said: I visited Rābiʿa when she was an old woman of eighty years of age. She looked like a shrunken, old waterskin, and appeared to be on the verge of collapsing. In her house I saw a worn, rectangular mat and a clothes rack made of Persian reeds, extending about two spans up from the floor. The door to the house was covered by a skin, perhaps made from mullet. There were also a jar, a mug, and a piece of felt that served as her bed and her prayer rug. On the clothes rack made of reeds she had hung her burial shrouds. Whenever Rābiʿa mentioned death or passed by people who were aware of her worshipfulness, she would shake and be overcome by tremors.

A man once said to Rābiʿa: "Make a supplication for me." She cringed against the wall and replied: "Who am I to ask God to have mercy on you? Obey your Lord and call upon Him yourself! For verily He answers the supplications of those who are troubled!"

18. Ibn al-Jawzī, *Ṣifat aṣ-Ṣafwa,* vol. 4, 27–31.

(٣)

رابعة العدوية

عبد الله بن عيسى قال: دخلتُ على رابعة العدوية [و هي في] بيتها فرأيتُ على وجهها النّور و كانت كثيرة البُكاءِ فقرأ رجلٌ عندها آيةً من القرآن فيها ذِكْرُ النّار فصاحت ثمّ سقطَتْ.

ودخلتُ عليها و هي جالسة على قطعة بورى خلق فتكلّم رجل عندها بشيئٍ فجعلتُ أسمعُ وقع دموعها على البُورى مثل الوكف، ثمّ اضطربت وصاحتْ فقُمْنا و خرجْنا.

مسمع بن عاصم و رياح القيسي قالا: شَهدنا رابعة و قد أتاها رجلٌ بأربعين ديناراً فقال لها: تستعنين بها على بعض حوائجك. فبكت ثمّ رفعت رأسَها إلى السّماء فقالت: هو يعلم أنّي أستحيي منه أن أَسأله الدّنيا و هو يمِلكُها، فكيف أريدُ أنْ آخُذها ممّن لا يمِلكُها ؟

محمّد بن عمرو قال: دخلتُ على رابعة و كانت عجوزا كبيرةً بنت ثمانين سنةً كأنّها الشّنّ تكاد تسقط و رأيتُ في بيتها كراخة بوارى و مشجب قصب فارسي طوله من الأرض قدر ذراعين، و ستر البيت جلد و ربّما كان بوريا و حبٌّ و كوز و لبد هو فراشها و هو مصلاّها. و كان لها مشجب من قصب عليه أكفانها و كانت إذا ذكرت الموت انتفضت و أصابتها رعدة وإذا مرّت بقوم عرفوا فيها العبادة.

قال لها رجل: ادْعي. فالتصقت بالحائط و قالت: من أنا يرحمُك اللّه؟ أطِعْ ربّكَ و ادْعُهُ فإنّه يُجيبُ المضطرّين.

Sayf ibn Manẓūr said: I entered Rābiᶜa's house while she was prostrating in prayer. When she sensed my presence, she raised her head. To my surprise, her place of prostration was shaped like a puddle of water from her tears. She greeted me and approached me, saying: "Oh my son! Are you in need of something?" "I only came to greet you," I replied. [Sayf ibn Manẓūr] said: She began to weep and said: "Oh God, may You protect us! May You protect us!" Then she made some supplications for me. When she stood up and resumed praying, I left.

Al-ᶜAbbās ibn al-Walīd said: Rābiᶜa said: "I ask God's forgiveness for my lack of truthfulness in saying, 'I ask God's forgiveness."

Azhar ibn Marwān said: Rabāḥ al-Qaysī, Ṣāliḥ ibn ᶜAbd al-Jalīl and Kilāb[19] visited Rābiᶜa. They brought up the world and began to criticize it. Rābiᶜa said: "Verily, I see the world in its entirety in your hearts!" They replied: "How did you come to imagine this about us?" She said: "Because you concerned yourselves with the closest thing to your hearts and spoke about it."

Abū Jaᶜfar al-Madīnī[20] related from a leader of the tribe of Quraysh: Someone said to Rābiᶜa: "Have you ever performed a deed that you deemed acceptable to God?" She said: "If there had been such a deed, I would have been afraid that it would be rejected."

Jaᶜfar ibn Sulaymān [aḍ-Ḍubᶜī] said: Sufyān ath-Thawrī took me by the hand and said about Rābiᶜa: "Come with us to the mentor in whose absence I can find no solace." When we entered her house, Sufyān raised his hand and said: "Oh God, verily I petition You for safety!" At this, Rābiᶜa wept. "What makes you weep?" he asked. "You caused me to weep," she replied. "How"? he asked. She answered: "Have you not learned that true safety from the world is to abandon all that is in it? So how can you ask such a thing while you are still soiled with the world?"

[Sufyān] ath-Thawrī said in Rābiᶜa's presence: "How sorrowful I am!" "Do not lie!" she replied. "Say instead, 'How little is my sorrow!' If you were truly sorrowful, life itself would not please you."

Jaᶜfar ibn Sulaymān said: I heard Rābiᶜa say to Sufyān: "You are but a set of numbered days. When one day goes, a part of you goes as well. And with the disappearance of the parts, the whole is nearly lost as well. You [Sufyān] are aware of this, so remember!"

19. Abū Sayyār Kilāb ibn Jurā was an ascetic and weeper (*bakkā'*) from Basra. It was said that none could equal him in the strength of his fear of God and fervor in his love for God. Ibn al-Jawzī gives no information about the date of his death. See idem, *Ṣifat aṣ-Ṣafwa,* vol. 3, 381.

20. Abū Jaᶜfar ᶜAbdallāh b. Jaᶜfar al-Madīnī was a well-known transmitter of hadith. His son, ᶜAlī ibn Jaᶜfar, died in 234/849. See Franz Rosenthal, *A History of Muslim Historiography* (Leiden, 1968), 363.

سيف بن منظور قال: دخلتُ على رابعة وهي ساجدة فلمّا أحسّتْ بمكاني رفعتْ رأسَها فإذا موضعُ سُجُودهَا كهيئة الماء المُسْتَنْقَعِ من دمُوعها. فسلّمت وأقبلت عليَ فقالت: يَا بُنيّ ألكَ حاجة؟ فقلت جئت لأسلّمَ عليك، قال: فبكت و قالت سَتْرُكَ اللّهمّ سَتْرُكَ ! و دعَتْ بدعواتٍ ثم قامت إلى الصلاة و انصرفتُ.

العباس بن الوليد قال: قالت رابعة: استغفر الله من قلّة صدقي في قولي أستغفر الله.

أزهر بن مروان قال: دخل على رابعة رباح القيسي، و صالح ابن عبد الجليل، و كلاب، فتذاكروا الدّنيا فأقبلوا يذُمّونها فقالت رابعة: إنّي لأرى الدّنيا بترابيعها في قلوبكم. قالوا: و من أين توهّمتِ علينا؟ قالت: إنّكم نظرتم إلى أقربِ الأشياء من قلوبِكُم فتكلّمتُم فيه.

أبو جعفر المديني، عن شيخ من قريش قال: قيل لرابعة: هل عملت عملاً تَرَيْنَ أنّه يُقبَلُ منكِ ؟ قالت : إنْ كان فمخافتي أن يُرَدّ عليّ.

جعفر بن سليمان قال: أخذ بيدي سفيان الثوري و قال مرّ بنا إلى المؤدّبة التي لا أجد من أستريح إليه إذا فارقتها. فلمّا دخلنا عليها رفع سفيان يده وقال: اللهمّ إنّي أسألكَ السّلامة فبكت رابعة. فقال لها: ما يُبكيك؟ قالت: أنتَ عرّضَتني للبكاء. فقال: و كيف؟ قالت: أما علمتَ أنّ السَلامة من الدّنيا تركُ ما فيها فكيْف و أنت متلطّخ بها. ؟

و قال الثوري بين يديّ رابعة: وا حُزْنَاهُ. فقالت: لا تكذب. قُلْ: وا قلّةَ حُزْنَاهُ، لو كنتَ محزونًا ما هنّاك [هنأ لكَ] العيشُ.

جعفر بن سليمان قال: سمعتُ رابعة تقول لسفيان: إنّما أنت أيامٌ معدوداتٌ، فإذا ذهب يومٌ ذهب بعضُك، و يُوشِك إذا ذهب البعضُ أن يذهبَ الكلّ وأنت تعلم، فاعلمْ.

ᶜAbīs ibn Marḥūm al-ᶜAṭṭār (the Spice-Merchant) said: ᶜAbda bint Abī Shawwāl (one of the best slave-women of God who also served Rābiᶜa) related to me: Rābiᶜa used to pray the entire night. When dawn began to break she would take a short rest until it had fully appeared. She would leap up from her place of sleep as if in alarm, and I would hear her say: "Oh soul! How long will you sleep? And how long will it be before you awaken? Your sleep[21] is nearly as deep as the sleep from which you will only awaken when the trumpet heralds the Day of Resurrection!"

ᶜAbda said: That was the way she lived her life until she died. When her death approached, she summoned me and said: "Oh ᶜAbda! Do not inform anyone of my death. Just wrap me up in this shroud of mine." This was a shroud made of hair that Rābiᶜa used to wear during her night vigils when everyone was asleep.

ᶜAbda said: So we wrapped her in that shroud and a woolen veil that she used to wear.

ᶜAbda said: After a year or so, I saw Rābiᶜa in my sleep dressed in a bright green dress and wearing a veil made of green silk brocade. Never before had I seen anything so beautiful. I said: "Oh Rābiᶜa! what happened to the shroud and the woolen veil in which we wrapped you?" She said: "By God, they were taken from me and were replaced with what you see on me now. My shrouds were wrapped, sealed, and lifted up to the highest heaven[22] so that God's forgiveness for me on the Day of Judgment would be complete."

21. In this notice the modern editors of *Ṣifat aṣ-Ṣafwa* have mistakenly used the construction *manāmī* (my sleep) instead of *manāmaki* (your [f.] sleep). This latter construction is preferable because Rābiᶜa is speaking not to herself, but to her lower soul (*nafs* [f.]).

22. *ᶜIlliyyīn*, "The High Places," is a reference to Qurʾān 83 (*al-Muṭafifīn*), 18–21.

عبيس بن مرحوم العطار قال: حدّثتني عبدة بنت أبي شوّال، و كانت من خيار إماء الّله، و كانت تخدُمُ رابعة. قالت: كانت رابعة تُصلي الليل كلّه فإذا طلع الفجرُ هجعَت في مُصلاّها هجعةً خفيفةً حتّي يُسْفرَ الفجْرُ، فكنْتُ أسمَعُها تقول، إذا وثَبَتْ من مرقَدها ذلك و هي فزعة: يا نفسُ كم تنامين؟ و إلى كم تَقُومين؟ يوشك أنّ منامَك نومةً لا تقومين منها إلاّ لصرخة يوم النّشور. قالت: فكان هذا دأبُها دهرَها حتّى ماتت. فلمّا حضرتْها الوفاة دعتْني فقالت: يا عبدة لا تؤذني بموتي أحداً و كفّنيني في جُبّتي هذه. جُبّةٌ من شعر كانت تقوم فيها إذا هدأت العيون. قالت: فكفنّاها في تلك الجبّة و خمار صوف كانت تلبسُهُ. قالت عبدة: رأيتها بعد ذلك بسنة أو نحوها في منامي عليها حلّة استبرق خضراء و خمار من سُنْدُس أخضر لم أرَ شيئا قط أحسن منهُ. فقلت: يا رابعة ما فعلتْ الجبّة التي كفنّاك فيها و الخمار الصّوف؟ قالت: إنّه و الّله نُزع عنّي و أُبْدلتُ به هذا الذي ترينه عليّ. و طُويت أكفاني و خُتِم عليها و رُفِعَتْ في علّيّين ليُكمَلَ لي بها ثوابها يوم القيامة.

ᶜAbda said: I said to Rābiᶜa: "Is this what you were striving for during your time in this world?" She said: "Is this not a miracle that God, the Glorious and Mighty, bestows on His saints?" ᶜAbda said: "How did ᶜAbda [ᶜUbayda] bint Abī Kilāb[23] fare?" I asked. Rābiᶜa answered: "What a question! What a question! By God, she has surpassed us and has reached the utmost degree!" ᶜAbda said: I asked Rābiᶜa: "How could this be, while you were so highly esteemed by people?" Rābiᶜa answered: "She paid no heed to the state in which she found herself, whether it be in the morning or at night." ᶜAbda said: Then I asked: "How did Abū Mālik [Ḍaygham ibn Mālik][24] fare?" She answered: "He visits God whenever he wants." "How did Bishr ibn Manṣūr[25] fare?" I asked. "Well, well!" (*bakh bakh,* a Persian term) she replied. "He was given far more than he had hoped for!"

ᶜAbda said: I asked Rābiᶜa: "Command me to do something by which I may come closer to God, the Glorious and Mighty." She answered: "Maintain constant remembrance of Him. This will bring you delight nearly all the way to your grave."

[Ibn al-Jawzī] said: I limited myself to this number of accounts concerning Rābiᶜa, because I have already dedicated a book to her in which I gathered all of her sayings and reports about her.[26]

23. On ᶜUbayda bint Abī Kilāb, see section VI below and as-Sulamī, *Dhikr an-niswa,* section XXVII above.

24. Abū Mālik Ḍaygham ibn Mālik, known as "The Worshipper" (*al-ᶜābid*) was a companion of al-Ḥasan al-Baṣrī. In his spirituality he was strongly influenced by his mother, who was of bedouin origin. His daily religious practices consisted of 400 prostrations (*rakᶜāt*). He was said to resemble no other person in his sadness and the extent to which he lived in awe of God and afflicted his body with austerities. He said: "If I knew that it would bring about God's satisfaction, I would call upon the cleaver to cut my flesh into pieces." Ibn al-Jawzī gives no date for his death. Idem, *Ṣifat aṣ-Ṣafwa,* vol. 3, 357–60.

25. Abū Muḥammad Bishr ibn Manṣūr as-Sulaymī was a noted preacher and specialist in Islamic doctrine. He was of Arab origin and studied under Sufyān ath-Thawrī (d. 161 /777–78), from whom he transmitted the hadith: "Religion is nothing more than good counsel" (*innamā ad-dīnu an-naṣīḥa*). It was said about him that if a person saw him, that person would remember God, and if one saw his face, he would recall the afterlife. See al-Iṣfahānī, *Ḥilyat al-awliyāʾ,* vol. 6, 239-243; and Ibn al-Jawzī, *Ṣifat aṣ-Ṣafwa,* vol. 3, 376–77.

26. According to Massignon (via Brockelmann and Goldziher), this work was entitled *Manāqib Rābiᶜa al-muᶜtazila* (Exploits of Rābiᶜa the Recluse). See idem, *Essay,* np. 149. In this particular case, the term *muᶜtazila* refers to *ᶜuzla,* the practice of withdrawl from human society. It has nothing to do with the later theological school of Islamic rationalism, also known as *al-Muᶜtazila.*

قالت: فقلت لها: لهذا كنت تعملين أيّام الدّينا؟ فقالت وما هذا من كرامة الّله عزّ و جلّ لأوليائه. قالت: فقلت: فما فعلت عبدة بنت أبي كلاب؟ فقالت هيهات هيهات، سبقتنا و الّله إلى الدّرجات العلى. قالت قلت و بمَ وقد كنت عند النّاس؟ أي أكثر منها. قالت: إنّها لم تكن تُبالي علَى أيّ حالٍ أصبحت من الدّنيا و أمست. قالت: فقلت: فما فعل أبو مالك؟ تعنى ضيغمًا. قالت: يزور الّله متى شاء. قالت: قلتُ: فما فعل بشر بن منصور؟ قالت: بخ بخ أُعطِيَ و الّله فوق ما كان يأمُلُ. قالت: قَلت فمُريني بأمر أتقرّب به إلى الّله عَزّ و جلّ. قالت عليك بكثرة ذكره. أوشك أن تغتبطي بذلك في قبرك.

قلت [الشيخ صاحب الكتاب] : اقتصرت ههنا على هذا القدر من أخبار رابعة لأنّي قد أفردت لها كتابًا [جمعتُ] فيه كلامها وأخبارها.

IV

ʿAJRADA AL-ʿAMIYYA[27]

(ʿAjrada the Blind)

Rajāʾ ibn Muslim al-ʿAbdī said: We used to visit ʿAjrada the Blind at her home. She used to spend her nights in prayers and vigils. Perhaps he also said: She would stand from the beginning of the night until the coming of dawn. When dawn broke she would lament in a sorrowful voice: "For Your sake, oh, God, the worshippers cut themselves off from the world in the darkness of night, glorifying You from nightfall until the pre-dawn hours, competing for Your mercy and the favor of Your forgiveness. So through You, my God, and none other, I ask you to put me in the first rank of the Foremost, that You raise me up to the level of Your Intimates, and that You include me among Your Righteous Servants.[28] You are the Most Generous of the generous, the Most Merciful of the merciful, and the Greatest of the great. Oh, Noble One!" Then she would drop to her knees in prostration and would remain weeping and supplicating in a prostrate position until the sun rose at dawn. This was her habit for thirty years.

ʿAbd ar-Raḥmān ibn ʿAmr al-Bāhilī reported through Dalāl the daughter of Abū al-Mudill: My mother Āmina bint Yaʿlā ibn Suhayl related to me: ʿAjrada the Blind would come at the end of the day and spend the night with us for one or two days. My mother said: When night came, ʿAjrada would put on her garments and veil her face. She would stand in the prayer niche and remain praying until the first part of the dawn. Then she would sit and make supplications until daybreak.

[Āmina bint Yaʿlā] also said: I said to her (or someone else from the family said to her): "If only you would sleep for part of the night!" ʿAjrada wept and replied: "The remembrance of death does not allow me to sleep."

Jaʿfar ibn Sulaymān [aḍ-Ḍubʿī] said: One of my women (my mother or another woman from my family) reported to me: I saw ʿAjrada the Blind on a certain holiday. She was wearing a woolen outer garment, a woolen head veil, and a woolen mantle. She said: I looked closely at her and found that she was nothing but skin and bone.

The same woman said: I heard people mention about ʿAjrada that she did not break her fast for sixty years.

27. Ibn al-Jawzī, *Ṣifat aṣ-Ṣafwa,* vol. 4, 31–32.

28. On God's "Foremost" and "Intimates," see Qurʾān 56 (*al-Wāqiʿa*), 10–11. On "Your Righteous Servants" see Qurʾān 27 (*an-Naml*), 19.

(٤)

عجردة العمية

رجاء بن مسلم العبدي قال: كنّا نكون عند عجردة العمية في الدّار. قال: فكانت تحيي اللّيل صلاةً. و ربّما قال: تقوم من أوّل الليل إلى السّحر فإذا كان السّحر نادت بصوت لها محزونٍ: إليك قطع العابدون دُجى الليالي بتبكير الدلج إلى ظلم الأسحار يستبقون إلى رحمتك و فضل مغفرتك. فبك إلهي لا بغيرك أسألك أن تجعلني في أوّل زمرة السّابقين إليك، وأن ترفعني إليك في درجة المقرّبين، و أن تُلحقني بعبَادك الصّالحين، فأنت أكرم الكرماء، و أرحم الرّحماء، و أعظم العظَماء، يَا كريم. ثمّ تخرّ ساجدة فلا تزال تبكي و تدعو في سجودها حتّى يطلعَ الفجرُ فكان ذلك دأبُها ثلاثين سنة.

عبد الرحمن بن عمرو الباهلي قال: حدّثتني دلال بنت أبي المدلّ قالت: حدّثتني أُمّي آمنة بنت يعلى بن سهيل قالت: كانت عجردة العمية تغشانا فتظلّ عندنا اليوم و اليومين. قالت: فكانت إذا جاء الليل لبست ثيابها و تقنّعت ثمّ قامت إلى المحراب فلا تزال تصلّي إلى السّحر ثمّ تجلس فتدعو حتّى يطلع الفجر. قالت: فقلت لها: أو قال لها بعضُ أهل الدّار: لو نمت من اللّيل شيئا. فبكت و قالت: ذكر الموت لا يدعني أنام.

جعفر بن سليمان قال: حدّثني بعض نسائي، أمّي أو غيرها من أهلي. قالت: رأيت عجردة العمية في يوم عيدٍ عليها جبّة صوفٍ، و قناع صوفٍ، وكساء صوف. قالت: فنظرتُ فإذا هي جلدٌ وعظم. قالت: و سمعتهم يذكرون عنها أنّها لم تُفطِرْ ستّين عاما.

V

GHUFAYRA AL-ᶜĀBIDA[29]

(Ghufayra the Worshipper)

Rawḥ ibn Salama al-Warrāq (the Copyist) said to Ghufayra the Worshipper: "I have been informed that you do not sleep at night." She wept and then replied: "Perhaps I desired to sleep but I was not able to do so. How can one sleep or even be able to sleep when her two guardian angels do not sleep either in the day or at night?" By God! She made me [Rawḥ ibn Salama] weep and I said inwardly: "I see myself in one spiritual state and I see you [Ghufayra] in another."

Yaḥyā ibn Bisṭām said: I visited Ghufayra with a group of friends. She had been worshipping for a long time and had become blind from weeping. One of our friends said to the person beside him: "Blindness is most devastating to the one who used to see." Ghufayra heard him and said to him: "Oh slave of God! The blindness of the heart from God is more devastating than the blindness of the eye from the world. By God! I would rather have God grant me the essence of His love. Then He could take whatever was left from my extremities."

ᶜAbd al-Wahhāb ibn Ṣāliḥ reported that he heard Muḥammad ibn ᶜUbayd say: We visited a woman in Basra who was called Ghufayra and someone said to her : "Oh Ghufayra! Make a supplication to God for us!" She replied: "If the wrongdoers became mute your old woman would not have to speak. But God the Good (*al-Muḥsin*) has commanded the sinner to supplicate Him. So may God make your stay in my house a taste of Heaven. And may He make both you and me aware of death."

Mālik ibn Ḍaygham [the son of Ḍaygham ibn Mālik] reported that he heard Ghufayra say: "I have sinned against You, oh God, with each of my extremeties. By God, if You aid me, I will do my best to obey You with every extremity with which I have disobeyed You."

29. Ibn al-Jawzī, *Ṣifat aṣ-Ṣafwa,* vol. 4, 33–34. Ghufayra's name is given as *ᶜUfayra* (with an *ᶜayn* rathar than a *ghayn*) in the edited version of this work. While the word *ᶜaffāra* means "dusty," *ᶜufayra* is not a common term in Arabic. *Ghufayra,* on the other hand, is derived from *ghufrān* (forgiveness), and means "one who forgives." This should not be confused with *ghafīr,* which is an adjective signifying abundance. This apparent mistake by an early copyist of *Ṣifat aṣ-Ṣafwa,* the source of which is the elimination of a single dot, was perpetuated in the ninth/fifteenth century by ᶜAbd ar-Raḥmān al-Jāmī in *Nafaḥāt al-uns* (617). Modern scholars who rely primarily on Ibn al-Jawzī and Jāmī for their information on early Sufi women continue to make the same mistake. See, for example, Nelly Amri and Laroussi Amri, *Les femmes soufies ou la passion de Dieu* (St-Jean de Braye, France, 1992), 138–39 and n.1.

(٥)

غفيرة العابدة

روح بن سلمة الورّاق قال: لغفيرة العابدة: بلغني أنّك لا تنامين بالليل. فبكت، ثمّ قالت: ربّما اشتهيت أن أنام فلا أقدر عليه، و كيف ينام أو كيف يقدر على النّوم، من لاينام عنه حافظاه ليلا و لا نهاراً؟ قال: فأبْكَتني والّله، و قلت في نفسي: أراني [أرى نفسي] في شيءٍ و أراكِ في شيءٍ.

يحيى بن بسطام قال: دخلت مع نفر من أصحابنا على غفيرة، و كانت قد تعبّدت و بَكتْ حتّى عَميَتْ. فقال بعضُ أصحابنا لرجل إلى جَنبه: ما أشدّ العمى على من كان بصيراً. فسمعته غفيرة فقالت له: يا عبد الله عمى القلب -و الّله! - عن الّله أشدُّ من عمى العين عن الدّنيا، و الّله وددتُ أنّ الّله وهب لي كنهَ محبّته و أنّه لم تبق منّي جارحة إلاّ أخذها.

عبد الوهّاب بن صالح قال: سمعت محمّد بن عبيد يقول: دخلنا على امرأة بالبصرة يقال لها غفيرة، فقيل لها: يا غفيرة ادعي الّله لنا. فقالت: لو خرس الخاطئون ما تكلّمت عجوزكم، و لكن المحسنَ أمر المسيءَ بالدعاء، جعل الّله قراكم من بيتي الجنّة، و جعل الموت منّي و منكم على بال.

مالك بن ضيغم قال: سمعتُ غفيرة تقول عصيتك بكل جارحة منّي على حدّتها، و الّله لئن أعنت لأطيعنّك ما استطعت بكل جارحة عصيتُك بها.

Muḥammad ibn al-Ḥusayn [al-Burjulānī][30] related from Saʾīd al-ʿAmā (the Blind) who reported: I said to Ghufayra: "Don't you get depressed from crying so much?" She wept and said: "Oh, my son! How could one who has become ill from something become weary of that which contains the cure for her illness?" He said: Then she wept again. So I stood up, went out of her house and left her.

It was reported to me that Yaḥyā ibn Rāshid said: We were at Ghufayra the Worshipper's when news reached her about a nephew of hers whom she had not seen for a long time. She began to weep and someone said to her: "Why do you weep? This is a day of joy and happiness." Her crying increased and she replied: "By God, I cannot find any place for joy in my heart while I am thinking of the Hereafter. The news of my nephew's arrival reminded me of the day of my encounter with God. So I am between joy and devastation." Then she was overcome and fainted.

30. Accounts in this work that are attributed to Muḥammad ibn al-Ḥusayn al-Burjulānī (d. 238/852) most likely came from his *Kitāb ar-ruhbān* (Book of Monks and Ascetics), which has not yet been located in modern manuscript collections. See as-Sulamī, *Dhikr an-niswa,* n. 40 above.

قال محمّد بن الحسين: و حدّثني سعيد العمى قال: قلتُ لغفيرة: أما تسأمين من طول البكاء؟ قال: فبكت ثمّ قالت: يا بنيّ كيف يسأم ذو داء من شيئ يرجو أنّ له فيه من دائه شفاءً؟ قال: ثمّ بكت. فقمتُ فخرجتُ فتركتُها.

بلغني عن يحيى بن راشد أنّه قال: كنّا عند غفيرة العابدة فقدمَ ابن أخ لها كانت طالت غيبته فبشّرت به. فبكت فقيل لها ما هذا البكاء؟ اليوم يوم فرح و سرور، فازدادت بكاءً ثمّ قالت: و اللّه ما أجدُ للسّرور في قلبي مسكنًا مع ذكر الآخرة، ولقد أذكرني [ذكّرني] قدومه [بِـ] يوم القدوم على اللّه، فمن بين مسرور و مثبور. ثمّ غشي عليها.

VI
ᶜUBAYDA BINT ABĪ KILĀB[31]

Shuᶜayb ibn Muḥriz reported that Salāma the Worshipper said: ᶜUbayda bint Abī Kilāb wept for forty years until she lost her eyesight.

Yāḥyā ibn Bisṭām al-Aṣghar (the Younger) reported that Salama al-Afqam, who used to visit the village of aṭ-Ṭufāwa, said: I asked ᶜUbayda bint Abī Kilāb: "What do you desire?" "Death," she replied. "Why?" I asked. She replied: "Because, by God, every morning I get up fearing that I would commit a sin against myself that would lead to my perdition in the Days of Judgment!"

[Muḥammad ibn] ᶜAbd al-ᶜAzīz ibn Salmān said: ᶜUbayda and my father [ᶜAbd al-ᶜAzīz ibn Salmān][32] used to visit Mālik ibn Dinār[33] for twenty years. My father said: I never heard her ask Mālik about anything except once, when she said: "Oh, Abū Yaḥyā! When does the God-conscious person reach the ultimate level, above which there is no other level?" Mālik said: "Bravo! Well done, ᶜUbayda! When the God-conscious person reaches that highest level, above which there is no other level, nothing is more dear to him than standing before God." [ᶜAbd al-ᶜAzīz] said: ᶜUbayda uttered one cry and fell to the ground unconscious.

31. Ibn al-Jawzī, *Ṣifat aṣ-Ṣafwa,* vol. 4, 34–35.

32. ᶜAbd al-ᶜAzīz ibn Salmān is called "The Enraptured" (*al-wālih*) by al-Iṣfahānī. His spiritual practice was based on the fear of God. It was said that when he mentioned the Day of Judgment in his sermons, he would cry out, and his cries would be answered by others who lived in fear of God. At times, people would drop dead in his teaching sessions. Rābiᶜa bint Ismāᶜīl, the wife of Aḥmad ibn Abī al-Ḥawārī, called him "Lord of the Worshippers" (*sayyid al-ᶜābidīn*). He kept an underground cell (*sardāb*) beneath his house for pious retreat. Like ᶜUbayda bint Abī Kilāb, he was a figure of the late Umayyad period. See al-Iṣfahānī, *Ḥilyat al-awliyāᵓ,* vol. 6, 243–45.

33. Abū Yaḥyā Mālik ibn Dīnār (d. 128/745) was the *mawlā* of a woman from the tribe of Banū Sāma ibn Luᵓayy. He was a preacher and a copyist of the Qurᵓān, and based his Sufi practice on sincerity. He once said, admonishing those who merely memorize the Qurᵓān: "Oh bearers of the Qurᵓān! What does the Qurᵓān sow in your hearts? For the Qurᵓān enlivens the believer like the rain enlivens the earth. When the rain falls on the earth it brings forth vegetation, whose seeds never cease to grow, thus beautifying the earth and making it green. So, oh bearers of the Qurᵓān, what has the Qurᵓān sown in your hearts? Where is the one who lives by a single *sūrā* or two? What have you done with them?" He also said: "The people of the world leave the world without tasting the most delicious thing in it. This is the knowledge of God Most High." Mālik ibn Dīnār was a companion of many famous Muslims of Basra, including al-Ḥasan al-Baṣrī and Muḥammad ibn Sīrīn. Although he is considered a Sufi by al-Kalābādhī, al-Iṣfahānī, and al-Hujwirī, he is not seen as such by as-Sulamī and his student al-Qushayrī. See al-Iṣfahānī, *Ḥilyat al-awliyāᵓ,* vol. 2, 357–88; and Ibn al-Jawzī, *Ṣifat aṣ-Ṣafwa,* vol. 3, 273–88. See also, al-Hujwirī, *The Kashf al-Maḥjūb,* 89–90; and Smith, *An Early Mystic,* 69–70.

(٦)

عبيدة بنت أبى كلاب

شعيب بن محرز قال: حدّثتني سلامة العابدة قالت: بكت عُبيدة بنت أبى كلاب أربعين سنة حتّى ذهب بصرها.

عن يحيى بن بسطام الأصغر قال: حدّثني سلمة الأفقم، و كان ينزل الطفاوة، قال: قلت لعبيدة بنت أبي كلاب ما تشتهين؟ قالت: الموت. قلت: ولمَ؟ قالت: لأنّي و الله ! في كلّ يوم ٍ أصبحُ أخشى أن أجْنِيَ على نفسي جنايةً يكونُ فيها عطبي أيامَ الآخرة.

عبد العزيز بن سلمان قال: اختلفت عبيدة و أبي إلى مالك بن دينار عشرين سنة. قال أبي: فما سمعتها تسأل مالكًا عن شيئ قطّ إلاّ مرّة، قالت: يا أبا يحيى متى يبلغُ المتقى الدّرجة العليا التي ليس فوقها درجة؟ قال مالك: بخ بخ يا عبيدة إذا بلغ المتّقي تلك الدّرجة العليا التي ليس فوقها درجة لم يكن شيئ أحبّ إليه من القدوم على الله. قال: فصرخت عبيدة صرخة سقطت مغشيا عليها.

Dāwūd ibn al-Muḥabbir reported that he heard al-Barrāʾ al-Ghanawī say on the day that ʿUbayda bint Abī Kilāb died: "No one better than she has ever been born in Basra."

ʿAbdallāh ibn Rashīd as-Saʿdī, who was a companion of ʿAbd al-Wāḥid ibn Zayd, said: I have seen old men, youths, mature men, and women among the worshippers of God, but I have never seen a woman or a man whose intellect was better than that of ʿUbayda bint Abī Kilāb.

ʿAbīs ibn Marḥūm reported from ʿAbda bint Abī Shawwāl who said: I saw Rābiʿa [al-ʿAdawiyya] in my sleep and said: "How did ʿUbayda bint Abī Kilāb fare?" Rābiʿa answered: "What a question! By God, she has surpassed us and has reached the utmost degree!" ʿAbda said: "How could this be, while you were so highly esteemed by people?" Rābiʿa answered: "She paid no heed to the state in which she found herself, whether it be in the morning or at night."

داود بن المحبّر قال: سمعت البراّ ء الغنوي يقول يوم ماتت عبيدة بنت أبي كلاب: ما خلّفت بالبصرة أفضل منها.

عبد الله بن رشيد السعدي، و كان قد صحب عبد الواحد بن زيد، قال: رأيت الشيوخ و الشباب و الرجال و النسا ء من المتعبّدين فما رأيت امرأةً ولا رجُلا أفضل و لا أحسن عقلاً من عبيدة بنت أبي كِلا ب.

عبيس بن مرحوم قال: حدثتني عبدة بنت أبي شوّال قالت: رأيت رابعة في المنام فقلتُ: ما فعلت عبيدة بنت أبى كلاب؟ فقالت: هيهات سبقتنا والّله إلى الدرجات العلى. قلتُ: و بمَ و قد كنت عند النّاس؟ أي أكثر منها. قالت: إنها لم تكن تبالي على ما أصبحت من الدّنيا أو أمست.

VII

UMM ṬALQ[34]

Muḥammad ibn Sinān al-Bāhilī said: I heard Shuᶜba ibn Dukhkhān mention that Umm Ṭalq used to pray four hundred prostrations every night and that she recited what God willed from the Qurʾān.

Shayba ibn al-Arqam reported from ᶜĀṣim al-Jaḥdarī, who said: Umm Ṭalq used to say: "Whenever I prevent my lower soul from attaining its desires, God makes me a ruler over it."

It was reported from Sufyān ibn ᶜUyayna,[35] who said: Umm Ṭalq said to her son Ṭalq: "How beautiful is your voice when you recite the Qurʾān. I only hope that your voice will not lead to evil consequences for you on the Day of Judgment." Ṭalq wept until he became unconscious.

Salama al-Ayham reported through ᶜĀṣim al-Jaḥdarī who said: Umm Ṭalq used to say: "The lower soul is a king if you indulge it, but it is a slave if you torment it."

34. Ibn al-Jawzī, *Ṣifat aṣ-Ṣafwa,* vol. 4, 37.

35. Abū Muḥammad Sufyān ibn ᶜUyayna b. Abī ᶜImrān (107–98/ 725–814) was a *mawlā* of the Banū ᶜAbdallāh ibn Ruwayba, a segment of the tribe of Banū Hilāl. He was born in Kufa but lived in Mecca. His father was a client of the Umayyad governor of Iraq, Khālid ibn ᶜAbdallāh al-Qasrī (r. 106/724–120/738). He was forced to leave Iraq when his patron was deposed. Sufyān was said to have known eighty-six of the *Tābiᶜūn.* Of possible Jewish origin, he was a major source of information about Jewish and Christian apocrypha and was the teacher of Sufyān ath-Thawrī and al-Awzāᶜī. He transmitted the famous hadith: "The Muslim does not inherit from the unbeliever and the unbeliever does not inherit from the Muslim." See al-Iṣfahānī, *Ḥilyat al-awliyāʾ,* vol. 8, 270–318; and Ibn al-Jawzī, *Ṣifat aṣ-Ṣafwa,* vol. 2, 231–37. See also, Michael Morony, *Iraq After the Muslim Conquest* (Princeton, 1984), 81; and Smith, *An Early Mystic,* 75–76.

(٧)

أمّ طلق

محمّد بن سنـــان الباهلي قال: سمعْتُ شعبة بن دخّان يذكُـر أنّ أمّ طلق كانت تُصلّي في كل يـوم و ليلـة أربعمائة ركعة، و تقرأ من القرآن ما شاء اللّه.

شيبـة بن الأرقم قال: سـمعتُ عاصـما الـجحْدري يقول: كـانت أمّ طلق تقُـــــــول: مـا ملّـكتُ نفسي مـا تشـتهي منذ جعـل اللّـهُ لي علـيـهـا سلطانًـا.

عن سفيان بن عـيـينة قال: قالت أمّ طلق لطلق: مـا أحسن صوتَكَ بالقرآن فليْـتَـهُ لا يكون عليك وَبَـالاً يوم القيامة. فبكى حتّى غـُشي عليه.

عن سلمة الأيهم قال: سمعتُ عاصما الجحدري يقول: كانت أمّ طلق تقول: النّفس ملِكٌ إن اتَّبَـعَـتْـها، و مَـمْـلوكٌ إن أتْعَبْتَـهَـا.

VIII

BAḤRIYYA AL-ᶜĀBIDA[36]

(Baḥriyya the Worshipper)

Rabāḥ ibn Abī al-Jirāḥ said: I saw Baḥriyya al-ᶜĀbida weeping and saying: "I abandoned You, oh God, when I was young and fresh, and I came to You when I was ragged and decrepit. So accept the decrepit one for what she used to possess."

Baḥriyya used to be beautiful, but afflicted herself with hunger. She would spend forty days at a time without eating anything but a little bit of hummus. She was a specialist in self-denial and held an assembly of Sufis where the remembrance of God was invoked. Whenever she spoke, she would become agitated and tremble violently.

Aḥmad ibn Abī al-Ḥawārī said: An old woman from the people of Basra told me that she heard Baḥriyya say: "When the heart abandons its desires, it becomes habituated to knowledge and pursues it, bearing everything that knowledge entails ."

36. Ibn al-Jawzī, *Ṣifat aṣ-Ṣafwa,* vol. 4, 39.

(٨)

بحرية العابدة

رباح بن أبي الجراح قال: رأيتُ بحرية العابدة تبكي و تقول تركتك و أنا رطبة، و أتيتك و أنا حشفة فاقبل الحشفة على ما كان منها.

وكان بها مسحة من الجمال، و كان الجوع قد أضرّ بها و مكثت أربعين يومًا لم تأكل فيها شيئًا إلاّ شيئًا من حمّص و كانت مجتهدة و كان لها مجلس تذكر فيه، و كانت إذا تكلّمت اضطربت و اقشعرت.

أحمد بن أبي الحواري قال: حدّثتني عجوز من أهل البصرة قالت سمعتُ بحرية تقول: إذا ترك القلب الشهوات ألِفَ العلمَ و اتّبَعَهُ و احتملَ كلّ ما يَرِدُ عليه.

Notices of the Elect among the Female Worshippers of al-Ubulla:

IX

SHAᶜWĀNA[37]

Muᶜādh ibn al-Faḍl (Abū ᶜAwn) said: Shaᶜwāna wept until we feared that she would become blind. So we spoke to her about it. She replied: "By God! Becoming blind from weeping in this world is more desirable to me than being blinded by Hellfire in the Hereafter!"

Mālik ibn Ḍaygham said: A man from the town of al-Ubulla used to visit my father [Abū Mālik Ḍaygham ibn Mālik] often. He would talk with him about Shaᶜwāna and how much she cried. My father said to him one day: "Describe her weeping for me." He said: "Oh, Abū Mālik, I will describe it for you. By God, she weeps day and night, almost without stopping!" My father said: "This is not what I asked you to describe. How does she begin her weeping?" He replied: "Yes, oh Abū Mālik. Whenever she begins a session of invocation,[38] you will see tears pouring from her eyelids like rain." My father asked: "Which were more abundant— the tears coming from the inner corner of the eye beside the nose, or the tears coming from the outer corner of the eye beside the temple?" He replied: "Oh, Abū Mālik, her tears were too numerous to distinguish one from another. From the moment she begins her invocation, they flow, all at once, from the four corners of her eyes."

My father wept and said: "It seems to me that fear has burnt up her entire heart!" Then he said: "It has been said that an increase or decrease of tears is proportional to the extent of the burning of the heart. When the heart has been fully consumed, the person who maintains the station of sorrow (*al-ḥazīn*) can weep whenever he wants. Thus, the smallest amount of invocation will cause him to weep."

37. Ibn al-Jawzī, *Ṣifat aṣ-Ṣafwa,* vol. 4, 53-56.

38. This passage refers to the *samāᶜ,* a session of "audition" or invocation (*dhikr*). In *Bidāyat al-murīd* (Basic Principles of the Sufi Path), the Andalusian Sufi Abū Madyan (d. 594/1198) describes the "Folk of Samāᶜ" in the following way: "The Folk of Samāᶜ are a group of people who moan, do penance, and blame themselves. They spend their days fasting and their nights standing in prayer. Then they break into weeping, wailing, (crying out), imploring, and sobbing. They completely renounce the material world and devote their hearts to their Beloved, irrevocably divorcing the material world." Cornell, *The Way of Abū Madyan,* 80.

(٩)

شعوانة

معاذ بن الفضل، أبو عون، قال: بكت شعوانة حتّى خفنا عليها العمى، فقلنا لها في ذلك، فقالت: أعمى و اللّه في الدّنيا من البكاء أحبّ إليّ من أن أعمى في الآخرة من النّار.

مالك بن ضيغم قال: كان رجل من أهل الأبلّة يأتي أبي كثيرا فيذكر له شعوانة و كثرة بكائها فقال له أبي يوما: صف لي بكاءها. فقال: يا أبا مالك أصفُ لكَ. هي و اللّه تبكي الليل و النّهار لا تكاد تفتر قال: ليس عن هذا أسألك، كيف تبتدئ بالبكاء؟ قال: نعم يا أبا مالك تسمع الشّيئ من الذّكر فترى الدموع تنحدرُ من جفونها كالقطر. قال: فمجاري الدّموع من المآق الذي على الأنف أكَثر أم مؤخَر العين ممّا يلي الصُّدْغ؟ قال يا أبا مالك إنّ دموعها أكثر من أن يعرف هذا من هذا، ما هي إلاّ أن تسمع [الذكر] فتجيئ عيناها بأربع نجوما [سجوما] متبادرة جداً.

فبكى أبي و قال: ما أرى الخوف إلاّ قد أحرق قلبها كلّه. ثمّ قال: كان يُقال إنّ كثرة الدّموع و قلّتها على قدر احتراق القلب، حتّى إذا احترق القلب كلّه لم يشأ الحزين أن يبكي إلاّ بكى، و القليل من التّذكرة يُحْزِنُهُ.

Mālik ibn Ḍaygham said: My father said to me one day: "Go with Manbūdh (Pariah) to this righteous woman (meaning Shaᶜwāna) and evaluate her." So I left with Abū Hammām [Manbūdh] for al-Ubulla. We arrived at her house at lunchtime and entered. Manbūdh greeted her and said: "This is the son of your Sufi brother Ḍaygham." She greeted me and welcomed me warmly, and said: "Welcome, oh son of the one whom we love without seeing him! By God, my son, I have long been yearning for your father. The only thing that has prevented me from seeing him is the fear that I will distract him from his service to his Master. For service to his Master is more worthy than talking to Shaᶜwāna."

Mālik [ibn Ḍaygham] said: Then she said: "But who is Shaᶜwāna? And what is Shaᶜwāna? Nothing but a sinful black slave!"

Mālik said: Then she began to weep. She remained crying, so we went out of her house and left her.

Yaḥyā ibn Bisṭām said: I often used to be present at Shaᶜwāna's gatherings and saw what she did to herself. I said to a companion of mine called ᶜImrān ibn Muslim: "What if we visit her when she is alone?" [Yaḥyā] said: So he and I left for al-Ubulla. Upon arriving, we asked Shaᶜwāna's permission to enter and she admitted us. The house was of a shabby and bare appearance. My companion said to her: "Be easy on yourself and refrain from crying a bit. This would give you more strength to attain your desire." Yāḥya said: She wept and replied: "By God! I want to cry until I run out of tears. Then I will cry blood until not a single drop of blood is left in my body. So how far am I from real crying!" Yaḥyā said: She kept on repeating this until her eyes rolled back into her head. Then she fell over, unconscious. So we stood up, went out, and left her in that state.

Rawḥ ibn Salama said: Muḍar told me: I have never seen anyone who could bear as much crying as Shaᶜwāna, nor have I heard a voice that was more burning to the hearts of the God-fearing as hers was when she lamented and cried out: "Oh dead ones, sons of the dead, and bretheren of the dead!"

Muḥammad said: I asked Abū ᶜUmar aḍ-Ḍarīr (the Blind): "Have you ever visited Shaᶜwāna?" He said: "I used to attend her gatherings often but I could not understand what she had to say because of her profuse weeping." Then I asked: "Did you preserve any of her sayings?" He said: "I did not retain any of her sayings that I can recall at this moment, except for one thing." "What is it?" I asked. He answered: "I heard her say: 'Any one of you who is able to weep should weep or at least be compassionate towards the one who weeps. For the weeper only weeps because of his awareness of what has affected his soul."

قال مالك بن ضيغم: قال لي أبي يومًا انطلق مع «منبوذ» حتّى تأتي هذه المرأة الصّالحة فتنظر إليها، يعني شعوانة، فانطلقت أنا و أبو همّام إلى الأبلّة ثمّ غدونا عليها فدخلنا فسلّم عليها منبوذ و قال: هذا ابن أخيك ضيغم. فرحّبت بيّ و تحفّت و قالت مرحبا بابن من لم نَرَهُ و نحن نحبّه، أمّا واللّه يا بنيّ إنّي لمُشتاقة إلى أبيك و ما يمنعُني من إتيانه إلاّ أنّي أخافُ أن أشغله عن خدمة سيّده، و خدمة سيّده أولى به من محادثَة شعوانة. قال: ثم قالت: و من شعوانة؟ و ما شعوانة؟ [شعوانة] أمة سوداء عاصية. قال: ثمّ أخذت في البكاء فلم تزل تبكي حتّى خرجنا و تركناها.

يحيى بن بسطام قال: كنت أشهد مجلس شعوانة كثيراً فكنت أرى ما تصنع بنفسها، فقلت لصاحب لي يقال له عمران بن مسلم: لو أتيناها إذا خلت. قال: فانطلقنا أنا و هو إلى الأبلّة فاستأذنّا عليها فأذنت لنا فإذا منزلٌ رثُّ الهيئة أثرُ الجدب عليه بَيِّنٌ. فقال لها صاحبي: لو رفقت بنفسك فقصرت عن هذا البكاء شيئاً كان أقوى لك على ماتُريدين. قال: فبكتَ ثم قالت: وَاللّه لوددْتُ أنّي أبكي حتّى تنفذ دَموعي، ثمّ أبكي الدّماء حتّى لا تبقى في جسدي جارحة فيها قطرةٌ من دم، و أنّى لي البكاء؟ قال: فلم تزل تردّد ذلك حتى انقلبت حدقتاها، ثمّ مالت ساقطةً مغشيًا عليها. فقمنا فخرجنا و تركناها على تلك الحال.

روح بن سلمة قال: قال لي مُضر: ما رأيتُ أحداً أقوى على كثرة البكاء من شعوانة، و لا سمعت صوتًا قطّ أحرق لقلوب الخائفين من صوتها إذا هي نشجت ثمّ نادت: يا موتى و بني الموتى و إخوةَ الموتى.

Al-Ḥārith ibn al-Mughīra said: Shaᶜwāna used to wail and lament at hearing these two verses:

> He hopes the world will stay with him forever,
> But death strikes him down before his hope can be fulfilled.
>
> Like compost, which nourishes the roots of the cutting,
> The cutting goes on living while the plant itself dies.

Al-Ḥasan ibn Yaḥyā said: Shaᶜwāna used to repeat this verse and weep, making the ascetics who were with her weep as well. She said:

> "The fool made the abode of his station a safe haven,
> "Anticipating a day when he would be as much unsafe as he is safe."

Al-Fuḍayl ibn ᶜIyāḍ[39] said: I once visited Shaᶜwāna and complained to her about my troubles. Then I asked her to petition God on my behalf. She replied: "Oh Fuḍayl! What is between you and God such that He would not answer you if you petitioned Him yourself?" [Ibn al-Jawzī] said: Al-Fuḍayl sighed and fell down, unconscious.

Muḥammad ibn ᶜAbd al-ᶜAzīz ibn Salmān said: Shaᶜwāna used to be overcome by grief to the point where she could neither continue to pray nor worship. Then she received a visitor in her dream who said:

> "Scatter tears from your eyes if you are truly distressed,
> "For grieving heals those who sorrow.
>
> "Strive, stand, and fast tirelessly at all times,
> "For steadfastness comes from the acts of the obedient."

Then she awoke and began to chant and weep, and her spiritual practice was restored to her.

39. Abū ᶜAlī al-Fuḍayl ibn ᶜIyāḍ ibn Bishr (d. 187/803) was of the Banū Yarbūᶜ segment of the Banū Tamīm tribe, whose home was in the region of Kufa in Iraq. He, however, was born in Khurasan —according to some, in a village called Fundīn near Merv, and according to others in the region of Samarqand. He returned to Kufa after his conversion to Sufism and ended his life in Mecca. It is said that he was originally a highwayman, but of chivalrous disposition, because he would not rob a poor person or a caravan that contained a woman. He was a student of Sufyān ath-Thawrī and was noted for his Sufi aphorisms. He said: "Three things harden the heart: an excess of food, an excess of sleep, and an excess of speaking." According to al-Hujwirī he said: "The world is a madhouse and the people therein are madmen, wearing shackles and chains. Lust is our shackle and sin is our chain." See as-Sulamī, *Ṭabaqāt aṣ-ṣūfiyya,* 6–14; al-Iṣfahānī, *Ḥilyat al-awliyāʾ,* vol. 8, 84–139; al-Qushayrī, *ar-Risāla,* 424–25; and Ibn al-Jawzī, *Ṣifat aṣ-Ṣafwa,* vol. 2, 237–47. See also, al-Hujwiri, *The Kashf al-Maḥjūb,* 97–100; and Smith, *An Early Mystic,* 74.

قال محمّد: وقلت لأبي عمر الضّرير: أتيتَ شعوانة؟ قال: قد شَهدْتُ مجلسَها مراراً ما كنت أفهمُ ما تقول من كثرة بُكَائها. قلت: فهل تحفظ من كلامها شيئًا؟ قال: ما حفظتُ من كلامها شَيئًا أذكرُهُ السّاعةَ إلاّ شيئًا واحداً. قلت و ما هو؟ قال: سَمعتُها تقول: من استطاع منكم أن يبكي فلْيَبْكِ و إلاّ فلْيَرحمِ الباكي فإنّ الباكي إنّما يبكي لِمَعرفتِهِ بما أتى إلى نَفْسِهِ.

عن الحارث بن المغيرة قال: كانت شعوانة تنُوحُ بهذين البيتين:

يُؤمِلُ دنيا لتبقى له	فوافى المنية قبل الأمل
حثيثًا يروي أصول الفسيل	فعاش الفسيل و مات الرّجل

الحسن بن يحيى قال: كانت شعوانة تردِّدُ هذا البيت فتبكي و تُبكي النُّسّاك معها، تقول:

لقد أمِنَ المغرور دار مقامه	ويوشك يومًا أن يخافَ كما أمِنَ

عن فضيل بن عياض قال: قدمتُ شعوانة فأتيتُها فشكوتُ إليها سألتُها أن تدعو بدُعاء، فقالت: يا فضيل ما بينَك و بين الّله ما إن دعوتَه استجاب لك؟ قال: فشهق الفضيل و خرّ مغشيا عليه.

عن محمّد بن عبد العزيز بن سلمان قال: كانت شعوانة قد كمدت حتى انقطعت عن الصلاة و العبادة فأتاها آتٍ في منامِها فقال:

أذري جفونك إمّا كنت شاجية	إنّ النّياحة قد تشفي الحزينينا
جِدّي وقومي وصومي الدّهر دائبة	فإنّما الدّوْب من فعل المطيعينا

فأصبحت فأخذت في التّرنّم و البكاء و راجعت العمل.

Ibrāhīm ibn ʿAbd al-Malik said: Shaʿwāna and her husband visited Mecca. When they started circumambulating the Kaʿba, her husband became exhausted and sat down, so she sat down behind him. While sitting, he said: "I am thirsty from loving You, oh God, but I cannot quench my thirst!" So she said in Persian: "In the mountains there grows a cure for every illness. But the cure for the lovers does not grow in the mountains!" May God be pleased with her.

ابراهيم بن عبد الملك قال: قدمت شعوانة و زوجها مكّة فجعلا يطوفان فإذا أكلّ أو أعيا جلس و جلسَتْ خلفَهُ فيقول هو في جُلُوسه: أنا العطشان من حبّك لا أروى. و تقول هي بالفارسية: أنبت لكل داءٍ دَواء في الجبال، ودواءُ المحبّين في الجبال لم ينبتْ.

رضي اللّه عنها.

Among the "Rationally Insane"[40] of al-Ubulla:

X

RAYḤĀNA[41]

Abū al-Qāsim ibn Saᶜīd reported that he heard Ṣāliḥ al-Murrī say: I saw Rayḥāna al-Majnūna (the Possessed) and greeted her. She said to me: "Oh Ṣāliḥ, listen:

"By Your countenance, do not torture me! For truly,
"I hope to attain the best of abodes.

"There You are the neighbor of the righteous—
"Were it not for You, the visit would not bring joy!"

[It was related that] ar-Rabīᶜ said: Muḥammad ibn al-Mukandar,[42] Thābit al-Bunānī and I spent the night at Rayḥāna al-Majnūna's in al-Ubulla. She spent the first part of the night upright in prayer and then recited:

"The lover drew near to One he longed for in such a way,
"That his heart nearly flew from his body from sheer happiness."

In the middle of the night I heard her say as well:

"Do not become intimate with the One whose sight you long for,
"For you will be prevented from finding Him in the darkness.

"Strive and persevere, and be in the night as one who sorrows,
"And He will pour you a glass of love from His glory and generosity."

40. Ibn al-Jawzī uses this term to distinguish saints and sages who are divinely possessed from people who are truly insane.

41. Ibn al-Jawzī, *Ṣifat aṣ-Ṣafwa,* vol. 4, 57.

42. Muḥammd ibn al-Mukandar b. ᶜAbdallāh (d. 130/747–48) was an Arab of the tribe of Tamīm ibn Murra. His father was related to the Prophet Muḥammad's wife ᶜĀʾisha. Muḥammad ibn al-Mukandar's mother was a concubine (*jāriya*) whom his father purchased with 10,000 dirhams that the governor of Syria, Muᶜāwiya ibn Abī Sufyān (d. 60/680), the founder of the Umayyad dynasty, sent to ᶜĀʾisha. He was a famous transmitter of hadith and was known for his piety and virtue. He lived in Medina and transmitted traditions from some of the best-known Muslims in the second generation after the Prophet Muḥammad. See al-Iṣfahānī, *Ḥilyat al-awliyāʾ,* vol. 3, 146–58; and Ibn al-Jawzī, *Ṣifat aṣ-Ṣafwa,* vol. 2, 140–44.

(١٠)
ريحانة

أبو القاسم ابن سعيد قال: سمعت صالحا المرّي يقول: رأيت ريحانة المجنونة فسلمت عليها فقالت لي: يا صالح اسمع:

بوجهكَ لا تُعذّبني فإنّي أؤمل أن أفوز بخير دار
و أنت مجاور الأبرار فيها و لولا أنت ما طاب المزار

عن الرّبيع قال: بتٌّ أنا و محمد بن المكندر و ثابت البناني عند ريحانة المجنونة بالأبلة فقامت أوّل اللّيل و هي تقول:

قام المحبّ إلى المؤمَّل قومة كاد الفؤاد من السّرور يطير

فلمّا كان جوف اللّيل سمعتها تقول أيضا:

لا تأنسنّ بمن توحشك نظرته فتُمنعنّ من التّذكار في الظُّلَم
واجهد وكِدّ وكن في الليل ذا شجن يسقيك كأس وداد العزّ والكرم

[Ar-Rabī^{c}] said: Then she cried out: "What a war! What a hardship!" "In regard to what?" I asked. She said:

> "In intimacy and closeness to God the darkness dissipates,
> "If only His intimacy could bring back the darkness as well!"

قال ثمّ نادت: واحرباه واسلباه. فقلت: ممّ ذا؟ فقالت:

ذهب الظّلام بأنســـه و بألفـــه   ليت الظّلام بأنســـه يتـــجـــدّد

Notices of the Elect among the Female Worshippers of Syria:

XI

ʿATHĀMA[43]

Muḥammad ibn Sulaymān [the son of ʿAthāma] related that ʿAthāma lost her eyesight. She was devoted to worship (*mutaʿabbida*).

Al-Jarwī said: ʿAmr ibn Abī Salama reported that Saʿīd ibn ʿAbd al-ʿĀzīz[44] said: "We know of no one who has made more vows to travel for the sake of religion and then has done so than ʿAthāma. For she made a vow and went to Mecca, where she spent five hundred dinars."

Muḥammad ibn Sulaymān ibn Bilāl ibn Abī ad-Dardāʾ related that his mother ʿAthāma lost her eyesight. Her son went to her one day after he had prayed. "Have you prayed, my son?" she asked. "Yes," he replied. So she said:

> "Oh ʿAthāma, why are you distracted?
> "Your house must have been invaded by a trickster!
>
> "Weep so that you may complete your prayers on time,
> "If you were to weep at all today!
>
> "And weep while the Qurʾān is being recited,
> "For once you too, used to recite it.
>
> "You used to recite it with reflection,
> "While tears streamed down from your eyes.
>
> "But today, you do not recite it
> "Without having a reciter with you.
>
> "I shall lament for you with fervent love,
> "For as long as I live!"

43. Ibn al-Jawzī, *Ṣifat aṣ-Ṣafwa,* vol. 4, 298.

44. Saʿīd ibn ʿAbd al-ʿAzīz was a traditionist and transmitter of rare hadiths (*gharāʾib al-ḥadīth*) from Syria. He also reported numerous sayings and accounts from Jewish and Christian apocrypha. Al-Iṣfahānī gives no information about the date of his death. See idem, *Ḥilyat al-awliyāʾ,* vol. 6, 124–29.

(١١)

عثامة

عن محمّد بن سليمان أنّ عثامة كُفَّ بصرها. و كانت متعبّدة.

قال الجروي: حدّثنا عمرو بن أبي سلمة عن سعيد بن عبد العزيز قال: ما نعلم أحدا أحنث في مشيٍ إلاّ عثامة فإنّها حنثت فمشت إلى مكّة فأنفقت خمسمائة دينار.

محمّد بن سليما ن بن بلال بن أبي الدّردا ء أنّ أمّه عثامة كُفَّ بصرُها، فدخل عليها ابنُها يومًا و قد صلّى، فقالت: صلّيْتُمْ أي بُنَيَّ؟ قال: نعم، فقالت:

عَـثـامَ مـالَكِ لاهِيَـة ... حَلَّتْ بدارك داهِيَـهْ
إبكي الصّلاة لوَقْتها ... إنْ كُنْت يومًا باكِيَهْ
وابكي القرآنَ إذا تُلِيَ ... قد كُنت يومًا تاليهْ
تَتْلِيَنَهُ بتفَكُّرٍ ... و دُموعِ عينِك جاريهْ
فاليوم لا تتلينَه ... إلاّ و عندك تاليهْ
لَهْفِي عليكِ صبابةً ... ما عِشْت طولَ حَياتِيَهْ

XII

ᶜABDA[45]

(Slave)

The Sister of Abū Sulaymān ad-Dārānī

[Aḥmad ibn Abī al-Ḥawārī reported that] Abū Sulaymān said: "I described for my sister ᶜAbda one of the bridges of Hell. After listening to this, she stood up for an entire day and night, uttering one scream without stopping. Then she stopped doing it any more. But whenever the story was mentioned to her, she would scream again." "What caused her to scream?" I asked. Abū Sulaymān replied: "She imagined herself on the bridge and it was collapsing beneath her."

Aḥmad ibn Abī al-Ḥawārī related that Abū Sulaymān said: I heard my sister say: "The Sufis are all dead, except the one whom God brings back to life through the glory of sufficiency and contentment in his poverty."

Abū ᶜAbd ar-Raḥmān as-Sulamī mentioned that Abū Sulaymān had two sisters: ᶜAbda and Āmina. He said: They both attained an exalted level of intellect and religious observance.

45. Ibn al-Jawzī, *Ṣifat aṣ-Ṣafwa,* vol. 4, 300.

(١٢)

عبدة

أخت أبي سليمان الداراني

أبو سليمـــان قـال: وصفتُ لأختـي عبـدة قنْطَـرة من قناطـر جهنّم، فأقـامت يومًا وليلـةً في صيحَـةٍ واحـدَةٍ مـا تسكُـت. ثمّ انقَطع عنهـا [الصيـاح] بعدُ. فكلّمـا ذكَرَتْ لهـا صَاحت. قُلتُ: من أيّ شـيئ كـان صياحُها؟ قال: مَثّلَـتْ نفسَها على القَنْطَرة تُكْفَأُ بِـها.

و قـد روى أحمـد بن الحواري عن أبي سليمـان أنّه قـال: سـمعتُ أُختي تقـول: الفقـراء كلّهم أمـوات إلاّ من أحيـاه اللّه تعالى بعزّ القنـاعة و الرّضا بفقره.

و ذكر أبو عبد الرحمن السّلمي أنّه كان لأبي سليمان أختان: عـبدة و آمنة قال: و كانتا من العقل و الدّين بمحلٍّ عظيـمٍ.

XIII

RĀBIᶜA [OR RABĪᶜA] BINT ISMĀᶜĪL[46]

The Wife of Aḥmad ibn Abī al-Ḥawārī

Abū Bakr ibn Abī ad-Dunyā[47] traced Rābiᶜa's lineage in this way. Abū ᶜAbd ar-Raḥmān as-Sulamī mentioned that Rābiᶜa al-ᶜAdawiyya shared the same first name as the subject of this section and that their fathers' names were also the same. Most of what is reported about Rābiᶜa the wife of Aḥmad [ibn Abī al-Ḥawārī] is that she is Rābiᶜa with a letter *bāᵓ* and that [Rābiᶜa] al-ᶜAdawiyya was from Basra whereas this one was from Syria.[48]

Ibn Nāṣir informed us that it was related about Abū al-Ghanāᵓim ibn an-Nursī that he said: *Rābiᶜa* with a stroke (*kasra*) under the letter *bāᵓ* is Basran and *Rabīᶜa* with a *yāᵓ* after the *bāᵓ* is Syrian.

Aḥmad ibn Abī al-Ḥawārī said: I said to Rābiᶜa (my wife) while she was spending the night upright in prayers: "We have seen Abū Sulaymān [ad-Dārānī] and we have worshipped with him, but we have not seen anyone spending the night upright in prayer as early as you do." She said: "Glory be to God! Would one like you utter such things? I stand up for prayer when I am called!" He said: I sat down to eat and then she started lecturing me. So I said to her: "Leave me alone! Let me enjoy my food in peace!" She replied: "Neither I nor you are among those who lose their appetites for food at the mention of the Hereafter!"

Aḥmad ibn Abī al-Ḥawārī said: Rābiᶜa said to me: "Oh brother! Do you not know that when the slave practices obedience to God, the Almighty makes him aware of his evil deeds, so that he becomes preoccupied with God instead of His creatures?"

Aḥmad ibn Abī al-Ḥawārī said: Rābiᶜa used to experience many spiritual states (*aḥwāl*). At times she was overtaken by love (*ḥubb*), at other times by intimacy (*uns*), and at other times by fear (*khawf*). Once I heard her say while she was in a state of love:

46. Ibn al-Jawzī, *Ṣifat aṣ-Ṣafwa,* vol. 4, 300–303.

47. Abū Bakr ᶜAlī ibn Muḥammad, known as Ibn Abī ad-Dunyā (d. 281/894) was a noted traditionist and teacher of the ᶜAbbasid caliph al-Muktafī Billāh (r. 289–95/902–8). He was known for composing many works on ascetics and saints, including monks (*ruhbān*), the "rationally insane" (*al-ᶜuqalāᵓ al-majānīn*), and a work called *al-Hawātif* (The Calls), on prophecies which foretell the future. See Rosenthal, *Muslim Historiography,* 399, 429, 432, 505.

48. Although this text reads "Rābiᶜa with a 'b'," it is more likely that the intended reading was "Rabīᶜa with a 'yāᵓ'." This would differentiate Rābiᶜa bint Ismāᶜīl al-ᶜAdawiyya the Basran from Rabīᶜa bint Ismāᶜīl the Syrian.

(١٣)

رابعة بنت اسماعيل

امرأة أحمد بن أبي الحواري

كذا [هكذا] نسبَها أبو بكر بن أبي الدّنيا. و قد ذكر أبو عبد الرحمن السّلمي أنّ رابعة العدوية تُشاركُ هذه في اسمها واسم أبيها وعموم ما يأتي في الحديث عن زوجة أحمد أنّها رابعة بالياء، و العدوية بصرية و هذه شامية.

و قد أخبرنا بن ناصر قال: أنبأ أبو الغنائم بن النّرسي قال: رابعة بالباءِ بنقطة من تحتها بصرية، ورابعة بالياء باثنتين من تحتها شامية.

أحمد بن أبي الحواري قال: قلتُ لرابعة، و هي امرأتي و قد قامت بليل: قد رأينا أبا سليمان و تعبّدنا معه، وما رأينا من يقوم من أوّل اللّيل. فقالت: سبحان اللّه مثلك من يتكلّم بهذا؟ إنّما أقوم إذا نُوديتُ. قال: و جَلسْتُ آكُلُ و جَعَلتْ تُذكّرُني. فقلتُ لها: دعينا يهنينا [يهنأ لنا] طعامُنا. قالت: ليس أنا و أنتَ مِمّن يَتَنَغّصُ عليه الطعام عند ذكْرِ الآخرة.

أحمد بن أبي الحواري قال: قالت لي رابعة: أيْ أخي أعَلمْتَ أنّ العبدَ إذا عمِل بطاعة الله أطلعَهُ الجبّارُ على مساوئ عمله فيتشاغل به دون خلقه؟

عن أحمد بن أبي الحواري قال: كانت لرابعة أحوالٌ شتّى فمرّةً يغلبُ عليها الحبّ، و مرّةً يغلبُ عليها الأنس، ومرّةً يغلبُ عليها الخوف فسمعتُها تقول في حال الحبّ:

"A Beloved no other beloved is equal to,
"And none other than Him has a share of my heart,

"A Beloved who, though absent from my sight and my person,
"Is never absent from the depths of my soul!"

I also heard her say while in a state of intimacy:

"I have made You the One who speaks to me in the depths of my soul,
"While I made my body lawful for the one who desires to sit with me.

"My body is my intimate gift to my worldly companion,
"While my heart's Beloved is my true Intimate in the depths of my soul."

I also heard her say while in a state of fear:

"My sustenance is meager; I do not see it as sustaining me.
"Is it for sustenance that I weep, or for the length of my journey?

"Will you burn me with fire, oh Ultimate Object of Desire?
"Where is my hope in You? And where is my fear of You?"

Aḥmad ibn Abī al-Ḥawārī said: I heard Rābi^{c}a say: "I withhold even a lawful morsel of food from myself, fearing that through it I might feed my lower soul (*nafs*). So when I see my upper arm getting fat, I grieve." He said: And sometimes I would say to her: "Are you fasting today?" She would reply: "A person like me does not break her fast in this world." He said: Sometimes I would look at her face and neck, and my heart would be moved at the sight of her. Not even conversations with our companions after worship would affect my heart in this way. She said to me: "I do not love you in the way that married couples do; instead, I love you as one of the Sufi brethren. I wanted to be with you only in order to serve you, and I desired and hoped that my fortune would be consumed by someone like you and your brethren."

Aḥmad said: She had seven thousand dirhams and she spent it all on me. Whenever she cooked a meal, she would say: "None of this, my lord, would have come to fruition were it not for the glorification of God." She also said to me: "It is not lawful for me to forbid you from myself or another. So go ahead and get married to another woman." He said: So I married three times. She would feed me meat and say: "Go with strength to your wives!" If I wanted to have sex with her during the day, she would say: "I implore you in the name of God to not make me break my fast today." And if I wanted her during the night, she would say: "I implore you in the name of God to grant me this night for God's sake."

حـبـيبٌ ليس يعـدله حـــبـيب و لا لسـواه في قلبي نصيـــب
حـبيبٌ غـاب عن بصري و شخصي ولكن عن فـؤادي مـا يغيــبُ

وسمعتُـها في حال الأنس تقول:

ولقـد جـعلتُـكَ في الفـؤاد مـحدّثي و أبحتُ جــسـمي من أراد جلوسي
والجـسم مني للجليس مـؤانس و حـبيبُ القلبِ في الفـُؤاد أنيسي

وسمعتُـها في حال الخوف تقول:

وزادي قليلٌ مـا أراهُ مُـبلـِّغـي ألِزّاد أبكي أم لِطول مسـافـتي؟
أتحـرقُـني بالنّار يا غـاية المُنى فـأين رجائي فـيك؟ أين مـخافـتي؟

أحمد بن أبي الحواري قال: سمعتُ رابعة تقول: إنّي لأضنّ باللقمة الطيّبة أن أطعمها نفسي، و إنّي لأرى ذراعي قد سمن فأحزن. قال: و ربّما قلتُ لها: أصائمة أنت اليوم؟ فتقول: ما مثلي يُفطِرُ في الدّنيا. قال: و ربّما نظرت إلى وجهها و رقبتها فيتحرّك قلبي على رؤيتها مالا يتحرّك مع مذاكراتي أصحابنا من أثر العبادة. و قالت لي: لستُ أحبك حبّ الأزواج إنّما أحبّك حبّ الإخوان، و إنّما رغبت فيك رغبةً في خدمتك، و إنّما كنت أحِبُّ وأتمنّى أن يأكُلَ [ملكي و] مالي مثلُكَ ومثل إخوانكِ.

قال أحمد: كانت لها سبعة آلاف درهم فأنفقتها عليّ. فكانت إذا طبخت قدرا قالت: كلْها يا سيّدي ما نضجت إلا بالتّسبيح. وقالت لي: لستُ أستحلُّ أن أمنعك نفسي و غيري، اذهَبْ فتزوّج. قال: فتزوّجتُ ثلاثًا، وكانتَ تُطعمُني اللحمَ و تقول: اذهَبْ بقُوّتكَ إلى أهلكَ. وكُنتُ إذا أردْتُ جماعَها نهاراً قالت: أسألك باللّه لا تُفطرنَي اليومَ، وإذا أردتُها بالليل قالت: أسألك بالله لما وهبتني للّه الليلةَ.

Aḥmad ibn Abī al-Ḥawārī said that he heard Rābiᶜa say: "I never hear the call to prayer without thinking of the Caller on Judgment Day; I never look at snow without thinking of the dispersal of the pages of destiny; I never see a swarm of locusts without thinking of the gathering of souls at the Resurrection."

Aḥmad ibn Abī al-Ḥawārī said: Rābiᶜa said to us: "Take that wash basin away from me! For I see written on it: 'Hārūn ar-Rashīd, the Commander of the Believers, has died!'" Aḥmad said: We looked into the matter, and found that he had indeed died on that day.

Aḥmad ibn Abī al-Ḥawārī said that he heard Rābiᶜa say: "Sometimes I see spirits in the house coming and going. At times they are Houris, who veil themselves from me with their sleeves." She said this swearing with her hand upon her head.

Aḥmad ibn Abī al-Ḥawārī said: Once I called for Rābiᶜa and she did not answer. After an hour had passed she answered me: "What prevented me from answering you was that my heart was filled with happiness from God Most High. For this reason, I could not answer you."

أحمد بن أبي الحواري قال: سمعتُ رابعة تقول: ما سمعْتُ الآذان إلاّ ذكرتُ منادىَ القيامة. و لا رأيتُ الثّلجَ إلاّ رأيْتُ تطايُرَ الصُّحُفِ، و لا رأيتُ الجرادَ إلاّ ذكرتُ الحشْر.

أحمد بن أبي الحواري قال: قالت لنا رابعة نحّوا عنّي ذلك الطّسْت، فإنّما عليه مكتوب : مات أمير المؤمنين هارورنُ الرّشيد. قال أحمدُ: فنظروا، فإذا هو مات في ذلك اليوم.

أحمد بن أبي الحواري قال: سمعتُ رابعة تقول: رُبّما رأيتُ الجنَّ يذهبون ويجيئون. و رُبّما رأيتُ الحُورالعين يستترن منّي بأكمَامِهِنَّ. و قالَت بيدها على رأسِها.

قال أحمد: و دعوتُ رابعة فلم تُجبْني. فلمّا كان بعد ساعة أجابتني، وقالت: إنّما منعني من أن أُجيبَكَ أنَّ قلبي كان قد امتلأ فرحًا باللّهِ، فلم أقدِرْ أنْ أُجيبَكَ.

XIV

UMM HĀRŪN[49]

c Abd al-cĀzīz ibn cUmayr said: Umm Hārūn, who was one of the God-fearing worshippers (*min al-khā'ifīn*), said: "I have put the world in its proper place." She used to eat nothing but bread.

Umm Hārūn said: "By my father! How delightful is the night. I am sad during the day until night comes! When night comes, I stand in prayer during the first part of it, and when the dawn comes, the Holy Spirit (*ar-rūḥ*) enters my heart."

Aḥmad ibn Abī al-Ḥāwārī said: Umm Hārūn left her village seeking her place of private worship. A boy shouted to another boy, "Take him!" Umm Hārūn fell to the ground. She fell upon a rock and started to bleed, and blood appeared on her veil.

[Aḥmad ibn Abī al-Ḥawārī] reported that Abū Sulaymān [ad-Dāranī] said: "He who wishes to see one who is thunderstruck should look at Umm Hārūn!" Abū Sulaymān also said: "I never thought that in Syria there would be a woman such as her."

Aḥmad ibn Abī al-Ḥāwārī reported that his wife Rābica said: "Umm Hārūn did not treat her hair with olive oil for twenty years. But when we uncovered our hair, her hair was in better condition than ours."

In a chain of transmission (*bi-l-isnād*), Abū Bakr al-Qurashī related through al-Qāsim al-Jūcī, who said: Umm Hārūn became ill, so a friend of mine and I paid her a visit. When we entered her house, she was sitting on the steps. We asked her how she was doing and I said to her: "Umm Hārūn! Is there anyone among the worshippers of God for whom preoccupation with the fear of Hellfire prevents him from desiring Heaven?" "Ah!" she said. Then she fell from the steps and lost consciousness. Qāsim said: Umm Hārūn used to travel on foot once a month from Damascus to Jerusalem. One day I visited her and she said to me: "Oh Qāsim! I was walking in Baysān (a village in Palestine to the south of Tiberias) when a fierce dog approached me. When it came close to me I looked at it and said: 'Come on, dog! If this is your lucky day, then devour me!' When he heard my words, he barked and turned away to leave."

Aḥmad ibn Abī al-Ḥawārī said that he asked Umm Hārūn: "Do you desire death?" "No," she said. "Why?" I asked. She replied: "If I disobeyed a human being, I would not want to encounter him. So how could I desire to encounter God when I have disobeyed Him?"

49. Ibn al-Jawzī, *Ṣifat aṣ-Ṣafwa,* vol. 4, 303–4.

(١٤)

أمّ هــارون

عبد العزيز بن عمير قال: قالت أمّ هارون، و كانت من الخائفين العابدين: قد أنزَلْتُ الدُّنيا منزلَتَهـا. و كانت تأكلُ الخبز وحده.

قالت: بأبي الليل ما أطيَبَهُ، إنّي لأغتمُّ بالنّهار حتّى يجيئ اللّيل، فإذا جاء اللّيل قُمتُ أوّلَـهُ، فإذا جاء السّحر دخل الرّوح قلبي.

قال أحمد بن أبي الحواري: و خرجت أمّ هارون من قريتها تريدُ موضعَها. فصاح صبيٌّ بصبيٍّ خُذوهُ. قال: فسقطت أمّ هـارون، فوقعت على حجرٍفدميت، فظهر الدّمُ مِنْ مقنعَتها. قال: و قال أبو سليمان: من أرادَ أن ينظُرَ إلى صَعْقٍ صحيحٍ فليَنْظُرَ إلى أمّ هارون. و قال أبو سليمان: ما كنتُ أرى أنّه يكون بالشّامٍ مثلها.

قال أحمد بن أبي الحواري: و قالت لي رابعة: ما دهَنَتْ أمّ هـارون رأسَها [شعرَها] مُنذُ عشرين سنة. فإذا كشفنا رؤوسنا كان شعرها أحسن من شعورنا.

و بالإسناد قال أبو بكر القرشي: و بلغني عن القاسم الجوعي قال: مرضتْ أمّ هارون فأتينا نعودها أنا و صاحب لي، فدخلنا عليها و هي على طرف الدّرجة فسألناها عن حالها. فقلت لها: أم هارون أيكون من العبّاد من يشغله خوف النّيران عن الشّوق إلى الجنان؟ فقالت: آه و سقطت عن الدّرجة مغشيا عليها. قال القاسم: و كانت أمّ هارون تأتي بيت المقدس من دمشق كل شهر مرّة على رجليها. فدخلت عليها فقالت: يا قاسم كنتُ أمشي ببيسان فإذا قد عرض لي هذه الكلب الأسد فمشى نحوي. فلمّا قربَ منّي نظرتُ إليه فقلتُ: تعال يا كلبُ، إنْ كان لكَ رزق فكُلْ. فلمّا سمع كلامي أقعى ثمّ ولّى راجعا.

أحمد بن أبي الحواري قال :قلتُ لأمّ هارون: أتُحبّيين الموت؟ قالت: لا.

قلتُ: و لِمَ؟ قالت: لو عصيتُ آدميًا ما أحببْتُ لقاءَهُ، فكيف أُحِبُّ لقاءَ اللّهِ و قد عصَيتُهُ.

Notices of the Elect among the Female Worshippers of Baghdad:

XV

THE SISTERS OF BISHR IBN AL-ḤĀRITH AL-ḤĀFĪ[50]

The daughters of al-Ḥārith [Bishr's father] were three: Muḍgha (Embryo) , Zubda (Essence), and Mukhkha (Marrow). Muḍgha was the eldest. As-Sulamī said that the sisters of Bishr were Mukhkha, Zubda, and Muḍgha. Zubda was called Umm ᶜAlī.

Muḍgha, the sister of Bishr, was older than Bishr and died before him. It was said that when Muḍgha died, Bishr grieved greatly for her and wept copiously. He was asked about this and said: "I read in some books that when the slave falls short in his service to His Lord, He deprives him of his intimate companion. My sister was my intimate companion in this world."

Al-Khaṭīb [al-Baghdādī][51] related through Ibrāhīm al-Ḥarbī that Bishr made the above statement on the day that Mukhkha died. But God knows best.

Abū ᶜAbdallāh ibn Yūsūf al-Jawharī said: I heard Bishr ibn al-Ḥārith say on the day his sister died: "When the slave falls short in obedience to God, the Glorious and Mighty, He deprives him of his intimate companion."

Abū ᶜAbdallāh al-Qaḥṭabī said: Bishr had a sister who was known for her fasting and her night vigils.

Ghaylān al-Qaṣāʾidī reported that Bishr ibn al-Ḥārith said: "I learned scrupulousness from my sister. For she strove not to eat anything that was prepared by human hands."

ᶜAbdallāh the son of Aḥmad ibn Ḥanbal said: I was at home with my father one day when there was a knock at the door. My father said to me: "Go out and see who is at the door." I went out and found a woman. She said to me: "Ask Abū ᶜAbdallāh [Aḥmad ibn Ḥanbal] if I may come in." I asked him if she could come in and he said: "Allow her to enter."

50. Ibn al-Jawzī, *Ṣifat aṣ-Ṣafwa,* vol. 2, 524–26.

51. Al-Khaṭīb al-Baghdādī (d. 463/1071) is the author of the immense *Tāʾrīkh Baghdād* (History of Baghdad), the model for an entire genre of local and regional histories. See R. Stephen Humphreys, *Islamic History: A Framework for Inquiry* (Princeton, 1991), 132–33.

(١٥)

أخوات بشر بن الحارث الحافي

و هنّ ثلاث مُضْغَة و مُخّة و زُبْدة بنات الحارث، و أكبرهنّ مضغة. قال السّلمي: أخوات بشر مخّة و زبدة و مضغة. و كانت زبدة تكنّى أم علي.

وكانت مضغة أخت بشرأكبر منه، و ماتت قبله، و قيل: لمّا ماتت مضغة توجّع عليها بشر توجّعا شديدا و بكى بكاء كثيرا. فقيل له في ذلك فقال قرأت في بعض الكتب أنّ العبد إذا قصّر في خدمة ربّه سلبه أنِيسَهُ، و هذه كانت أنيستي من الدّنيا.

قال الخطيب: و ذكر إبراهيم الحربي أنّ بشراً قال هذا يومَ ماتت أختُه مُخّة، و الله أعلم.

أبو عبد الله بن يوسف الجوهري قال: سمعت بشر بن الحارث يوم ماتت أخته يقول: إنّ العبدَ إذا قصّر في طاعةِ الّله عزّ و جلّ سَلبَهُ مَنْ يُؤنِسهُ.

أبو عبد الّله القحطبي قال: كان لِبشر أختٌ صوّامةٌ قوّامةٌ.

غيلان القصائدي قال: قال بشر بن الحارث تعلّمت الورع من أختي فإنّها كانت تجتهد ألاّ تأكل ما للمخلوق فيه صُنْعٌ.

عبد الله بن أحمد بن حنبل قال: كنت مع أبي يوما من الأيّام في المنزل فدقّ الباب داقّ فقال لي: اخرج فانظر من بالباب؟ فخرجتُ فإذا امرأة، فقالت لي: استأذن لي على أبي عبد الله: قال فاستأذنته. قال: أدْخِلها.

ʿAbdallāh said: She came in, greeted my father, and said to him: "Oh Abū ʿAbdallāh, I am a woman who spins at night in lamplight. Sometimes, the lamp goes out and I continue spinning in the moonlight. So it is incumbent upon me to distinguish between the spinning made in the moonlight and the spinning made in the lamplight." ʿAbdallāh said: My father said to her: "If you see that there is a difference between the two [types of spun cotton], then it is incumbent upon you to make it known." ʿAbdallāh said: She replied: "Oh Abū ʿAbdallāh! Is the moaning of the sick a complaint?" He said: "I hope that it is not. Rather it should be a lamentation to God, the Glorious and Mighty."

ʿAbdallāh said: Then she said goodbye to him and left. My father said: "Oh my son! I have never heard a human being asking about things such as these. Follow this woman and see what is her destination." ʿAbdallāh said: So I followed her and she entered the house of Bishr ibn al-Ḥārith, for she was his sister. I returned and told my father about this. He said: "It is impossible for a person like this to be anybody's sister but Bishr's!"

The author [Ibn al-Jawzī] said: I believe that the woman who asked Aḥmad this question was Mukhkha. I have transmitted another story about her in which her name was mentioned that was similar to this story.

ʿAbdallāh ibn Aḥmad ibn Ḥanbal said in Baghdad: Mukhkha the sister of Bishr ibn al-Ḥārith came to see my father and said: "I am a woman whose investment capital is two *dānaqs* (one-third of a silver dirham). I buy cotton, spin it, and sell it for half a dirham. Thus, I sustain myself with one *dānaq* per week [from Friday to Friday]. Once, Ibn Ṭāhir aṭ-Ṭāʾif passed by me holding a torch. When he stopped to speak to the soldiers bearing arms, I took advantage of the light of his torch and spun a large amount of cotton. Then the torch disappeared, and I understood that I owed God an obligation. Release me, so that God may release you." Ibn Ḥanbal said to her: "Spend the two *dānaqs* so that you will be left without any capital. Perhaps God will reward you with something better."

ʿAbdallāh said: I said to my father: "Oh, Father! Why did you not tell her to get rid of what she had spun so much of [under the torch light of Ibn Ṭāhir]?" Oh my son," he answered, "Her question will not bear that interpretation." Then he said: "Who is this woman?" "Mukhkha, the sister of Bishr ibn al-Ḥārith," I answered. He said: "This is where she gets it!"

I read in the handwriting of Abū ʿĀlī ar-Rudhānī: Among the sisters of Bishr, it was Mukhkha who used to seek out Abū Ḥanbal and ask him about scrupulousness and asceticism. Aḥmad used to be amazed at the difficulty of her legal questions.

As-Sulamī said: Zubda, the sister of Bishr, said: "The heaviest thing for the slave is sinfulness and the lightest is repentance. So why does one not relinquish that which is heavy for that which is light?"

قال: فدخلت فسلّمت عليه و قالت له: يا أبا عبد الله أنا امرأة أغزل بالليل في السّراج فربما طفئ السّراج فأغزل في القمر فعليّ أن أبيّن غزلَ القمر من غزل السّراج؟ قال: فقال لها: إن كان عندك بينهما فرق فعليك أن تُبَيِّني ذلك. قال: قالت: يا أبا عبد اللّه أنينُ المريض الشّكوى؟ قال: أرجو ألاّ يكون، و لكنّه اشتكاء إلى اللّه عزّ و جَلّ . قال فودّعَتْهُ و خرجَتْ: فقال: يا بنيّ ما سمعتُ قطّ إنسانا يسأل عن مثل هذا. اتبع هذه المرأة فانظر أين تدخل؟ قال: فاتّبعتها فإذا قد دخلت إلى بيت بشر الحارث و إذا هي أخته قال: فرجعت فقلت له، فقال: مُحال أن تكون مثلُ هذه إلاّ أخت بشر.

قال المصنّف [الشّيخ مؤلّف هذا الكتاب] : قلت هذه المرأة التي سألت أحمد هي مُخّة و قد نقلتُ عنها حكايةً سُمّيَت فيها تُشْبِهُ هذه الحكاية.

عبد اللّه بن حنبل ببغداد قال جاءت مُخّة أخت بشر بن الحارث إلى أبي فقالت: إنّي امرأة رأس مالي دانقان، أشتري القطن فأغزله و أبيعُه بنصف درهم، فأتقوّتُ بدانق من الجمعة، فمرّ ابن طاهرالطائف و معه مشعل، فوقف يكلّم أصحاب المسالح، فاستغنمت ضوء المشعل فغزلت طاقات، ثمّ غاب عنّي المشعل، فعلمتُ أنّ للّه فيّ مطالبة، فخلّصني خلصكَ اللّه فقال لها تُخْرِجين الدانقين ثم تبْقين بلا رأس مال حتّى يعوضك اللّه خيرا منه. قال عبدَ اللّه: قلت لأبي: يا أبة لو قلت لها لو أخرجت الغزل الذي درجت فيه الطاقات؟ فقال: يا بني سؤالها لا يحتمل هذا التّأويل. ثمّ قال: من هذه؟ قلت مخّة أخت بشر بن الحارث. فقال: مِنْ هَا هُنَا أُتِيتْ.

قرأتُ بخطّ أبي علي الراذاني قال: كانت مُخّة من بين أخوات بشر تقصد أحمد بن حنبل و تسأله عن الورع و التّقشّف، و كان أحمد يُعْجَبُ بِمَسائِلِهَا.

السّلمي قال: قالت زبدة أخت بشر: أثقل شيئ على العبد الذنوب، و أخفّه عليه التوبة، فما له يدفع أثقل شيئ بأخفّ شيئ.

Notices of the Elect among the Female Worshippers
Who are Bedouins and Country-Folk:

XVI

UMM SĀLIM AR-RĀSIBIYYA[52]

In a chain of transmission, [Abū Bakr] al-Qurashī reported that Muḥammad ibn al-Ḥusayn [al-Burjulānī] related from Abū Samīr through a man from the tribe of Azd, who said: I visited Umm Sālim ar-Rāsibiyya between the midday and afternoon prayers. I asked her permission to come in and she allowed me to do so. When I entered, she was standing in prayer. She did not abandon her prayers and did not turn her face toward me until the afternoon prayer had been called. So I left, prayed, and returned to her house. She said: "If you are in need of something, do not come to me at this time. For anyone who neglects his prayer at this time is sure to squander his good fortune."

52. Ibn al-Jawzī, *Ṣifat aṣ-Ṣafwa,* vol. 4, 388–89.

(١٦)

أم سالم الرّاسبيــة

وبالإسناد حدّثنا القرشي قال: قال محمّد بن الحسين: حدّثني أبوسمير، رجل من الأزد، قال: أتيتُ أمّ سالم الرّاسبية بين الظّهر والعصر. فاستأذنتُ عليها فأذِنت لي. فدخلتُ عليها و إذا هي تُصلّي قائمةً فلم تنفتل من صلاتِها ولم تلتفتْ إليّ حتّى نودي بصلاة العصْر فخرجت فصليّتُ ثمّ دخلتُ عليها فقالت: إذا كانت لك حاجة فلاَ تأتني في هذا الوقت فإنّ الذي يَدَعُ الصّلاةَ في هذا الوقت فإنّما يُضيّعُ حَظَّ نفسِه.

INDEX

ᶜAbbasid caliphs, 22–23
ᶜAbbasids, 22–23, 25
ᶜAbda the sister of Abū Sulymān ad-Dārānī, 194, 312
ᶜabd Allāh, 54, 56
ᶜAbd ar-Raḥmān III, 21
ᶜAbdūsa bint al-Ḥārith, 236
Abū Ḥafṣ of Nishapur, 58, 67, 162, 168, 176
Abū Saᶜīd Abū al-Khayr, 42, 69
Adharbayjan (*see* Azerbaijan)
ᶜAḍud ad-Dawla, 23, 35
ᶜĀfiyya the Infatuated, 98
ᶜĀᵓisha bint Aḥmad aṭ-Ṭawīl, 258
ᶜĀᵓisha of Dīnawar, 152
ᶜĀᵓisha of Merv the wife of Aḥmad ibn as-Sarī, 32, 196
ᶜĀᵓisha the daughter of Abū ᶜUthmān al-Ḥīrī, 184
ᶜĀᵓisha the wife of Abū Ḥafṣ of Nishapur, 58, 156
ᶜAjrada al-ᶜAmiyya (*see* ᶜAjrada the Blind)
ᶜAjrada the Blind, 130, 284
ᶜAlī ibn Abī Ṭālib, 76, 264
ᶜamal, 39, 41, 218, 246
Amat Allāh al-Jabaliyya, 208
Amat al-ᶜAzīz, 222
Amat al-Ḥamīd, 154
Āmina al-Marjiyya, 254
Āmina the sister of Abū Sulaymān ad Dārānī, 194
ᶜAmra of Farghana, 190
Amri, Nelly and Laroussi, 36, 44, 286
al-Anṣārī, ᶜAbdallāh, 43–44
Arberry, A. J., 16–17, 40, 42, 264
al-Ashᶜarī, Abū al-Ḥasan, 30
Ashᶜarī Sufis, 30
Ashᶜarī theology, 28, 30, 35
Asrār at-tawḥīd fī maqāmāt ash-shaykh Abī Saᶜīd (The Secrets of Divine Unity in the Exploits of Shaykh Abū Saᶜīd), 69
ᶜAthāma, 64, 68, 110, 112, 310
ᶜAthāma the daughter [niece?] of Bilāl ibn Abī ad-Dardāᵓ (*see* ᶜAthāma)
ᶜAwna of Nishapur, 220
al-Azdī, al-Ḥusayn ibn Muḥammad, 31–32, 88
Azerbaijan, 24, 150

Baghdad, 22–23, 26–27, 30, 32, 37–38, 42–43, 47–48, 52–53, 55, 57, 65, 67, 74, 80, 86, 96, 110, 122, 148, 156, 158, 172, 182, 186, 192, 212, 216, 222, 248, 250, 252, 270, 322, 324
al-Baghdādī, Abū Ḥamza, 67, 158
al-Baghdādī, al-Khaṭīb, 38–39, 41–42, 52–53, 114, 322
Baḥriyya, 148, 296
Baḥriyya al-ᶜĀbida (*see* Baḥriyya)
Balkh, 20, 24, 28, 67, 148, 152, 168, 170
al-Balkhī, Shaqīq, 148
Banū Sulaym, 23–24
al-Bāqillānī, Abū Bakr, 35
Basra, 12, 17, 47–48, 52–53, 59–64, 74, 76, 78, 80, 84, 90, 94, 96, 98, 102, 108, 114, 116, 118, 122, 126, 128, 130, 132, 134, 136, 138, 148, 158, 182, 202, 210, 212, 264, 266, 268, 278, 286, 290, 292, 296, 314
Basra, female asceticism in, 61–63
Bāyazīd al-Bisṭāmī, 20, 58
al-Bayhaqī, Abū Bakr, 37–39

Böwering, Gerhard, 31–33, 35, 37, 39, 41–42, 45, 184
bukāʾ, 61, 156
Bulliet, Richard, 24, 27–28, 32–34, 37, 42, 224, 226, 244, 250
al-Burjulānī, Muḥammad ibn al-Ḥusayn, 52–53, 64, 96, 102, 104, 106, 110, 114, 118, 136, 164, 182, 288, 326
Buyids, 22–23, 25, 27–28

Damaghan, 48, 208, 230, 232, 234, 236
ad-Daqqāq, Abū ᶜAlī, 37
Darajāt al-muᶜamalāt (Degrees of Ethical Conduct), 41
ad-Dārānī, Abū Sulaymān, 20, 47, 63, 126, 146, 194, 312, 314, 320
Daygham ibn Mālik, Abū Mālik, 282, 298
Daylam, 22, 24
adh-Dhahabī, Muḥammad, 31–32, 34–35, 39, 41–42
Dhakkāra, 182
Dhamm takabbur al-ᶜulamāʾ (Condemnation of the Arrogance of Scholars), 41
Dhikr an-niswa al-mutaᶜabbidāt aṣ-ṣūfiyyāt (Memorial of Female Sufi Devotees), 9, 45–48, 51, 53–54, 69
Dhū an-Nūn al-Miṣrī, 15, 17, 20, 45, 59, 76, 122, 138, 142, 144, 174, 258
ad-Dīnawarī, Abū al-ᶜAbbās, 180

Egypt, 19, 21–22, 27, 39, 48, 65, 74, 76, 138, 142, 182, 186, 210, 212
Essay on the Origins of the Technical Language of Islamic Mysticism, 52, 60, 76

Fakhrawayh bint ᶜAlī, 32, 36, 176, 178
al-Fārisī, Abū Bakr, 246
Fars, 22, 30, 35, 37, 246
Fāṭima al-Bardaᶜiyya, 150
Fāṭima al-Khānaqahiyya, 68, 256
Fāṭima bint ᶜAbdallāh known as Juwayriyya (The Little Slave), 172
Fāṭima bint Aḥmad al-Ḥajāfiyya, 180
Fāṭima bint Aḥmad ibn Hānīʾ, 198
Fāṭima bint Aḥmad the mother of Abū ᶜAbdallāh ar-Rūdhbārī, 214
Fāṭima bint ᶜImrān, 234
Fāṭima nicknamed az-Zaytūna (Olive), 158, 160
Fāṭima of Baghdad, 67
Fāṭima of Damascus, 204
Fāṭima of Nishapur, 20, 45, 58–60, 63, 126, 142, 144, 258
Fāṭima Umm al-Yumn the wife of Abū ᶜAlī ar-Rudhbārī, 186, 188
Fatimid caliphs, 22
Fatimids, 21
female ethic of chivalry, 65–69
fiqh al-ᶜibādāt, 63, 82, 84
fityān, 66–68, 190, 196, 198, 256
Fuṭayma the wife of Ḥamdūn al-Qaṣṣār, 56–57, 206
futuwwa, 12, 32–33, 40, 66–68, 168, 176, 200, 226, 256

Ghufayra al-ᶜĀbida, 57, 61, 96, 286, 288

Ḥabība al-ᶜAdawiyya, 202
hadith, 13, 29, 32, 36, 42, 46, 49–50, 54, 57–59, 74, 76, 78, 90, 92, 100, 110, 114, 122, 156, 186, 226, 240, 264, 266, 268, 278, 282, 294, 306
al-Ḥāfī, Bishr ibn al-Ḥārith, 47, 192, 322, 324
Ḥafṣa bint Sīrīn, 62, 122, 270, 272, 274

Ḥanafī school of law, 25
Ḥaqā'iq at-tafsīr (Realities of Exegesis), 41–42, 54–55
Ḥasnā bint Fayrūz, 120
Heilbrun, Carolyn G., 18
Herat, 18, 24, 28, 43, 242
hermeneutic of remembrance, 48–49
Ḥikāyāt al-awliyā' (Tales of the Saints), 53, 110
Ḥilyat al-awliyā' wa ṭabaqāt al-aṣfiyā' (Adornment of the Saints and Generations of the Pure), 38, 40, 74
Hind bint al-Muhallab, 136
al-Hujwīrī, ᶜAlī ibn ᶜUthmān, 20, 34, 57, 67, 76, 80
Ḥukayma of Damascus, 59–60, 63–64, 126

Ibn Abī al-Ḥawārī, Aḥmad, 63, 65, 76, 82, 84, 86, 120, 124, 126, 128, 138, 140, 146, 148, 194, 202, 290, 296, 312, 314, 316, 318, 320
Ibn Asbāṭ, Yūsuf, 92, 104, 124, 192
Ibn al-Aᶜrābī, Abū Saᶜīd, 53, 90
Ibn ᶜAṭā', Aḥmad, 54–55, 57
Ibn ᶜAyyāsh, Ismāᶜīl, 100
Ibn Dīnār, Mālik, 80, 134, 290
Ibn Ḥamdān, Aḥmad, 51, 68, 156, 238
Ibn Ḥanbal, Aḥmad, 32, 52, 54, 138, 192, 322, 324
Ibn Ḥassān, Hishām, 122, 270, 272, 274
Ibn ᶜIyāḍ, al-Fuḍayl, 106, 302
Ibn al-Jawzī, Jamāl ad-Dīn Abū al-Faraj, 12, 36, 43, 45–47, 57, 60–62, 64–65, 74, 78, 80, 84, 86, 88, 92, 96, 104, 106, 108, 110, 114, 116, 118, 122, 124, 126, 128, 132, 138, 142, 148, 152, 154, 156, 158, 168, 176, 186, 192, 206, 212, 216, 234, 248, 252, 263–264, 266, 268, 270, 276, 278, 282, 284, 286, 290, 294, 296, 298, 302, 306, 310, 312, 314, 320, 322, 324, 326
Ibn al-Junayd, Ibrāhīm, 52, 64, 96, 98
Ibn Khaḍrawayh, Aḥmad, 20, 67, 168
Ibn Khafīf, Abū ᶜAbdallāh Muḥammad, 35, 59, 226
Ibn Munāzil, ᶜAbdallāh, 31–32, 34, 240
Ibn Nujayd, Ismāᶜīl, 32–33, 35, 37–38, 52, 102, 176, 226
Ibn Saᶜd, Muḥammad, 32, 50, 88, 114, 118, 122,
Ibn as-Sarī, Aḥmad, 190, 196
Ibn Shaybān, Ibrāhīm, 152
Ibn Sīrīn, Muḥammad, 62, 122, 270, 274, 290
Ibn Taymiyya, 42
Ibn Ushaym, Ṣila, 88, 264, 266
Ibn Zayd, ᶜAbd al-Wāḥid (Ḥammād), 108, 128, 268, 292
al-Ikhwa wa al-akhawāt min aṣ-ṣūfiyya (Brothers and Sisters among the Sufis), 39
ᶜilm, 29, 39, 49, 78, 218, 248, 250
iqṭāᶜ, 26–27
Iraq, 22, 24, 27, 36, 48, 52, 64, 138, 150, 212, 226, 252, 264, 294, 302
al-Iṣfahānī, Abū Nuᶜaym, 37–38, 40, 42, 46–47, 51–53, 74, 76, 78, 80, 82, 90, 92, 96, 100, 104, 108, 110, 112, 114, 118, 122, 124, 126, 138, 142, 148, 152, 154, 156, 158, 168, 176, 182, 186, 192, 200, 206, 212, 216, 226, 230, 246, 248, 252, 264, 266, 268, 270, 282, 290, 294, 302, 306, 310
isnād, 50–51, 88, 136, 174, 182, 202

Ja^c^far aṣ-Ṣādiq, 42
al-Jāmī, ^c^Abd ar-Raḥmān, 10, 18, 31–32, 43–44, 88, 286
al-Jarīrī, Abū Muḥammad, 248
Jum^c^a bint Aḥmad ibn Muḥammad b. ^c^Ubayd Allāh (*see also* Umm al-Ḥusayn al-Qurashiyya), 34, 224, 250
al-Junayd, Abū al-Qāsim, 32, 37, 55, 67, 90, 96, 102, 110, 154, 156, 158, 186, 200, 216, 248, 252, 258
jurisprudence of religious practice (*see fiqh al-^c^ibādāt*)

al-Kalābādhī, Abū Bakr, 15–17, 20, 27, 37, 40, 42, 70, 92, 124, 154, 290
Kashf al-maḥjūb (Unveiling the Veiled), 34, 67, 80, 110, 112, 114, 120, 122, 126, 142, 148, 154, 156, 158, 168, 176, 186, 192, 206, 216, 224, 226, 248, 252, 258, 290, 302
al-Kawākib ad-durriyya (The Glittering Spheres), 43
al-Kharrāz, Abū Sa^c^īd, 154, 172
al-Khashshāb, Muḥammad, 31, 38
al-Khawwāṣ, Ibrāhīm, 53, 216
al-Khiḍrī, Abū al-Ḥusayn, 250
al-Khuldī, Ja^c^far, 40, 52–53, 216
Khurasan, 7, 23–24, 27–28, 30, 32, 34–36, 40–41, 48, 53, 55, 65, 69, 78, 80, 84, 90, 142, 148, 150, 152, 156, 158, 190, 200, 212, 224, 242, 258, 302
al-Kirmānī, Shāh ibn Shujā^c^, 33, 176
Kitāb alfāẓ aṣ-ṣūfiyya (Book of Sufi Terms), 41
Kitāb al-fihrist (Bibliographical Index), 53, 96, 110, 182
Kitāb al-firāsa (Book of Clairvoyance), 41
Kitāb al-futuwwa (Book of Sufi Chivalry), 40–41, 66
*Kitāb al-luma^c^* (The Inspired Treatise), 35
Kitāb al-luma^c^ fī at-taṣawwuf (The Inspired Treatise on Sufism), 37, 40, 204, 210, 212, 226
Kitāb al-malāmatiyya wa ghalaṭāt aṣ-ṣūfiyya (The Path of Blame and the Errors of the Sufis), 40
Kitāb al-muntakhab min ḥikāyāt aṣ-ṣūfiyya (Selections from "Tales of the Sufis"), 53, 110
Kitāb ar-ruhbān (Book of Monks), 52, 64, 96, 182, 288
Kitāb at-ta^c^arruf li-madhhab ahl at-taṣawwuf (Introduction to the Methodology of the Sufis), 15–16, 92, 124, 154, 290
Kitāb ^c^uyūb an-nafs wa mudāwātuhā (The Faults of the Soul and their Cures), 40
Kurdiyya bint ^c^Amr, 116

love-mysticism (*see maḥabba*)
Lubāba al-^c^Ābida (*see* Lubāba al-Muta^c^abbida)
Lubāba al-Muta^c^abbida, 47, 63, 82, 124

maḥabba, 62, 64, 84, 142, 182, 228
malāmatiyya, 31, 67, 142, 156, 168, 192, 206, 240
Malika the daughter of Aḥmad ibn Ḥayyawayh, 232
Manāhij al-^c^ārifīn (Approaches of the Gnostics), 41
Marhā^o^ of Nisibis, 212
Martin, Dale B., 55–56
Maryam of Basra, 63, 84
Massignon, Louis, 52, 60, 63, 76, 78, 80, 90, 96, 104, 108, 110, 114, 122, 126, 128, 134, 138, 154, 174, 192, 266, 268, 282
mawlāt, 60, 74, 266

Maymūna the sister of Ibrāhīm al-Khawāṣṣ, 216
Merv, 24, 28, 32, 37, 56, 70, 158, 164, 190, 192, 196, 258, 302
muʾaddiba, 59
Muᶜādha bint ᶜAbdallāh al-ᶜAdawiyya, 51, 61–62, 88, 264, 266, 268
Muḍgha the sister of Bishr al-Ḥāfī, 47, 192, 322
Muᶜizz ad-Dawla, 23
Mukhkha (*see also* The Sisters of Bishr ibn al-Ḥārith al-Ḥāfī), 192, 322, 324
Muʾmina the daughter of Bahlūl, 51, 86
al-Munāwī, ᶜAbd ar-Raʾūf, 43–44
Muʾnisa aṣ-Ṣūfiyya (*see* Muʾnisa the Sufi)
Muʾnisa the Sufi, 64, 174
al-Muqaddasī, 25, 27–28
Musnad (Collection of Authenticated Traditions), 54
Muᶜtazilites, 28–30
Muᶜtazilī theology, 28, 30
muwālāt, 60, 74

Nafaḥāt al-uns (Breaths of Intimacy), 10, 18, 31–32, 43–44, 78, 88, 150, 286
nafs, 55, 57–58, 61, 168, 176, 196, 280, 316
Naṣīḥat al-umarāʾ wa al-wuzarāʾ (Advice for Princes and Viziers), 41
an-Naṣrābādhī, Abū al-Qāsim Ibrāhīm, 34–35, 37, 224, 226, 240, 244, 250
Nishapur, 7, 20–21, 23–25, 27–28, 31–35, 37, 41–42, 45, 48, 51, 58–60, 63, 67, 69, 76, 78, 126, 144, 156, 162, 176, 180, 184, 198, 206, 220, 224, 226, 238, 240, 242, 244, 246, 250, 258
niswa, 54, 66
niswān, 12, 45, 66–69, 168, 210, 214, 222, 238, 258
an-Nūrī, Abū al-Ḥusayn, 53, 67, 90, 124, 158, 160, 186
Nusiyya bint Salmān, 57, 92

oral tradition, 49–51

practitioners of female chivalry (*see niswān*)
Prophet Muḥammad, 21, 29, 32, 38–40, 42, 49–50, 54, 74, 86, 88, 104, 108, 110, 114, 132, 186, 190, 266, 268, 306
al-Qaṣṣār, Ḥamdūn, 56, 206, 240
al-Qaṭṭān, Muḥammad ibn Yūsuf, 41–42
al-Qaysī, Rabāḥ, 78, 276, 278
Qurashiyya of Nasā (*see also* Umm al-Ḥusayn al-Qurashiyya), 224
Qusayma the wife of Abū Yaᶜqūb of Tinnīs, 210
al-Qushayrī, Abū al-Qāsim, 31–32, 37–38, 51, 76, 80, 102, 110, 114, 124, 142, 148, 152, 154, 158, 168, 176, 180, 184, 186, 192, 206, 212, 216, 226, 240, 246, 248, 252, 290, 302
Rābiᶜa al-ᶜAdawiyya, 17, 36, 44, 47, 59–63, 74, 76, 78, 80, 82, 84, 88, 108, 128, 138, 202, 234, 276, 278, 280, 292, 314
Rābiᶜa al-Azdiyya, 128
Rābiᶜa [Rabīᶜa] bint Ismāᶜīl, 63–65, 138, 140, 314, 316, 318
Rayḥāna, 94, 306, 308
Rayy, 24–25, 33, 76, 78, 162, 176
rijāl al-ᶜilm, 49
ar-Risāla fī ᶜilm at-taṣawwuf (Treatise on the Science of Sufism), 37

Roded, Ruth, 32, 44, 46, 138
ar-Rūdhbārī, Abū ʿAlī, 186, 210, 212, 214, 224

sacred biography, 16, 34, 39–40, 43, 45, 47, 49–51, 53, 57, 63–64, 69, 224
Ṣafrāʾ of Rayy, 162
Saʿīda bint Zayd, 108
as-Salaf aṣ-Ṣāliḥ, 42, 49
as-Saʿlūkī, Abū Sahl, 33–34, 226
Samanids, 24–26
as-Sarrāj, Abū Naṣr, 37, 40, 204, 210, 212, 226
as-Sayyārī, ʿAbd al-Wāḥid, 258
semimatrilineal ascription, 32
Servitude
culture of, 26, 54–58,
disciplined practice of, 26, 54, 58
formal ties of, 26, 60
rhetoric of, 55–57
theology of, 54–60
Shabaka of Basra, 90
ash-Shāfiʿī, Muḥammad ibn Idrīs, 28
Shāfiʿī school of law, 28–29
ash-Sharīʿa, 22
ash-Shāshī, Abū Bakr, 37
Shaʿwāna, 59, 106, 116, 298, 300, 302, 304
ash-Shiblī, Abū Bakr, 212, 224, 232, 252
Shiʿism, Ismāʿīlī, 21–22, 42
Shiʿite century, 21, 26
Shiʿites, Imāmī, 23, 27–28, 30
Shiʿites, Zaydī, 22, 28, 30
Shuhda bint al-ʿIbarī, 46
ash-Shukhtanī, Zakarīyā, 180
Shurayba, Nūr ad-Dīn, 31–32, 36–37, 39, 63, 76, 88, 138, 182
as-Sijzī, Abū ʿAbdallāh, 200
Slavery as Salvation, 55–56
Smith, Margaret, 12, 43–44, 74, 88
spiritual marriage, 64–65
Sufi doctrine, 16, 37–39, 64, 126, 158, 186, 192, 248
Sufi "path of blame", 31
Sufi practice, 39–40, 124, 176, 192, 290
Sufyān ath-Thawrī, 36, 47, 59, 63, 74, 76, 80, 84, 92, 96, 100, 192, 206, 222, 242, 278, 282, 294, 302
as-Sulamī, Abū ʿAbd ar-Raḥmān, 31–42, 45, 51–53, 58–59, 65–69, 76, 88, 164, 270, 312, 314
as-Sulamī, Aḥmad ibn Yūsuf, 32
as-Sulamī's book of Sufi women, 19, 41, 43–48, 52–53, 66–67, 69
Sunan aṣ-ṣūfiyya (Traditions of the Sufis), 39, 43
Sunna, 29, 31, 38, 40, 86, 108, 152, 158, 164, 180, 192
Surayra ash-Sharqiyya, 58, 246
Syria, 15, 20, 22, 47–48, 63–65, 69, 100, 110, 124, 126, 138, 146, 174, 212, 268, 306, 310, 314, 320
Syrian women's Sufism, 63–65

taʿabbud, 26, 54, 67
ṭabaqāt literature, 49–53
aṭ-Ṭabaqāt al-kubrā (The Greatest Generations), 50
Ṭabaqāt an-nussāk (Categories of the Ascetics), 53, 90
Ṭabaqāt aṣ-ṣūfiyya (Generations of the Sufis), 31–37, 39, 43–45, 48–49, 51–53, 62, 76, 78, 88, 90, 96, 100, 102, 110, 112, 124, 126, 142, 148, 150, 152, 154, 156, 158, 164, 168, 176, 180, 182, 186, 190, 192, 200, 206, 212, 216, 224, 226, 232, 238, 240, 246, 248, 252, 258, 266, 302

Tabaristan, 24–25
Ta^ʾrīkh Baghdād (The History of Baghdad), 38–39, 42, 52–53
Taʾrīkh aṣ-ṣūfiyya (History of the Sufis), 39, 41, 43
ath-Thaqafī, Abū ʿAlī, 176, 240
The Sisters of Abū Sulaymān ad-Dārānī (*see* ʿAbda and Āmina)
The Sisters of Bishr ibn al-Ḥārith al-Ḥāfī (*see also* Muḍgha and Zubda), 192, 322, 324
Turkish period of Islamic history, 26–27

ʿUbayda bint Abī Kilāb, 134, 282, 290, 292
ʿubūdiyya, 55, 57–58, 154, 206
al-Ubulla, 48, 59, 106, 298, 300, 306
Umayyads of Spain, 21
Umm ʿAbdallāh the daughter of Khālid ibn Maʿdān, 100
Umm ʿAbdallāh the wife of Abū ʿAbdallah as-Sijzī, , 200
Umm Aḥmad bint ʿĀʾisha the grand daughter of Abū ʿUthmān al-Ḥīrī, 218
Umm al-Aswad bint Zayd [Yazīd] al-ʿAdawiyya, 47, 104, 166, 268
Umm ʿAlī the daughter of ʿAbdallāh ibn Ḥamshādh, 58, 244
Umm ʿAlī [Fāṭima] the wife of Aḥmad ibn Khaḍrawayh, 168–69
Umm Hārūn, 64, 146, 320
Umm al-Ḥusayn al-Qurashiyya, 34, 47, 224, 242, 246, 250
Umm al-Ḥusayn al-Warrāqa, 252
Umm al-Ḥusayn the daughter of Aḥmad ibn Ḥamdān, 68, 238
Umm Kulthūm, 31, 34, 240
Umm Saʿīd the daughter of ʿAlqama an-Nakhaʿī, 114
Umm Sālim ar-Rāsibiyya, 132, 326
Umm Ṭalq, 58, 118, 294
Unaysa bint ʿAmr, 47, 61, 88, 102, 164
ʿUnayza of Baghdad, 57, 248
ustādh, 45, 59–60, 63, 126, 144
Ustuvā, 32
uṣūl al-fiqh, 29
uṣūl
  methodology of, 29, 38
uṣūlization, 37–40

al-Wahaṭiyya Umm al-Faḍl, 35, 59, 226, 228
walī Allāh, 56, 82
al-Wāqidī, Muḥammad, 50
waraʿ, 58, 61–62, 90, 124, 156, 182
Women
  deficient in religion and intellect, 17–19, 56, 58–59, 63
  exceptional, 18, 48–49, 57, 58–59

az-Zāhid, Abū ʿAbdallāh, 234
Ziyāda bint al-Khaṭṭāb of Ṭazar, 230
Ziyādat ḥaqāʾiq at-tafsīr (Addendum to "Realities of Exegesis"), 41
Zubda the sister of Bishr al-Ḥāfī, 47, 192, 322, 324p